Teacher's Manual to Accompany

HUMAN RESOURCE MANAGEMENT
A GENERAL MANAGER'S PERSPECTIVE

Text and Cases

Bert Spector
Michael Beer

THE FREE PRESS
A Division of Macmillan, Inc.
NEW YORK

Collier Macmillan Publishers
LONDON

The Free Press
A Division of Macmillan, Inc.
866 Third Avenue, New York, N. Y. 10022

Collier Macmillan Canada, Inc.

Printed in the United States of America

printing number

2 3 4 5 6 7 8 9 10

Case material of the Harvard Graduate School of Business Administration is made possible by
the cooperation of business firms and other organizations which may wish to remain
anonymous by having their names, quantities, and other identifying details disguised while
maintaining basic relationships. Cases are prepared as the basis for class discussion rather than
to illustrate either effective or ineffective handling of administrative situations.

Separate copies of cases for classroom and other use should be ordered from HBS Case
Services, Harvard Business School, Boston, MA 02163. The availability of cases is subject to
change. An order form with information on how to order cases will be found at the
back of this manual.

ISBN 0-02-902440-4

Contents

Appendix II. *SUPPLEMENTARY CASES*

CHAPTER 1

Introduction

Human Resource Management: A General Manager's Perspective is not a traditional personnel textbook. We do not review theory, research, and practice in personnel administration, labor relations, and organization behavior and development, the three major research and practice traditions represented in many personnel functions and courses. It is a book for *any* manager, or prospective manager, particularly general managers, who want to learn about the critical issues and the strategic questions they will have to consider in managing large aggregates of employees in the 1980s and beyond.

The development of our approach to human resource management (HRM) was stimulated through our contacts and experiences in the field, as well as our reading of academic literature, all of which indicated to us that HRM problems were significantly influencing the effectiveness of corporations. Competitive pressures, changing values in the work force and society, government legislation, slower growth or decline in mature industries, and rapid growth in high-technology firms are making human resources an increasingly important competitive factor.

The rising importance of human resources has led us to rethink traditional approaches to the management of an organization's human resources. That rethinking is reflected in the content of *Human Resource Management: A General Manager's Perspective*. The general management perspective, elaborated upon in Chapter 1 of the text, places HRM within the context of business strategy and society. It attempts to stimulate students to ask important questions about managing human resources in a

1

changing environment, while at the same time giving them sufficient information about existing institutional arrangements and known personnel practices to facilitate a realistic discussion. It asks them to grapple with the many dilemmas and problems general managers encounter in fashioning short- and long-term solutions and taking action.

The text and cases in the book reflect the HRM course as it was originally offered in 1981 and 1982, but we have included recently developed cases and notes as well. This required course was developed jointly by a team of faculty representing three quite different perspectives—labor relations, personnel administration, and organizational behavior/development. The goal was to develop a course that integrated these perspectives into a general management perspective. Thus the text, cases, readings (in *Readings in Human Resource Management*), and audiovisual materials represent an effort to develop a very different personnel management course than is typically taught in many business schools. We were interested in developing a course that all students in our MBA and Executive programs would find meaningful and useful, not just students who are interested in becoming personnel and labor relations specialists.

The emphasis is on presenting students with case material, readings, and audiovisual material that will stimulate discussion of the most important and strategic questions they as managers or prospective managers will have to tackle. In our experience, many traditional personnel courses attempt to teach the concepts and techniques that are of interest to the personnel and labor relations specialist, and present these concepts and techniques in a way that only specialists would find interesting by emphasizing practice methods such as job evaluation, compensation, selection, and so on. Our cases and text do not present all that specialists need to know about collective bargaining, employee selection, training, compensation, or organization development, for example. Indeed, specialists may not even recognize that their specialty is represented in our materials if they are looking for extensive discussions of personnel management practice. In our view, each of our respective specialties is adequately represented if we accept that the basic purpose of the course is the education of managers, particularly general managers.

The implication of all this is that adoption of the book will demand a willingness to rethink what the required personnel and labor relations course (what we are calling HRM) should include. Just as the development of the business policy curriculum at the Harvard Business School (HBS) represented a breakthrough in the School's pedagogy with respect to the education of general managers, so the HRM course represents a new approach in teaching managers and prospective managers how to think about and act on human resource problems of the firm.

We continue to offer two organizational behavior (OB) courses in our required curriculum: one concerned with interpersonal and group issues (micro OB), taught prior to the HRM course, and one concerned with organizational design and change which follows the HRM course. The former is a building block which offers fundamentals about relationships, communication, motivation, and action taking in organizations. These are needed by students before they can think about formulating human resource policies and practices for large aggregates of employees. The latter (the macro OB course in design and change) attempts to integrate learning from the micro OB and HRM courses into an organizational effectiveness perspective with special emphasis on how leaders might design and change organizational structure and human resource systems and practices to improve organizational effectiveness. A course on labor relations and personnel administration continues to be offered in our second-year elective curriculum.

Teaching the Course

After the two introductory chapters, students will find one chapter for each of four major human resource policy areas, and a concluding integrative chapter. Each chapter presents conceptual background as well as some knowledge about institutional arrangements and personnel practice needed to tackle the cases. While we do not review research, theory, and practice in exhaustive detail, the text material is based on our knowledge of both research and practice. We have tried to synthesize that knowledge in the interest of articulating more general issues and questions of concern to general managers. We realize full well that in doing this we are leaving unstated many important qualifications that a detailed review of research and theory would allow. We have tried to deal with this potential problem by only making assertions about general directions, considerations, and questions rather than about specific solutions. The issues and questions we raise can, of course, only provide a general framework for analysis and action. Human resource management problems and practices found in each situation require a situation specific analysis such as the one we require in a case discussion.

Consistent with the pedagogy of HBS, we teach HRM by the case method. The case method puts students in a real situation and forces them to diagnose that situation and take action. If the case presents a given company's approach to HRM, it offers students the opportunity to evaluate the effectiveness of that approach.

The text that precedes each section is aimed at giving students the general background and perspective required to analyze and discuss the cases in that section. By asking students to diagnose, evaluate, and take action with classroom challenges from peers and faculty, we are helping students develop their own research findings, ones they are likely to remember because they come from their own experience. So long as the discussion is guided by someone who knows the research and understands the constraints of reality, this approach is, we believe, preferable to providing them with our own analysis of the cases or with comprehensive reviews of research studies which deal with the problem.

Naturally, instructors are an important part of this type of learning process. They guide the discussion by asking relevant questions, providing expertise and experience where needed and encouraging students to grapple with important questions. The following chapter in the teacher's manual contains some specific suggestions on teaching by the case method.

We have limited our text to a more general treatment of HRM. Instructors and students will have available to them a companion book of supplementary readings: *Readings in Human Resource Management.* These readings are intended to provide the minimum knowledge of concepts, institutional arrangements or current law, or practice needed by students as background for an informed discussion. Reference will be made throughout the teaching manual to the articles contained in *Readings in Human Resource Management,* as well as to other articles and books that might be especially useful and important in thinking about the cases. In most instances, however, the supplementary readings book is intended to provide background material which will help in the discussion of the more fundamental questions the instructor raises about the cases. The questions that should dominate the discussion are, "What is the problem here, and what short- and long-term action do you recommend?" Or, if the case is descriptive of HRM policies and practices in a given company, the key questions are, "How do you evaluate the company's approach and under what circumstances can it be applied elsewhere?" Given the varied experience and values of students, the class can arrive at a much more complete understanding of the situation and a more complete plan of action than can any single individual. Of course this complete understanding requires that the instructor bring out the different viewpoints in the class rather than lecture about the case or use it as an illustration. An alternative approach is to subdivide the class into small groups which are asked to present their analyses and recommendations for action.

Teaching Cases

It might also be useful here to state our feelings on what purpose cases can serve. We include cases not as examples of revealed truths or as illustrations of the proper, or for that matter, improper ways of handling a particular HRM problem. Readers would seriously err, we believe, in seeking *the* answer or answers within the cases. The cases present HRM problems and approaches in a variety of real-world settings. Companion readings provide background information about the content of relevant personnel practices to help students diagnose problems and consider action alternatives. We urge that cases be used to trigger ways of thinking about HRM issues; that they be read and discussed to illuminate the dilemmas, the issues, the problems, and the possibilities for action inherent in the task of managing human resources.

The teacher's manual itself presents brief introductory material to each of the text sections—Introduction, Conceptual Overview (these two sections are discussed together in Chapter 3 of the manual), Employee Influence, Human Resource Flow, Reward Systems, Work Systems, and Integrating Human Resources. The bulk of the manual is given over to detailed analyses of each case. We also suggest how the case fits into the overall course, with references to both earlier and later cases. Appendix I provides instructors with information for ordering audiovisual material which may be used to supplement case teaching. Appendix II includes follow-on cases that instructors will want to hand out in class. In many instances these follow-on cases are critical to a full discussion of the case problem. An order form for obtaining these follow-on cases from Harvard's HBS Case Services is included.

Using the Teaching Notes

We suggest that instructors start their preparation by reading the teaching manual section introduction for each book chapter. This will provide an overview and position each case in the course, indicating how it fits and relates to other cases. Next, the case to be taught should be read quickly for an overview of its content and thrust. After this we suggest that the teaching note for the case be read for the analysis of the case and the ideas about how to teach it. Finally, the instructor will want to return to the case for a more careful reading of the issues discussed in the teaching note.

All class plans provided in the teaching manual assume a 1½-hour class. We have indicated approximately how long you will want to spend on each segment of the class (indicated by key questions to be asked to focus discussion). However, we urge you to be flexible in time allocation to each of these segments depending on the energy each question generates. In general, we suggest going with the energy and interest of the class. Thus, the questions we provide may be used in a somewhat different order and for a longer or shorter period of time depending on what is happening in class.

In many of the teaching notes we have provided tables which summarize analyses of issues or numbers. We have also provided illustrations that summarize conceptual points. In many instances these were overhead transparencies used by one or more instructors in the HRM course. You may want to use them in the same way.

CHAPTER 2

Teaching by the Case Method

Upon approaching *Human Resource Management: A General Manager's Perspective,* instructors, particularly those whose previous exposure to the case method of teaching has been limited, may be somewhat baffled at first by the abundance of case material presented in the book. For that reason, in addition to the case-by-case teaching notes contained in this manual, we thought we might say just a few words about the *method* of teaching cases.

First, it is important to understand precisely what a case is. A case presents students with an experience: a depiction of real life which places them in the middle of a real-life situation and asks them to respond as managers. The data provided are not always as clear-cut as students would like, are sometimes contradictory, and occasionally even wrong (that is to say, the data reflect the biases of individuals rather than the "truth" of a situation), just as are data in real life. Managers—and students who become managers in the classroom—must sift through the data and take actions or make analyses based on their own reading of what is important and what is real. Challenges, questions, and alternative suggestions provided by fellow students and the instructor all serve to sharpen a student's analytical, problem-solving, and reasoning skills.

In preparing this chapter, we would like to acknowledge the ideas and insights of John S. Hammond, E. Raymond Corey, and Mortin Marshall for their notes on learning by the case method; C. Roland Christensen, *Teaching by the Case Method* (Boston: Harvard Business School Division of Research, 1981); and John J. Gabarro, "Teaching and Using Cases" in Phyllis F. Schlesinger et al., *Instructor's Manual to Accompany Managing Behavior Organizations* (New York: McGraw-Hill, 1983), pp. 3–9.

Some of the cases in *Human Resource Management: A General Manager's Perspective* are primarily descriptive in nature ("Air Traffic Controllers," "Assessing Managerial Talent at AT&T," "General Motors and the United Auto Workers," "Human Resources at Hewlett-Packard") and ask students to analyze and evaluate actions that have already taken place. The bulk of the cases, however, are "action oriented." They plunk students down in the middle of a crisis and say, "Given the realities and constraints imposed on you (as described in the case), what actions should you take now?" The recognition of realities and constraints is a critical part of that process. There is a tendency for students to tackle an action question by saying, "In the best of all possible worlds where I am able to manipulate any and all aspects of reality, here's what I would do." While there is some value to the "omnipotent overseer" approach (by comparing their ideal model to the reality of the situation, they can dissect, analyze, criticize, and better understand the real model with which they are faced), instructors should always encourage students to assume the view of the "trench fighter." Students should be pushed to recognize that there are constraints to action. The president of a company operates under certain constraints; so does a manager and a supervisor considerably further down in the organization's hierarchy. Constraints can be imposed by the environment (government regulations, societal values, labor markets, competition, and so forth) or by organizational arrangements. And one of the most important and immutable constraints is the one imposed by time: Wynn Evans must respond to the union's organizing campaign in the *next 30 days* ("First National Bank of Lake City"); Dirk van Berkel must report back to his Management Board on the progress of the Amersfoort sale *tonight* ("Workers' Councils: Hobbema and van Rijn, N.V."); and Bob Carter must submit recommendations for trimming his personnel *next Wednesday* ("Webster Industries").

Instructor Preparation

In preparing to teach a case, instructors have two basic chores: mastering the *content* of the case, and carefully planning the *process* of the classroom discussion. The content requirement is self-evident (and we hope the individual notes provided in this manual will be of great help here), so we will devote our attention to the process side.

We suggest that you approach each class discussion with an outline that covers both the main topics you wish to cover during the discussion, and the approximate length of time you wish to allocate to each aspect of that discussion. While we have provided a specific outline like this for each case (which we hope will be viewed by instructors as a *suggestion* rather than as *the* way to teach the case), we can suggest in more general terms a four-step approach to the allocation of time in the classroom:

7

1. *What are we doing here?* Instructors can set aside five to ten minutes at the beginning of class for setting the stage by showing what purpose the case serves in the overall course and how it flows from previous cases. Each individual teaching note in the manual provides some suggestions for articulating the place of the case in the HRM course.
2. *What is the problem?* A longer period of time can now be devoted to identifying and defining the problem as posed in the case.
3. *Now what?* The bulk of the class can now be devoted to proposing and managing various alternatives to management action.
4. *So what?* A short period of time at the end of class, usually five to ten minutes, can be given over to the instructor's summary of the main points of the case, as well as a "bridge" forward to show how this case fits with the ones that are coming in the course. Again, we have made suggestions in the individual teaching notes that may help you think about your concluding comments.

Instructors can think not only about how to divide up the class time, but also about how to move from one part of the discussion to the next. How do I get from analyzing the problem to action planning? The key tool at the instructor's disposal is the ability to ask questions.

"All right," the instructor can say after 20 minutes, "we've identified most of the major problems faced by this organization. Now what can we do?" These transition questions are critical in moving the class discussion along, and we suggest you give careful thought before entering class to what those questions might be and when they should be put into the discussion. Once again, we have made suggestions for transition questions in the teaching plans which accompany each case note.

One final tool which can be made use of prior to entering the classroom is the assignment questions. By providing students with a set of analytical questions beforehand, you can help guide them toward what you consider to be the main purposes and points of the case. We have suggested assignment questions for each of the cases.

Teaching the Class

Armed with a detailed teaching plan, one of the first decisions you must make once the class begins is how closely and strictly you will stick to that plan. Basically, you are faced with a balancing act. Rigid adherence to the plan imposed by strict controls from the instructor runs the danger of sapping spontaneity and freshness from the class discussion. Total abandonment of the plan by allowing students to "go with the flow" wherever it might lead them risks conducting a class in which key points are missed and the students are given no clear, logical analysis of what the case was all about. Obviously, the ideal solution is to strike some balance between the two. On this point, we cannot help you much other than to say that the distance between the two poles is wide. You need to find a style and approach that is comfortable to you and that seems to work with the particular set of students with whom you are dealing. This is where the "art" of teaching comes into play. Be assured there is no single correct way of striking that balance. We have all seen excellent teachers whose approaches to the case method differ dramatically.

While we are placing the issue of control in your hands, we would like to suggest that the case method requires some rethinking of the role of an instructor. In a lecture or even a traditional seminar setting, the instructor becomes the fount of wisdom and knowledge. Students may ask questions, but the flow of information is generally one way. The case method changes all that. While the knowledge of the instructor must still serve as the anchor of the discussion, information flows in every direction: from student to student, from instructor to student, and from student to instructor. (Don't underestimate your own opportunities for learning as well as teaching.) The proper role of the instructor in a case discussion is one of a *facilitator*: guiding, shaping, integrating, and questioning the discussion.

What are the tools that are available to you as a facilitator once the discussion begins? John J. Gabarro has suggested a number of tools, among which are:

1. *Questions*. Broadly posed questions can be used to start an area of discussion ("What's going on here?"; "What's the problem?"), while more specific, probing questions can be used to focus and tighten the discussion ("What is it about John Fortier that makes him such an effective supervisor?"; "Why are Jim Boyd's people *really* leaving Megalith, Inc.?").
2. *Rephrasing*. The instructor can often rephrase a student's comments, carefully retaining the jist of what the student has said but repeating the comment in such a way that makes it more understandable, closer to the focus of the discussion, or even places the comment on a higher level of abstraction. Rephrasing requires careful listening on the instructor's part. Make sure that you understand what students are trying to say so that you can avoid putting words into their mouths.
3. *Soliciting other opinions*. The instructor should take particular care to elicit the entire range of opinions that exist in the classroom. Because the nature of the material in this course often touches upon matters of personal values, we can predict that there will be a wide range of deeply felt opinions on many of the cases. Allow students an opportunity to express those opinions and create and maintain

an atmosphere where students will not feel inhibited in expressing opinions that may be different from the consensus or somehow unpopular. Make sure judgments, debates, and challenges focus on the content of the opinion rather than on the person who is expressing that opinion.

4. *Transition questions.* As discussed above, this is one of the key ways of moving class discussion along.

5. *Asking students to summarize* the discussion of the class and to identify key points, ideas, or conclusions that can be drawn.

6. *Lecturettes.* Case teaching is primarily *not* a lecture format. However, instructors may find it useful to drop in lecturettes (five to ten minutes) to summarize, bridge forward or backward, or to introduce some key points from the text material. Lecturettes usually come at the beginning or end of a class, but they can be used sparingly in the middle of a class where some confusion or lack of understanding has interrupted the flow of the discussion, and could be overcome by a lecturette from the instructor.

It is often in this "summing up" process that instructors can tie the discussion that has preceded it in with some of the broader, more academic concepts introduced either in the text chapters or in assigned supplementary reading. The decision on how much to emphasize theory versus discussions of the case is, of course, up to the individual instructor. We would like to make the point, however, that the case method can be used to deal with and teach theory. One of the common complaints about teaching with cases is that students will not be grounded in any of the academic theories that tend to make up the bulk of more traditional textbooks. We have found instead that cases and case discussions allow students an opportunity to develop their own "theories" about how and why things are as they are. Once this process of analysis has taken place, instructors can introduce classical theory that will now be grounded in the reality of the discussion. Theory that flows naturally from an analysis of reality, we believe, is more meaningful to the student than theory that precedes reality. Thus, Hackman and Oldham's theories on job enrichment, for example, can follow a discussion of how and why work teams in "Sedalia Engine Plant" operate rather than preceding that discussion. That way, students may latch onto the theory as a good way of explaining the phenomenon that they have just experienced. But at all times we warn students that a conceptual framework should not be used rigidly to analyze all situations. Nor should conceptual frameworks be used in the same way to analyze similar situations. We tell students that conceptual frameworks offer "port holes" to the world that can help analyze and direct thinking. Ultimately, however, the student must sharpen his or her analysis of the situation using his or her ability to think critically.

Conclusions

Just as we tell students there is no one correct answer to the problems raised by the cases in the book, so too we tell instructors that there is no one correct way to teach a case. We hope that the discussion here and the detailed individual teaching notes will provide useful suggestions. More than that, we hope that this material will give you the instructor, the confidence to approach the case method in a way that fits best with your individual characteristics, talents, and feelings about the art and science of teaching.

CHAPTER 3

The HRM Perspective

Chapters 1 and 2 of *Human Resource Management: A General Manager's Perspective* outline the four-policy approach we have taken to human resource management (HRM), as well as the conceptual perspectives that guide our approach. The four-policy framework not only eliminates the need for a long, potentially cumbersome listing of assorted practice areas, but it is consistent with what we see as a need for greater emphasis on *strategic* issues central to organizational effectiveness. Each of the policy areas defines a major HRM task to which managers must attend:

—*Employee influence.* This policy area has to do with one of the key questions all managers must ask: How much influence should employees at all levels of the organization be given? How much responsibility, authority, and power will managers delegate and to whom? The manager's task here is to provide an appropriate amount of influence to employees and employee groups in matters such as business goals, pay, working conditions, advancement, employment security, and the task itself. Managerial and societal values, the maturity of the work force, needs for employee development, and the nature of the task will determine how much influence is appropriate and how much occurs.

—*Human resource (HR) flow.* This policy area has to do with the necessity of managing the flow of people into, through, and out of the organization. Traditional personnel practice areas such as recruitment, internal staffing, performance appraisal, and outplacement are all subsumed into this area. But the task goes further. Functional specialists and line managers must work in concert to ensure that personnel flows meet the corporation's long-term, strategic requirement for the "right" number of people and mix of competencies. Selection, promotion, and termination decisions can also meet the needs of employees for job security, career development, advancement, and fair treatment, just as they must meet legislated standards of society. Managers must ask themselves whether they consider employees to be assets or variable costs. Their answer will determine how much employment security employees will have, and how much the corporation will invest in employee development. When characterized as a whole, the pattern of practice in this area constitutes the organization's HR flow policies. To be effective, these policies must be consistent with the strategy and task of the firm, the values of management and society, and the expectations and capacities of employees.

—*Rewards.* This policy area has to do with another key question managers must ask: How shall we use rewards to develop the behaviors and attitudes required for the organization to be effective? It is up to top management of an organization, and not just pay specialists, to attend to certain questions under this HRM task. On what basis do we want employees to become involved in the organization? Should the basis for involvement only be money and promotion, or should involvement also come from commitment to corporate goals, participation in decisions, and opportunities for such intrinsic rewards as challenge, recognition, and responsibility? In other words, should monetary rewards provide equitable treatment based on performance stimulated by intrinsic motivation, or should money be used as the primary incentive to induce desired behaviors? Should monetary rewards be tied to individual performance or to organizational performance and how might these be mixed? Answers to these questions will help shape the response of managers to questions concerning the reward system itself: how competitive should our wages be? How shall industrial pay for performance systems (merit pay or bonus systems) be used to reward initiative and competence without creating undue competitiveness between individuals and groups that must cooperate? Can they be used without reducing collaboration and coordination? Should profits of the organization or gains from productivity improvements be shared with various employees or employee groups? The answers to these questions lead to the task of designing and administering, equitably and fairly, rewards that will attract, retain (satisfy), and motivate employees at all levels. Policies must be guided by accurate assumptions about what people want and are capable of doing, about the labor market in which the organization competes, and what reward mix best suits the task and culture of the organization.

—*Work systems*. This policy area has to do with the task of arranging people, information, tasks, and technology at all levels of the organization; in other words, how to define and design both work and decision-making processes around the task. Management choices about these arrangements affect the quality of decisions people make, coordination developed between functions and tasks, the extent to which people's competencies are utilized, the extent to which people are committed to the organization's goals, and the extent to which people's needs for development and quality of work life are met. Decisions about manufacturing processes at the plant level (extent of division of labor and application of technology, for example), about new information technology in the office (computerized information systems, for example), and about planning and goal-setting systems at the management level are all examples of policy decisions in the work systems area. Decisions about work systems must be consistent with employee capabilities and the potential for developing those capabilities. Decisions must also be consistent with the supervisory and managerial skills available to the organization.

By placing a stakeholder perspective at the core of our HRM approach, we are saying that the end results of an organizations's operations can be judged not just in terms of meeting the needs of the shareholders, but in responding as well to the *legitimate needs of various stakeholders in the organization*. We are suggesting that there are different groups, or "constituencies," whose interests, attitudes, and behaviors may well be quite distinct from those of shareholders. Thus, the impact of HRM policy choices can be viewed from the perspective of top management, whose interests may not always be consistent with those of shareholders, as well as from the perspective of such stakeholders as unions, minority employees, government agencies, customers, the host community, subsidiaries, and various functional groups within the organization.

In Chapter 2 we suggest a series of analytical levers which can be brought to bear on the HRM issues raised by our cases. We suggest situational factors—laws and societal values, task technology, unions, work force characteristics, labor market conditions, business strategy, and management philosophy—that need to be considered when making HRM policy choices. We suggest a way of evaluating the impact of policy decisions: the four C's of competence, commitment, congruence, and cost effectiveness. And we propose that, ultimately, the consequences of HRM policies be viewed on three levels: organizational effectiveness, employee well-being, and societal well-being.

Chapter 2 in the text concludes with "Air Traffic Controllers," the introductory case in the course. The case allows students to identify the four policy areas that make up an HRM system, and analyze how these policies are working (or not working) together by looking at their impact on each of the four C's. The case also presents the first opportunity for analysis of the ultimate consequences of HRM policy choices—both those made in the case and those which students might propose as part of their "action plan"—on organizational effectiveness, employee well-being, and societal well-being.

Subject Matter Matrix

Although the text is organized around the four policy frameworks, the traditional practice areas of the personnel/HR field are represented in the various cases. Instructors can turn to the subject matter matrix to see which cases contain material on these more traditional subheadings.

Audiovisual Material

Instructors may wish to accompany the teaching of "Air Traffic Controllers" with a 20-minute film, "Flight 52," produced by the Federal Aviation Administration (FAA) which depicts the daily work done by air traffic controllers. Information on how to order this film, as well as all other audio-visual material referred to throughout this manual, can be found in Appendix I.

Supplementary Reading Assignments

The following supplementary reading assignments can be made from *Readings in Human Resource Management*:

TEXT MATERIAL	SUGGESTED READINGS
Chapters 1 and 2—"Air Traffic Controllers"	David C. Ewing, "The Endless Wave"
	R. Edward Freeman, "Managing in Turbulent Times"
	Shoshana Zuboff, "The Work Ethic and Work Organization"
	Lodge, McCormick, and Zuboff, "Sources and Patterns of Management Authority"

Subject Matter Matrix

Case	The HRM System	Environmental Context	Equal Employment Opportunity	Human Resource Planning	Recruitment	Selection/Placement	Motivation/Satisfaction	Performance Evaluation
Air Traffic Controllers	X	X		X	X	X	X	X
First National Bank of Lake City		X					X	
Bethoney Manufacturing							X	
Coal Strike of 1977/1978		X						
Workers' Councils: Hobbema & van Rijn, N.V.		X						
Nippon Steel Corporation	X	X		X				
Webster Industries				X				X
Colonial Food Services Company							X	X
Assessing Managerial Talent at AT&T						X	X	
Highland Products, Inc.			X			X		
Medical and Environmental Electronics, Inc.		X		X	X	X		
Alcon Laboratories, Inc.	X			X		X	X	
Megalith-Hay Associates							X	
LEP Corporation								
First Federal Savings								
Dana Corporation —The Richmond Camshaft Plant	X						X	
New Technology and Job Design in a Phone Company							X	
Kalamazoo Plant Parts Division —Acme Motors	X						X	
Sedalia Engine Plant	X						X	X
Office Technology, Inc.							X	X
General Motors and the United Auto Workers	X	X					X	
Human Resources at Hewlett-Packard	X				X	X	X	
People Express	X	X			X	X	X	

Compensation Systems	Incentive/Individual and Group Bonuses	Work Force Reduction	Labor Relations	Union Organizing and Collective Bargaining	Employee Relations	Job Design	The Future of HRM
X		X	X	X	X		
			X	X	X		
			X	X			X
			X	X			
					X		
		X	X		X		
		X					
X	X					X	
X							
X	X						
X	X						
X	X		X				
					X	X	
			X		X	X	
X		X			X	X	X
					X	X	X
X			X			X	X
				X	X	X	X
				X	X	X	X

17

AIR TRAFFIC CONTROLLERS
Teaching Note

On August 3, 1981, approximately 12,000 federally employed air traffic controllers, members of the Professional Air Traffic Controllers Union (PATCO) went on strike. The President of the United States, declaring the strike to be illegal, immediately announced that any striking controller who failed to report back to work within 48 hours would be dismissed. Three days later, approximately 12,000 dismissal notices were mailed, and the Secretary of Transportation announced, "It's over. Our concern is rebuilding the system."

This case introduces students to a HRM system and allows them to analyze that system as it existed prior to the strike, to evaluate the action plan taken by the government (will it solve the human resource problems of the air traffic control system?), and to suggest further actions for changing the employment conditions of the air traffic controllers.

ASSIGNMENT QUESTIONS

Students should read the case and come to class prepared to discuss the following questions:

1. What is your analysis of the situation leading up to President Reagan's decision to terminate the striking air traffic controllers? Do you agree with his decision? Why or why not?
2. What recommendations would you make to Secretary of Transportation Lewis about the employment conditions of the air traffic controllers and why?

CASE ANALYSIS

The case offers an excellent opportunity to introduce the four-policy HRM framework—employee influence, HR flow, reward systems, and work systems—elaborated upon in Chapters 1 and 2. Case discussion can start with a thorough analysis of employment conditions prior to the strike done in such a way to show how these policies and procedures interacted with each other as the case events progressed.

All teaching notes in this manual, unless otherwise indicated, were prepared by Michael Beer and Bert Spector.

Copyright © 1984 by the President and Fellows of Harvard College. Harvard Business School teaching note 5-485-002.

Employee Influence

Analysis in the Employee Influence area can not only identify the various stakeholders in the air traffic control system, but show how these stakeholders acted upon each other, while discussing also the multiplicity of interests that each of the stakeholders might have. For example:

1. *The FAA.* Established by the act of Congress in 1958, the FAA is "to provide for the *regulation* and *promotion* of civil aviation" (emphasis added). In other words, the FAA is supposed to promote both aviation and safety, aims which may occasionally be contradictory. Controllers complain, for example, that the FAA's handling of "access" indicates a priority on promotion over regulation. The FAA's policy of allowing private airlines virtually unlimited access to airports means that more planes are flying into the same airports at the same peak hours. Indeed, FAA data show that the size of the gap between peak and valley activity at air traffic facilities is strongly correlated with job pressures felt by controllers.
2. *Airline pilots.* These highly paid employees of the airlines are engaged in a constant tug-of-war with controllers. They are represented by separate unions, although both are affiliated with the American Federation of Labor–Congress of Industrial Organizations (AFL–CIO). The sharpest battle is over which group bears ultimate responsibility for the aircraft. Both feel that they do, although the law seems to give pilots the final responsibility.
3. *Union/nonunion controllers.* Because of the way work is organized (split shifts, long "off" periods), controllers tend to socialize both on and off the job with other controllers, and thus develop strong peer relations. This peer pressure can exert a strong influence on controllers to join the union and support the strike. Most controllers (94 percent) are members of PATCO. Even though 95 percent of the controllers voted to reject the June 22 contract, a smaller number, 69 percent (74 percent of PATCO members) actually went on strike.
4. *The AFL–CIO.* The International Federation has a strong interest in supporting PATCO. Public employees represent the only sector of the work force where unionization is increasing (43.4 percent of public employees were in unions in 1980 compared with 21.7 percent in the private work force). At the same time, PATCO has alienated itself from the AFL–CIO in several ways. PATCO was one of only four AFL–CIO affiliates to endorse Republican Ronald Reagan over Democrat Jimmy Carter in the 1980 Presidential race (the Airline Pilots Association was another). And PATCO had failed to consult with other unions before embarking on their strike. The di-

lemma for fellow unions was increased by the fact that direct support for an illegal strike (such as honoring picket lines) is itself an illegal act.

5. *The federal government/President Reagan.* During the 1980 campaign, Ronald Reagan responded to the PATCO endorsement with a commitment to help rebuild the air traffic control system (see casebook Exhibit 1–5). However, the Republican Party generally and Ronald Reagan specifically (despite his own union affiliation as president of the Screen Actors Guild) are not considered to be strong supporters of unionism, having called for an extension of "right to work" laws in their 1980 platform.[1] The President can be said to have had five specific goals in this situation:

   a. Keep the air traffic control system running
   b. Preserve air safety
   c. Help control inflation
   d. Send "messages" to other unions, particularly public employee unions (and specifically the powerful postal unions just getting ready to vote on a contract) that wage settlements must help fight inflation and that illegal strikes will not be tolerated
   e. Retain his generally conservative constituency support

6. *PATCO.* The split between PATCO president Robert Poli and the man he defeated in 1980, John Leyden, apparently still affects the union. Poli admits to being the more militant of the two. Even under Leyden, however, PATCO has a long history of conflicts with the FAA (sick-outs and slowdowns) and of illegal activities (their 1978 slowdown in violation of a 1970 court injunction). But Poli has rejected sick-outs and slowdowns as being ineffective, and is on record as saying, "The only illegal strike is an unsuccessful one." In addition to the militant/moderate split, other interest groups can be identified within the union: controllers at the busiest airports versus those who work in towers that handle light traffic; tower versus en route controllers; younger versus older controllers, with the latter group being more interested in retirement benefits while the former group is more interested in immediate pay increases.

After identifying the various stakeholders, discussion can focus specifically on the controllers and ask what influence mechanisms are available to them within the constraints of the law (because of government employment, management "rules" have the force of law) and past practice. The 1979 Federal Labor Relations Act (FLRA) allows for *some* collective bargaining, but specifically prohibits bargaining over such matters as wages, job classifications, benefits, work assignments, layoffs, and so forth. The law also continues the 1955 ban on strikes by public employees. But the "practice" of labor relations in the federal government has established its own set of norms. The government has engaged in "behind the scenes" collective bargaining with the postal union, for instance, over precisely the matters prohibited by law. And even though air traffic controllers, like other federal employees, must take a no-strike oath upon being hired, there is a past record of treating illegal government strikes with different degrees of enforcement. A 1970 illegal strike by 175,000 postal workers, for instance, resulted in the return to work of all but 90 workers. And prosecutions of the 1978 illegal slowdown by PATCO had declined because employees had not been notified in advance that they could be subject to criminal prosecution.

HR Flow

Analysis of the flow policies of the FAA can look at recruitment, selection, and promotion practices, and the degree of "fit" between the organization's human resources and the tasks to be done by air traffic controllers. Recruitment is from the civil service register, and the requirement that only a high school education is needed means that most job applicants are not qualified for this highly demanding job (in 1980, only 5 percent of the applicants actually became controllers). Those selected tended to be former military air traffic controllers (50 percent) with high school educations. Only 15 percent of successful applicants were women.

A particularly troublesome point seems to be at the supervisory level. There is no standard performance appraisal system for controllers, and no system for appraising potential. Promotion to supervisor, made entirely from within, was based, therefore, on a "buddy" system. Furthermore, there was no real training for supervisors. There was no requirement for them to seek further education beyond the high school level, and the FAA cancelled internal supervisory training when budgets became tight.

Another problem relating to the movement of controllers through and out of the system related to the issue of "burnout" caused by stress. Nearly 90 percent of the controllers are forced to retire early because of medical disabilities. Yet the FAA offers no alternative career planning or guidance. Some controllers insist that the demands for high salaries and generous pensions are fueled, in part at least, by their almost sure knowledge that they will be forced to retire early without knowledge of where their careers might move from there.

Reward Systems

Although air traffic controllers are extremely well paid, there were nonetheless problems raised by the FAA's reward system. Controllers are well paid in comparison with other federal employees, but for purposes of external equity they tend to compare themselves not with other federal employees, with whom they have little direct contact, but with private airline pilots. Many controllers feel that their job entails greater responsibility than the pilots' jobs ("They're flying an airplane with 150 people on board. . . . We're sitting at a scope working ten airplanes at once with 150 on each plane.") Furthermore, in comparison with air traffic controllers around the world, U.S. controllers work longer weeks and get fewer vacation days and paid sick days. Also, the pay range is based entirely on the type of facility the controllers work at (high versus low level, tower versus en route center) rather than on individual duties within the facility (which can differ considerably sector by sector within the same facility) or by performance.

The federal annual pay cap ($50,112.50 in 1980) created problems of its own, having to do with salary compression and perceived fairness. Because of the cap, the highest-paid controllers earned not only as much as their supervisors, but as much as facility chiefs and regional FAA directors, all of whom were under the same pay cap. Such compression can serve to build resentments on both sides. Management feels inequitably paid compared with higher-level controllers, while controllers resent taking orders from supervisors who do not get paid any more than they do. Adding to the problems caused by the pay cap, the 1/26th and no carry-over rule (no federal employee can earn more than 1/26th of the cap in any two-week period; and if overtime or night and Sunday differentials place the employee above 1/26th of the cap, that time cannot be carried over to another period when the employee might fall below the cap level) means that some controllers can be deprived of earned income.

An analysis of rewards should also look at the FAA's retirement benefits. Although the benefits are generous compared with other federal employees, this is a benefit that has more immediate meaning to older controllers nearing retirement. Exhibit 2–7 in the casebook shows clearly that over three times as many pension-eligible controllers did not strike as did.

Work Systems

There is a good deal of evidence that working as an air traffic controller induces a great deal of stress (although the job is not necessarily unique in this), which affects controllers' lives, the health of their families, and the length of time they spend on the job. Stress may be inherent to the job itself and may, in part, be what attracts controllers to the job. But there are certain aspects of the work system that appear to increase both stress and the impact of stress on employees:

1. *Supervision.* There is a high degree of distrust and alienation between controllers and supervisors who used to be their colleagues. The lack of supervisory training and promotion from within based

on a "buddy" system rather than evaluation of potential means that a highly autocratic, militaristic style of supervision will be used for highly motivated, skilled controllers. Controllers may well be over-supervised.

2. *Job content*. The FAA policy of virtually unlimited access during peak periods leads to great variability in job demands and apparently enhances stress. Most system errors, for instance, occur during "valley" periods, probably because of reduced concentration and boredom.

3. *Work rules*. Rigid split-shift assignments remove the possibility of flexibility or individual participation in work assignments to help create schedules more tailored for individual needs. Many of the other work rules (sick leave, hours per week, vacation days) are standardized for all federal employees, even though the controllers' job is significantly different, that is, in terms of levels of stress, from other federal jobs. The comparison with other controllers indicates a possible need for greater flexibility.

4. *FAA Response*. The case contains several examples of the Agency's apparent insensitivity to the stress issue, their refusal to admit that the issue is a real one, and their disinclination to act on specific proposals (for example, the Rose Report).

Another aspect of a work system discussed in the case has to do with new technology. Much of the new technology introduced by the FAA during the 1970s threatened both the job security and status of the controllers. Because of such new technology, the FAA believes it was overstaffed at the time of the strike by between 20 percent and 50 percent, and that further technological innovations (more sophisticated display screens, for example) will make further reductions likely. Despite the publicly acknowledged overstaffing problem, the FAA claims that PATCO resistance has prevented the Agency from acting to reduce manpower levels. Other technological innovations, like an automated anticollision system (which FAA director Helms announced shortly after the first tentative agreement) will tend to give greater responsibility to pilots, while diminishing the role of controllers. There is no evidence that any technological innovation is being considered or implemented in consultation with the union or with controllers.

Analysis of the Government's Handling of Dispute

Students should be asked to take a stand on President Reagan's termination decision. In deciding to take a support or nonsupport stand, students should consider matters such as:

1. The impact of enforcing/not enforcing the law
2. The impact of past enforcement/nonenforcement of no-strike laws

3. The meaning of Helm's warning letter and the no-strike oath
4. Did the "punishment" fit the crime (termination during a recession)?
5. Could the President have enforced the law any other way (decertification and amnesty, for instance) and what would the impact have been?
6. To what extent did termination solve the basic HR problem shown earlier (that is, alienation and its causes).

Of course, there is no one right or wrong answer to any of these questions, but discussion can look at the impact of Reagan's decision on a number of factors.

Societal Impact. The termination sent a signal to other unions relating both to enforcement of the law and holding down inflation. Past practice in regard to law enforcement was, as already noted, inconsistent. Postal workers were able, by and large, to escape punishment in 1970 because of their clout (175,000 members). While PATCO also escaped punishment for their 1978 slowdown, the FAA had legally notified all controllers of the consequences of a strike in 1981 (casebook Exhibit 1–6), so criminal prosecution can occur. There is also the loss of jobs during a period of high unemployment. Not only have 12,000 controllers been terminated, but the airlines cut back about 10,000 people, and probably half of these cutbacks are related directly to the strike and flight cutbacks. The President has agreed that terminated controllers may apply for other federal jobs, but federal unemployment has risen 22 percent in 1981.

Political Impact. Polls show that the public supports Reagan's "tough" stand, but that there is also a large amount of concern with content of the controllers' complaints. There seems to be a political opportunity for Reagan to improve the air traffic control system.

Air Traffic Impact. The financial costs of the termination are enormous. There is a significant loss of skills and competencies that will not be immediately recoverable. There are huge costs (estimated at between one and six billion dollars) to airlines, hotels, cargo deliveries, and so forth, associated with cutbacks in flights. The cost of training new controllers will be about $175,000 per controller, and the demand for increased training will, as the case notes, place a tremendous strain on the training facility at Oklahoma City. While there is apparently no adverse impact on airline safety, there are warnings that the system's safety is being strained by the excess hours nonstriking controllers and supervisors are being forced to work.

FAA Impact. An imbalance of power apparently existed between FAA management and PATCO (inability to achieve manpower reductions due to fear of union would be an example of this power imbalance). Now with PATCO decertified, a new power disequilibrium exists. The FAA now has the opportunity to move toward optimum staffing levels. Helms announced that the Agency will fill only 5,500 of 12,000 lost jobs. However, that reduction was made not as part of a careful HR planning process that looked at needed competencies, but on the basis of support of the strike.

Analysis. Analysis can move now to ask the question: to what extent has the government addressed the issues raised in our earlier analysis of the HRM policies and practices at the FAA? The answer can look both at the "package" rejected by PATCO but that Lewis will recommend to Congress, and at the real impact of the termination:

> —*Employee influence.* A new power imbalance exists as the controllers have no mechanism for exerting influence. At the end of the case, the Teamsters are considering organizing controllers, and this may once again alter the power balance.
>
> —*HR flow.* While the package does contain some money for alternative career retraining, none of the other flow issues are addressed. The termination and need to hire quickly over 5,000 new controllers, has created a new recruitment and training problem. The training academy is severely strained in terms of staffing. The lowering of entrance requirements, speeding up of training, and hiring of new trainers has doubled the failure rate at the academy.
>
> —*Reward systems.* The package would give controllers an average increase of more than twice that given other federal employees. It also removes the pay cap restrictions on overtime or premium time pay.
>
> —*Work systems.* The work week will not be shortened, although controllers who work 40-hour weeks will be paid for 42 hours. Lewis has appointed an independent panel to make further recommendations on employment conditions.

Analysis of the government's handling of the case could also look at the negotiation process itself, and recognize that employment considerations were not the only reason for the break-down of talks. PATCO entered the negotiations not only with a militant history, but also a new president who had won on a platform of increased militancy. A strike fund had been developed by 1981. The case raises the question of how much communication was actually taking place between the union leadership and its members. Why, for instance, was the June 22 agreement hailed by Poli and then rejected by 95 percent of the membership?

The case also provides information about the government's own role, particularly in gearing up for a strike: flow control developed by the FAA under President Carter to get the maximum use of air space with a severely reduced work force; a "hit list" developed by the FAA six months before the strike to single out controllers for prosecution; going into the actual negotiations with "last best offer" on the table; discussing further automation to replace controllers while the membership was considering the proposal; Lewis' public acknowledgment of employment problems in the FAA. What impact did the government actions have on the process, and what do those actions say about the intent of the government?

Outside influences such as the role of the media can also be seen as important to the public posturing of both parties. Students can recognize the need for symbolic victories, the difficulties of "giving in," and the inability to maneuver behind closed doors because of the wide stakeholder interests and publicity.

Action Planning

In analyzing possible actions, students can look at conditions as they existed after the terminations (understaffing, fewer people working as supervisors, no union, most PATCO members gone). Action plans can be framed in recognition of that reality, as well as the existing historical and legal restraints on action. Action recommendations must look at all four policy areas:

—*Employee influence.* The union has been decertified and a power imbalance now exists on the side of the FAA. What, if anything, should the FAA do about this? Run organization without influence mechanisms? Create mechanisms? How? Which ones? Deal with a new union? How?

—*HR flow.* The system is understaffed and controllers are working 48 hour weeks. What can be done to ensure safe and efficient functioning? Should terminated controllers be rehired? All of them? If so, overstaffing will not be dealt with. Hire only a limited number? If so, which ones? How will selection be made: talents and skills, or role in the strike? What will be the impact on the work environment in the towers and centers if strikers are allowed back to work with nonstrikers? What signals would be sent to other public employee unions? Could recruitment policies be changed? Bring in more non-military people? Better educated people? More women? Can controller/supervisor alienation be reduced? How?

Specific suggestions for training, job descriptions, performance criteria for supervisors should be proposed. What, if anything, can or should be done to ease displacement by new technology? Employment security? Changes in retirement age? Retraining and/or outplacement counseling?

—*Reward systems.* Recommendations should address the pay cap (should changes be made in the non-carry-over rule? Should an exception be made for controllers? If so, what will the impact be on other federal employees?) and compression (should supervisors be allowed to rise above cap? What will be the impact of this on equity?). Can nonpay rewards—working conditions, time off, job satisfaction—be used to make rewards seem more equitable in comparison with pilots, other controllers?

—*Work systems.* Supervisor/controller tension is now low because most supervisors are working as controllers, but will future problems arise? Has the philosophy of management changed? Can it be changed? How? Should or can anything be done to address future problems (students' recommendations can address role and scope of supervision, and how many—if any—supervisors are needed). Other recommendations can look at other ways of improving working conditions (work schedules, assignments, access) and ways of involving controllers in decision about their work.

Action suggestions must either work within existing legal restraints or move to change the law. Should the FLRA be changed? If so, how? Can government employees have real influence within the current legal framework? Can or should they be given the right to strike or to binding arbitration? Should the system be moved from the public to the private sector? Would this give greater flexibility in rewards (work week, time off, pay cap, for instance). Strikes would be legal, but what would be the impact on economy? On public safety?

A specific action plan might include some of the following elements:

—*Employee influence.* Regular surveys of employee attitudes. Results could be summarized for all employees and discussed between management and employees. Participation committees to allow employees influence in such matters as new technology, scheduling, and so forth. In the absence of a union, the FAA can create new influence mechanisms (committees, task forces, ombudsmen, open door, speak-out programs, and so forth).

—*HR flow.* Flexible staffing to meet predictable peak demand. Part-time controllers (perhaps controllers who wish to pursue further education or training, or to begin transition to retirement or another career) could be used during peaks. Selected full-time controllers could control traffic during peak periods and perform staff work and training during valleys. An objective controller performance appraisal system could be developed by use of machine testing and on-the-job evaluation by a trained evaluation person other than the daily supervisor. Managers can be evaluated on human resource and collaborative management performance; quality of work life (QWL) employee attitude surveys could be used in evaluating performance. Select supervisors on basis of (1) above average technical knowledge,

(2) peer respect, and (3) direct assessment of management potential. Emphasize early identification of controllers with management potential and provide them with opportunities for management orientation, training, and experience. Require some college education for advancement; offer time off, partial or full tuition rebate. Establish career paths for nonmanagement employees that allow greater flexibility to move to assignments according to job pressures employees feel they could handle.

—*Reward systems.* Do something about the cap: either eliminate it entirely, or seek exception for FAA managers.

—*Work systems.* Working conditions—recognize that air traffic control system is different from other federal employment; bring it more in line with other countries. Reduce stress: better management of access—a pricing mechanism on user fees to encourage use at nonpeak hours (like the phone company) or market auction for operating opportunities to ease flow and reduce gap between peaks and valleys. Management needs to be more understanding of controller problems during peaks, more demanding of concentration during valleys. To ease stress, some program of job assignment flexibility, particularly for senior controllers who may be especially affected by stress.

Update on Case

On March 17, 1983 the task force appointed by Drew Lewis (Lawrence Jones, president of the Coleman Company, a manufacturer of sailboats and heating equipment; Stephen Fuller, vice-president of personnel, General Motors; and David Bowers of the University of Michigan Institute for Social Research) issued its 150 page report, accusing the FAA of having developed "a rigid and insensitive system of people management."[2]

The study said that many of the controllers still on the job believe the FAA "has little concern for employees, poor upward communication, and weak management support systems," and that management attitudes were regarded as "centralized, rigid, and insensitive." The report acknowledged that a spirit of cooperation had emerged in the period immediately after the strike. "The period after August 3, 1981 was marked by a renewed spirit of dedication, hard work, cooperation, care and courtesy within and between employees at all levels in the FAA. 'Them' and 'Us' disappeared, and a 'We' returned." However, it was soon apparent that "Most factors that had caused problems in the past are reasserting themselves, and the FAA seems headed toward more people-related problems in the future."

Among the specific findings of the task force were:

1. One in 20 controllers still working suffers from burnout, with the percentage rising to nearly 70 percent among controllers with an average of 19 year of service.

2. While some supervisors have tried to communicate more freely with controllers, some continue to have "a propensity to be high-handed" and authoritarian.
3. The complaints expressed about FAA management by controllers who struck and those who stayed on the job "are almost identical."

The report urged a return to the cooperative spirit that immediately followed the strike. "This asset (cooperation) is more powerful than any set of electronic gear. It is worth preserving, worth caring for, worth enriching in every possible way. This asset appears to be slipping away from the FAA. To retain and enhance this renewed teamwork, an immediate and energetic effort is needed." Helms responded to the report by saying, "it identifies and documents some significant management problems that we must resolve."

A study of the air traffic system by the *New York Times* one year after the strike noted that traffic volume had risen to about 83 percent of pre-strike levels with a negligible impact on the number of passengers being serviced, no evidence of hampered airline safety, but with considerably higher flight delays. At least two thirds of the fired PATCO members were reemployed, according to the union. Two hundred were working as controllers abroad, and the rest had found jobs with average wages considerably less than what they had been receiving. About 25 percent of working controllers were still working above 40 hours per week; at the larger centers, controllers worked 6 days a week. Serious questions were being raised about both the quality of the training taking place in the Oklahoma City facility and the ability of the FAA to restaff the towers to prestrike levels.

By the summer of 1983, the number of working controllers (including on the job trainees and supervisors working as controllers) had risen to 12,258 as compared with 16,300 prior to the strike. In June 1984 former PATCO president John Leyden (currently director of the AFL-CIO's Public Employee Department) announced that his organization would help organize current controllers. With that announcement, an airline lobbyist observed, "I have an uneasy feeling we are about to repeat the whole problem."[3]

TEACHING PLAN

30 min.   1. What is your evaluation of President Reagan's decision to terminate striking controllers?
a. You can start by asking students to vote pro and con, listing the reasons for their vote.
b. Students can be queried on the impact of their decisions, if any, in each of the four HRM policy areas.

45 min.   2. What recommendations would you make to Drew Lewis about the employment conditions of the air traffic controllers? Stu-

15 min.

dents can again be taken through each of the four policy areas to articulate what changes they would make and why.

3. Closing lecturette—review material in Chapters 1 and 2 on the four-policy perspective and general manager's perspective. The case can also be used to illustrate the stakeholder perspective, the social capital perspective, and the importance of considering the impact on employees and society when formulating and administering HRM policies.

While the discussion of this case allows students to see how HR problems and actions may be categorized into the four-policy framework, this revelation should emerge rather than be imposed. A looser discussion of problems and action is to be preferred to a discussion that forces students into listing problems by policy area.

NOTES

1. The 1947 Taft-Hartley Act specifically outlawed "closed shops" (agreements that permit the hiring only of union members) and allowed states to pass their own laws banning "union shops" (stipulations that while anyone may be hired, union membership is a requirement for continued employment). State laws outlawing union shops have come to be known as "right to work" laws, and by 1980 20 states had such laws on their books. See Bert Spector, "Note on Labor Relations in the United States," in Michael Beer and Bert Spector, eds., *Readings in Human Resource Management* (New York: Free Press, 1985) for further details.
2. Instructors may wish to read and assign as supplementary reading after the case discussion an article by David Bowers summarizing his analysis of the task force's findings. David G. Bowers, "What Would Make 1,150 People Quit Their Jobs," *Organizational Dynamics*, Volume 2, Winter 1983, pp. 5–19.
3. *Business Week*, June 18, 1984, p. 25.

CHAPTER 4

Employee Influence

The objective of the employee influence section is to help students understand the differences in interests and perspectives between stakeholders, particularly between employees and managers, in the firm. In our experience, business students assume that workers have or should have the same perspective as management, that unions are bad, and that they serve no useful purpose in society. The cases, notes, and audiovisual materials are intended to broaden students' views on these issues. This section is also intended to introduce students to the first of four major human resource management (HRM) tasks: deciding on how much influence to provide, and managing mechanisms for employee influence. The objective is not only to expose them to the legal and institutional frameworks for providing influence such as unions or, as in the case of the Dutch company, workers' councils, but to help them to explore their own attitudes toward these institutional mechanisms. Thus, traditional labor relations is subsumed under the broader policy question of employee influence: How much influence should employees have, and how should a company manage legislated mechanisms for influence such as collective bargaining? In particular, can and should management develop a collaborative relationship with unions? What are the difficulties, costs, and gains?

Among the key issues raised by the cases are:

1. *Why do employees join unions?* Students will learn that pay, security, fringes, and working conditions are not the only reasons employees join and support unions. Needs for influence, status, iden-

tity, community, and participation may also be important, and can be provided or precluded by management's HRM policies and practices (see the cases "First National Bank of Lake City," "Bethoney Manufacturing").

2. *The dynamics of conflict.* Students learn about how conflict develops and escalates. They see in "Bethoney Manufacturing" (as they already have in "Air Traffic Controllers") some strategies used by management to end that conflict. In later sections of the course, they will see other examples of companies attempting to end a conflictual union–management relationship by moving to greater collaboration ("Dana Corporation—The Richmond Camshaft Plant" and "General Motors and the United Auto Workers").

3. *The structure and process of collective bargaining.* In "First National Bank of Lake City," students are exposed to an organizing campaign and will be asked to evaluate management and employee response. "Note on Labor Relations in the United States"[1] can be assigned from the supplementary reading book to provide further details on the major laws and institutions that govern the process, as well as the history of the labor movement in the United States (to provide students with an historical perspective on the matter of employee influence). "Air Traffic Controllers" has already raised the general problems of providing influence, dealing specifically with unions in the public sector.

4. *Other legislated mechanisms for providing influence.* In "Workers' Councils: Hobbema and van Rijn, N.V.," students can learn about the legal framework for employee influence in Europe.

5. *Managing employee influence.* The "Workers' Council" case also introduces students to the issue of managing influence process: how much influence is appropriate, useful, and manageable, and what skills are needed by management and workers. This issue will be raised again in several later cases ("Dana Corporation," "Sedalia Engine Plant," and "Office Technology, Inc.").

Sequence of Cases

We are suggesting the following sequence of cases:

1. *First National Bank of Lake City.* The "Air Traffic Controllers" case opened the course by offering students a broad perspective on the overall HRM policies and practices of an organization, as well as introducing them to the importance of employee influence and of influence mechanisms (or lack of mechanisms). "First National Bank of Lake City" opens the employee influence section by allow-

ing a more specific focus on the question of why employees might consider joining a union. Students can explore the possible ramifications of a lack of internal mechanisms by which employees can exert influence or exercise voice over their working environment. In this instance, employees looked to an *external* influence mechanism: a trade union. As students deal with the question of how to create internal influence mechanisms, they can also begin to explore some of the dilemmas involved in building these mechanisms, particularly those that surround traditional managerial concerns about the loss of flexibility and power.

"First National Bank of Lake City" introduces an issue that is key to the entire HRM course: one of the main tasks of general managers is to provide a means of influence for employees. The bank has failed to provide for such influence for many of its white-collar workers, so employees must look for external mechanisms to enable them to exert influence. In this case, they look to a union. As we move through the employee influence section, we will see cases in which the forces of past union–management relations ("Bethoney Manufacturing") and of legislation ("Workers' Councils") have helped determine the boundaries in which management finds itself. The bank, on the other hand, seems to be relatively free and flexible in its ability to allow for influence. Their failure to do so has direct consequences in a union drive.

2. *Bethoney Manufacturing.* "Bethoney Manufacturing" describes an adversarial relationship between a local union and plant management, culminating in a wildcat strike and a 109-day authorized strike. A key question is what are the causes of this adversarial relationship, and what should management strategy be at the time of the wildcat strike and after the strike is over? For the first time, students can see the specific costs of a long-standing adversarial relationship: the loss of management influence on the shop floor, a disruptive wildcat strike, and an $8 million loss in profits during the longer strike. The case also allows students to continue the exploration begun in "First National Bank of Lake City," of how an adversarial relationship came to exist in the first place. Another new element is added in "Bethoney Manufacturing": a possible management strategy for breaking out of that adversarial mold (a power strategy). Thus, "Bethoney Manufacturing" takes students a major step beyond "First National Bank of Lake City."

The (C) case, to be handed out in class, provides a description of what the plant manager did to turn the union–management relationship around. An atmosphere seems to exist where both union and management are willing to work together to move from an adversarial to a cooperative mode. But how can such cooperation be institutionalized? Some prospects are mentioned in the (C) case, and other models for cooperation will be explored in some depth later in the course. "Dana Corporation—the Richmond Camshaft Plant," for instance, looks at how rewards (specifically, the Scanlon plan) can be used as a vehicle for encouraging and institutionalizing cooperation, while "General Motors and the United Auto Workers" will describe a more thorough and all-encompassing model for institutionalizing cooperation despite a long-standing history of union-management conflict.

3. *The Coal Strike of 1977/1978.* In "First National Bank of Lake City" and "Bethoney Manufacturing," students saw union–management relations being played out mainly on a local level. With this case, they move for the first time to industrywide negotiations, a pattern followed by only a few other industries in the United States (trucking and maritime, for instance), and more commonly in Europe. As negotiations move to a higher level, however, a greater multiplicity of stakeholders become involved. In "First National Bank of Lake City" and "Bethoney Manufacturing," the stakeholder groups were relatively few and easily identifiable. With "The Coal Strike of 1977/1978," students see that there can be a multiplicity of stakeholders *within* both union and management. The interests of society are also made explicit for the first time, showing the public as a major stakeholder with a vital interest that is threatened by this adversarial relationship. Government thus becomes an important player here, and a pattern of government helping to shape or even determining HRM policies will be carried throughout the course ("Workers' Councils: Hobbema and van Rijn, N.V." and "Nippon Steel Corporation" overseas and "Highland Products, Inc." in the United States).

Perhaps more than any other case in the course, "The Coal Strike of 1977/1978" illustrates the importance of history and culture in shaping HRM policy choices. The idea that unions serve a psychological function by providing a sense of community and power, introduced in "First National Bank of Lake City," is expanded upon here. Also, students will be given a chance to listen to, understand, and perhaps sympathize with blue-collar workers, and to see them as a vital asset of the business enterprise. Another issue made explicit for the first time is that money is often not the only, or even primary, reason to strike. Matters like safety, health benefits, the strength of their union, and pride in their work can be prime motivators for workers.

4. *Workers' Councils: Hobbema and van Rijn, N.V.* What alternatives exist for the adversarial relationships found in "Air Traffic Controllers" and "Bethoney Manufacturing"? This is the first case

34

in the course that exposes students to a non-U.S. and non-collective-bargaining approach to employee influence. Indeed, institutionalized employee influence in the form of legally constituted workers councils may be seen as one way of allowing for employee influence *outside* of traditional union–management relations. Moreover, the Hobbema case raises many questions about how much real participation is appropriate or effective when a legislated framework for participation already exists.

5. *Collective bargaining exercise.* Though not included in the case textbook, the original HRM course at Harvard Business School (HBS) included a collective bargaining exercise. Students were organized into management and labor teams, given a case ("American Metals and Machinery Company," available from Harvard Business School Case Services, Harvard Business School, Boston MA 02163) which provides information about a company and union (including data on wages, profits, and a copy of the current contract) just prior to negotiations. Students were asked to negotiate a contract and then in a subsequent class were asked to report on the contract negotiated and the experience of negotiation itself. We found this to be an extremely valuable experience for students as they learned about wage packages, supplemental unemployment benefits, considered profit-sharing, and learned (particularly those who were assigned to the union team) about the perspective of labor unions.

Audiovisual Material

Instructors may wish to consider using the following films to supplement or accompany the cases in the employee influence section of the text:

1. "Close the Gate—88"—a 25-minute film produced by the United Steelworkers of America during a local strike dramatizes the emotional as well as the rational appeal of unions. This film can be used to accompany "First National Bank of Lake City" and/or assigned with "Note on Labor Relations in the United States" and "Note on Why Employees Join Unions" by Bert Spector in the HRM reader.
2. "Taylor Chain"—a 30-minute documentary covering the inner workings of a local union and its relationship with the international during a strike. Can be used to supplement the case material and/or assigned with "Note on Labor Relations in the United States" and "Note on Why Employees Join Unions."
3. "The Wilmar 8"—a 50-minute documentary covering the struggle of a group of women bank employees who strike in an attempt to end what they perceive as sexual discrimination by their employer.

Can be used to supplement the case material and/or assigned with "Note on Labor Relations in the United States" and "Note on Why Employees Join Unions."

4. "Between a Rock and a Hard Place"—a one-hour documentary which explores attitudes toward work, fellow workers, and employers on the part of American coal miners. Can be used to accompany "The Coal Strike of 1977/1978."

5. "Harlan County, U.S.A."—a 90-minute Academy Award-winning documentary. This powerful film (also commercially available in VHS format) has been used by us in teaching "The Coal Strike of 1977/1978." We strongly recommend its use.

6. Interview with the plant manager and union president at Bethoney Manufacturing after an adversarial relationship was transformed into a collaborative one. In the interview the plant manager and union president describe how and why union–management relationships have turned around (order through HBS Case Services).

Supplementary Reading Assignments

The following supplementary reading assignments can be made from *Readings in Human Resource Management*:

TEXT MATERIAL	SUGGESTED READINGS
"First National Bank of Lake City"	Richard B. Freeman and James L. Medoff, "The Two Faces of Unionism"
"Bethoney Manufacturing"	Bert Spector, "Note on Labor Relations in the United States"
"The Coal Strike of 1977/1978"	
	Bert Spector, "Note on Why Employees Join Unions"
"Workers' Councils: Hobbema and van Rijn, N.V."	Ted Mills, "Europe's Industrial Democracy: An American Response"
	Don H. Fenn, Jr. and Daniel Yankelovich, "Responding to Employee Voice"
	Rosabeth Moss Kanter, "Dilemmas of Managing Participation"

Note

1. In Michael Beer and Bert Spector, eds., *Readings in Human Resource Management* (New York: Free Press, 1985).

FIRST NATIONAL BANK OF LAKE CITY
Teaching Note

The president of First National Bank of Lake City (FNBLC), Wynn Evans, has received formal notice from the National Labor Relations Board that a representative election will be held at the bank within 30 days. The bank management is taken by surprise at the extent of interest in a labor union on the part of its white-collar work force. Even though FNBLC's wages are not top among area banks, and the bank does not offer employees any kind of health care plan, FNBLC has counted on the prestige of the job, favorable working conditions, and a generous profit-sharing plan to maintain employee loyalty.

Much to the surprise of bank officials, 80 percent of the employees sign union cards, and old-time employees become organizers. Not in the case is the fact that the International Metalworkers Union (IMU) gains recognition.

The purpose of this case is to acquaint students with unions, the legal framework in which they operate, why employees join unions, and the management practices and environmental forces that might lead to unionization. The case can be used to help students see the role that unions can play in giving employees a voice and the dilemmas management faces in dealing with an organizing campaign.

ASSIGNMENT QUESTIONS

Students should read the (A) case and come to class prepared to discuss the following questions:

1. Why are employees at the bank seeking representation by a union?
2. What is your evaluation of the bank's response to the union organizing campaign? How should they respond?
3. What could the bank management have done to respond to the concerns of their employees? What can be done now?

CASE ANALYSIS

One of the critical questions with which the case deals is the matter of why the bank employees are considering a union. Traditionally, unions have had less appeal among white-collar workers than among their blue-collar counterparts.[1] Although nearly 51 percent of all employees found themselves in white-collar jobs in 1980, only about 10 percent of non-management white-collar workers belonged to a union. There are, of course, certain roadblocks to unionization among white-collar workers. Middle-class employees are less likely than lower-class employees to feel a need to affiliate with an organization like a union for the purpose of achieving power, identity, and dignity. Indeed, a 1977 survey of American workers[2] indicated a special appeal of unionization among nonwhite workers. Union membership offers, for these generally powerless individuals, some group power, an appeal which may not be quite so attractive to individuals who generally feel somewhat more powerful. Also, middle-class, white-collar workers may be more likely to accept the individualistic ethos of American culture.

The above factors, combined with a higher level of responsibility on the job, make it more likely that white-collar workers will identify, at least in their aspirations, with management. It is possible that in the past, white-collar workers may have viewed unions as rabble-rousing organizations beneath their dignity.

It has also been suggested that, as a result of the perceived value of their jobs, white-collar workers have developed a "threshold level" below which job dissatisfaction will be tolerated. When that threshold is passed, unionization can follow, particularly if an articulate leader arises to transform latent into manifest discontent.[3] As new technology turns white-collar jobs into fragmented tasks, some white-collar workers may come to feel as if they are working in a factory. It is only possible to speculate that such changes could move the "threshold level" down and the likelihood of white-collar workers supporting unionization up.

Already unions are beginning to sense a potential for growth among the country's 50.5 million white-collar workers. "Everyone sees the future of the trade union movement in white-collar workers," an Office and Professional Employees International organizer said recently. But will unions rest their appeal to white-collar workers on the same bread-and-butter issues they have historically called upon when organizing blue-collar workers? The Teamsters Union, for instance, is counting on financial issues, always their strongest card among blue-collar workers, to become increasingly important for white-collar workers. "The white-collar worker is coming around to realizing that while he is enjoying titles and so-called professionalism," said a Teamster official, "the guy in the warehouse is earning more." On the other hand, another blue-collar union, the United Auto Workers, has begun to chart a slightly different course, attempting to exploit workers' desires for greater participation and on-the-job pride by cooperating with management on a quality of work life program.

A model for illustrating an employee's decision concerning unions is presented in Figure 4–1. Employees satisfied with both their jobs and the

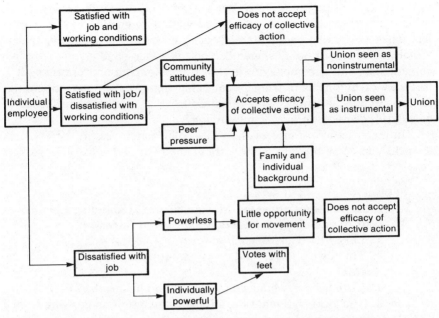

FIGURE 4–1

From Individual Employee to Union

working conditions are unlikely, of course, to support a union-organizing campaign. Employees dissatisfied with the job itself can "vote with their feet" by seeking more satisfying employment elsewhere. They may also remain in the organization; but if they feel they have enough individual power to improve their situation, they are unlikely to support an organizing campaign.

Employees who are dissatisfied with the job itself and either see little opportunity for outside movement or feel they possess inadequate individual power to improve the situation might be ready to turn their dissatisfaction into collective action. So might employees who are satisfied with their jobs but dissatisfied with working conditions.[4]

The acceptance of unionism, however, requires more than the presence of dissatisfaction. Employees must also accept a belief in the need for *collective* action to address causes of dissatisfaction. Often, this need is articulated by a leader, from either inside the work group or outside. That leader articulates both the existence of widespread employee dissatisfaction and the need for a formal collective organization to improve conditions. But even once this criterion is met, employees must still make an individual decision—recognizing that factors such as peer pressure, personal and family background, and community attitudes will exert a strong influence over that decision. Employees will ask whether a union would be "instrumental" in meeting their concerns. Part of that instrumentality has to do with the perception of what the union can do to improve such causes of dissatisfaction as wages and working conditions. But instrumentality cannot be viewed just in this narrow sense. Unions will also be viewed by employees as potential instruments of power—both internally against a powerful company, and externally as a form of political and ideological power—and involvement in a community (with accompanying feelings of belonging and prestige). It is this view of unions as instruments of achieving goals—broad, long-range goals as well as narrower, short-range goals—that is likely to influence an employee's decision on supporting a union.

In the specific instance of the white-collar employees at the FNBLC, students can come up with a checklist of the pros and cons of employees considering the union.

PROS
1. Close relationship with IMU members: traditional white-collar fears of unionization are weakened by four factors:
   a. Lake City is a strong union town.
   b. The town's largest industry, an automobile plant, is under the IMU.
   c. Virtually every bank employee has family members in the IMU.
   d. The local National Educational Association, in growing from a professional organization into a union, has set an example for white-collar workers.
4. The profit-sharing plan emphasizes long-term rather than short-term benefits. Although employees become eligible after two years of employment, the money was not paid out until an employee either quit or retired at age 65.
5. Other benefits: there are fewer holidays and vacation days than at the automobile plant
6. There is no medical plan, due to philosophical opposition of major stockholder Fred Savage.
7. No blue-collar union at bank exists to win better benefits for white-collar employees.
8. Management style: Frank Lockhard ran an efficient and autocratic customer loans department for ten years (department eventually supported union 100 percent).
9. There was a lack of *direct* communication between top management and employees, plus lack of voice or influence mechanisms.
10. Bank benefits like pension and profit-sharing plans may have greater appeal to older workers closer to benefit eligibility and less appeal to younger workers who see such benefits as being somewhat remote.

These "pros" are summarized in Table 4–1.

TABLE 4-1

Possible Reasons *For* Joining Union

—Lake City *strong union town*
—IMU already organized *automobile plant*
—*Teacher's union* set successful precedent for professional union
—*Lower salaries* than employees of other banks
—*Pension plan* difficult to understand, doesn't serve as motivator
—*Profit-sharing* plan emphasizes long-term rather than short-term benefits
—Fewer *holidays* and *vacation days* than automobile plant
—No *medical plan*
—No *grievance procedures, influence mechanisms*

CONS

1. FNBLC has always been a "prestige" place to work.
2. There are good working conditions.
3. Good personal development and training process without degree are available.
4. Job security—employees are never laid off and rarely discharged for poor work.
5. Profit-sharing plan is generous; this is particularly good for older employees; FNBLC is the only bank in area with such a plan.
6. The pension plan is better than that of other banks.

These "cons" are summarized in Table 4-2.

These lists of pros and cons, however, should not be viewed as static. Changes in the environment, both external and internal, have an important effect on how employees view their relationship to the organization. Five examples from the case seem particularly significant:

1. In the past, employees were willing to trade off something in wages (as compared with other neighboring banks) in order to get the prestige of working at FNBLC. *A shifting economy*, particularly an inflationary one, could dramatically affect the relative weighing involved in such a tradeoff, lowering the importance of prestige, for instance, and increasing the significance of wages.
2. The past benefit of *job security* had largely disappeared over the past decades as the IMU negotiated for the town's automobile

TABLE 4-2

Possible Reasons *Against* Joining Union

—Prestigious place to work
—Good working conditions
—Personal development and training: upward mobility
—Job security
—Generous profit-sharing, pension plans

workers supplementary unemployment benefits (SUB) and then a guaranteed income stream (GIS).

3. *Technology* was changing the relationship between the bank and its employees. Long-time employee Esther Douglas, for instance, was moved from a responsible bookkeeping job which placed her in direct and daily contact with the bank president to a job that put her in the company of lower-paid, lower-skilled workers and broke off her contact, both literally and figuratively, with the bank's president. That she became an active union supporter may have been the result of such technology-induced changes. FNBLC's new move to computerization of savings accounts might also influence the way some employees viewed their employment relationship.

4. As women became more sensitive to on-the-job *sex discrimination* in the 1970s, it may have become clear that upward mobility at FNBLC was largely reserved for males. Again, Esther Douglas's case is instructive. She had been with the bank 14 years longer than Wynn Evans. Like Evans, Esther had no college degree and had started as a clerk. But while Evans had risen to the bank presidency, Esther had been relegated to an isolated desk at the back of the main floor. Remembering that unions are often viewed as vehicles to power for groups of employees with relatively little power, it is possible that sex discrimination could have been contributing to employees' willingness to support the union.

5. The case gives several examples of the *changing nature of the work force*. FNBLC's recent move to branch banking may have worked to undermine the feelings of loyalty and pride associated in the past with working at the bank. There is evidence that union support is particularly strong among the 30 workers in the data processing center. These employees were all relatively new, often left the bank for the automobile plant, and were the only employees in the bank on shift work. They felt little loyalty to the bank management and were probably strong supporters of the union.

These changes are summarized in Table 4–3.

TABLE 4–3

Changes in the Human Resource Environment

—Prestige becoming less important than wages due to inflation
—Job security less an advantage over automobile industry (SUB, GIS)
—Technology changing relationship between bank and employees
  (Removes Esther from responsible job, close contact with president)
—Growth also changes relationships—branch banking
—Sex discrimination coming under closer scrutiny
—Changing nature of work force
  (Shift work in data processing—workers not loyal to bank, compare themselves to automobile workers)

One of the main lessons to be derived from the case, in fact, is how the human resource policies and practices of an organization are affected by changes in the internal and external environment, and the possible consequences to an organization when these policies and practices are not constantly reviewed and updated to respond to those changes.

Organizing Campaign

Under the NLRB, the primary steps of an organizing campaign are[5]:

1. One or more employees invite union in.
2. Union asks employees to sign card authorizing union as bargaining agent.
3. When at least 30 percent of employees have signed cards, union petitions NLRB for secret ballot election.
4. Election unit set (by mutual agreement or by NLRB) and election held, usually within 30 days.

If the majority of workers vote "no," the organizing campaign ends (all new campaigns must start at the card-signing step). If the majority of the workers vote "yes," the union becomes the authorized bargaining agent for *all* covered workers in the unit.

If and when a union becomes an official bargaining agent, the two parties—union and management—are required to bargain in good faith. Management does have available to it, however, various legal avenues of appeal, and may thus actually delay entering into negotiations for as long as a year. The various steps of this process are illustrated in Figure 4–2, p. 44.

Management Reaction

The two noticeable features of FNBLC's reaction are the unpreparedness of management and its inadequate or poorly timed responses.

The case recounts a number of times where management is "surprised" by events:

1. Surprised that IMU thought there was enough union interest among employees to send out direct mailing
2. Paul Blanton (Personnel) surprised that emp:~ .es had little "knowledge" or "appreciation" for wage and benefit package
3. Surprised (and shocked) at organizing efforts among assistant auditors
4. Surprised at Esther Douglas's pro-union activities

The following actions or inactions were taken by management in response to union activities. Students should be asked to list them and discuss their efficacy and legality.

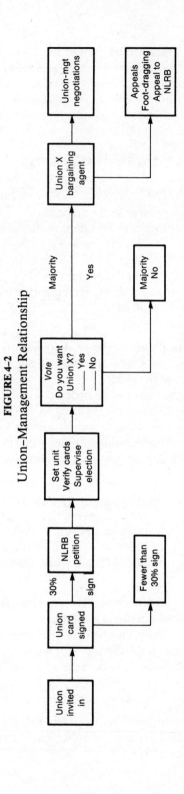

FIGURE 4-2
Union–Management Relationship

Week 1	As case opens, management tightens security in response to appearance of union cards.
Week 16	Management takes no action in response to IMU direct mailing; Blanton appointed as "clearinghouse" for all facts and rumors.
Week 20	In response to second IMU letter and first union meeting (between 75 and 100 employees attended), Blanton proposes active anti-union campaign, calls Q & A sessions with small groups of employees where he tries to raise uncertainties about union.
Week 22	Management calls halt to assistant auditors' activities.
	Union informs bank that 80 percent of employees have signed cards; bank attorney Grant expresses "honest doubt."
Week 23	In response to second union letter, President Evans sends memorandum to all employees. In that letter, the first written communication between anyone in management to the employees on the union matter, he made the following points:

1. "If we were distrustful of an employee, he or she would not be working for us." That statement at least implies the possibility that employees have been weeded out on some vague criterion of trustworthiness.
2. "You have a right to deal with us directly without the intervention of a union on any matter." That statement implies the existence of some sort of formal or informal voice mechanism. Employees can at least ask what those mechanisms are and how they can deal with management. There is no evidence in the case that any mechanisms for employee voice or influence exist.
3. "Both our pension and profit-sharing plans are purely voluntary on the part of the bank. . . . We hope to continue them, but there is nothing in the law to require us to do so if we feel economic conditions warrant a change. If you vote in favor of a union, all these items are subject to negotiation." Thus, management issued a thinly veiled threat regarding the continuation of the pension and profit-sharing plans.

Week 25	Bank files request for 100 percent bank-paid medical plan (Fred Savage had died eight months earlier), notifies department heads, branch managers, and supervisors of plan, and asks supervisors to inform employees rather than informing them directly. Should the bank offer this medical plan now? Will it persuade employees to vote against the union or will it convince them that a union is indeed an effective means for influence? Is it legal?
Week 27	Union files unfair labor practice (ULP) petition with NLRB, resulting in a delay in the election.
Week 31	NLRB hearing on ULP petition; bank produces evidence that planning for medical plan had begun *before* unionization drive.
Week 35	Management declines lawyer's advice to fire Esther Douglas for passing out union cards during work.
	Union withdraws ULP petition; president writes letter to employees informing them that medical plan would become effective in two months.

Week 37   Bank insists on formal NLRB hearing of election petition.
Week 41   Bank challenges cards and composition of bargaining unit.
Week 43   After NLRB election call bank asks for formal review of election petition.

With the promise of health care benefits in the middle of the campaign, the IMU filed a ULP charge with the NLRB. The union claimed that the bank had promised the health care program for the sole purpose of discouraging unionization. The bank responded at the hearing that the plan had actually been in the works *before* the unionization drive had commenced. The law hinges on whether a promise was made contingent on acceptance or rejection of the union. In this case, the union withdrew the complaint before the NLRB ruled. Nevertheless, the promise probably worked against the bank. "The bank is offering a health care program now only because they are afraid of us," the union could claim (justifiably or not). "Think of how much more you'll gain if you actually have a union!" Furthermore, if the union drive succeeds, the bank could find itself "locked in" by this promise during its first bargaining session.

Action Plan

Before deciding what specific actions might be taken in the remaining 30 days, management must first decide on what the *objectives* of such action might be. The alternatives available to management include:

1. Fight the union at all costs.
2. Fight the union, but do so in such a way that will not seriously jeopardize labor/management relations once the election is over.
3. Do nothing.

Students should see that the different sets of objectives will require different sets of actions, each of which will have a different consequence. And the consequences of such action should not be viewed only in terms of immediate impact on the organizing campaign. Different actions will also have different consequences in terms of employee relations *after* the campaign is concluded. If selecting the first objective (fight the union at all costs) involves taking actions that are deemed by workers to be dishonest (even if they are, in fact, legally permissible under NLRB rules) or making statements that indicate a stereotyped, negative, or somehow degrading view of workers or the union, those actions can have an important impact on future employee relations. If the union wins, workers and their representatives may see little reason to trust in or communicate honestly with bank management. The likelihood of collaborative, problem-solving behavior can be seriously diminished. Even if the union loses, such actions may serve to block up channels of communication between management and workers.

By seeking alternative two, management can move to create an atmosphere of "informed choice" and to do so in such a way that creates a model of behavior that will positively influence employee relations (regardless of whether they are unionized) after the election. Two examples of such actions might be:

1. Management could develop an employee benefit handbook and ensure that benefits are explained so that employees understand them. If students suggest this option, they can be pushed on what would be included. Specifically, what would the handbook say about employees' voice or influence?
2. Management could perform a survey of comparative benefits at other banks and the automobile company, compile this information, and communicate it to employees either directly or through a memorandum.

Management might also take steps to indicate its concern with the employees' well-being. Such steps might be seen as an attempt to fight the union, but they could also serve as a model for a new kind of management behavior which will continue after the election regardless of the results. Some steps might include:

1. Establishment of a formal grievance procedure
2. Creation of some sort of voice or influence mechanisms such as an ombudsman, open door policy, speak-out program, and so forth
3. Work closely with Lockhard to improve relations with employees under him
4. Begin to open direct communications channels between top management and employees. Perhaps this could be started by holding open meetings in which the president addresses employees directly (rather than through letters) and answers their questions about the bank.

If students suggest that last step, particularly the president meeting directly with employees, the instructor can use the opportunity to engage in role playing. Have a student who suggested the idea role-play Evans. Have the rest of the class role-play bank employees and ask Evans questions. The instructor can also add questions. Some specific questions that can be raised are:

1. Why don't you want us to have a union? What are you afraid of?
2. Do you intend to bring our wages in line with other banks?
3. In your letter, you wrote that "if we were distrustful of an employee, he or she would not be working for us." What did you mean by that? Have you fired employees for being "distrustful?" Will you do so in the future? What are your criteria? What rights of due process do we have to protect against such firings?

4. Why did you wait eight months after Savage died to announce a medical plan? Wasn't it really to keep us from voting for a union?
5. Your letter states that we have the right to "deal with us directly." What do you mean by that? How can we deal with you? On what issues? What power will we have? Why didn't you say this before the union came to organize? Will you be so open if we don't vote for a union?

Aftermath of Case

The case closes 30 days prior to the election. The following is a summary of subsequent events[6]:

1. In the 30 days the bank adopted a low-key approach: workers approached informally and asked to give bank a chance to improve working conditions.
2. Two days before election, President Wynn Evans retired.
3. Union won election: 99 to 90.
4. Bank bargained for nine months before reaching contract.
5. Contract provisions:
   a. No strong union security clause or dues check-off.
   b. Number of job descriptions reduced from 97 to 35; many salary inequities eliminated.
   c. Wage increase: 50¢ per hour first year; 40¢ per hour second and third years.
   d. Benefits: hospitalization plan approved; continuation of profit-sharing, pension.
   e. Four-step grievance procedure implemented.
6. Paul Blanton worked during contract period to build cooperative relationship with union; several managers felt he was weakening management's prerogatives.

These events are summarized in Table 4–4

TABLE 4–4
Aftermath

—Bank strategy for 30 days—low-key approach: employees approached informally, asked to give bank chance to improve working conditions.
—Two days before election, Wynn Evans retires.
—Union wins, 99 to 90.
—Bank bargains 9 months before signing contract.
—Three-year contract
   —Grievance procedure established
   —Wage increases staggered over term of contract: 50¢, 40¢, 40¢
   —No dues check-off
   —Hospitalization plan improved: bank continues to pay 20 percent of value
   —Pension and profit-sharing plans untouched

TEACHING PLAN

30 min.   1. Why would you vote for or against a union?

One way to open class would be to take an actual vote among students, put the tally on the board, then alternate back and forth between those who voted for and against the union. A set of subquestions would involve identifying various stakeholder groups within the bank (young versus old workers, males versus females, data processing versus other employees) and asking how *they* might see the union differently.

25 min.   2. How would you evaluate management's tactics so far? Discussion here can be directed to several points:

a. How effectively have they communicated with workers? Look at both the *content* and *process* employed in communicating with workers.

b. What has been the relationship between the bank and the NLRB? Why did the union drop its Unfair Labor Practice charge concerning the medical plan? Make sure students have some understanding of the law

c. How did management get into the position it is now in? What have been changes in external (economy, sex discrimination awareness) and internal (technology, shifting nature of work force) environment and what impact have those changes had on the bank's human resource policies and practices? Why did management get so out of touch with its employees (lack of feedback or employee voice mechanisms).

25 min.   3. What should management do now, in the next 30 days? Discussion here should be directed to several points:

a. Is the issue decided? Is it too late to do anything?

b. What are your objectives over the next 30 days? Fight the union? Improve labor–management relations? What are the long-term implications of the actions you are suggesting?

c. Given the objectives, what actions would you recommend? Make sure action suggestions are specific. If the bank should communicate with workers, how? Who should do it? Large groups? Individuals? What would you say? This is the opportunity to engage in role playing with a student acting as Evans and the class and the instructor raising questions that the workers themselves might raise.

10 min.   4. Conclusion. Tell students what happened (see above). Draw some conclusions.

a. Management should keep in touch with the (perhaps shifting) needs and interests of the employees.

b. Formal voice or influence mechanisms can help management keep in touch.

c. If there are no internal influence mechanisms, workers may turn to unions to provide that influence.

d. Unions are the means by which our society gives employees (through the legal framework that protects employees' rights to organize) voice and influence in determining their relationship with employers when they are dissatisfied with that relationship and/or when employers have not created provisions for employee voice or influence.

NOTES

1. See Bert Spector, "Note on Why Employees Join Unions," In Michael Beer and Bert Spector, eds., *Readings in Human Resource Management* (New York: Free Press, 1985).
2. Reported in Thomas A. Kochan, "How American Workers View Labor Unions," *Monthly Labor Review* (April 1977), pp. 23–31.
3. See Vincent Lombardi and Andrew J. Grimes, "A Primer for a Theory of White Collar Unionization," *Monthly Labor Review* (May 1967), pp. 46–49.
4. There are studies that indicate it is this latter group (satisfied with job/dissatisfied with working conditions) who make up the bulk of union supporters in an organizing campaign. They generally express satisfaction with the jobs they are doing, but are displeased with the conditions under which they must work. Instead of leaving their jobs, they seek a union to improve those working conditions. See Julius German et al., *Union Representation Elections: Law and Reality* (New York: Russell Sage Foundation, 1976) and W. Clay Hamner and Frank J. Smith, "Work Attitudes as Predictors of Unionization Activity," *Journal of Applied Psychology* (August 1978), pp. 415–421.
5. For a more detailed discussion see Bert Spector, "Note on Labor Relations in the United States," in Beer and Spector, eds., *Readings in Human Resource Management*.
6. For more details, see "First National Bank of Lake City (E)," No. 1-679-072, HBS Case Services.

BETHONEY MANUFACTURING
Teaching Note

Long and violent strikes are costly both in economic and human terms. Lower profits and cash flow can drastically affect future plans for capital investment. Market share can be affected in the near and long term. Adversarial relations between union and management can continue well beyond the strike, affecting negatively the potential for developing higher commitment to the organization and greater job satisfaction among employees in the future. Alternatively, efforts can be made to improve relationships. Why do strikes occur? What, if anything, can be done to turn the adversarial relationship into a cooperative one?

The purpose of this case in the HRM course is to introduce students to the potential for severe labor–management conflict. The case allows an analysis of the factors that have led to this situation (business strategy of groups, management practices at the plant and at corporate headquarters), an analysis of prestrike tactics and bargaining as a contributing factor to the strike. The case allows students to grapple with the problem of what to do after the strike to improve labor relations. This case, in particular, sets the stage for later quality of work life (QWL) cases in the work systems section.

ASSIGNMENT QUESTIONS

Students should read the (A) and (B) cases and come to class prepared to discuss the following questions:

1. What has caused the bad labor relations climate?
2. What were the causes of the wildcat strike? Is Arn Nelson's get-tough approach the right way? What were the alternatives?
3. What are the causes of the long strike which followed six months later? Consider the issues, union–management relations, and the bargaining process itself.
4. What should Arn Nelson do now that the strike is over? What problems can he expect and what opportunities exist? Develop a short- and long-range action plan.

CASE ANALYSIS

The (A) case focuses on the wildcat strike. Responding to pressures from Bethoney's Glass Division, plant manager Arn Nelson pressures workers to improve housekeeping, quality, and efficiency. Finally, when he prohibits coffee on the plant floor, the workers strike.

Arn's key characteristic is his religious outlook. It is more important to him to be honest and fair than to be popular. He has a long-range perspective and a strong sense of right and wrong. An earlier incident at another plant when a striker pointed a loaded, cocked shotgun at him convinced him that all future union–management confrontations involved a test of inner strength.

Arn's personality is a strong contrast to that of his predecessor, Ernie Bowen. Everyone liked Bowen, we are told, because he wasn't afraid to get his hands dirty. He involved himself in details, particularly employee relations. Within Bethoney, any manager with a history of union troubles was not likely to be viewed favorably, so Bowen tried to be cozy with the union. He made many individual exceptions in the contract to avoid potential grievances.

Arn is transferred to Plant G during the 1974 recession. Diminished demand places greater stress on quality, and Arn is expected to improve the plant's quality and "clean up the plant." This task progresses slowly because of Arn's inexperience in such a large plant, and his naive belief that workers share his sense of right and wrong. By 1976, division management is placing pressure on Arn to speed up the process. In response, he takes the dramatic step of banning food and coffee from the plant floor. His stated goal is to reduce litter, and his action results in a wildcat strike. Was this the best way to turn the plant and its labor relations climate around? Were there alternatives? Did this incident make the longer strike inevitable?

Arn is left to weigh pressures from the division to get tough and clean up the plant against Bethoney's historical taboo against work stoppages, particularly when customers were on allocation as they were in 1977. To complicate things, new contract talks are scheduled since the contract is due to expire in six months. Arn does not want to place management in a weak position.

In the (B) case, the wildcat strike ends when the International does not support it, but bad feelings persist. Workers look forward to getting back at management in the upcoming contract negotiations. Division executives, most of them new, send their manager of organizational development, Jim Riley, to survey the situation. His attitudinal survey indicates a high level of dissatisfaction among hourly employees, especially around the issues of working conditions and equipment maintenance. A survey of issues of values, based on the work of Scott and Susan Meyers, shows most workers have a "tribalistic" need to feel like members of a community. This survey also uncovers a large group of young workers with a high level of self-direction and leadership. The fact that these surveys are taken so late makes them of little use in preventing a strike. The fact that they are not taken earlier indicates a lack of employee–management communication. What is the role of employee surveys in employee relations? What role can someone like Riley play in improving management–labor relations?

In early 1977, division management learns that the employee relations supervisor at Farmington is not performing his job. In March they send Russell Walters to replace him. Though Walters' qualifications are good, his personality seems to make him incompatible with the people around him. Workers feel that bringing in someone like Walters is "insanity."

Negotiations begin badly, with Walters insisting that the parties break with their traditional negotiating pattern and segregate themselves from each other except over the bargaining table. The old contract expires before an agreement can be reached, and the strike begins.

The long strike is accompanied by violence and sabotage. The negotiations are unproductive until a mediator is brought in. The first negotiated contract is rejected by the union membership. Then Bethoney's president sends a letter to the families of all strikers. Because of the unstable labor market in Farmington, he hints broadly, the plant might have to move. A second vote soon after ratifies the contract.

Arn is then faced with getting the plant started again. He has to choose an appropriate attitude toward the returning workers. His challenge is to diffuse any tensions that might have remained and to take positive action to create a better atmosphere in the plant.

In analyzing the case, it is possible to identify four distinct phases in the development of union–management relations: the Ernie Brown phase, the "toughening up" under Arn Nelson leading to the wildcat strike, the events leading up to and including the longer strike, and the aftermath of that strike.

The Ernie Bowen Phase

Bethoney purchased its Glass Division from the Brownfield Company in 1956. For 20 years, that Division was run, by and large, by holdovers from Brownfield. The structure, attitudes, and behaviors manifest at Plant G and represented by plant manager Ernie Bowen (who worked his way up through the ranks of the Brownfield Company) came largely from the Brownfield Company.

Before analyzing those attitudes, it is necessary to know something about the business of Plant G. Their primary customers are automobile companies, so their own business ebbs and flows with the cycles of the automobile industry. In prosperous times (and, despite occasional recessions, prosperity dominated the automobile industry during the years covered in this case), the Glass Division could sell whatever it produced, with customers waiting for their allocations. As we are told in the case, during these times Plant G and the rest of the Division operated at full capacity and customers said little about the products they were receiving. (Although it is not mentioned in the case, they probably said little about cost, since the increased cost of components could simply be passed along to the customer in the price of the finished car.) Recession, of course, created a very different set of dynamics. Glass manufacturing plants would operate at far less than capacity and customers, no longer on allocation and themselves having a difficult time selling automobiles, became fussier about the quality (and probably the cost) of the products they were purchasing. As will be explored below, the realities of the Glass Division's business—and shifts in that business environment—will have a significant impact on employee relations at Plant G.

Before turning to the specifics of those relations, five other points about how Plant G was run that will have a direct impact on employee relations need to be recognized:

1. *Control systems.* Plant performance was measured by adherence to budget rather than plant profitability, with part of the plant manager's pay being tied to budget performance. We are told in the case that the budgets given the plant included inadequate funding for machinery maintenance, either long-run maintenance or immediate repairs. Once repair funds allocated in the budget ran out, there was no further repair money in the budget and a disincentive in the pay system for managers to spend over budget. Machine breakdowns were frequent. Ernie Bowen apparently made the situation even worse. He seemed unwilling or unable to schedule routine maintenance. Occupational Safety and Health Act (OSHA) injuries at Plant G ran ahead of the rest of the Glass Division, and workers, we are told, were enormously frustrated by the state of disrepair of their machinery (a frustration enhanced by the incentive pay system that will be discussed below).

2. *Supervision.* Plant G relied on a multilevel supervisory structure. Several employees operating a machine were overseen by a machine chief, who reported to the foreman, who reported to the shift foreman, who reported to a superintendent. The small span of control that necessarily results from such a profusion of supervisory levels can work to increase tensions between workers and their supervisors. Workers may feel they are being monitored too closely which can deprive them of feelings of autonomy and responsibility. (The importance of autonomy and responsibility will be addressed in greater detail in the work system section.) They may come to resent what they see as constant and unnecessary interference. In fact, the attitude survey reported on in the (B) case indicates that workers at Plant G are less likely than workers in the rest of the company to agree that their supervisors are either fair or know their job well.

    The possibility of a positive and close working relationship between foreman and workers is further undercut by the plant's policy of rotating foremen across shifts rather than allowing them to build a rapport with a group of workers.

Finally, the company's—and plant's—manner of dealing with the union leads to frustration among supervisors, as will be discussed in more detail below.

3. *Pay.* The incentive pay plan negotiated with the union involves a bonus based on the productivity of a single machine line above pre-established standards (less reported scrap). The performance or profitability of the plant as a whole, then, plays no part in the bonus provided workers, possibly lessening commitment to the overall performance of the plant. On the other hand, poor machine maintenance (as discussed above) will have a direct and negative impact on workers' take-home pay.

4. *Demographics.* Both the Farmington plants and the shifts within Plant G tended to be somewhat segregated by age. Since the seniority system of plant assignments covered all three plants in Farmington, older workers tended to shun the least desirable plant: Plant G. Within Plant G, workers with the least seniority were assigned to the A shift (midnight to 8:00 A.M.). In other words, the youngest workers in town tended to be at Plant G and the youngest workers at Plant G tended to be all together on the A shift. The case tells us that younger workers were more "unsettled" and "aggressive" than their older counterparts. The attitude survey in the (B) case finds that older workers tended to be "tribalistic" (strongly influenced by tradition and the power exerted by the boss), while younger workers tended to be "egocentric" (rugged individualists). Studies not reported on in the case have shown younger workers in general to be more resistant toward "abusive" and "arbitrary" authority and more interested in expanding their influence over their working environment than their older counterparts.[1] It is perhaps not surprising that the wildcat strike started on the A shift.

5. *The community.* Two facts are important to know about the community that hosts Plant G. First, Farmington is a strong union town with the United Auto Workers setting the standard for good wages. And second, it is a rural community in which most people maintained at least a part-time farm. It might be possible, then, for workers to endure a longer strike because of their farming interests.

Union–Management Relations. When it came to labor relations the premium during this phase was on peace at virtually any cost so that the line would be kept running. There were business-related reasons behind this approach. With the plant selling everything they could produce and customers on allocation, there was little concern for quality. The overriding concern was: keep the line running and the product moving out. Under the old

Brownfield regime (even after it was purchased by Bethoney), any manager with a history of labor strife was unlikely to get promoted.

Ernie Bowen fit well into this system and became something of a master politician. He engaged in what might be termed deal bargaining, and traded so many favors that he had to carry a looseleaf notebook to keep track of all the "special arrangements" and "exceptions" he, his employee relations people, and the union leaders made to the contract. (This atmosphere of deal bargaining and the possible negative impact of that approach to labor relations will be seen again in "The Kalamazoo Plant Parts Division" case in the Work Systems section.) What impact does such a deal bargaining system have on employee trust in their union and management? Does it increase their voice and influence or does it decrease their influence?

Bowen's style of operating may have pleased his superiors, himself, and the union leaders who engaged in the deal bargaining with him. But it likely displeased two important groups within the plant: the foremen and the workers. We are told that the foremen were constantly finding their decisions about grievances and discipline overturned after the union committee, Ernie, and his employee relations people got together. The merit of the content of such decisions is less important to this discussion than the process. Foremen decisions were reversed regularly, but the reasons behind that reversal were rarely if ever communicated to them by either Bowen or the employee relations people (a situation which we will see repeated almost exactly in the "Kalamazoo" case). Instead, foremen learned of the decisions from the union representatives or the affected employees themselves. Not surprisingly, foremen felt frustrated, powerless, confused, alienated, and angry, and it is likely that their frustration had a direct and negative impact on their relationship with their subordinates. (Again, this issue will be explored in greater depth in "Kalamazoo.")

Although not mentioned explicitly in the case, it can be implied that workers themselves may have been somewhat displeased with the deal bargaining conducted at the plant. We are told that Ernie occasionally made deals that circumvented the grievance procedure. That procedure has been negotiated and placed into union contracts to provide workers with a mechanism for due process on the job. By circumventing that mechanism, Ernie—and the union leaders who made the deals with him—deprived Plant G workers of that contractually protected sense of justice.

The Coming of Arn Nelson

The assignment of Arn Nelson to Plant G should be seen in the context of a shifting strategy regarding the plant and its labor relations. Arn arrived at the plant during a recession, when concerns about quality and efficiencies were high. His attempts to clean up the plant and improve maintenance proved rather ineffective; in part because of his inexperience in running a large plant, and in part because he was still operating under a management that said the only way to get promoted in the Division was to maintain labor peace. The changes in upper management in 1976 with the arrival of Ed Sherman coincided with the end of the recession. Now the change in strategy becomes clearer. Plant G must be made efficient. If Arn cannot do the job, Sherman will find someone else who can. The rules have changed. Perhaps because of his earlier experiences with unions, Arn translated his mission into action by pitting his personal authority against the union and workers. Despite positive signs of improved morale due to a much improved maintenance program initiated by a new plant engineer, Arn pushed cleanliness as the issue on which to test authority and power.

Power Inequities and Conflict. The case introduces the issue of power as being central to Arn's thinking. He believes that the union has become too powerful, and that his demands concerning cleanliness will help redress that power imbalance. Compromise over the coffee cups in such a context becomes "giving in" to the union by going back to the old power imbalance.

Because power is an issue that runs through the development of the case—along with conflict—it is worth exploring the relationship between power and conflict. Richard Walton has written that the perception of power imbalance between parties can lead to distrust between them, inhibit candid expression of views, and foster the growth of negative, often stereotypical and inaccurate perceptions of the other party. Blake, Shepard, and Mouton[2] add that once such distrust exists, it can set off its own dynamics that move parties through the following steps of ever-escalating conflict:

1. *Closing ranks.* When one party is identified as an adversary, the other party will become more cohesive in preparation to defend and/or attack; dissenters within that party (those calling for collaboration rather than conflict) will be ostracized.
2. *Pride and reputation.* As the two parties close ranks, the stakes of the conflict seem to go up. Individuals in each party, particularly leaders, tend to think their personal pride and reputation are at stake, as well as the issues on which the conflict was originally based; believe their side *must* win to preserve pride and reputation.
3. *Distortion.* Conflicting parties distort information about the other side to enhance their own position, while downgrading the position of their adversary. Contrary evidence will be rationalized away. For these same reasons, the content of the other side's proposals for ending the conflict will also be distorted.
4. *Stereotyping.* As mutual respect and confidence between conflicting parties erode, each party develops strong, negative, and hostile attitudes toward the other, leading to strong stereotype formations.
5. *Differences highlighted.* Even when similarities between parties do

exist, those similarities will be virtually ignored; thus highlighting differences even where they do not really exist.

6. *Loss of capacity for empathy.* With communications and views distorted, neither side can understand the position being taken by the other side. This attitude can persist even once the conflict is resolved.

It is worth noting, as the events progress in the (B) case, how the dynamics of conflict unfold at Plant G.

Walton suggests that a necessary first step to breaking out of this cycle is the achievement of some level of power equalization between parties. Only when two parties perceive themselves as being relatively equal in power will they begin to put their full efforts toward ending the conflict, talking honestly with each other, and collaborate on solving mutual problems. Employee influence mechanisms such as unions or workers' councils in Europe (as will be explored in "Workers' Councils: Hobbema and van Rijn, N.V.") are attempts to create mechanisms to ensure such power parity. When power inequities exist within a unionized setting, then mechanisms such as joint committees may be employed (see two later cases: "Dana Corporation" and "General Motors and the United Auto Workers").

Walton also suggests that when inequities become severe, the weaker party may have to confront the stronger party in some type of "power strategy."[3] There are some conflicts that are amenable only to power solutions; that is, one side attempts to get its way over a "zero-sum" issue (one in which when one side wins, the other necessarily loses) through a show of superior power. The pursuit of a power strategy, Walton warns, almost always leads to some immediate disintegration of friendliness and trust between the parties. In the long run, however, the result *can* be real and positive attitude changes. Walton cites three reasons why power strategies may eventually improve relations:

1. The conduct of one side in pursuing the power strategy may engender respect, after a while, on the part of the other side.
2. Power strategies may lead to power equalization; by getting rid of power inequities, parties may be getting rid of a major roadblock to building open communications and trust.
3. When a party gains power, the other party must treat them differently, and in doing so they will eventually assume a new attitude to justify that treatment.

Only when the issue of power inequity is addressed can the conflictual relationship be moved toward decreased conflict and, perhaps, collaboration and problem-solving behaviors. It is worth asking whether Bethoney, perceiving itself to be at a power disadvantage vis-à-vis the union at Plant G, is pursuing its own power strategy.

The Strike

Once the wildcat strike ends (at a cost of $100,000 in lost production), the dynamics of conflict continue to be played out at Plant G. Consider the following points:

1. Not only does Arn hold fast to his "no coffee" rule, but he disciplines every worker on the A shift (a move that Ed Sherman, Division general manager, terms "adding fuel to their fire"). Students can debate Arn's post-wildcat stance and suggest alternative ways of dealing with the strikers within the context of both an upcoming contract negotiation and the demands of management to straighten the plant out.
2. Feeling that they have lost power, the union begins to view the upcoming contract talks as a way of getting even. Workers begin to make financial arrangements for a strike.
3. Union leaders are angered by Bethoney's announcement that while the company plans to spend $250 million updating its Glass Division, none of that money will be spent in Farmington. This is an example of how capital investment decisions affect human resources and why such decisions need to be influenced by human resource considerations.
4. Russell Walters, who became the new employee relations manager for Farmington, serves as a divisive rather than a healing figure. Management people dislike him; workers despise him. He is a totally new player, and although the union views his coming as "pure insanity" on the company's part, it is possible that Walters has been brought in precisely because of these two traits: he is an outsider and he is tough. Such a move would be consistent with Walton's notion of a power strategy. The decision to bring in Walters is also an example of what can happen when local management is not involved in selecting the industrial relations manager.
5. Walters adds a further degree of adversarialism to the talks themselves by ordering an end to the traditional after-hours socializing between the parties.

The fact that the company is playing "hard ball" with the union is reemphasized during the strike itself: first with Walters' intimation that strikers would be permanently replaced (probably an unfair labor practice), and then with the letter written by Bethoney's president.

The strike ends after over 100 days and with a cost of nearly $8 million in profits. The company seems to have "won" on most of its issues (wage offer and cost of living). And the power balance is clearly altered. One of the questions that can be asked at this point is whether Arn and the company squandered any opportunities to improve relations at the plant with-

59

out a strike. While no simple answer to that question is possible, there are some indicators in the (B) case:

1. Sherman's statement after the wildcat indicates that Division management would have tolerated a more conciliatory approach by Arn, but only if it worked (which is to say, if he was still able to "clean the place up").

2. There were some positive steps being taken. As seen at the end of the (A) case, the arrival of new plant engineer Larry Johnson had improved maintenance and "significantly" improved morale. The company had brought in an organization development (OD) person from headquarters and an attitude survey was giving employees a chance to voice their feelings and concerns directly for the first time. And even though there were many negative findings in the survey (morale was low, working conditions were poor, equipment was poorly maintained), those were the very issues that Johnson was working successfully to improve. There was also, apparently considerable dissatisfaction with the work rules at Plant G (40 percent of all Bethoney employees agreed that "Bethoney's rules and policies help me," while only 19 percent of Plant G employees agreed). Even so, there were some positive signs in the survey. A majority of Plant G employees, for instance, agreed with the following statements:

   "My job is secure at Bethoney."
   "I find my work satisfying."
   "I am proud to work for Bethoney."

   There were, apparently, some strong and positive feelings on the part of hourly employees toward the company that changes in work rules and policies and continued improvements in maintenance might have exploited.

3. In contrast to the antagonism felt toward Russell Walters, the employee relations supervisor at Plant G apparently had a high degree of credibility with the union. Atkins, however, seemed to play a virtually nonexistent role in the actual contract talks.

The Aftermath of the Strike

Once the workers are returned, students are left with another difficult question: was it worth $8 million to the company? Again, there is no simple answer. Much of the answer, of course, depends on what will happen next. Arn ponders what attitude to take toward returning workers, and students can debate whether he should repeat his earlier attitude (after the wildcat strike) or adopt a more conciliatory approach. Those who opt for the latter can be pressed on precisely what that approach would involve (return coffee privileges?). Perhaps they can role-play a speech by Arn to returning workers or to union leaders. What work rules or policies, if any, should Arn attempt to change? Can anything be done, for instance, about supervision (assigning supervisors to work with specific groups of workers, training supervisors, helping facilitate communications between supervisors and employees, eliminating supervisory levels such as machine chief and/or shift foremen)? At this point in the course, students may be able to deal more with attitudes and rule changes than with more basic changes in union–management relations, but the instructor can bridge forward to the work system section by introducing the idea of joint union–management committees, work teams, redefining the role of supervisor, plantwide gainsharing and so forth.

Finally, students can be given the (C) case. This case is set three years after the first two. Arn and new local president Bob Graham (formerly the union's vice-president) put into action several plans for improving the climate at Plant G. Housekeeping and maintenance have been improved. The union president and committee have been given much more information about the business and plant goals. Many social and sports activities are now supported by the company, and company sports teams have been formed by the workers. The foremen are now given better training and more information to do their jobs. A videotape of an interview with Arn Nelson and Bob Graham is available through Harvard's HBS Case Services.

Postscript

A discussion with plant manager Arn Nelson in late 1980 revealed the following developments since the end of the (C) case.

The (C) case states that Arn had intended to expose shop stewards to Scott Meyers's seminar on managing with a union. The seminar, which deals with labor–management collaboration, had been presented to all foremen in the plant. As it turned out, the seminar for shop stewards was never held because of the objection of a union committee member. The committee member, according to Arn, is one of the "old school," and had strong feelings that union and management should not cooperate. To overcome this barrier, Arn recently asked a local college professor to put together a one-day seminar on "new ideas." The seminar, modeled after some of General Motor's QWL training programs (see "General Motors and the United Auto Workers"), will include films on quality circles, NBC-TV's 90-minute program, "If Japan Can, Why Can't We?," and other audiovisual material on productivity matters. Arn explained his problem to the local professor and asked him to be his "facilitator." The idea of the program was accepted by the committeeman because union–management collaboration is not its *announced* theme or objective.

Furthermore, Arn is planning a program for all foremen and key hourly workers which would take them out of the plant to customers who are using Plant G products. Presumably, workers will learn about the competitive environment of the firm.

This program has been adopted by the division, and will also be applied to other plants in the division. This is an indication of the growing credibility of Arn Nelson in the division and in Bethoney. Indeed, Arn reported that on a recent visit to headquarters, the division general manager hinted strongly that he will be asked to take a promotion to a division-level job. Arn says that he will probably not take it because he feels a responsibility to continue what he started at Plant G, at least for another three years.

TEACHING PLAN

The Bethoney cases may be taught in one or two classes, depending on the amount of time available in the course. The one-day teaching plan is crowded given all that can be done with the cases. The two-day teaching plan assumes that students will read the (A) and (B) case for the first class. The (B) case will continue to be discussed in the second class and the (C) case will be handed out mid way through this class. Additionally, the videotape interview with the plant manager and the union president can be shown at the end of the second class. At Harvard we have taught this case in one day and have always found the class crowded, particularly if a lot of time is used to analyze the causes of poor labor relations in the plant described in the (A) case.

One-Day Teaching Plan

15 min. 1. Ask students to analyze the causes of poor labor relations in the plant. Some responses might be (full analysis in notes above):
  a. Ernie Bowen's style and deal-making
  b. The control system in company leading to poor maintenance
  c. Corporate strategy of avoiding strikes to maximize sales
  d. Bonus system for production employees
  e. Supervision and communication

10 min. 2. Ask students to analyze the causes of the wildcat strike and to evaluate Arn Nelson's tactics. What were the alternatives?
  a. Contrast in style between Bowen and Nelson
  b. Change in management strategy from pacifying union to regaining power due to:
    (1) Recession puts emphasis on quality.
    (2) New chief executive officer (CEO) wants to appear strong and effective to the board.
  c. Nelson chooses to make labor relations a test of strength. Was this the best strategy? Alternative?

15 min. 3. Analyze the events leading up to the long strike.
  a. The collective bargaining process

b. Walters's role

c. Investments of capital ($250 million) outside of Farmington threatens union and workers. If the company is going to be less dependent on the plant to meet sales goals this may be the union's last chance to get what it wants.

d. The wildcat strike itself caused the longer strike. Union leaders who lost must reexert political muscle to retain credibility. Ask students to imagine what is going on in the union. What factions were there and what pressures did they bring to bear?

10 min. 4. Why did the strike last so long?

a. Union membership votes to give up right to vote on union proposals; gives its leaders a lot of freedom in negotiations.

b. The international has low power. This allows exploration of the relationship between locals and internationals.

c. There was community support for the union.

d. Many striking workers were farmers who had other sources of income.

e. The image of union was damaged in wildcat strike.

f. Analyze the impact of letter about closing down the plant. Did it shorten the strike? What can/should management do ethically and legally?

g. Who has won?

20 min. 5. What should Arn Nelson do now that the workers are returning from the strike?

a. What should he do on the first day? Ask students for specifics.

b. What should be his longer-term strategy? This is an opportunity to explore briefly issues that will come up later in the work systems section when QWL will be discussed. For example:

(1) Union–management communication

(2) Improving maintenance

(3) Involving workers

(4) Training supervisors

(5) Using earlier attitude survey data and those of the OD consultant Riley

15 min. 6. Hand out (C) case and tell the students briefly what is in the case. There will be no time to discuss it. Then show the videotape of interview with the plant manager and union president. While it describes in some detail how the relationship improved, the dynamics of the interview (dominated by Nelson) clearly shows that Nelson is in control. Students should be reminded that the old union leadership was voted out and Graham voted in since the strike. Does the balance of power in the interview reflect the balance of power in the union–management relationship?

5 min. 7. Lecturette on lessons of the case. We see in this case a whole cycle of labor relations from poor management practices that lead to unrealistic expectations by the union and low trust between management and workers to strikes and finally more collaborative relations.

    a. Discuss the importance of power balance in creating conditions for improving union–management relations (see Watson reference earlier in note).

    b. But to establish a power balance the company lost $8 million (cost of strike). The company has not yet leveraged this investment into a full-blown QWL effort (union–management committees, work restructuring, employee participation). Its success in establishing better relationships has positioned it to do so. This can be a bridge to the later work systems section and cases like "General Motors and the UAW" and "Dana Corporation—The Richmond Camshaft Plant."

Teaching Plan for Two-Day Class

Day 1. Assign the (A) and the (B) cases.

30 min.	1.	Ask students to analyze the causes of poor labor relations in the plant.
20 min.	2.	Ask students to analyze the causes of the wildcat strike and evaluate Nelson's tactics.
20 min.	3.	Ask students to analyze the events leading up to the long strike.
15 min.	4.	Ask students to evaluate why the strike lasted so long.
5 min.	5.	Lecturette on the causes of poor labor relations and the dilemmas companies are in once they are in an adversarial relationship.

Day 2. Assignment is to evaluate the Company's strategy up to the end of the (B) case and plan for what Nelson should do now.

20 min.	1.	Evaluate the company's strategy. Was Bethoney using a power strategy and what were the elements of that strategy? Was it worth $8 million? What are the implications for the future?
25 min.	2.	What should Nelson do now? Get students to discuss short- and long-term strategy. See if they can anticipate how management might move to collaboration and how higher commitment might be obtained from workers.
10 min.	3.	Hand out (C) case for reading.
15 min.	4.	Ask students to evaluate Nelson's program. Can they anticipate what else he might want to do?
15 min.	5.	Show videotape of interview with Nelson and Graham (union president).
5 min.	6.	Lecturette on the importance of power balance before moving to collaboration and on approaches that companies like General Motors have used to improve relations. Bridge forward to the work systems section by showing how Nelson's program is a step in the right direction but falls short. What else he might have done will be explored more fully the work systems section.

NOTES

1. *Work in America* (Cambridge, MA: MIT Press, 1973); R. P. Quinn and G. L. Staines, *The 1977 Quality of Employment Survey* (Ann Arbor, MI: University of Michigan Survey Research Center, 1978).
2. Richard Walton, *Interpersonal Peacemaking: Confrontation and Third-Party Consultation* (Reading, MA: Addison-Wesley, 1969); R. R. Blake, H. A. Shepard, and J. S. Mouton, *Managing Intergroup Conflict in Industry* (Houston, TX: Gulf Publishing, 1964).
3. Richard Walton, "Two Strategies of Social Change and their Dilemmas," *Journal of Applied Behavioral Science*, 1 (1965), pp. 167–179.

THE COAL STRIKE OF 1977/1978
Teaching Note

Bituminous coal is an industry central to America's future energy strategy. It is also an industry replete with labor problems. From the late 1960s to 1977, for example, labor productivity declined rapidly. Furthermore, the United Mine Workers (UMW), after years of one-man rule by John L. Lewis, had become a largely undisciplined example of participatory democracy. Wildcat strikes were common in the coal fields. In 1977 the coal companies, the union, and the government tackled these problems in the negotiations for a national collective bargaining agreement. A four-month strike resulted.

The cases describe the negotiating, bargaining, and ratifying process, the role played by mine owners, the union, and the federal government. It is told mainly from the national viewpoint and follows the activities of UMW leadership, the Bituminous Coal Operators Association (BCOA) negotiating team, and President Carter and his advisors. Students will also be asked to view the film "Harlan County, U.S.A.," which introduces them to the lives of mine workers and provides an understanding of the social context in which the negotiations took place.

The purpose of this two-class series is to expose students to the complexity of industrywide bargaining with its multiple stakeholders and to explore the management practices and historical forces that have led to such poor labor–management relations. Industrywide bargaining may be compared with the plant-level bargaining in the Bethoney case in terms of the extent to which these two bargaining forums provide a vehicle for employee influence. Students should come to understand that while industrywide bargaining is an imperfect mechanism for employee influence, there are provisions for labor–management negotiations over local issues.

CASE ANALYSIS

The entire coal industry was in a state of flux when these negotiations got under way. Prior to 1900 coal accounted for 90 percent of U.S. energy. That proportion fell to around 45 percent in the 1940s, and 25 percent in 1960. That slide was reflected in coal production—down from 631 million tons in 1947 to 392 million in 1954—and employment—down from 461,911 in 1942 to 169,400 in 1960. But in the 1970s with the country's search for energy independence, there was renewed interest in coal.

Coal operators are hardly a unified group. They are divided geographically—east versus west—and by style of mining—pit versus strip. But perhaps the most important split relates to who the owners are. There are three major groups of operators, each with its own interests and needs:

1. *Independents.* Many are small operators. They produce about half the U.S. coal and are concerned mainly with the efficiency of mining. They view labor primarily as part of the production process.
2. *Steel companies.* They need coal to make steel and are less concerned with the coal market than with the impact of coal prices on the steel market. In negotiations, they are considered the "hardliners," since their need for cheap coal to keep U.S. steel companies competitive leads them to press for low wage settlements.
3. *Oil companies.* They have lately begun to dominate coal production. They are committed to coal only if return on investments are adequate. They are considered to be the "liberals" of labor relations.

These three diverse groups form the BCOA. That association was begun in the early 1950s (with prodding of UMW President John L. Lewis) and negotiated its first national contract in 1951. Between 1968 and 1981 they failed to come to an agreement with the UMW in each of their negotiating settlements (and the union has a strict no-contract/no-work policy). There are three main reasons why the companies stay in the BCOA:

1. Gives companies united negotiations
2. Companies have mutual interests in joint pension funding
3. Affords opportunities for discussions among companies that might otherwise be prohibited by antitrust legislation

The UMW members are also in a period of change. After being dominated by one president, John L. Lewis, for 39 years (1920–1959), they went through a succession of less-charismatic leaders: Thomas Kennedy (1959–1963), Tony Boyle (1963–1972), convicted for murdering a union opponent, Jock Yablonski, and Arnold Miller (1972–1980). The dominance of the UMW in the mine fields was clearly eroding: 75 percent of the nation's coal was mined by UMW workers in 1933, while this figure had diminished to about 50 percent in 1977. While Lewis had enforced strict penalties against wildcat strikes in the 1950s, wildcats were spreading in the 1970s. The miners themselves were changing: they were younger and better educated.

This brings us to the 1977 negotiations. The most obvious issue on the table was money. The miners wanted to move from $64 to $100 a day. But there were other issues as well:

1. Restoration of benefits
2. Stability for mine owners
   a. Reduce absenteeism
   b. Penalties for wildcats
   c. Nonstrike clause with teeth

    d. Liberal interpretation of safety rules

    e. Right to install incentive bonus

3. Royalties on nonunion coal
4. Equalization of pension between miners on the 1950 plan and those on the 1976 plan
5. Restrictions on overtime for miners

    a. Drop compulsory overtime

    b. Reduce work week to 4 days

Chronology

What follows is a chronology of events in the three cases:

(A) CASE

June 20, 1977	Trustees of funds cut benefits; cuts to take effect July 1.
June 24	Wildcat strikes begin.
July 2	Miller wins reelection with 40 percent vote.
July 18	Miller seeks to reopen contract, BCOA refuses.
	Secretary of Labor Marshall and Wayne Horvitz of the Federal Mediation and Conciliation Service work to settle wildcats.
Late August	Wildcats end when trustees get loans to keep benefits.
Fall	Government tells utility companies through Federal Power Commission to stockpile coal to make possible coal strike ineffective.
October 6	Negotiations start, Miller being challenged from within; constant struggle over control of BCOA.
November 27	BCOA accepts Washington lawyer, Harry Huge, as part of UMW negotiating team.
December 5	Miller of UMW and Joseph Brennan of BCOA leave negotiations.
December 6	Strike!
December 23	Rod Hills, president of Peabody Coal (nation's largest producer) takes over negotiations.
January 21, 1978	First settlement reached by Hills, Huge, and Miller.
January 23	Settlement rejected by UMW bargaining team.
February 6	Second agreement reached.
February 12	UMW bargaining council rejects agreement, unhappy over pay and strike clauses.
	Bruce Johnson of U.S. Steel and Bobby Brown of Consolidation Coal (owned by Continental Oil) take over BCOA negotiations.
February 20	UMW bargaining council approves separate agreement with Pittsburgh and Midway (P&M) Company (owned by Gulf Oil).
February 21	Nicholas Camicia, an independent, takes over BCOA negotiations.

| February 27 | UMW suggests local agreements based on P&M settlement, BCOA rejects proposal. |

(B) CASE

February 24, 1978	President Carter meets with CEOs of five major coal companies; also present is Robert Strauss, a key figure in discussions of steel import quotas; Carter threatens to go on television and denounce coal operators if settlement is not reached; at 7:15 P.M. he announces "negotiated settlement."
February 26	Miners reject P&M settlement two to one.
March 5	Miners reject BCOA settlement two to one; Carter declares Taft-Hartley injunction.
March 9	Stonie Barker of Inland Creek Coal (owned by Occidental Petroleum), and Camicia seek new agreement with UMW.

(C) CASE

March 13, 1978	Court order to return to work is ignored by most miners.
March 14	Third agreement by Miller and Camicia; agreement features sharp reductions in health plan deductibles; pension payments under 1950 plan would be increased to come closer to 1974 plan; provisions calling for productivity incentives and allowing operators to fire leaders of wildcat strikes would be dropped.
March 16	UMW bargaining council accepts new proposal.
March 24	UMW ratifies agreement 57 to 43 percent.
May 1979	Consolidation Coal withdraws from BCOA.

Points About Case

The case does not deal as much with the specifics of the various proposals and counterproposals as with the negotiating process. Here are some of the major points to be derived from the case:

1. This is an example of *industrywide association bargaining*. The Bethoney model involved a single plant negotiating with a local union:

    Plant ⟶ Collective Bargaining Agreement ⟵ Union

    Single-company collective bargaining models in the United States include most manufacturing, banking, and automobile companies. Association models are far less frequent in the United States than in Europe, but include the following industries: trucking, coal, copper, construction, steel, supermarket, and maritime.

2. One of the special concerns of HRM—*stakeholder interests*—is dramatically represented in this case. There are multiplicity of stakeholders competing for influence in the collective bargaining process:

BCOA	UMW
East versus West	East versus West
Strip versus pit miners	Strip versus pit miners
Oil versus utilities versus steel	Young versus older workers
	Active versus pensioners

Other stakeholders involved either directly or indirectly include: non-BCOA mines, nonunion mines, and the federal government.

3. Almost all major industries are involved in coal: oil, steel, and so forth.

4. Division within each side is as great as division between sides.

5. It takes three agreements to make one:

Union ◄——1.——► Union negotiator ◄——2.——► Management negotiator ◄——3.——► Management

6. Has BCOA outlived its usefulness? Who is BCOA favoring? The "king of the hill" in BCOA can set labor relations policies for entire industry.

7. The issue is not really money, since margins have improved so much; operators are more concerned with productivity, wildcats, control of mines.

8. Operators do not like health benefits because they cannot allocate payments equitably between strip mines—where output is high (three times higher than pit mines), but incidence of black lung disease is low—and pit mines—where output is low and black lung is high.

9. The government is deeply involved in this process. Both sides think the government is favoring the other side. Government is seen as favoring operators when it advises utilities to stockpile coal, and is viewed as favoring miners when President Carter forces negotiated settlement, favoring operators when Carter issues Taft-Hartley injunction, and favoring miners when there is no enforcement.

10. Collective bargaining represents a particular social policy. One of the alternatives—worker participation—will be illustrated in the "Workers' Councils: Hobbema & van Rijn, N.V." case.

Film

Between the first and second class, students will be asked to view "Harlan County, U.S.A." Among the important points that the film will add to the discussion are:

1. Labor negotiators must pay attention to more than simply economic factors.
2. There are limitations to the law.
3. History and culture are important factors.

The film dramatizes the separate and unique culture of the Eastern coal fields. That culture is deeply rooted in a long history of bitter struggle and is passed on through stories and songs from generation to generation. The film depicts the tremendous pride the miners feel for their work and the ownership they feel toward the land and even the mines. Violence is clearly just beneath the surface in these communities. For students who wonder why the government did not enforce the back-to-work order, the film should hint at least at the consequences of such an attempt. It is also clear that money is a secondary issue to these miners—well behind health care concerns, safety, and the strength of their union. The strong, pro-union ethos makes it highly unlikely that miners would cross a picket line regardless of whether the context was a wildcat or an authorized strike.

Update

What happened since the closing of the (C) case?

October 1979	U.S. Steel threatens to leave BCOA.
February 1980	NLRB bans picketing at nonunion mines.
March 1980	BCOA reorganizes; there is a three person negotiating committee to deal with UMW, and a nine-person CEO policy committee to deal with government.
	Consolidation Coal rejoins BCOA; president Bobby Brown will head negotiating team in next sessions.
January 1981	Negotiations begin on new contract between Brown and Sam Church, UMW's newly elected president.
March 9, 1981	177,000 miners stage two-day walkout to protest President Reagan's proposed cutbacks in federal funding of the black lung trust.
March 27, 1981	Old contract expires without agreement, strike begins.
April 1981	Miners reject first agreement; Sam Church accuses Bobby Brown of being tool of "Big Oil."
May 1981	Miners reject new agreement negotiated by Church and Brown.
June 1981	New contract approved by rank-and-file; includes royalties on coal purchased from nonunion suppliers to be paid by operators into union's health and retirement fund; total cost to industry, including 38 percent boost in wages and benefits, estimated at $1.5 billion annually.
November 1982	Rich Trumka, a young lawyer, overwhelmingly defeats Sam Church in the union's presidential election.
September 1984	With Rich Trumka heading the UMW negotiating team and Bobby Brown leading the BCOA group, an agree-

ment for a 40-month contract is reached and ratified by the membership without a strike. Brown says, "It's all upbeat. The most positive thing we start with is 40 months of stability." Trumka adds that the settlement should erase any lingering doubts about the union's willingness to help the industry survive.[1]

TEACHING PLAN

Students will prepare the (A) case for the first day, read the (B) case and view "Harlan County, U.S.A." for the second day, and be handed the (C) case during the second class.

Because of the complexity of the (A) case, opening the first class with an action question like "What should the BCOA do now?" might elicit only a weak response. Instead, it might be preferable to start with a more general analysis question:

Day 1

30 min.	1. Why can't an agreement be reached? After a general discussion, go back and isolate the key factors:
10 min.	2. Who are the primary stakeholders on the BCOA side?
10 min.	3. Who are the primary stakeholders on the UMW side?
10 min.	4. Who are the other stakeholders involved in the negotiations?
10 min.	5. What are the key issues being debated?
10 min.	6. What are the cultural–historical forces at work here? What are the effects of those forces on the negotiations? That question will bridge into students' viewing of the film.
5 min.	7. Summarize the point that it takes three agreements to make two.
5 min.	8. Close by asking what the government should do now.

Day 2

For the second day, the film will most likely have a powerful effect on many students, and a discussion of the film should carry much of the class:

40 min.	1. What did the film add to your understanding of the situation?
10 min.	2. What was the government's stake in the process?
10 min.	3. Hand out and read (C) case.
20 min.	4. Now, what do you think of the process? a. What do you think of the association bargaining? b. What do you think of the future of BCOA?
10 min.	5. Summary of events since close of (C) case, lecturette on collective bargaining as social policy.

NOTE

1. *New York Times,* September 29, 1984.

WORKERS' COUNCILS: HOBBEMA AND VAN RIJN, N.V.
Teaching Note

The case focuses on the 1974 decision by the management board of Hobbema, a Dutch office supply and design company, to sell off an unprofitable division, and management's attempt to win the approval of their legally constituted workers' council for that sale. The case allows students to become familiar with the tactical problems of managing within the Dutch legal framework. More importantly, it allows students to explore the dilemmas of managing participation. Employee participation has its costs. It is time consuming for managers and requires special managerial attributes and competencies. The costs will also be present and must therefore be weighed in another form of institutionalized participation described in the later "Sedalia Engine Plant" case. Students can see in industrial democracy a distinct alternative approach to employee influence with its own set of assets and liabilities.

ASSIGNMENT QUESTIONS

Students should read the (A) case and "Note on Worker Participation" and come to class prepared to discuss the following questions:

1. What should van Berkel do now?
2. What has caused the problems faced by van Berkel? What, if anything, could he have done differently?
3. What is your evaluation of workers' councils as a societal response to the issue of employee influence?

CASE ANALYSIS

Because of the somewhat complex set of events described in the (A) case, it might be wise to open discussion with a brief review of the chronology and content of the events. Table 4–5 provides a brief overview of those events.

One of the critical lessons of the case is that managers can, through their own actions, have a considerable impact on both *how much* influence employees will have and the *manner in which* that influence is exercised. Even though the involvement of workers through councils is mandated by Dutch law, there is still a good deal of flexibility: questions about *which workers councils* should be consulted, the *issues* about which they should be consulted, and the *extent* of their power. Thus, van Berkel's handling of the Amersfoort sale should be viewed in terms of both short- and long-term im-

TABLE 4–5

Brief Chronology of Events in (A) Case

1974		Hobbema discontinues a manufacturing line of its Amersfoort Division. Management approached with offer to buy Division, reaches take-over agreement.
Nov. 7, 1974		Management reports agreement to union.
Nov. 8, 1974		Van Berkel calls meeting of Central Workers' Council, outlines plan for sale; Council proposes questions on sale.
Nov. 15, 1974		Van Berkel calls meeting of Central Workers' Council to review answers and consider sale; Council adjourns to await advice of Amersfoort Division Workers' Council
Dec. 2, 1974		Amersfoort Division Workers' Council delivers 65-page report to management condemning proposed sale and suggesting partial sale to leave Hobbema with 49 percent interest in Division.
Dec. 10, 1974		Central Workers' Council holds meeting on "neutral" grounds, adjourns until next day without decision but with "aggressive" and "negative" tone. Van Berkel, excluded from next day's Central Workers' Council Meeting, prepares to meet with management board.

pact: not only how it will affect his capacity to implement a specific decision that the management board has already made (the decision to sell the Amersfoort Division), but also how it will impact in the long run on the pattern of participation that will become institutionalized at Hobbema. Should participation be minimized and councils used primarily as means of communicating management's decisions? Or should councils become a governance structure which approve all major decisions?

Such questions have broader application than Dutch management practices. Managers in the United States who encourage participation by workers (as seen in the "Sedalia Engine Plant" and "General Motors and the United Auto Workers" cases), must ask a similar set of questions:

1. What will the mechanisms be for influence? Should influence be exercised solely through traditional mechanisms like unions (through expanding the role of unions) or through some sort of nonunion governance boards, committees, or task forces? What about some combination, as suggested under Dutch law?
2. What issues will workers be asked to participate in? In later cases in the course, workers will be seen to have increasing influence over matters relating to the job itself and be allowed to participate in decisions regarding both the design and implementation of pay systems. By and large, worker participation in the United States has not extended much beyond these issues, although there are beginning to be a number of examples of exceptions to that rule. In return for concessions made to Chrysler Corporation, the president of the UAW was granted a seat on the Chrysler board. Also in return for concessions, the United Steelworkers demanded and received a let-

ter of understanding from the steel conference members as to precisely how money generated from the new contract would be invested. As the *expectation* of participation by workers increases, so too might the expectation of the scope of issues in which workers can participate also increase.

3. How well prepared are workers for increased participation? The assumption on which expanded worker participation over the doing of their jobs is based is that nobody knows better how to do the job than the workers themselves. The Hobbema case, however, points to the fact that worker participation and influence can, and often does (especially in European countries) expand well beyond the job itself. And the comment managers often make is: workers may know a lot about how to do their jobs, but they lack the special training, expertise, and resources to make well-informed decisions about broader business issues like whether to sell off a division. Although there are indications that the Amersfoort Workers' Council had considerable sophistication in drawing up its lengthly report, it is still an issue that managers must face. But managers can do more than merely ask the question. They can seek to *develop* in their employees the kinds of skills and competencies necessary to make business decisions, and then provide them with all the relevant data to make an informal decision. The extent to which an organization will commit time and resources to such development is a management choice.

4. How can workers be expected to make decisions that are good for the company as a whole when their own self-interests are involved? The question is, of course, a difficult one when asked of employees at *any* level of the organization. Managers, after all, can make short-term decisions to maximize their bonus at the expense of the long-run effectiveness of the organization. In all cases, organizations can attempt to create and administer HRM policies and procedures that encourage employees to adopt a long-range and broadly based view of the organization. Communicating realistic and complete information concerning the competitive position of the company (information traditionally shielded from workers, particularly in union settings where control of information is used to enhance management's bargaining position) will at least allow employees the opportunity of developing a realistic view of the organization and its market position. In this case, although van Berkel does provide the Workers' Council with considerable information, he does so late in the process. He informs the Council of the sale only one day prior to their meeting to consider that sale, and then provides further details only after the Council officially requests it. Students may discuss whether a more proactive process with much longer lead time

would have led to different results. American companies have attempted to instill a "we're all in it together" view of the organization through the use of stock plans and organization-wide bonuses (see "Dana Corporation—The Richmond Camshaft Plant").

It is in the context of understanding management's ability to impact the influence process that van Berkel is faced with a number of tactical decisions as events unfold. While legally the Central Workers' Council has the right to "advise" on the question of selling the Amersfoort Division, it does not have the right to veto the decisions. Yet, practically speaking, could Hobbema's management board sell a division against the advice of the council? The Central Workers' Council has two members from the Amersfoort Workers' Council who will more than likely oppose the decisions.

Given the stakes, the Amersfoort Division's Workers' Council insists that since they are being sold, they should be able to advise management directly as a Council. The Central Workers' Council, in an effort to assert its power, opposed this and says that the two Amersfoort members should bring the views of the Amersfoort Council to the deliberations of the Central Workers' Council. Management attempts to resolve this issue by agreeing to accept advice from both councils. Fearing that their voice may not be heard, the members of the Amersfoort Division Workers' Council ask that they and the Central Council could approve the sale even if their council is unanimous in its disapproval. Because it wants to preserve its prerogative, the Central Council rejects the proposals for joint meetings. Since the law upholds this position, joint meetings are not held.

These dynamics and management's decision to take advice from both councils create some of the difficulties later encountered by van Berkel. A negative recommendation by the Amersfoort Council, a likely possibility, can hold hostage the decision to sell. Furthermore, van Berkel does not have any formal relationship with the Amersfoort Council, whereas he is chairman of the Central Council.[1] By agreeing to hear from the Amersfoort Council as a whole he has strengthened their position and the influence they will have on the decision to sell. As the (A) case ends, van Berkel is about to meet with the management board. Its members must decide what to do about this turn of events given their conviction that sale of the Amersfoort Division is necessary for the company's health. But they also recognize that a formal vote by the Workers' Council in opposition of the sale presents a formidable barrier in implementing the sale of the division, to future relations with the workers, and to the future of worker participation at Hobbema. The case provides an opportunity to critique management's decisions about how much participation to allow and the tactics of van Berkel as events unfold. It raises the question of who the stakeholders are in this company. This discussion can be followed with the action question about what van Berkel and the management board should do now.

The (B), (C), (D), and (E) cases are short and designed to be handed out sequentially in class following a discussion of the (A) case.

1. The (B) case provides information about a compromise solution sought by the management board which was later implemented in modified form. A reading of the case in class should be followed by a critique of the board's decision, a discussion of problems this decision will create, and the development of anticipatory action plans.

2. The (C) case provides a description of a meeting of van Berkel with the Amersfoort Division Workers' Council and the Central Council, and a final compromise solution agreed to. Again, a discussion of the solution, and its implications should follow. Particularly, will the board of directors accept this decision and what is the implication of the compromise for the future of worker participation at Hobbema? Van Berkel's decision to tell the Central Workers' Council that a negative recommendation on the sale would constitute a veto deserves special attention. One of the key questions in managing participation is how to get participating parties to feel truly responsible for the actions they take. Van Berkel is, in effect, voluntarily increasing the Council's power in order to let its members know that their decision in this matter will have important, far-reaching consequences. Students can debate van Berkel's actions in this regard.

3. The (D) case indicates that the board of directors accepted the compromise solution, its reservations about the solutions, and van Berkel's reflections about the process.

4. The (E) case provides the final irony. The prospective purchaser of the Amersfoort Division backs out of the deal because of the purchaser's claims of a weak business picture and inability to obtain financing. The case describes the reaction of the workers' councils and subsequent cooperative efforts between workers, union, and management to stem financial losses at Amersfoort.

This final turn of events raises questions about whether delays resulting from worker participation and changes in the purchase agreement were responsible for this final outcome. This leads to questions about the handling of the whole affair. Was there too much or too little worker participation? One could argue that involving the Amersfoort Workers' Council in the problems at Amersfoort should have been the place to start. One can also argue that if the Amersfoort Council had been shut out completely, none of the events in the case would have occurred. It is a dilemma that students need to understand. A choice about the extent of worker participation has long-term policy implications and requires quite different managerial approaches.

Through the use of the short (B), (C), (D), and (E) cases, students can be involved in "real-time" deliberations and decisions. Thus they can experience the real dilemmas, problems, and opportunities inherent in worker participation. More importantly, the cases allow students to learn about and evaluate a wholly different approach than that found in the United States for resolving conflict between employees and management. What are the implications of worker participation legislation for organization effectiveness, employee well-being, and society as a whole? What are its underlying assumptions? Would this approach work or be desirable in the United States? Is it inevitable? If so, what are its implications for management?

CONCLUSION

Because the case closes the employee influence section of the course, it can be used as an opportunity to discuss, in more general terms, trends in the policy area of employee influence. There can be little doubt that a growing number of organizations are seeking to increase participation and influence by employees at all levels of the organization. A recent survey conducted by the New York Stock Exchange indicates that 70 percent of U.S. corporations (with 500 or more employees) have some program to involve rank and file workers to some degree in decision making.[2] Chapter 2 provides an overview discussion of what those forces are (see Table 4–6 for a summary).

But students should also see that management can influence that process by the decisions it makes. After discussing van Berkel's handling of the situation, the following list of questions concerning how influence is to be managed can be generated:

1. How do you as a manager create realistic expectations on the part of employees?

TABLE 4–6
Reasons for Expanding Employee Influence

Limitations of hierarchical control mechanisms
Increasing international competition—Japanese model of high commitment and lower conflict through employee involvement
Changing characteristics of the work force
    —Employees better educated
    —Changing values concerning authority
    —Women and blacks entering work force
Greater government involvement
    —Codetermination/workers' councils in Europe
    —Labor–management–government cooperation in Japan
    —Collective bargaining laws in United States
Growth of "knowledge workers"/new technological work which relies heavily upon individual and team skills

2. How do you as manager match the growth of employee influence with the development of employee expertise?
3. How do you as manager develop responsibility for actions?
4. When do you as manager engage in integrative problem-solving and when do you engage in distributive bargaining?
5. How do you as manager keep issues fluid while informing and discussing with participants?
6. How do you as manager get one side to see the other side's point of view?
7. How do you as a manager solve immediate issues while retaining a long-range view of the precedents being set?

A model for conceptualizing employee influence is presented in Figure 4–3. Management can seek either to *minimize* or to *maximize* influence of employees. It may also seek to develop in employees a tendency to act in the interest of the enterprise rather than in their own interests. As other forces push to increase the *amount* of employee influence (pushing into quadrants three and four), managers must seek a way to develop an organization-wide view (quadrant 4). For if employee influence grows, but the view taken by employees is strictly narrow in focus, management could find themselves

FIGURE 4–3
Conceptions of Employee Influence

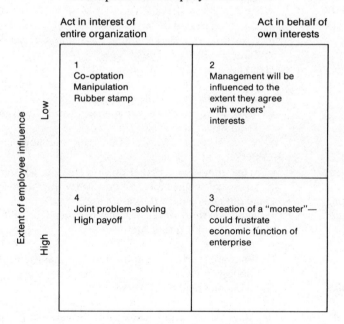

with a "monster" on their hands: increasing employee influence which could actually frustrate the economic functioning of the organization.

TEACHING PLAN

There are several alternatives to teaching this material. All the cases (A–E) may be read and prepared in advance of class. Using this approach the decisions of van Berkel may be critiqued and his tactics reviewed. But the main focus would be on the broader question of workers' councils in Europe and their implications. A second approach would involve providing the students with only the (A) case in advance. The (B), (C), (D), and (E) cases would be handed out in class to provide an opportunity for "real-time" action planning. The second alternative is likely to be more involving and exciting. Of course, any number of other options are possible such as preclass preparation of the (A), (B), (C), and (D) cases and handing out the (E) case, or preclass preparation of the (A), (B), and (C) cases and handing out the (D) and (E) cases. The plan below assumes that students will have read the (A) case. The other cases are to be handed out in class.

You might open class discussion by either eliciting from a student or presenting yourself a chronology of the (A) case. Then move to the action question.

5 min.	1. Review chronology of (A) case.
25 min.	2. What should van Berkel do now?
	a. What has caused the problems?
	b. How can van Berkel make sure that Central Workers' Council will act responsibly?
5 min.	3. Hand out and read the (B) case.
10 min.	4. What do you think of the management board's decision, and what problems do you think might now arise?
	a. How do you evaluate the management board's decisions? From whose perspective?
	b. What problems do you anticipate and how should van Berkel deal with them?
	c. What should van Berkel do now? Again ask, how would you make people more responsible for their actions?
5 min.	5. Hand out and read the (C) case.
10 min.	6. What do you think of the deal that has been reached?
	a. What are the future implications for the company's performance?
	b. What are the future implications for management–worker relations?
5 min.	7. Hand out and read the (D) case.
10 min.	8. Do you agree with van Berkel's evaluation? Class discussion at this time should begin focusing on broader issues of worker participation.

           a. How would you evaluate the whole process and its out-come?

           b. What would you predict for the future situation at Hob-bema?

           c. What is your evaluation of worker participation in Europe?

5 min.   9. Hand out and read the (E) case.

10 min.   10. What is your evaluation of this process?

           a. What did the company get out of it?

           b. What did the workers get out of it?

           c. What are the dilemmas, problems, and opportunities of managing employee influence? This final question can be turned into a summary lecturette on employee influence.

Note: The teaching is very tight on time. Combining the handout of cases (D) and (E) can result in gaining more time for discussion of both cases and their implications.

NOTES

1. In the case, van Berkel was by law a member and chairman of the Central Workers' Council. Dutch law has since removed the chairman of the company from the workers' council.

2. *People and Productivity: A Challenge to Corporate America* (New York: New York Stock Exchange Office of Economic Research, 1982). See also James O'Toole, *Making America Work* (New York: Continuum Publishing, 1981) and John Simmons and Walter Mares, *Working Together* (New York: Knopf, 1983).

CHAPTER 5

Human Resource Flow

The objective of this section of the course is to give students an understanding of a second major human resource management (HRM) task: managing the flow of people *in*, *through*, and *out* of an organization. Students learn that societal expectations, government policy, unions, legislation, and business strategy all influence management's policies in hiring, promoting, and terminating employees. This is particularly true in the area of employment security, fair practices, and employee development. We want students to recognize these constraints, to appreciate the reasons for them and to understand their implication for managing human resource (HR) flow. This section contains a non-U.S. case, "Nippon Steel Corporation," to point out societal and cultural differences regarding the question of employment security and business, union, and government relations. Additionally, we hope students will recognize that competent people are not always available in the firm or in labor markets, and that careful planning and fair treatment of people in this area is necessary if the required number of competent and committed people are to be available. The following key issues are dealt with in the cases:

1. *The implications of business conditions and government policy for personnel planning.* Students learn about the implications of rapid growth (and decline) on personnel planning. They learn that a declining economic climate can lead to serious problems if an organization's flow policies have not been kept up to date ("Nippon Steel Company," "Webster Industries"). Likewise, equally difficult recruitment and employee development

problems can occur in a rapid growth economy with tight labor markets [Medical and Environmental Electronics Devices (MEED)].

2. *Effective management of human resource flow requires good employee evaluation and development systems and practices.* Students learn about performance appraisal systems and processes, particularly about the potential for conflict in attempting to serve the dual goals of employee evaluation and development. They learn about the importance of considering both business results and personal characteristics in making evaluations of performance and managerial potential.

Students also have an opportunity to examine various systems and practices ("Webster Industries," "Colonial Food Services Company," and "Assessing Managerial Talent at AT&T")

3. *Fairness is an important consideration in personnel decisions.* Students learn how unfair personnel decisions can evolve from supervisor bias about personal habits, dress, sex, and so forth, and about the due process employees might seek through government regulatory apparatus to redress these grievances. They are forced to reexamine personnel systems for appraisal, assessment, and promotion decisions in light of the fairness question and the threat of government and the courts ("Colonial Food Services" and "Highland Products").

Sequence of Cases

We suggest the following sequence of cases:

1. *Nippon Steel Corporation* opens the HR flow section of the course by presenting students with a cross-cultural alternative, lifetime employment, as a way of attracting people with needed competencies and of developing needed commitment. "Human Resources at Hewlett-Packard" will introduce students to an American company using a modified version of lifetime employment as part of its overall HRM approach. It also helps students see the connection between HRM policies—in this case, flow policies—and strategic business planning. The case provides as example of the clanlike approach to management that will be discussed in Chapter 7 of the text; a theme that will be revisited in "Sedalia Engine Plant," "People Express," and "Human Resources at Hewlett-Packard." To a greater degree than in any other case in the course, government will be seen as a major stakeholder in the enterprise, although the issue of government as a stakeholder has already been raised in "Workers' Councils: Hobbema & van Rijn, N.V." and will come up in "Highland Products" as in regards to affirmative action.

"Nippon Steel Corporation" bridges back to the stakeholder influence perspective introduced in Chapter 2 of the text by showing how various stakeholders—management, full-time male workers (and, by implication, part-time and women workers who are not covered by lifetime employment policies), government, and society—are all affected by and in turn attempt to influence a particular HR policy (lifetime employment) and a management decision on how to deal with one of the outcomes of that policy: excess employees. The high level of commitment achieved by the flow policy also bridges forward throughout the course. Slow promotions, which are a critical part of the Japanese approach to HRM, relate directly to how reward systems are devised. Furthermore, work systems can achieve high commitment more effectively when they are built on a foundation of employment security (see "Sedalia Engine Plant," "Office Technology, Inc.," "General Motors and the United Auto Workers," "People Express," and "Human Resources at Hewlett-Packard"). As such, "'Nippon Steel Corporation" is a pivotal case. It is the one place in the course where students can become familiar with the Japanese model and consider its relevance to U.S. management.

2. *Webster Industries.* In "Nippon Steel Corporation," students saw an explicit psychological contract for a HR flow policy—lifetime employment—and were asked to evaluate the costs and benefits of breaking such a contract. In "Webster Industries," that psychological contract is more subtle, but it is still there. The question put to Bob Carter is not *if* to break the contract, but rather *how* to do it and *what* the costs might be. Like "Nippon Steel Corporation," "Webster Industries" shows the problems that ensue when HR planning has been allowed to drift away from the realities of the marketplace, and the traumatic, though perhaps unavoidable, costs of suddenly realigning those policies with reality. "Webster Industries" also differs dramatically from "Nippon Steel Corporation" in terms of the governmental and societal context under which managers operate, and brings down to a micro, even interpersonal, level the stresses and costs of acting. But this is not to say that society does not have an interest in the HR policy decisions at Webster. The host community will bear the burden, even the costs, of layoffs. Unlike the situation in many European countries, however, there is no political mechanism whereby the community can seek to protect its interests.

3. *Colonial Food Services Company.* "Nippon Steel Corporation" concentrated mainly on how to manage HR flow into and out of the organization. "Webster Industries" also raised the question of how to manage internal flow, although the case was explicitly concerned with outflow (termination). In "Colonial Food Services," there is no talk of laying off or firing employees. Rather, the point is how to manage flow through the organization by better performance appraisal and developmental systems. Colonial Food Services has created a performance appraisal system, and students will be placed directly in the middle of one such appraisal. Through struggling with how to have an effective performance discussion, students will learn

that managing an effective HR flow policy requires managers to possess the will and skill to engage in a dialogue with subordinates about difficult issues.

4. *Assessing Managerial Talent at AT&T.* In "Webster Industries," Bob Carter was unsure of the validity of the data at hand upon which to base important human resource decisions. "Colonial Food Services" developed a system in which appraisal depended almost entirely on the perception of an individual manager regarding his subordinate's performance and potential for growth. To move away from this reliance on individual perceptions and toward more valid criteria for judging potential, AT&T has introduced assessment centers as an additional source of data about potential. What new problems do these types of systems present?

5. *Highland Products, Inc.* The possibility of discrimination in Human Resource Flow policies was raised as early as the "First National Bank of Lake City" case (in the case of Esther Douglas). The fact that government can move in to help shape human resource policies in the name of protecting the "greater good" of society has been demonstrated in many of the earlier cases, although "Highland Products" represents the most pronounced intervention in a U.S. case. In this instance, the two issues—sex discrimination and government involvement—come together. But while the case is primarily about equal employment opportunity, it is also about managing flow as part of an overall HRM approach. Sex discrimination, as much as poor advanced planning and lack of systematic performance appraisal data, can lead to underutilization of available human resources. "Highland Products" also raises again the notion of "fit" or congruence between various HR policies (an issue implicit to all cases but explicitly addressed previously in "Air Traffic Controllers" and "Nippon Steel Corporation"). Job posting is seen in this case as a way of eliminating discrimination in promotion decisions. But successful implementation of a job posting system will not occur unless accompanied by a wide array of policies that will work to overcome institutional, managerial, and even self-imposed barriers to equal opportunity. Indeed, the culture of the corporation must support the behaviors required (openness, cooperation, development) for job posting to work.

6. *Medical and Environmental Electronic Devices Corporation* concludes the flow section of HRM by showing the relationship between corporate strategy (growth projections, in this case), HR availability (the short supply of competent managers and engineers), and flow policies. Building on the need for fit seen in "Highland Products," students will be asked to integrate all the various elements that make up a flow policy: recruitment (who to recruit and how to attract them, how geography affects recruitment, how to do advanced planning that meshes with the availability of talent for the future), internal flow (how shall performance and potential, par-

ticularly management potential, be appraised; what kind of training needs to be initiated), and outflow (what to do about high turnover, how all the various HR policies and business strategies affect turnover).

Audiovisual Material

"Colonial Food Services Company" is a case on a particular performance appraisal process and should be accompanied by the videotaped record of the Cranston–Kirby appraisal interview: "Colonial Food: Performance Appraisal Interview." (Order through HBS Case Services.)

Supplementary Reading Assignments

The following supplementary reading assignments can be made from *Readings in Human Resource Management:*

TEXT MATERIAL	SUGGESTED READINGS
Chapter 4	James W. Walker, "Managing Careers: Policies and Systems"
"Nippon Steel Corporation"	Stephen Marsland and Michael Beer, "Note on Japanese Management and Employment Systems"
"Webster Industries"	James F. Bolt, "Job Security: Its Time Has Come"
	Douglas A. Benton, "A Guide to Work Force Reduction Planning"
"Colonial Food Services Company"	Michael Beer, "Note on Performance Appraisal"
"Assessing Managerial Talent at AT&T"	William C. Byham, "Assessment Centers for Spotting Future Managers"
"Highland Products, Inc."	Gloria J. Gery, "Equal Opportunity-Planning and Managing the Process of Change"
"Medical and Environmental Electronic Devices Corporation"	Edgar H. Schein, "Increasing Organizational Effectiveness Through Better Human Resource Planning and Development"

NIPPON STEEL CORPORATION
Teaching Note

Nippon Steel Corporation (NSC) faces declining sales in the wake of the 1973 "oil shock" and finds itself with at least 3,500 excess employees. At the same time, their union is pressing the company to raise the retirement age from age 55 to 60 years. The case provides the data for students to determine the financial and people impact of the problem, and the consequences of various solutions. Should lifetime employment be continued? What would be the consequences, particularly on cost improvements from self-management groups, of discontinuing it? If lifetime employment is continued, what specifically should Nippon do to bring headcount and costs into line with business needs? There are sufficient numbers in the case for students to do some flow planning (see casebook Exhibit 8-4 and casebook page 273). Finally, the case provides an opportunity to explore how lifetime employment fits into the context of Japanese society and business structure.

ASSIGNMENT QUESTIONS

Students should read the case and Stephen Marsland and Michael Beer's "Note on Japanese Management and Employment Systems,"[1] and come to class prepared to discuss the following questions:

1. How serious is NSC's problem and what should management do? Students should be prepared to recommend specific steps for dealing with the excess employees, and the impact of their recommended steps on employment levels, costs, profits, as well as on commitment and competencies of the work force.
2. What are the advantages and disadvantages of lifetime employment? Should NSC consider modifying the policy?

CASE ANALYSIS

The following is a summary of the material presented in the case:

DEVELOPMENTS IN THE GROWTH OF
THE JAPANESE STEEL INDUSTRY
1. Japanese government sets up country's first steel works—1901.
2. Government consolidates smaller steel companies into Japan Steel Corporation (JSC), half private, half government-owned—1934.

3. Allied forces split JSC into two companies after World War II.
4. Government assists in managing economy and rationalizing industry, allocates loans and credits for steel mill upgrading—early 1950s.
5. Japanese steel production surpasses French in 1959, British in 1961, West Germans in 1964.
6. Two former JSC companies merge, form Nippon Steel—1970.
7. Output of Japanese steel industry up to 120 million metric tons; Japan third behind United States (second) and USSR (first)—1973.

NSC's LABOR RELATIONS

1. Viewed as one of Japan's most prestigious employers; top students rank it among top ten employers; reputation for good management; employees consider themselves part of the elite group; managers and blue collar employees expect lifetime employment; "closed world" created for employees.
2. In post–World War II years, plants organized by communist-led unions, leads to period of labor unrest and severe strikes throughout 1950s.
3. NSC begins revising employment practices: allows more upward mobility for blue collar workers (1958), creates new pay system that relates 15 percent of pay to the job itself instead of relying totally on seniority (1962); strikes end at NSC (1965).
4. Moderates win control of NSC union: win 53 percent of vote in 1968, 82 percent in 1978.
5. Self-management (*Jisho Kanri*) system encourages blue collar workers to be involved in safety, energy, and process improvement; initiated in 1965; can save ¥50 billion a year.

NSC's CORPORATE STRATEGY

1. Dual allegiance of management: to company *and* country
2. World's largest producer of crude steel
3. Invest heavily in latest steel-making technology
4. Fully integrated with broad product line; lowest-cost steel producer in the world; dominates Japanese market
5. Maintain flexible skilled work force; use exports to maintain employment stability when domestic market lags
6. Increasing cost-cutting in late 1970s due to stagnant demand

WHAT IS THE SITUATION FACED BY NSC IN 1979?

1. Still in recession from 1973 oil shock: output down 20 percent since 1973, employment down 8 percent, income fluctuating.
2. NSC did not begin to trim work force until 1977.
3. Operating all facilities, although some at 40 percent capacity
4. Excess work force of 3,500 employees
5. What should NSC do about excess work force? What about lifetime employment?

1. Union proposing to move back retirement age from 55 to 60. The Japanese government has just moved the retirement age of civil servants to 60. That, plus the "aging" of the Japanese population[2] increases pressure on companies to follow government.
2. 3,500 excess personnel (3,000 of them blue collar) costing ¥50 million a day.
3. Employment costs, running ¥350 billion per year, key variable cost.
4. Is it time to change NSC's personnel policies? Proposals gaining management consensus call for shutting down or phasing out four of five mills, transferring personnel to other plants. Transfers opposed by unions and workers.

WHAT ARE NSC's FLOW OPTIONS?
1. Retirement age—move it back gradually, all at once, or not at all.
2. Blue collar retirement—7,000 scheduled to retire between 1980 and 1984.
3. Rationalization reducing the number of people required for operators.
4. Hiring—has been significantly reduced, but management is worried about long-range impact on NSC work force; think NSC should hire 700 persons per year.
5. Stopgap measures—accelerated career training, "loaning" workers to other firms, "restructuring" work assignments given to subcontracting companies, transfer of personnel to help start up new ventures, early placement of workers in post retirement jobs.
6. "Western-style" adjustments like layoffs and early retirement. Some evidence that voluntary early retirement may work in Japan.
7. Cutting costs per employee—take tough stand on wage increases, cut fringe benefits 10 percent, unilaterally cut retirement bonus, reduce annual seniority-based increase.

REMAINING QUESTIONS
1. How should decisions by made?
2. What would be the financial and morale costs?
3. How should decision, once it is made, be presented to the work force?

Action Plan Analysis

Analysis of the work force indicates that maintaining it at present levels would be extremely expensive. It is clear that 3,500 is a conservative number since 3,000 blue collar workers were in excess while NSC was running facilities at 40 percent capacity. If NSC immediately shut down mills and rationalized production, 6,000 employees would be out of work. Thus, NSC's ex-

TABLE 5-1

Savings from Maximum Use of NSC Stopgap Measures

Category	Salary Saved (%)	Salary (¥ million)	No. People	Total Savings (¥ billion)
"Loaning"	70	3.68	400	1.0
"Restructuring"	60	3.68	200	0.5
Accel. training	0	—	—	—
Transfers to new subsidiary	100	3.68	100	0.4
"Job trials" at subcontractors	60	4.8	200	0.6
Total				2.5

cess labor costs would be nearly ¥100 million per day, or ¥35 billion per year.

Costs can be figured from the case. Assuming 3,000 excess blue-collar workers *times* ¥230,000/month *times* 16 months (including bonus) *plus* total annual fringe benefit cost of ¥50,000 month *times* 12 months *equals* ¥12.84 billion. Five hundred excess white collar workers make substantially more than blue collar workers, about ¥8 million, for a cost of ¥4 billion. Total cost is nearly ¥17 billion.

A number of short-term factors operate in NSC's favor, however. Table 5-1 shows savings from maximum use of all stopgap measures. Reduced wages costs can yield ¥2.5 billion per year, self-management programs ¥50 billion per year, retirement saves ¥4.28 billion per 1000 employees. This excess labor can be brought into line quickly if retirement age changes can be held off for several years. Table 5-2 shows actual costs of keeping excess work force while still gaining self-management savings.

This analysis points to a gradual move of the retirement age to 60, thereby maintaining good relations with the work force. Table 5-3 shows

TABLE 5-2

First-Year Cost of NSC Excess Work Force*

(Assuming 1980 Retirement of 1,400 Men)

	Excess Work Force	
	3,000 Blue-Collar (¥ billion)	6,000 Blue-Collar (¥ billion)
Excess work force times ¥4.28 million annual salary	12.84	25.68
Less total savings from stopgap measures	2.5	2.5
Less 1980 retirement of 1,400 men times ¥4.28 million annual salary	6.0	6.0
Total cost of excess work force in first year	4.34	17.18

*Annual savings from "self-management" = ¥50 billion.

TABLE 5-3
Move Back Retirement Age One Year Each Odd Year Starting 1981

	1980	1981	1982	1983	1984	1985
Work force at start of fiscal year	51,000	49,600	49,600	48,200	48,200	46,600
Less retirement	−1,400	0	−1,400	0	−1,600	0
Less turnover	− 200	− 200	− 200	− 200	− 200	− 200
Less promotion of white-collar workers	− 200	− 200	− 200	− 200	− 200	− 200
Plus hiring	+ 400	+ 400	+ 400	+ 400	+ 400	+ 400
Work force at end of fiscal year	49,600	49,600	48,200	48,200	46,600	46,600
Less work force required for operations (reduced annually due to rationalization)	−47,500	−47,000	−46,500	−46,000	−45,500	−45,000
Excess work force	2,100	2,600	1,700	2,200	1,100	1,600
Less stop-gap measures						
Accelerated training	− 200	− 200	− 200	− 200	− 200	− 200
"Loaning workers"	− 400	− 400	− 400	− 400	− 400	− 400
"Restructuring" subcontracting	− 200	− 200	− 200	− 200	− 200	− 200
Transfers to new firm	− 100	− 100	− 100	− 100	− 100	− 100
"Job trials" at subcontractors	− 200	− 200	− 200	− 200	− 200	− 200
Excess work force assigned to make-work projects	1,000	1,500	600	1,100	0	500

TABLE 5-4

Move Back Retirement Age One Year Each Odd Year Starting 1982

	1980	1981	1982	1983	1984	1985
Work force at start of fiscal year	51,000	49,600	49,600	48,200	48,200	46,600
Less retirement	−1,400	−1,400	0	−1,600	0	−1,600
Less turnover	− 200	− 200	− 200	− 200	− 200	− 200
Less promotion of white-collar workers	− 200	− 200	− 200	− 200	− 200	− 200
Plus hiring	+ 400	+ 400	+ 400	+ 400	+ 400	+ 400
Work force at end of fiscal year	49,600	48,200	48,200	46,600	46,600	45,000
Less work force required for operations (reduced annually due to rationalization)	−47,500	−47,000	−46,500	−46,000	−45,500	−45,000
Excess work force	2,100	1,200	1,700	600	1,100	0
Less stop-gap measures						
Accelerated training	− 200	− 200	− 200	0	− 200	0
"Loaning workers"	− 400	− 400	− 400	− 400	− 400	0
"Restructuring" subcontracting	− 200	− 200	− 200	0	− 200	0
Transfers to new firm	− 100	− 100	− 100	0	− 100	0
"Job trials" at subcontractors	− 200	− 200	− 200	− 200	− 200	0
Excess work force assigned to make-work projects	1,000	100	600	0	0	0

the impact of moving back the retirement age one year each odd year starting in 1981, and Table 5–4 shows the impact of moving back the retirement age one year for each even year starting in 1982.

Seeing Flow Policies as Part of an HRM System

One of the key points of the case relates to the interconnectedness of an organization's HRM policies, as well as the importance of congruence or fit between those policies and the environment in which that organization operates. In Japan, lifetime employment does not stand alone, but rather is supported by an array of other employment and management systems (slow promotions, frequent transfers, sharing of information, formation of work groups, and so forth), as well as external forces such as the history, culture, and values of the host country, the labor market, the role of government, and the structure of Japanese private enterprise and unionism. The elaborate interconnectedness of Japanese employment systems is discussed by Marsland and Beer[3] and summarized in Figures 5–1 through 5–3 and Tables 5–5 through 5–8. In reading and discussing the case, students can also generate a listing of "costs" and "benefits" that accrue from the Japanese lifetime employment system (see Table 5–9, p. 97).

HRM policies must also be considered in terms of their impact on business strategy and policies. Writing in *The New York Times,* Steve Lohr[4] has suggested that the very policies that have benefited Japanese companies in terms of high levels of employee commitment and competencies will have important costs to the companies in terms of their long-range competitive

FIGURE 5–1
Japanese Employment System

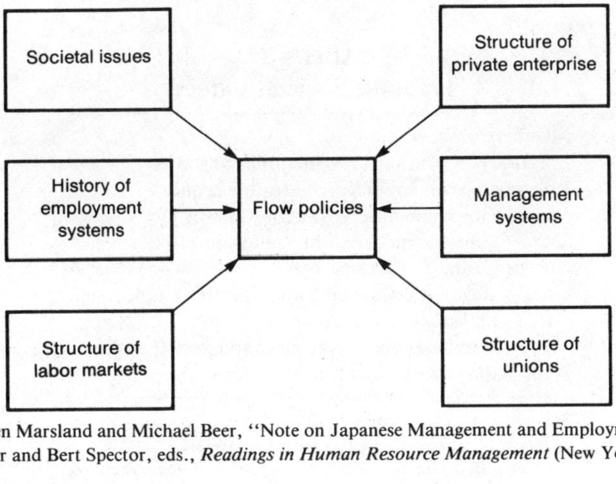

Source: Stephen Marsland and Michael Beer, "Note on Japanese Management and Employment Systems," in Michael Beer and Bert Spector, eds., *Readings in Human Resource Management* (New York: Free Press, 1985).

FIGURE 5–2
Japanese Employment System

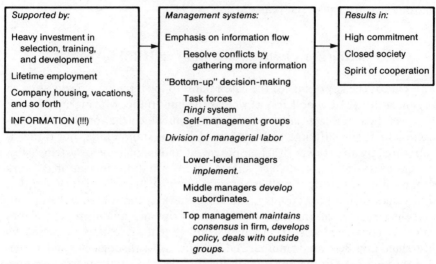

Supported by:	Management systems:	Results in:

Heavy investment in selection, training, and development
 	
Lifetime employment
 	
Company housing, vacations, and so forth
 	
INFORMATION (!!!)
	Emphasis on information flow
	   Resolve conflicts by gathering more information
	   "Bottom-up" decision-making
	     Task forces
	     Ringi system
	     Self-management groups
	
	Division of managerial labor
	   Lower-level managers *implement.*
	   Middle managers *develop* subordinates.
	   Top management *maintains consensus* in firm, *develops policy, deals with outside groups.*
		High commitment
		
		Closed society
		
		Spirit of cooperation

Source: Stephen Marsland and Michael Beer, "Note on Japanese Management and Employment Systems," in Michael Beer and Bert Spector, eds., *Readings in Human Resource Management* (New York: Free Press, 1985).

position. Students can be asked to generate their own list of pluses and minuses in terms of the impact on competitive position or be given Lohr's analysis, and then discuss the relative weights of the pluses and minuses of the overall approach to the management of HR in Japan. Lohr's list of possible future problems includes the following:

1. "Japan's hierarchical, seniority-based system of management, which has been so effective at coordinating the high-volume pro-

TABLE 5–5
Japanese Societal Values

Membership in *group*
Emphasis on relationships/hierarchical status
Role of government in "orchestrating economy"
   —Government serves as coordinator, preventing
    conflicts on behalf of "public interest"
Role of business in society
   —Business responsible for providing employment
    and security to *regular* employees
   —Emphasis on market share and growth rather
    than on high profits

Source: Stephen Marsland and Michael Beer, "Note on Japanese Management and Employment Systems," in Michael Beer and Bert Spector, eds., *Readings in Human Resource Management* (New York: Free Press, 1985).

FIGURE 5-3
Structure of Private Enterprise
Emphasis on debt financing, market share, and size rather than profits

Long-term perspective

Firm in one industry

Intense inner-industry competition

Subcontracting/satellite firms

Supports lifetime employment

Major firms	*Satellite firms*
Production	Warehousing
Marketing	Fabrication of spare parts
R&D	Maintenance
	Shipping

Zaibatsu *(business groups) — alliance of*
large firms in different industries

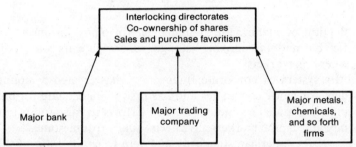

Interlocking directorates
Co-ownership of shares
Sales and purchase favoritism

Major bank | Major trading company | Major metals, chemicals, and so forth firms

Source: Stephen Marsland and Michael Beer, ''Note on Japanese Management and Employment Systems,'' in Michael Beer and Bert Spector, eds., *Readings in Human Resource Management* (New York: Free Press, 1985).

TABLE 5-6
Structure of Labor Market

Hierarchical Banking of Employee Groups
Regulars
    —School-leaver men (elite)
    —Midcareer men
    —Women (blue- and white-collar)
Temporaries
Day Laborers

Lifetime Employment for Elite

Wages Function of Length of Service and Position of Responsibility

Source: Stephen Marsland and Michael Beer, ''Note on Japanese Management and Employment Systems,'' in Michael Beer and Bert Spector, eds., *Readings in Human Resource Management* (New York: Free Press, 1985).

TABLE 5-7

History of Employment Systems

1870s: Industrialization
  —Competitive advantage through subsistence wages
1910: High absenteeism, strikes, high turnover lead to incentives to remain at work
  —Improved working conditions
  —Wages tied to seniority
  —Retirement bonuses
Post–World War II: Labor unions shift power balance
  —Living wage
  —No layoffs
  —Seniority-based pay
1950s: Depolarization from work force to "co-opt" radical unions
  —Promotion from blue- to white-collar ranks
  —Extension of benefits to blue-collar workers
  —Company consults with and supports moderate unions

Source: Stephen Marsland and Michael Beer, "Note on Japanese Management and Employment Systems," in Michael Beer and Bert Spector, eds., *Readings in Human Resource Management* (New York: Free Press, 1985).

duction of manufactured items, has in many instances not been flexible and fast-moving enough to navigate its way to lead in emerging markets."

2. "Its system of corporate finance . . . has created a mountain of debt for many companies and has proved inadequate for bankrolling innovative new industries. . . . Efforts to raise funds in the equity and capital markets have been equally troublesome."

   "By American standards, the debt to equity ratio of the average Japanese concern is alarmingly high, with about 85% debt and 15% equity. 'There is little doubt whether this system will be viable in the future as we have to develop new industries,' Akio Mikuni, a Tokyo financial consultant to many companies, said."

3. "Perhaps most important, the country's emphasis on community obedience, and uniformity, all of which have been crucial to its

TABLE 5-8

Structure of Unionism

Enterprise unionism
  —Membership includes all regular employees up to assistant section manager
  —Violent opposition to layoffs
  —Support moves to improve company's competitiveness
  —Industrywide federations to enhance collective bargaining
  —Growth of mutual cooperation and trust in private sector

Source: Stephen Marsland and Michael Beer, "Note on Japanese Management and Employment Systems," in Michael Beer and Bert Spector, eds., *Readings in Human Resource Management* (New York: Free Press, 1985).

TABLE 5-9

Costs and Benefits of Japanese Lifetime Employment System

Costs	Benefits
Depends on stable or growth environment	Opportunity to transfer people
Cost of excess employees in decline	High loyalty
Loss of flexibility in changing skill mix	Opportunity to reduce jobs and costs
High training cost	Low turnover/high stability
Slower promotions and career progression	Continuity in experience
Vulnerable to major and rapid upset	Opportunity to increase motivation and commitment
Lower diversity (innovation) in slow growth	Opportunity to develop cooperative union/ management relations; inbred work force

Source: Stephen Marsland and Michael Beer, "Note on Japanese Management and Employment Systems," in Michael Beer and Bert Spector, eds., *Readings in Human Resource Management* (New York: Free Press, 1985).

highly efficient assembly lines, has discouraged individual creativity and, with it, far-reaching product inventions."

Whatever the conclusions students may draw, the important point is that HRM policies must be judged by how well they work together, by how well they work with the environment and conditions under which the company must operate, and by the various outcomes of those policies. Figure 5–4 presents a brief analysis of the mix of policies, conditions and outcomes that can be derived from the "Nippon Steel Corporation" case. Students can undertake similar analyses of all other cases and examples of HRM policies and practices.

TEACHING PLANS

Option A

This option involves starting with the action plan and working back to more generalized observations about management and employment systems.

40 min.   1. How serious is NSC's problem and what can be done? Press students on numbers here to demonstrate how HRM policies have a direct impact on costs and profits.

40 min.   2. What are the primary elements of NSC's management and employment system?
     a. What has been NSC's market strategy?
     b. What are the outside conditions that affect management and employment conditions?
     c. What have been NSC's policies in regard to stakeholder interest, rewards, and flow?

FIGURE 5–4

Mix of Conditions, Policies, and Outcomes at Nippon Steel

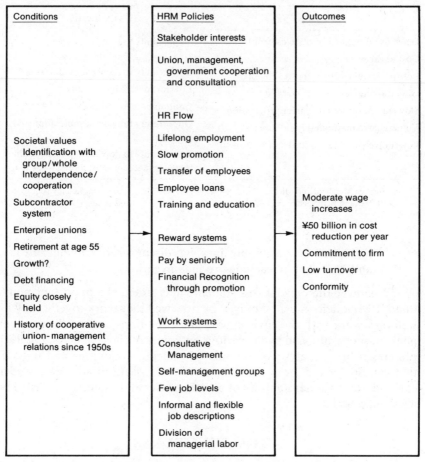

d. What outcomes have those HRM policies produced for NSC?

10 min.   3. Lecturette on alternative flow policies, benefits, and costs of lifetime employment.

Option B

Start with a question on stakeholder interest in Japan as a bridge between the stakeholder interests and flow section of HRM:

30 min.   1. Who are the main stakeholders at NSC and what does each party want?

          a. What is *management* looking for? (Flexibility of tasks, innovation by workers leading to cost reductions, no strikes, and so forth).

          b. What are *workers* looking for? (Lifetime employment, favorable working environment, training, self-management, prestige of working for NSC, and so forth.)

          c. What does *government* expect? (Low-cost steel, favorable export position, labor-management peace, loyalty, and the like.)

20 min.   2. What is NSC's marketing strategy and how does it compare with U.S. companies?

          a. What is NSC's strategy?

          b. How does it differ from the strategies of U.S. companies?

             (1) Is emphasis short- or long-term?

             (2) Who are the primary stakeholders?

             (3) What is NSC's investment in new technology?

             (4) What is relationship between the company and government?

20 min.   3. What should NSC do to solve its problem of excess employees?

10 min.   4. What should company's position on retirement be? What are the alternatives and what are their costs?

10 min.   5. Instructor summary of differences between Japanese and U.S. employment systems.

NOTES

1. In Michael Beer and Bert Spector, eds., *Readings in Human Resource Management* (New York: Free Press, 1985).

2. Japan is still a relatively "young" society. In 1982, the ratio of working people to retirees in Japan was 7.5:1 compared to 3:1 in the United States and Western Europe. However, the average life expectancy in Japan has risen from 55 years in 1949 to 76 years in 1982, and Japan is expected to reach the 3:1 ratio by the year 2000. See Steve Lohr, "Japan Struggling with Itself," *New York Times*, June 13, 1982.

3. "Note on Japanese Management and Employment Systems," in Beer and Spector, *Readings in Human Resource Management*.

4. Steve Lohr, "Japan Struggling With Itself," *New York Times*, June 13, 1982.

WEBSTER INDUSTRIES
Teaching Note

A manager receives a directive from the corporation to reduce the work force. The manager is given guidelines and a strict time limit. What should he do and how? The case presents information on the implicit life employment contract that has existed, and the performance appraisal system (PAS) that might be used as a data base. The (B) case and an audiotape of the manager being played during class describes what happened.

One of the specific problems faced by Bob Carter has to do with the lack of a good, consistently used data base for making effective decisions about advanced planning and immediate layoffs. Future cases will cover such data gathering devices as performance appraisal interviews ("Colonial Food Services Company") and assessment centers ("Assessing Managerial Talent at AT&T"), as well as the question of "fairness" in making such decisions ("Colonial Food Services Company" and "Highland Products"). Students can be reminded that, unless some specific procedure is used, managers can find themselves in Carter's uncomfortable position.

The purpose of this case in the HRM course is to contrast the Nippon case with the U.S. approach to managing people (they are typically treated as a variable cost) and to place them in the difficult situation of managing an employee reduction. Is Webster pursuing the right strategy given the company's situation? What short- and long-term impact will the employee reduction have on the commitment of employees? How might the reduction be managed to minimize the negative impact? As a by-product, students will learn about performance appraisal systems.

ASSIGNMENT QUESTIONS

Students should read the (A) case and come to class prepared to discuss the following questions:

1. How should Carter go about deciding who should be terminated? Students should be prepared to discuss in detail the criteria, information, and processes to be used.
2. How should Carter implement the personnel reduction decision he makes?
3. What should Carter do about the performance appraisal system? What recommendations should he make about future use of the system?

CASE ANALYSIS

Bob Carter has been manufacturing manager of the Fabrics Division of Webster Industries for one year when, on a Friday, he is told by Ike Davis, head of the Fabrics Division, that Fabrics will be reducing its personnel by 20 percent. Carter must trim his 289 managers by 43 individuals. President Abe Webster has set the following Friday as the deadline for submitting termination lists, and Carter must be prepared by Wednesday to review his decision with Davis and other top divisional managers.

Carter must operate under certain constraints. The first is the culture and history of the company. Webster has been operating out of a small company town since just after the Civil War. It is a nonunion company, known as a "first class" place to work, and characterized by a good deal of implicit paternalism, including the assumption that, after 10 years, an employee will have a guarantee of lifetime employment.

The second major constraint is a five-point set of guidelines provided by Abe Webster. The reduction will focus on the managerial level, early retirement should not be counted on for meeting targets, minorities are not to be terminated any more aggressively than any other groups. Point 3 states that seniority is not to be considered as a major determining factor. While this point seems to signal a shift in the Webster culture, that signal is somewhat overshadowed by the point that Abe placed on the top of his list: no one with 20 years of service and 50 years of age can be terminated without a review by the president. The culture apparently will not be changed entirely.

The third constraint faced by Carter is the data base available. The Human Resource Division has designed a PAS and a personnel audit to track each employee's career and development. The PAS, initiated three years earlier, was designed to help each manager define his or her goals within the organization [management-by-objective (MBO)], help managers review the behavior of their subordinates (developmental review), and evaluate and review salary levels. The system is voluntary, and has a 29 percent corporate-wide usage, 40 percent in manufacturing. The audit consists of a yearly visit from the HR division's auditor to managers in which the performance of subordinates is discussed. This process leads to a performance rating for each employee. There are audit ratings for 97 percent of Carter's management personnel.

As Carter considered his actions that night, he thought over the following points:

1. Carter realized that he had not gotten around to using the PAS on a regular basis.
2. He admitted that his department had "fat" at the managerial level.
3. He recalled trying to demote three individuals, including his second-in-command, and being overruled by Ike Davis.

4. Because he wanted to demote his production superintendent, Russell Brown, and promote Brown's assistant, Cecil Stevens, he decided to involve Stevens in his deliberations.

Carter and Stevens got together later that night and drew up a timetable. They would meet on Monday morning with their production managers (except for the home furnishing manager) to develop a strategy; begin to implement that strategy by Monday afternoon; and have a list for review on Wednesday.

On Monday morning, Stevens suggested five guidelines to be used, and admitted that each one had certain weaknesses:

1. *Seniority*. Webster's guidelines would permit this criterion to be used only sparingly.
2. *Fairness*. Stevens admitted that operationally, he didn't know what "fairness" meant.
3. *"Fat."* The problem here was that some good people were in "fat" positions.
4. *Performance*. But what are the data? Some felt that PAS was flawed. Carter had relied on it very little in the past, and to use it suddenly as a criterion for laying people off when they had received little feedback seemed unfair. Using the audit material might seriously jeopardize its future integrity.
5. *Potential*. Again, what are the data? Stevens also wondered whether they should terminate people with low potential, even though they might be performing satisfactorily at their current level.

The case will allow students to raise, and then begin to answer, several questions concerning HR flow:

1. How do you plan for a reduction? There are several points a company can follow in order to create effective contingency plans for layoffs:
   a. Examine the psychological contract and keep it up-to-date with business realities.
   b. Do advanced planning of personnel requirements. Visualize how the organization will look after the reduction. What positions? What skill requirements?
   c. Think through the mix of performance, potential, and seniority as layoff criteria in light of the business environment.
   d. Design a performance appraisal system (PAS) with the needs of layoff information in mind.
   e. Prepare reduction plans consistent with company philosophy. These plans must be in touch with the business environment. Managers should know not only what those realities are, but what they will be in the future. What directions will their busi-

ness be taking? What direction would they like the business to be taking? Those questions can have an important bearing on personnel plans.

2. What will the data base be? The case implicitly raises the question of whether a PAS, no matter how it is structured, can provide all the necessary data. The Webster example is far from perfect on the matter of advanced planning. It does, however, clearly indicate the importance of entering into a process for reaching work force reduction decisions. The case clearly illustrates the difficult position in which managers find themselves when they have little or no data. Future HRM cases will cover such data gathering devices as personal performance appraisal interviews and assessment centers. Students can be reminded that unless those—or, some specific alternative—procedures are used, managers can find themselves in Carter's position: layoffs to be made and no data on which to base those decisions. Nevertheless, students should also be reminded that no data base, regardless of how complete or elegant, can substitute for managerial judgment about who should be terminated at the time the terminations are to take place. The definition of satisfactory performance changes when reductions are needed.

3. What are the opportunities and the costs of layoffs? Layoffs can be made specifically to fire people and save the company money. They can also be used to change the structure, even the culture of an organization. While there is no evidence that Abe Webster had anything in mind other than short-term savings, the Webster layoffs did create the opportunity for reorganizing—an opportunity taken advantage of by Carter. They also "shattered" the old psychological contract, and there is evidence that the old contract had gotten in the way of dealing with business realities. (Carter's decision to demote three individuals was overturned by Davis.)

   But, if there are opportunities, there are also costs. Could the culture have been changed and the department reorganized without the traumatic "shattering" caused by the 20 percent layoff? The answer seems to be "yes." And what will the costs be? That is a question mark. If Stevens is right, the company lost a lot more good performers than bad performers. Some think the company has lost loyalty and commitment. Has it? Was it necessary?

4. What is fairness? Stevens says that, operationally, he cannot define fairness, but that he wants to avoid gross unfairness. Presumably, he will know gross unfairness when he sees it. Students can be asked to grapple with the same problem: What is fairness? Should unfairness be avoided at all costs? What are the costs of unfairness? What are the obligations of a corporation to its employees, even those that are performing below par? Who is responsible for their performance: the corporation or the individuals?

The most obvious point on which the issue of fairness will be raised concerns the lack of a consistently applied performance appraisal system. Employees have received little or no feedback in the past. Is it fair to terminate them now? If not, what are the alternatives? What are the costs of unfairness?

5. What are the restraints on action? Different societies impose different constraints on management actions. When it comes to work force reduction, for instance, the constraints that are societally imposed are far different in the United States than in many European countries. In France, for instance, national law requires employers to supply the economic, financial, production, and other data to the elected council of workers for consultation before any layoff can take place. Employers must then gain the approval of the regional council of labor. If that approval is not forthcoming, they must appeal to a joint industrial committee. French law also mandates an annual *social audit* in which an employer must provide workers with a report on employment levels, pay and fringe benefits, health and safety training, industrial relations development, and living conditions of the workers and their families.[1] Students can compare the various constraints to action, as diagrammed in Table 5-10. The cost to Webster of violating the expectation of lifetime employment is an unknown. Students can speculate on just what those costs might be as compared with the benefits.

6. When is it time to say "No!"? Some students, when asked to develop an action plan, may suggest that Carter, Davis, and other top managers should tell Abe Webster that they will not comply with his demand for a list by the end of the week. Seeing "no" as an alternative is more common among executives classes than among MBAs. Occasionally, executives have suggested that, if Webster still insists on a list, then the top managers should turn in their own names. This, they insist, is a case where defiance is called for.

Students who express this point of view should be pressed on the implications of such defiance. Perhaps role-playing in which one

TABLE 5-10
Constraints to Reduction of Work Force

Type of Constraint	France (National Law)	Nippon Steel	Webster Industries
Contractual, legal constraints	High	Low	Low
Political, governmental constraints	High	Moderate	Low
Constraints imposed by expectations and estimated costs of violating	Moderate to high	High	?

student plays Webster, another Carter, would be useful here. While the bulk of the discussion should focus on an action plan for work force reduction, some time can be spent on this matter of "saying no." Such a discussion will also help focus attention on the perceived costs of such a layoff.

Follow-Up

The (B) case records the actions taken by Carter the following Monday and Tuesday:

On Monday and Tuesday, the following actions were taken (as reported, in Carter's words, in both the (B) case and the audiotape);

1. Because of his long tenure, Russell Brown was offered the opportunity to take the demotion and then invited to participate in the deliberations.
2. Carter's department was reorganized: one plant was closed, and the home furnishing department manager's position was eliminated.
3. Carter and his group then sought the best people for the reorganized staff positions. Audit data were used as a "check on our perceptions." PAS was of little use because "we just did not trust it." Assessments were based on both performance and potential.
4. "Excess" list then drawn up, rechecked against audit material. The list now had 48 names.
5. They then looked at who was available from other departments, took 7 of those people, and revised the list up to 55 names.
6. The list was presented to Davis and the divisional managers on Wednesday. They disagreed with three recommendations. Six additional individuals were demoted to weekly payroll. This gave the final list.

Many of the people involved in the process discussed their reactions. Carter emphasized the personal trauma involved in making such a decision. Cecil Stevens felt that the process was too rushed and that consequently, "75 percent of these released were at least 'satisfactory' employees." Carter also gave Abe Webster high marks for selling the company's position to the community, and talked about the "shattering" of the belief structure (the assumption of lifetime employment). There were different views on whether the impact of that shattering was positive or negative.

One of the strongest reactions was that something had to be done about the PAS. Abe Webster called for honest and clear feedback. There was talk about how to redesign PAS and how to achieve 100 percent usage. How would students do that? This is one of the most consistently troubling HRM problems in corporations.

TABLE 5-11
Important Points About Webster Industries Case

1. Examine the psychological contract and keep it up to date with business realities.
2. Do advance planning of personnel requirements.
3. Prepare reduction of work force contingency plans consistent with company philosophy.
4. Think through mix of merit versus service as layoff criteria in light of business environment.
5. Design performance appraisal system with needs for layoff information in mind.
6. Decide when you will say *no*.

TEACHING PLAN

25 min. 1. How should Carter go about deciding who to lay off?
   a. What criteria should be used? People? Jobs? Performance? Potential?
   b. What data? PAS? Audit? Supervisory opinion?
   c. What sequence of steps should be followed? By whom?
   d. How should decision be implemented?

20 min. 2. What will be the consequences for Webster?
   a. How did Webster get into this bind? How could they have avoided it?
   b. Why is Webster doing this? Save money? Change culture?
   c. Has Webster broken psychological contract? What will be the consequences (costs and opportunities) of that?
   d. Why is management breaking the psychological contract so abruptly? Pressures from Wall Street? An opportunity to manage major changes that have been previously resisted?

15 min. 3. What do you think of the PAS?
   a. What are the strengths and weaknesses?
   b. If not this system, what system? Bridge to "Colonial Food Services" and "Assessing Management Talent at AT&T."

15 min. 4. What do you think of Carter's actions?
   a. Hand out (B) case, and allow students time to read it.
   b. Critique Carter's actions.

5 min. 5. Closing lecturette on main points of case. (See Table 5-11.)

NOTE

1. Thomas Kennedy, "Labor Relations in France," Harvard Business School case 1-481-130.

COLONIAL FOOD SERVICES COMPANY, JAMES CRANSTON, AND EUGENE KIRBY
Teaching Note

In order for organizations to make decisions about pay, promotions, and terminations, and in order to develop employees and improve their performance, most corporation have some type of performance appraisal system (PAS). Appraisal discussions provide one of the main links between the individual employee and the organization. During such discussions, expectations are set and the psychological contract is implicitly reviewed and re-negotiated. Thus, the quality of the discussions and the appraisal system itself will have an important impact on the employees's perception of the organization's standard of performance, fairness, and opportunity to communicate its expectations about performance and to influence employee development.

Despite its acknowledged importance, appraisal is filled with difficulties which can create dissatisfaction and misunderstandings. This set of cases and film will shed light on the sources of these problems, and raise the question of what can be done.

In particular, the material provides the reflections of a regional vice president—Jim Cranston—and one of his district sales managers—Gene Kirby—prior to an appraisal interview. The 50-minute videotape is an edited version of the two-hour interview. The material brings down to the boss–subordinate level questions about performance appraisal: what is managerial potential, and what is a fair and effective way of evaluating that potential? The case and videotape will allow an evaluation of the Colonial Food Services appraisal systems (the form and administrative practices associated with it). The videotape also allows students the opportunity to critique the fairness and effectiveness of the appraisal interview conducted by Jim Cranston. Students should come away with the realization that effective performance appraisals depend on the skills of managers to engage in dialogue about difficult problems more than they depend on the appraisal system.

But even with such a system in place, the issue of *fairness* and *effectiveness* is not avoided. Would the kind of data provided by Colonial Food's performance appraisal system have helped Bob Carter? Have Gene Kirby's interests been looked after, or even the interests of the company? The question bridges back to the employee influence section of the course. The organization has an interest in evaluating and developing employees. Employees have an interest in receiving valid and useful feedback in order to enhance their standing in the organization. Students must grapple with the question of whether this performance appraisal system serves either set of those interests. If not, why not? What are the alternatives? "Assessing Managerial Talent at AT&T" will provide one such alternative: an assessment center.

"Colonial Food Services" also raises two other problems that will be seen again in "Assessing Managerial Talent at AT&T." One is the possible confusion caused by mixing together *performance* and *developmental* appraisals. The fact that the system under which James Cranston is operating mixes the two leads to apparent ambiguity of results, perhaps undermining the effectiveness of the system. Students can also raise a question that is critical to both the Colonial Food's and AT&T process: how *valid* is the appraisal?

ASSIGNMENT QUESTIONS

These materials are ideally taught in a two-day sequence, though it is possible to teach them in one day. In the two-day sequence students are asked to read the three cases and to plan for the upcoming appraisal interview as if they were Jim Cranston, the boss. The first class lends itself to role-playing. The second class is devoted to an evaluation of the appraisal interview itself which they will have viewed on videotape the night before.

Day 1 Assignment

Read "Colonial Food Services Company," "James Cranston," and "Eugene Kirby (A)"

QUESTIONS
1. What is your assessment of Kirby's performance?
2. What is your plan for conducting the appraisal interview? How will you start? What will you tell him and how? How will you use the form? Plan to participate in a role-playing session as Cranston or Kirby.
3. If you were Kirby, what would you do to prepare for the interview?
4. Given your knowledge of the two people, what do you predict will happen?

Day 2 Assignment

View videotape of Cranston–Kirby interview and read "Note on Performance Appraisal" in *Readings in Human Resource Management.*

1. What are the strengths and weaknesses of the Cranston–Kirby interview?
2. How do you account for the interview process and content?
3. What would you have done differently if you had been Cranston?

CASE ANALYSIS

Colonial Food Services provides food services to a variety of companies. The mid-Atlantic sales region, headed by vice president Jim Cranston, services mainly colleges and prep schools. Typically, Colonial's contracts run one to three years, and the company places great emphasis on maintaining good customer relations as well as recruiting, training, and developing new talent.

Cranston is 32 years old, Kirby 42. Cranston is healthy-looking and athletic, Kirby noticeably overweight. Cranston oversees eight food districts, each supervised by a district manager of which Kirby is one. Recently, Cranston decided to reactivate the regional operations manager's position and appointed one of Kirby's good friends—also 42 years old—to that position.

The central feature of Colonial's performance appraisal includes annual interviews. Cranston made plans to meet with each of his district managers in 1977. Prior to that interview, he would fill out a new company form (Exhibit 10–2 in the casebook), and that form would provide the basis for a discussion between Cranston and his manager. After the interview, the appraisee would sign the form and add any additional comments. The form would then be submitted to Cranston's immediate supervisor for review and placed in the appraisee's personnel file.

The interview itself would also include a discussion of salary. At Colonial, bonuses were based on profits exceeding forecasts, while base salary depended on merit as determined by the employee's superior. Cranston insists that profits are not the whole story; that merit increases address the capacity and potential of the individual as a manager.

Prior to his interview with Kirby, Cranston filled out the appraisal form and made the following comments about Kirby's strengths and weaknesses:

STRENGTHS	WEAKNESSES
1. "Very good with people"	1. "He seems to take criticism pretty well, but underneath he's basically an insecure person . . . he needs to listen longer and not get so defensive."
2. "A *tremendous* developer of people"	
3. "Good with clients, very innovative, and good on working out new contracts"	

STRENGTHS	WEAKNESSES

STRENGTHS

4. "He has a very strong operations background. He knows his stuff, and he's a very hard worker."
5. "Has all the technical skills"
6. "Shrewd with finances; he has an outstanding profit performance record."
7. "He's never had an account terminated. . . . Operationally, he does almost everything right."

WEAKNESSES

2. "He is very overweight and smokes to excess. He is in poor physical condition. . . . He has endurance limitations."
3. Clients "can think he's a shrewdy, and manipulative."
4. "He needs to get out [of his house] and get more accounts."
5. "He is very good at keeping me informed, *but* he calls too frequently."
6. "He loses his temper and talks when he should be quiet. . . . He opens his mouth and doesn't know when to shut up. . . . He creates malice that I have to clean up. He *causes* problems (particularly with staff groups)."
7. "His potential to go up in the organization is limited."

In planning the interview with Kirby students need to take into account the following factors.

1. Cranston is ten years' Kirby's junior and obviously on the "fast track."
2. Kirby is obviously viewed as a valued employee by Cranston given his experience, technical knowledge, and the consistent results he gets.
3. Cranston obviously feels that Kirby has little potential to move up the organization. How should this be handled by Cranston? Should he ask Kirby about his aspirations, thereby raising the issue or should he avoid the issue, only giving his opinion if directly asked? What are his and the corporation's responsibilities?
4. How should the health issue be handled? Is it an appropriate subject for an appraisal interview?
5. How do students plan to proceed in the interview?
   a. Start with positives and then go to negatives and finish with positives (sandwich approach).
   b. Do they plan to start by giving Kirby his ratings? What would be the impact on the interview climate?
   c. How do students plan to use the form? Follow it? Leave it in the background? Can you do that if you already have filled it out?
   d. Do students plan to have Kirby fill out the form jointly with Cranston? Can you let a subordinate influence his evaluation?

e. How will students (playing Cranston) motivate Kirby to change those aspects of his behavior that are a problem?

f. To what extent do students intend to lead Kirby through the interview into areas they want to cover or to what extent do they plan to let Kirby lead (see the problem-solving interview in Michael Beer's "Note on Performance Appraisal").

VIDEOTAPE ANALYSIS

The Cranston–Kirby interview allows students to see first hand the difficulties in conducting an appraisal interview. Many of the classic problems in appraisal interviews are displayed. In evaluating the interview you should instruct students to consider the following:

1. Content: What points did Cranston cover? Did he deal with all the issues that he talked about before the interview?
2. Process: How did Cranston conduct the interview? Did he listen? How did he use the form? Other relevant points?
3. How will the interview affect:
   a. The relationship between Kirby and Cranston?
   b. Kirby's motivation and performance?
   c. Cranston's understanding of Kirby as a person?
   d. Kirby's understanding of himself and where he stands in the company?

The class analysis of the interview is typically conducted by asking students to list the strengths and weaknesses of the interview given the criteria above and their reading of the "Note on Performance Appraisal." The following list typically emerges:

STRENGTHS
1. Cranston covers all of the issues that were of concern to him.
2. Cranston seems to conduct a fairly candid interview given the difficulty of such interviews.
3. Cranston and Kirby's relationship seems to come out intact.
4. Cranston handled the health issue appropriately.

WEAKNESSES
1. Cranston does not listen, does most of the talking.
2. He follows the appraisal form rigidly, thereby preventing Kirby from really exploring his behavior and feelings.
3. Cranston is uncomfortable with Kirby's feelings. Every time he tries to talk about them Cranston interrupts.
4. Cranston talks about his ratings of Kirby when he knows Kirby does not like to be graded.

5. Cranston "waffles" all over the place. He never tells Kirby exactly where he stands.
6. Cranston uses humor inappropriately, ridiculing Kirby (there is room for disagreement here).
7. Cranston does not have a right to discuss Kirby's health, fitness, and so forth (issues of privacy and relevance may be discussed in this regard).
8. Cranston uses the three-month period in which Kirby had health problems as an excuse to justify his moderately satisfactory rating of Kirby. This is an important issue because it suggests that Cranston is trying to find a way to justify his rating of Kirby's performance despite the excellent results Kirby obtains. Could it be that Cranston must provide a lower rating of performance consistent with his estimate that Kirby has low potential for promotion? In other words, because performance and potential are not clearly distinguished on the appraisal form or in Cranston's mind, one might infer that Cranston is led into a trap of giving a lower rating of performance than is really justified. Does he do this to be able to justify his estimate that Kirby has little potential for promotion? A high rating would make it difficult to deny Kirby a promotion.
9. Kirby is being given an unfair rating considering the results he obtains. This raises another critical point which can be explored and lectured on. Should employees be evaluated on measurable results or whether they behave or appear in a way that fits the corporation's culture. Figure 5–5 illustrates that the "off quadrants" present some real dilemmas in evaluation. Is Kirby being discrimi-

FIGURE 5–5
Potential–Results Dilemma

Results

		High	Low
	High	Promote	?
Fit with expected behavior (potential)			
	Low	? (Kirby)	Discharge

nated against because he does not fit in appearance or behavior? Is behavioral fit as valid a criterion as results? Many students have never confronted the fact that results are not the only factor in their evaluation and promotion. But if "fit" is a valid criterion, what does it do to fairness, what are the implications for equal employment opportunity? If "fit" is not allowed as a criterion, what is the implication for developing a strong culture important for corporate effectiveness?

10. Students will also recognize that one of the problems with the interview is that Cranston is trying to achieve the incompatible objectives of evaluation and development at the same time. This may account for his lack of listening and efforts to justify. It certainly accounts for his sticking too clsely to the form thus precluding a more open-ended discussion in which Kirby can learn about himself and take part in problem solving.

11. No action plan for developing Kirby is presented, perhaps because Cranston does not really believe that Kirby has potential. Kirby is never told this, however.

The filmed interview typically evokes a lively discussion and allows the instructor to deal with almost all performance appraisal issues, issues of process, systems, and corporate policy. Classes are typically critical of Cranston (as he was of himself when he saw the interview videotape). But students need to be reminded that as appraisal interviews go this is probably about average if not slightly above average. It is more thorough than most and certainly longer. Almost all of the issues in the "Note on Performance Appraisal" are raised by the interview.[1]

Afternote

Given the importance of the health issue it is important to report that approximately one year after the case was written, Gene Kirby died on the job of a heart attack. It can be reported also that in a "debriefing" interview with a case writer, Kirby stated that this appraisal interview was the best he had ever had.

Performance Appraisals

The following points from the Michael Beer "Note on Performance Appraisal" can be made about performance appraisals in general:

1. There are two goals of performance appraisal: *evaluation* goals and *development* goals. Since both of the parties to the appraisal pro-

cess—the organization and the employee—each have their own set of goals for evaluation and development, there are in fact four separate sets of goals (see Table 5-12).

There is not a perfect congruence or fit between these four sets of goals. There is, in fact, noncongruence both *within* and between the two parties:

a. *Within the organization.* When the goals are evaluation, managers use the appraisal system as a tool for making difficult judgments that affect their subordinates' future. When development is the goal, however, the manager must play the role of helper. Thus, for the organization the goals of evaluation and development are not identical, particularly in the case of a poorly performing individual.

b. *Within the individual.* Employees want feedback to help them develop and tell them where they stand. But if the goals of the appraisal are evaluation, there is a strong incentive to avoid any unfavorable feedback.

c. *Between the two parties when the goals are evaluation.* Because there is a fixed sum of rewards, the organization and the employee will enter into a distributive bargaining mode.

d. *Between the two parties when the goals are developmental.* Here is where the goals of the two parties are most compatible; where the organization and the employee can enter into a problem-solving process.

e. *Between the two parties when the employee seeks a development appraisal and the manager is planning to conduct an evaluation appraisal.* This is where there is the least congruence.

Because of this noncongruence and potential for conflict, it has been suggested that evaluation and development be separated. Less defensiveness and an open dialogue can be obtained if managers split their roles of helper and judge and have two separate performance appraisal interviews. Have one focus on evaluation and the

TABLE 5-12

Differing Goals of Appraisal

	Evaluation	Development
Organization	Seeking information from employees on which to base rewards and make personnel decisions	Seeking the development of individuals through counseling, coaching, and career planning
Employee	Seeking important rewards and maintenance of self-image	Seeking valid performance feedback so they know where they stand and can develop

other on development, and hold the interviews at different times of the year.

2. There are three methods of conducting an appraisal interview:

    a. *Tell-and-sell.* Manager seeks to communicate evaluation accurately and gain the subordinate's acceptance of the evaluation; places employees in dependent position, does not allow them to participate in development of plan for improvement, may not motivate them to improve.

    b. *Tell-and-listen.* Manager seeks to communicate evaluation to subordinate and let subordinate respond. Will result in better understanding between supervisor and subordinate than will "tell-and-sell," subordinate will be less defensive, may not result in clear understanding by subordinates of where they stand, subordinates may not have clear idea of how to improve, may lack commitment to improving behavior.

    c. *Problem-solving.* Manager's objective is to help subordinates discover their own performance deficiencies and jointly develop plan for improvement; has no provision for communicating the supervisor's evaluation.

    d. *Mixed model.* If evaluation and development appraisals were uncoupled, then one of the first two methods could be used in evalaution, and problem-solving could be used in development.

3. The following guidelines can be used to evaluate an appraisal interview:

    a. *At the beginning*

      1. Did supervisor create open and acceptant climate?

      2. Was there agreement on purpose and process of interview?

      3. Were both parties equally prepared?

    b. *During interview*

      1. To what extent did supervisor try to understand employee?

      2. Were broad and general questions used at outset?

      3. Was supervisor's feedback clear and specific?

      4. Did supervisor learn some new things—particularly about deep feelings and values of subordinate?

      5. Did subordinate disagree and confront supervisor?

      6. Did interview end with mutual agreement and understanding about problems and goals for improvement?

    c. *Appraisal outcomes*

      1. Did appraisal session motivate the subordinate?

      2. Did appraisal build a better relationship?

      3. Did subordinate come out with clear idea of where he or she stood?

      4. Did supervisor arrive at fairer assessment of subordinate?

      5. Did subordinate learn something new about supervisor?

6. Did subordinate have clear idea of what actions to take to improve performance?

The following points can be made more specifically about the Colonial Food cases:

1. The evaluation and development goals were not clearly delineated. Many of the weaknesses cited by Cranston have to do with Kirby's potential for development rather than an evaluation of his results. When the two are confused within the same process, the results can be ambiguity and unfairness. Figure 5–5 (which appeared earlier) presents a chart illustrating that uncertainty. When an employee combines high results with high potential, the organization's decision will likely be to promote. When the employee combines low results with low potential, the decision is equally unambiguous. But what happens on the other diagonal? In the Colonial Food case, Kirby falls in the bottom left square: high on results, low on potential (he's often overbearing and insulting to people, stays at home when he should be out hustling new accounts, fat and unwell in an organization that places a premium on trimness and physical fitness, and so forth). Because the appraisal goals—evaluating results and potential—are confused in this interview, the results are ambiguity and unfairness:
   a. *Ambiguity.* Does Kirby really know where he stands at the end of this interview? There is reason to doubt that Kirby fully understands his position with Cranston. While Cranston spends a good deal of time discussing Kirby's weaknesses, he never makes clear his view that those weaknesses limit Kirby's "potential to go up in the organization." At the conclusion of the interview, Kirby seems to think that his problems all came in a bad few months, and have now gone away. It will be worth raising with students the question of whether telling employees exactly where they stand is best for employees, or even desired by them. Yet, unless they are told, they are subject to surprise while the organization is exposed to legal challenge.
   b. *Unfairness.* Kirby is being judged by his potential for organizational fit as well as his results, but he is never told that explicitly, and never told what the criteria are for arriving at that judgment. Fairness would seem to dictate that the goals of the appraisal and the criteria on which that appraisal will be made should be revealed to the appraisee at the outset. The organization, too, would benefit from distinguishing between performance and potential.
2. Of the various methods listed above for conducting an interview, Cranston's falls somewhere between "tell-and-sell" and "tell-and-

listen." He does allow Kirby to respond to the evaluation, but often limits that response (sometimes by insisting that they continue to the next point, sometimes by displaying physical signs of disinterest in what Kirby is saying). And he spends as much time trying to sell his position as he does listening to Kirby.

3. There is a privacy issue raised in this interview. Implicitly and explicitly (although often through barbed jokes), Cranston brings Kirby's health and fitness into the appraisal. That raises the question of just what *are* legitimate issues for an appraisal interview.

There are various levels at which an appraisal interview can theoretically probe:

a. Results
b. Energy level, stamina, hours at work
c. Health indexes, rest patterns, motivation level, dress
d. Weight, smoking, off-the-job activities like gambling
e. Diet, exercise
f. Psychological needs, coping mechanisms
g. Personality

We can all agree that results are a legitimate topic to be covered, and that each subsequent level has a direct impact on the one above it. But how far down can an appraisal go without violating privacy and fairness? First, we must ask: what are the guidelines (legal, ethical, company culture and norms, interpersonal contracts)? Then, what is our competence to judge on these various levels? Also, what are we appraising—performance or potential—and does a potential appraisal allow us to go to lower levels?

CONCLUSION

What are the objectives of performance appraisal?

EVALUATION
1. Let subordinates know where they stand.
2. Provide valid data for pay and other personnel decisions.
3. Document discharge decisions.
4. Provide warnings.

COACHING AND DEVELOPMENT
1. Counsel and coach subordinate.
2. Develop commitment to organization.
3. Discuss career opportunities.
4. Motivate subordinate.
5. Strengthen supervisor–subordinate relations.
6. Diagnose performance and organizational problems.

What conclusions can be drawn from the case?

1. Performance appraisal validates or changes psychological contract.
2. Don't mix developmental interview with evaluation goals.
3. The appraisal form and system influences interview.
4. Results and "right" characteristics don't always coincide.
5. Listening is key to developmental interview.
6. Supervisor's values and perspectives affect evaluation.
7. Implementing performance appraisal in organizations means influencing the behavior of all managers and subordinates.

TEACHING PLAN

Day 1

5 min.   1. Open with a lecturette positioning performance appraisal in the HR flow section. In many ways, a corporation's policies and practices in performance appraisal determine the effectiveness with which it can manage HR flow.

15 min.   2. What is your evaluation of Kirby? What are his strengths and weaknesses? How effective is he?

30 min.   3. What is your plan for the appraisal interview? Have the class discuss their plans. Start with one student's plan and put it on the board. Class critiques this plan and offers alternatives. Generate a discussion of the issues listed earlier in this note.

25 min.   4. Divide class into trios, assigning each student a role as Cranston, Kirby, or an observer. Instruct them to role play the appraisal interview. This usually generates a lot of energy and interest.

10 min.   5. Report out from groups (particularly observers) about the interview. Compare approaches taken by the different Cranstons.

5 min.   6. Bridge to the next class. Prepare students for viewing the actual appraisal interview by building it up. "It is not very often we get to sit in on someone else's appraisal interview." Then tell them that the quality of the videotape is not very good and the 50-minute interview is not a Hollywood film in terms of drama, but it is a slice of real organizational life. They will have to pay attention to many subtleties of behavior.

Before viewing the video tape students should be given the one-page orientation sheet which follows this teaching plan. It provides some of the information above and informs them about a weekend in New Hampshire that Cranston and Kirby talk about in the interview.

Day 2

5 min.   1. Open with a discussion of what criteria can be used to evaluate performance appraisal interviews—content, process, outcomes (see above).

55 min.   2. What are the strengths and weaknesses of the interview? Many of the points listed above in analysis of the videotape should be brought out. Students should be asked to compare with their own experience.

10 min.   3. Was the interview fair? This issue should be brought up explicitly if it has not surfaced to this point.
   a. By what criteria should performance be judged, results or "fit."
   b. This is a good time to put Figure 5–5 on the board and lecture about it.

10 min.   4. Was the interview too personal? Was it appropriate to raise the health issue?

10 min.   5. Summary lecturette—can be drawn from the "Note on Performance Appraisal."

A one-class teaching plan should follow the Day 2 plan. Students will be assigned to read the cases and view the Cranston–Kirby interview film before class.

NOTE

1. Michael Beer, "Note on Performance Appraisal," in Michael Beer and Bert Spector, eds., *Readings in Human Resource Management* (New York: Free Press, 1985).

ORIENTATION TO THE
CRANSTON-KIRBY APPRAISAL INTERVIEW

Jim Cranston and Eugene Kirby had a two-hour appraisal interview in June 1977. A videotape of this interview was edited and shortened to represent the full interview and capture the spirit of the interactions between the two men. Obviously not all of the content could be retained. But an attempt has been made to keep the most important portion of the dialogue. To make the videotape easier to view, a fade-out and -in technique has been used to bridge gaps in the interview. Bleeps have been inserted to mask the mention of names and places that might reveal the identity of the company or individuals.

In the opinion of the casewriter, the videotaping of the interview had only a minor impact on the participants and their behavior is consistent with the casewriter's expectations based on prior interactions. This became more and more true as the interview progressed and the participants became accustomed to the television camera.

In early May, approximately one and a half months before the appraisal interview, Jim Cranston arranged for a special weekend meeting for all district managers in his region and himself. The purpose of the meeting was to go through a program designed and conducted by the staff of a local university at a management resort in the woods of New Hampshire. The intent of the program was to help each manager explore his personal capacities and skills, and to increase self-awareness through measurement of his vital medical signs. Jim Cranston felt that this particular university program was a good one for CFS managers because it uncovered information on each of the participants on several levels, among them, interpersonal and communication skills, willingness to trust and to delegate, physical condition, and willingness to work as a team. In addition to a variety of discussions and tests, the managers were asked to participate in several physically demanding tasks which required that they work together. Discussion of the experiences generated by these tasks provided individuals with an opportunity for learning about their interpersonal relations, communication, and physical condition. This weekend is discussed by Cranston and Kirby in the interview.

ASSESSING MANAGERIAL TALENT AT AT&T
Teaching Note

The decisions to promote and develop managers are among the most important made in an organization. These decisions can have a significant impact on the development of subordinates and indeed the long-run development of the organization as a whole. Organizations that want to be effective in the long run need a process for continually assessing and developing management potential. A scarcity of management talent at critical stages of the organization's life can arrest its growth and development as much as a scarcity of financial resources. But what constitutes management potential? How does one know whether or not an individual has it?

Managers have been assessing manager potential for years by using their own personal yardsticks. Over the last 25 years, industrial psychologists have been working to develop predictive measures of that potential. Despite their efforts, the prediction of managerial potential has remained elusive, in large part because of the complexity of managerial work. Within the last 20 years, a new approach has been developed: assessment centers.

Many corporations are finding that assessment centers can be an important tool for assessing and developing managerial effectiveness. These cases provide background data on AT&T's assessment centers and the roles they play in that corporation's promotion decisions. The focus is on the evaluations of two candidates and the assessment process.

In contrast with Colonial Food Services, AT&T has introduced a third party into the assessment process, presumably to improve the validity of the results. But the AT&T system is not problem-free. Privacy is a concern. Donna Lawrence feels that hers has been violated to some extent. Both Donna and Walt Jackson wonder whether their performance at the Center is truly reflective of how they would handle a Level 5 job. Despite the sophistication of the tests and the fact that the Equal Employment Opportunity Commission (EEOC) has found no sexual bias in them, employees (and students) might still perceive inequality by asking whether factors like sex, along with age and socialization, have been accounted for adequately. In the end, however, the system must be judged when compared with a more individualized system ("Colonial Food") or an infrequently used system ("Webster Industries").

The purpose of these cases is much more than to introduce students to the assessment center method. We see these cases as introducing students to the question of what is management potential and how corporations might make these assessments fairly and objectively. Students generally react negatively to the assessment center and other third-party assessments because somehow they believe such methods lessen their control of their own future. But how else are large corporations to select those with potential out of a large pool of employees? AT&T has that problem, particularly when individual manager judgments are not always comparable. Moreover, if students do not like the assessment center, do they prefer their future to be determined by individual bosses as at Colonial Food? Finally, these cases are intended to raise practical, political, and ethical questions about how data on employee potential should be handled. Should assessment center data be the sole determinant of promotions (at AT&T it is only one source of information to be considered with others)? To what extent can assessment data be used for developmental purposes?

In short, these cases should be used to raise a whole host of issues about that part of managing human resource flow that has to do with the question of what is effectiveness, how it should be measured, and how these data should be utilized in the organization. As a by-product, students also learn about assessment centers, a method that is increasingly being used by corporations.

ASSIGNMENT QUESTIONS

Students read the (A) case and come to class prepared to discuss the following questions:

1. Based on your reading of the case, what rating would you assign to Walt and Donna: excellent, good, moderate, or poor? Students may be given an evaluation sheet (Table 5–13) prior to class discussion and asked to fill it out.
2. What are the specific assets and liabilities of each candidate? What developmental plans would you recommend for them?
3. Do you think the qualities being assessed by AT&T are valid predictors of managerial potential?
4. What is your evaluation of AT&T's assessment center? Can you suggest alternatives?

CASE ANALYSIS

Management structure at AT&T follows a ten-level pyramid pattern for both corporate and telephone company personnel. Level 3 (district manager) is considered the beginning of "middle management," and level 5 (department head) begins "top management."

AT&T began systematically assessing managerial talent in 1958 when it put hourly workers through a two-day program to assess promotability to

TABLE 5-13
Variable Rating Form*

	WALT JACKSON	DONNA LAWRENCE
Personal Qualities		
1. Energy	_____	_____
2. Self-objectivity	_____	_____
3. Tolerance of uncertainty	_____	_____
4. Resistance to stress	_____	_____
5. Range of interests	_____	_____
6. Scholastic aptitude	_____	_____
Communication Skills		
7. Leadership	_____	_____
8. Oral defense	_____	_____
9. Written communication	_____	_____
Interpersonal Skills		
10. Leadership	_____	_____
11. Impact	_____	_____
12. Behavior flexibility	_____	_____
13. Awarness of social environment	_____	_____
14. Autonomy	_____	_____
Administrative Skills		
15. Decision-making	_____	_____
16. Decisiveness	_____	_____
17. Organizing and planning	_____	_____
Analytical Skills		
18. Fact-finding	_____	_____
19. Interpreting information	_____	_____
20. Problem-solving	_____	_____
Career Orientation		
21. Inner work standards	_____	_____
22. Goal orientation	_____	_____
23. Need advancement	_____	_____
24. Development orientation	_____	_____
Overall Rating: Indication of the potential to perform effectively at fifth level is: Excellent	_____	_____
Good	_____	_____
Moderate	_____	_____
Low	_____	_____

*Each quality or skill is rated by assessors on a five-point scale with each point on the scale illustrated by a descriptive statement which defines the extent to which the person demonstrated the behavior.

level 1. Ten years later, a similar program was begun to assess level 1 personnel, and in 1978 the company initiated its Advanced Management Potential Assessment Program (AMPA). Seventy-seven Level 3 participants nominated by their supervisors and vice presidents of personnel arrived in groups usually of 12 at AT&T's assessment center in Atlanta for a 3½ day program.

The AT&T Assessment Center

The assessment center staff consisted of the center's director, Joel Moses, three part-time clinical psychologists, and 15 level 5 managers who went through a six-day training program and would act as assessors.

Generally, AMPA attempted to look at the promotability of level 3 managers for level 5 assignments. Specifically, the stated goals were:

1. To identify individuals for placement in a pool as potential officers of the company
2. To examine the individuals in existing pools as potential officers
3. To identify individual development needs
4. To examine closely potential managers in order to understand more clearly the company's HR strengths and weaknesses

The Assessment Tools

Six major tools, designed specifically for the program, were administered to each of the participants:

1. *Group discussion.* Groups of six participants role-play members of the Riverview city council. Given a considerable amount of data, the participants must decide how to allocate a large federal grant. This exercise measures interpersonal and communication skills.
2. *Complex business game.* Groups of six sit as the board of a small mutual fund investment company, buying and selling stocks based on continually changing price quotations. This technique measures interpersonal skills.
3. *In-basket.* One at a time, participants spend three hours sifting through a substantial amount of material dealing with a variety of complex long- and short-term issues. An interview afterward with a staff person helps measure administrative skills.
4. *Problem-solving exercise.* Participants must develop a program of stress management by analyzing written material and questioning a staff analyst. Measures administrative skills.
5. *Personal interviews.* For an hour, participants meet individually with a clinical psychologist to discuss themselves, their experiences, and their careers.

6. *Paper-and-pencil tests*
   a. Projective tools—participants are presented with ambiguous stimuli—incomplete sentences and pictures—and asked to respond by completing the sentences and explaining the pictures.
   b. Bell System Qualifying Test—measures mental ability.

These paper-and-pencil tests are considered less significant assessment tools than the exercises. They are used only if they support behavioral data based on performance during the exercises. If they do not support such data, they are ignored.

After the 3½ days, assessors are divided into two teams with a staff person heading each team. They evaluate the participants along three lines:

1. *Dimension rating.* Assessors assign a number between 1 and 5 for each dimension listed on the AMPA form (the broad categories are personal qualities, communication, interpersonal, and analytical skills, and career orientation). Significant differences in rating are discussed, and a consensus reached.
2. *Overall rating.* This takes place after each dimension is rated. Candidates scored either excellent, good, moderate, or low based on exercise performance and assessors' understanding of what is required of a top management job.
3. *Developmental recommendations.* Based on all pertinent information, these recommendations are shared with vice-presidents of personnel and participants.

Feedback

A staff psychologist meets with each of the participants within two weeks of the program when possible to discuss performance, self-perception, and developmental needs. In addition, a written report is sent to the personnel vice-presidents consisting of:

1. Overall rating of potential
2. Description of performance
3. Overview of strengths and weaknesses in each dimension
4. Suggested developmental assignments and activities

This written report is stored in a private personnel file and not made part of the individual's general personnel record.

How are the results used by superiors? One personnel vice-president says:

It would be difficult to promote somebody who did poorly at AMPA. However, AMPA results can't be the only tool . . . we *certainly* take developmental recommendations seriously. . . . But if our own perceptions are not confirmed, we owe it to ourselves and the individual we sent to think twice.

The Participants

Among the participants at the first AMPA were Walt Jackson and Donna Lawrence.

Walt Jackson's Results. After the personal interview, the psychologist assessed Walt Jackson as "extremely pleasant and self-assured." Jackson was in his mid-40s and felt that opportunities for promotion were limited. He had no major advancement goals beyond the possibility of one promotion before he retired in 15 years.

In his qualifying test, he scored in the 78th percentile on verbal skills, in the 10th percentile on quantitative skills.

In the exercises, Jackson showed himself to be energetic, confident, and articulate. He did his homework, made effective presentations, and was often able to sway other members of his group to his own position.

Donna Lawrence's Results. Donna Lawrence scored considerably higher than Jackson on the qualifying test: 95 in verbal, 97 in quantitative. She was younger than Jackson—29—and had hopes of being promoted in the next two years. She had enjoyed past Bell positions as manager and general manager, but was bored with the position of plant engineer. She seemed to be an analytical thinker, well organized, and uncomfortable with bossing or being bossed.

In her exercises, she was usually well prepared, but tended to make ineffective presentations. She often spoke softly and deferred to others. She also had trouble of seeing relationships between different pieces of information.

(B) Case—To Be Handed Out in Class

Walt received a "good" rating, and within five months was promoted to level 4. He found the Atlanta experience quite stressful and competitive. He was particularly upset with the paper and pencil tests ("I kept thinking that if I had a choice I wouldn't go through with it.") He was unsure of how he did when he left Atlanta and somewhat surprised about his perceived lack of motivation. On the whole, he felt that AMPA did well at measuring certain skills but not at predicting day-to-day performance.

(C) Case—To Be Handed Out in Class

Donna received a "moderate" rating. She had been "very anxious" about AMPA, thinking it was a "do-or-die situation." She was surprised by the amount of "back-biting" among the participants, and sometimes felt intimidated. She disagreed with the assessment that her written skills were poor, since nobody had ever complained about the letters she had written on the job. Overall, she felt that the program had "intruded" upon her and had measured her reaction to anxiety rather than how she might perform at a level 5 job. She felt that the recommendation that she go back to school for an MBA was also intrusive.

Assessment Centers

First, there are some important points that can be made about assessment centers in general. In measuring management "potential," what abilities or characteristics should an assessment center be looking for? Research on assessment centers at a number of companies has suggested that certain abilities may be necessary for achieving management success:

1. Leadership impact
2. Energy
3. Persuasiveness
4. Flexibility
5. Perceptivity
6. Decision-making skills
7. Decisiveness
8. Ability to plan, organize, and delegate
9. Capacity to acquire information, ascertain factual information, and solve problems
10. Skills in oral presentation, oral defense, and written communication

In addition, centers devoted to measuring potential look for certain other characteristics:

1. Need for achievement and advancement
2. Self-awareness
3. Stress and ambiguity tolerance
4. Need for autonomy
5. Contemporary knowledge
6. Range of interests
7. General intellectual skills

TABLE 5–14
American Corporate Leaders Rate
Strengths and Weaknesses

Strengths	Weaknesses
Integrity	Limited point of view
Ability to get along with others	Inability to understand others
Industriousness	Inability to work with others
Intelligence	Indecisiveness
Business knowledge	Lack of initiative
Leadership	Failure to take responsibility
Education	Lack of integrity

It is interesting to note that in a recent Gallup poll, American corporate heads came up with their own list of the most important strengths and weaknesses, which are listed in Table 5–14.

Reliability

What are the various criteria for reliability? A measurement of criterion is considered reliable when repeated application of the measure to the same person yields consistent results. Reliability is typically determined by taking two or more measurements over time and correlating the results to determine consistency.

Assessment centers combine exercises and simulations which place participants in situations similar to those they might encounter on a management job. By training other managers to observe and evaluate the way participants handle these situations, a direct measurement of participants' skills can be obtained. This avoids both the problem of inadequate criteria for measuring management effectiveness, and the problem of credibility. The criterion problem is eliminated, it is said, because the observable behaviors are close to the ones the evaluators might want to predict. The credibility problem is eliminated by the fact that actual behavior, as opposed to psychological testing, for example, is observed and measured, and the fact that managers rather than psychologists do the measuring.

Problems of Assessment Centers

What are some of the general problems of assessment centers?

1. Is the criterion problem truly eliminated? Is observed behavior under the special conditions of an assessment center in fact predictive of "on-

the-job'' performance? That point is raised in the case when Walt observed: "On the whole, I feel that AMPA is a pretty good measure of certain skills, but I'm not convinced that it really can predict how you do on the job in the day-to-day work environment.'' Donna also wonders whether the assessment center experience is truly reflective of how she would handle a level 5 job.

Of course, such skepticism by participants does not mean that assessment centers are invalid. Indeed, AT&T has done a large amount of predictive research and shown correlations between assessment center ratings and career progress.

However, the assessments made at such a center are not—or should not be—the sole criterion for making a judgment about someone's potential. We are told that at AT&T the results are weighed and tested against the experience and impression of immediate supervisors. This is critical, since research indicates that the correlation between results at an assessment center and future performance as a manager range from 0.27 to 0.64.

2. The results of an assessment center can disappoint assessees and discourage them concerning their future with the company. In this case, Donna is disappointed in her "moderate" rating, disbelieving about some of the specific assessments, angry over what she considers to be an intrusion into her life by the company. The assessment center experience has, in this instance, left a woman who has performed well in the past and who had impressed some people with her management potential disappointed, angry, and confused over her future with AT&T.

3. How are assessees selected? In most cases, they are recommended by their supervisors. But this raises another question: Is management potential self-evident? Could such a system of selection end up perpetuating a common mold of managers (one of the very traps the assessment center was set up to avoid)? What other system could be used in place of this selection process?

Important Points of the Case

How do you take into account factors like age, sex, socialization, and training? It can be argued that at least some of the results obtained by both Walt and Donna were affected by one or more of the above factors. Walt is downgraded for his apparent lack of ambition. But he is 45 years old, has been working since high school, and has managed a slow but steady climb through his jobs. The fact that he does not easily or readily express intense ambition may say more about his age and socialization than about his management potential, though skeptics would have to contend with the argument that ambition has been shown to be correlated with upward mobility at AT&T and will be even more important in the future.

Donna, on the other hand, is downgraded for her rather timid oral presentations. Could it be that socialization as a woman has encouraged her to present herself in that way? Also, the pressures of going through an intense three days at an assessment center tend to emphasize individual competitiveness, a trait which is often not part of a woman's socialization. While EEOC has found no sexual bias in the tests used by AT&T, the question can be asked nonetheless whether the results of the assessment center might not tend to work against women. Alternatively, defenders of assessment centers would argue that oral presentation has been found to be correlated with promotability and if women score lower it is indicative of a societal problem, not a problem with the criterion on the method of assessment.

Development

Which weaknesses are correctable and which are not? A corollary to this question would be: what type of follow-up training does AT&T offer assessees? It would seem that while the assessors found significantly more weaknesses in Donna's performance than in Walt's (Donna received a "moderate" rating, Walt a "good" rating), they also believed Donna's weaknesses to be more correctable. The follow-up interviewer recommended that she return to college for an MBA to improve both her administrative abilities and her writing skills. Walt, on the other hand, was given no specific suggestions to help him overcome his perceived weaknesses. The psychologist "said that I should just behave the way I always behave."

It should be noted that even in Donna's case, the follow-up training was to be provided by Donna herself rather than the firm.

Was it fair to conclude that Donna's weaknesses were correctable and Walt's were not? If they were correctable, was it fair to label (and perhaps stigmatize) Donna as only a "moderate" performer? Should the company provide its own follow-up training to the assessments? These kinds of questions should come up in class discussion.

Alternatives

If an assessment center seems like an unsatisfactory way of judging management potential, what then are the alternatives? To rely on individual boss–subordinate appraisal runs the risk of identifying as promotable only those individuals who meet the preconceived, perhaps narrow and not very predictive, criteria selected by each individual boss. Also, that boss may not have the training and/or ability to make informed appraisals of an individual's potential. The one-on-one arrangement probably runs a greater risk than an assessment center of mixing together and confusing developmental assessment from performance appraisal.

On the other hand, the lack of any systematic approach to assessing management potential can leave a company particularly vulnerable during periods of rapid growth or cutbacks, and can lead at other times to a vast underutilization of its human resources.

TEACHING PLAN

A good way to teach this case might be to allow students to participate in the assessment of the two candidates—Walt Jackson and Donna Lawrence—and use that participation as a springboard to a discussion both of the specifics of the case and the general matter of assessment centers and assessing managerial talent.

20 min.   1. Ask students to break up into groups of between four and six people (this can be done informally by asking them to cluster around their neighbors). Based on their reading of the (A) case, each group must assign a rating—excellent, good, moderate, or poor—to the two candidates. Warn them that there are apt to be some differences within the groups and tell them that each group must come to a consensus rating (as evaluators must do in actual assessment centers).

Allow 15 minutes for the groups to confer, and write on the blackboard a chart for scoring their ratings. Then spend five minutes tallying how many groups voted for each rating, and fill in the appropriate figures.

30 min.   2. Allow students to report on their conclusions. Pick sample teams (perhaps one from each extreme on each assessee) and ask them to explain their rating. Ask if any individual students within the group strenuously disagree with the "consensus" rating, and allow them to articulate those differences, perhaps debating other members of their own group. Most of the above-mentioned issues concerning the pros and cons of assessment centers—is performance at an assessment center really predictive of on-the-job managerial performance? Are matters like socialization, sex, and age being adequately considered?, and so forth—should begin to emerge from this discussion. It is important that students recognize that the assessment center method has been *extremely well researched* and studies have demonstrated its *validity*. Thus, their discomfort with the method is in itself an issue that corporations must deal with if they are to use third-party assessments.

20 min.   3. Now ask the class to pinpoint precisely what the assets and liabilities of each assessee were. This will force students back to the data while at the same time allowing continued discussion of those broader issues. What are their assets and liabilities? What recommendations would they make for development of Walt and Donna?

The following list might be generated:

WALT'S ASSETS	WALT'S LIABILITIES
All skills of a good manager	Not enough ambition
Good leader	Quantitative scores limit him
Good sense of who and where he is	
Take-charge person	
Well organized	

DONNA'S ASSETS	DONNA'S LIABILITIES
Good on details	Can't put ideas into action
Good planner	Doesn't express herself well
Good at gathering information	Doesn't work well in groups
Gets results	Is fine at current level, but not
Smart	ready for higher level

5 min. 4. Hand out and read (B) and (C) cases.

10 min. 5. You can ask students to respond to the reactions of Walt and Donna.

    a. Were they evaluated and treated fairly?

    b. How do you respond to Donna's anger over the perceived "intrusion" by the firm?

5 min. 6. Closing comments by instructor.

    a. What are the dangers to the organization of not having a systematic approach to gathering such data? (Use "Webster Industries" as an example.)

    b. What are the alternatives? (Use "Colonial Food Services" as an example.)

    c. What are the main assets and liabilities of an assessment center? (See Table 5–15.)

TABLE 5–15

Assets and Liabilities of Assessment Centers

Assets

    —An additional valid source of data on potential, free of limitation inherent in manager judgments

    —Force participating assessors who are managers to consider what makes a good manager

    —Train managers in assessing potential

    —Allow assessment of *behavior* rather than assessment based entirely on paper-and-pencil test results

    —Perhaps the only way for large company like AT&T to accomplish the difficult task of identifying high potentials in a large pool of employees

Liabilities

    —Do exercises really represent reality (validity)?

    —Do negative assessments cause permanent damage to a person's career?

    —Perpetuate existing culture rather than promoting change.

    —Weak developmental follow-up could undermine effectiveness

    —Privacy?

    —Expensive (AT&T spends several million dollars a year on assessment centers)

    —Will employees and managers accept and use assessment center data?

HIGHLAND PRODUCTS, INC.
Teaching Note

The executive officers of Highland Products have received a letter from a woman employee accusing the company of systematic sex discrimination in their hiring and promotion policies, and threatening to take those complaints to the government and the media. The case provides that letter, along with the responses of Highland's managers, as well as a summary of equal opportunity legislation, and asks students to decide what they would do next. The case focuses on the impact of government policies on the management of human resources within a company.

ASSIGNMENT QUESTIONS

Students should read the (A) case and "Note on Job Posting" and come to class prepared to discuss the following questions:

1. If you were Raymond Kirk, what would you do? Students should develop an action plan to deal with this crisis, and be prepared to discuss how it deals with the immediate problem as well as the long-term implications.
2. How do you account for the problems Susan Lesley cites in her letter given top management statements about equal opportunity and the open posting system?

CASE ANALYSIS

Highland Products is a large, U.S.-based manufacturer. Corporate headquarters are in Baltimore, but management is strongly decentralized within six major divisions. The Hampton Division, a manufacturing division, employs 10,000 people including 3,000 women and 2,000 minorities. Their North Haven, Connecticut plant manufactures metal components. The plant manager for the past nine years, Michael Benson, is 54, a long-time Highland employee, and "not a strong supporter of social change."

The Problem

On February 11, 1980 Ray Kirk—vice president and general manager of the Hampton Division, received a letter from a woman employee of the

North Haven plant, Susan Lesley. The letter was addressed to Kirk, John Robie, Highland's CEO, and George Wilkes, vice-president for personnel. Susan Lesley charged that, despite positive statements by both Kirk and Robie that at Highland "all applicants for employment and all current employees will be judged on the basis of their ability and skills alone" (see casebook Exhibits 14-1 and 14-2), "barbaric" discrimination was still being practiced at the North Haven plant.

The specific complaints contained in the Lesley letter were as follows:

1. 390 of the 1,375 North Haven employees were women, yet not one supervisory position was filled by a woman.
2. A specific job posting for a technician dated 1/15/80 was a "sham." The position was, in fact, filled by an overly qualified male before it was ever posted.
3. Women are told that they must have a technical degree if they wish to move beyond secretarial-type jobs, while men are given supervisory positions without that degree. Women with degrees in English are told they do not qualify for supervisory jobs, even though there are currently men in those positions with degrees in sociology and elementary education.
4. Women are generally denied the opportunity for lateral movement, while men are often given lateral moves plus raises.
5. All women are hired at minimum pay levels, while men come in somewhere between minimum and midpoint. Women are, in fact, occasionally paid below the minimum of their job level.

There were also charges of "double standards," "lies," and "deceitful practices." Lesley had been told, by whom she does not specify, that if she continued to question "the system," her future raises and promotions would be in jeopardy, as well as the career of her husband, a blue-collar supervisor with Highland. But such threats would not work, she insisted.

This letter was to be the first prong of her "attack." If she did not hear from Kirk, Robie, or Wilkes within the week, she would move to step two, which would involve mailing letters to newspapers—both local and national—politicians—the President, congressmen, local mayors, and so on—federal and state agencies, and the Hampton Products [sic] board of directors.

After reading the letter, Kirk received a call from John Robie. Kirk was to use George Wilkes and his staff as he saw fit to "fix it."

EEO Background

Kirk had been briefed by Highland's legal staff on important aspects of affirmative action law (casebook Exhibit 14-5). The lawyers pointed out that Equal Opportunity Employment (EEO) involved two distinct but occasionally overlapping categories:

1. The "passive" obligation of nondiscrimination. Congress prohibited discrimination through a series of federal laws usually echoed at the state level.
2. The "active responsibility" of affirmative action promulgated by an executive order in 1965. Affirmative action programs designed to improve the utilization of minorities and women without regard for whether discrimination has occurred against them is required of employers who contract with the federal government. The failure to achieve affirmative action goals, however, does not, per se, amount to discrimination.

Enforcement authority over discrimination claims is in the hands of the EEOC. Litigation can be filed either by individual claimants (as either an individual or "class" action) or by the EEOC itself. Court rulings have extended the definition of discrimination to include both "disparate treatment"—where an individual is intentionally discriminated against—and "disparate impact" any systematic personnel practices that adversely affect minorities or women to a disproportionately greater extent than whites or males (intent need not be proved).

The Supreme Court has also sanctioned the use of statistical proof in litigation, so that a complaining party may establish a prima facie case for relief on the basis of the absence of minorities or women from particular job classifications. The employer must then show a compelling nondiscriminatory reason for a particular personnel system with "no other reasonable alternatives" available.

Affirmative action performance, on the other hand, is solely the responsibility of the employer subject to performance reviews conducted by the U.S. Department of Labor, Office of Federal Contract Compliance (OFCCP). Companies doing business with the government must develop and submit a written affirmative action plan (which must include a comparison between existing work force utilization and the "availability" in the "relevant labor market" to indicate "underutilization," as well as both short- and long-range goals for improving that utilization), allow complete on-site compliance reviews, and correct any deficiencies found by the OFCCP. Private complainants may not bring suit.

After reading Lesley's letter, Kirk examined the affirmative action program at North Haven. He knew that the Hampton Division's performance, which was to be coordinated and monitored by Nancy Hobbs, had been only "modest," and that North Haven's goals were far from being met (casebook Exhibit 14–6). Despite stated goals, there were no women at the official or managerial level:

Position	Plant Female Population (%)	Plant Female Goal (%)	Plant Minority Population (%)	Plant Minority Goal (%)
Official/manager	0.0%	26.4%	4.8%	8.3%
Foreman	0.0	30.5	5.9	16.8
Professionals	15.8	25.1	5.3	8.1
Technical	20.0	33.4	0.0	13.2
Sales	14.3	15.0	0.0	8.0

Part of the problem at North Haven, Kirk felt, had to do with community standards: a strong ethnic community with rigidly defined sex roles.

Job posting, which had been extended to cover office/clerical jobs (in the late 1960s) and lower-level specialists (mid-1970s) was designed to open up opportunity in the plant. Management and supervisory job applicants were solicited by management recommendations, ads, and employment agencies.

(B) Case—To Be Handed Out in Class. After receiving Lesley's letter Kirk called in Daniel Trowbridge, corporate director of salaried personnel. On March 11 Trowbridge reported that the following steps had been taken:

1. Interviews with women personnel at North Haven. He met with 11 women, including Susan Lesley, almost all of whom indicated their frustration and belief that sex discrimination did exist. Trowbridge hopes to interview 20–25 more women employees, names supplied by Lesley.
2. Lesley felt that she was discriminated against when she was turned down for a buyer's job, and was now considering filing a suit.
3. Lesley had not indicated when, or if, she would proceed with step two as outlined in her original letter.

Trowbridge came to the following conclusions:

1. "Ms. Lesley is dedicated to opening up opportunities for women . . . articulate, well read or advised . . . does have a following."
2. There is no evidence of unequal pay for equal work, and the evidence of Lesley's particular discrimination charge seems weak.
3. "I feel that some of our practices—unintentionally, I believe—do impact negatively on promotional opportunities for women."

Trowbridge promised specific recommendations following completion of his interviews.

(C) Case—To Be Handed Out in Class. The Hampton Division announced a new affirmative action program on May 14. Some of the main points were:

1. Sensitivity programs for supervisors
2. Open posting for salaried (including exempt) jobs
3. Affirmative action committees at each unit
4. Establishment of new objectives, and considering attainment of those objectives as "a primary consideration" when awarding management incentive payments

(D) Case. On August 12 Susan Lesley wrote to Trowbridge (with copies to Robie, Kirk, Wilkes, Alfred Kraft—Kirk's new personnel manager—and Highland's Board of Directors). "I can't uncover or find any signs of progress," she said. "Highland Products still remains a mighty fortress of inequality." Her specific complaints were:

1. The way the affirmative action committee was picked undermined the "glimmer of hope" in the action plan. The committee was "hand picked" by the very people who practiced or condoned discrimination.
2. "Even though we have qualified women who could have gone into many job openings (even supervisory) in the last six months, we were not afforded the opportunities. . . . Action delayed is justice denied."

She then announced her intention to file suit against Highland as well as against "the State of Connecticut and the United States Federal Government."

Overcoming Barriers to Equal Opportunity

Gloria Gery[1] has provided a model for planning and managing the process of equal opportunity change: (see Figure 5–6). There are three levels of change with which an organization must be concerned:

1. *Organization barriers*: policies, practices, personnel systems, benefits, communication, expectations, accountability, rewards systems. These barriers exist both within the total organization and at each operating level.
2. *Managerial barriers*: barriers that exist within individual managers and supervisors, including attitudes, values, expectations, and beliefs or stereotypes about minorities and women that are the result

of past conditioning by society and/or the organization, as well as the behaviors that are based on those beliefs.

3. *Women's and minority barriers*: attitudes, behaviors, expectations, confidence, education and experience, definition of what can be done, and role definitions. Many women and minority workers have developed a "self-limiting philosophy."

All three sets of barriers must be attacked if genuine equal opportunity is to be achieved. Affirmative action plans aim at organizational barriers. Supervisory awareness training may help to overcome managerial barriers. Career development workshops for women and/or minorities can dramatically increase individual confidence and expectations, says Gery.

She further warns of the dangers of attacking barriers on just one or two levels. Career development workshops are "programmed" to fail without the necessary organizational support system in place. Overcoming organizational barriers could come to naught if blocked by backward-looking attitudes and behaviors on the part of supervisors. A company that has

FIGURE 5–6
Overcoming Barriers to Equal Opportunity

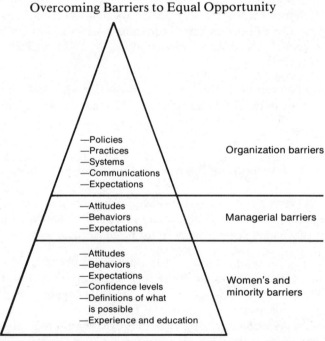

Source: Gloria J. Gery, "Equal Opportunity—Planning and Managing the Process of Change," in Michael Beer and Bert Spector, eds., *Readings in Human Resource Management* (New York: Free Press, 1985).

overcome managerial and organizational barriers can find itself with a scarcity of women and minorities interested in moving up.

HR Planning

While this case is primarily about EEO, it is also about managing flow as part of an overall HR policy. If Susan Lesley's charges are correct, Highland is passing over many highly qualified personnel, promoting less-qualified people. Even besides the EEO ramifications, Highland may be making inefficient use of of its available human reources because individuals do not have an opportunity to choose the job that might fit their competence and/ or ambition. In a 1967 article Theodore M. Alfred referred to companies that did not involve employees in career decisions as engaging in a "checkers" or arbitrary and haphazard approach to HR planning.[2] HR practices that do not allow the individual employee to participate meaningfully in organization career decisions invite failure in getting the right people for the right jobs. There are four broad areas of shortcomings in this regard, he writes:

1. Managers are allowed to hoard good people to the detriment of the organization.
2. Managers are allowed to promote within their own departments or among their own acquaintances without considering others within the organization.
3. An individual's opportunity to promotion depends too much on present supervisor's opinions and knowledge.
4. Those who do not get promoted are often not told why they did not get the promotion or even that they were considered.

Poor utilization of a firm's human resources can lead, Alfred writes, to the following problems:

1. Dilution of individual initiative and development
2. Loss of good people from organization
3. Underutilization of available talent
4. Politicization of career issues
5. Distrust in supervisor–subordinate relationships; dependency on supervisor
6. Coexistence of hoarding and understaffing

The internal labor market needs to be opened and formalized to avoid these pitfalls. Among the steps that Alfred recommends are:

1. Every job must be advertised throughout the organization.
2. No organizational barriers to applicants should exist.

3. Systematic information on career opportunities must be available.
4. Each unsuccessful candidate must be told why.

Job Posting

Alfred and others have suggested job posting as a method to enhance individual control over career. This system, currently being used in one form or another by a majority of American companies, considers the organization's internal staff to be an important labor market, and advertises open positions within that internal market either just as it would on the outside or by giving some preference to internal employees. Students should also be assigned "Note on Job Posting" in the text for a fuller discussion of job posting. The article also describes some of the potential benefits that both the organization and the individual can derive from a job posting system. Individuals will be given more control over their own careers. And by allowing individuals an "informed choice," the organization may gain enhanced commitment from the individual employee toward the organization that afforded the opportunity for such a choice.

There are also limitations to the system, mainly found in the implementation process. The successful administration of an open posting system will require a set of competencies and values on the part of managers that are different from the competencies and values used in a more traditional system. Managers must be able to communicate honestly and openly with subordinates the reasons for promotional decisions; including providing candid feedback about job performance. Managers must also be willing to relinquish some of their authority to determine career paths of their subordinates to the subordinates themselves. Such a shift implies a broader change in organization culture and management values concerning power and delegation.

Table 5–16 offers a summary of the possible advantages and disadvantages of an open posting system.

Barriers at Highland Products

There is evidence in the case that part of the problem at North Haven may well have to do with managerial barriers. The rigid views of the community in regard to women's roles may well be affecting the attitudes, expectations, and behaviors of local managers and supervisors. The particular sticking point may well be plant manager Michael Benson.

Highland has already tried to overcome the organizational barriers that Gery talks about. There is some evidence (the Lesley letter—not really conclusive) that there are women who have overcome their own inner barriers

TABLE 5-16

Open Posting

Opportunities
    —Opens opportunities for informed choice
    —Provides information abour career options
    —Increases individual control over career
    —Creates a competitive internal labor market
      —Feedback to organization and managers on HR effectiveness
    —Increases the number of candidates available
    —Helps meet legal definitions of EEOC

Problems
    —Depends on effectiveness and fair practice of supervisors
      —Good skills in assessment
—Unbiased
—Willingness and skill in giving feedback to unsuccessful candidates
    —Depends on willingness of supervisors to give up career authority
    —Difficult to implement in geographically dispersed companies
    —May increase turnover
    —Requires change in organization culture

and have the confidence to seek advancement. The blockage may well be coming from the middle part of Gery's triangle (see Fig. 5-6).

If such is the case, it is encouraging to note that much of the May 14 affirmative action plan is aimed at these managerial barriers; particularly, a supervisory training program, and the tying of incentive payments to the achievement of affirmative action goals.

Is this enough? That depends on answers (speculative) to these two questions:

1. Can the (presumed) intransigence of Benson be overcome, or must he be removed before any real progress can occur?
2. Has Highland really removed the barriers from the first (organizational) and third (inner) level?

While no definitive answers to these questions are available, they should be part of the discussion.

In regard to Susan Lesley, Highland seems to have made at least one of the mistakes mentioned by Alfred: failure to tell somebody why they were turned down for a promotion. Some of her anger seems to stem from that turndown, which she is convinced was based on sex discrimination. Trowbridge is equally convinced that the decision was fairly based on qualifications. However, management seems to have made no effort to explain their decision to Lesley. Such an explanation may not have convinced her, but the possibility exists that the effort could have helped to calm down the situation somewhat.

Action Plan

What should Kirk do? At the conclusion of the (A) case, Kirk is told to "fix it." But what is "it?" Is he being asked to somehow quiet down a potentially explosive situation and keep Highland out of court? Almost certainly he is. But is he also being asked to fix the discriminatory practices in existence at the North Haven plant? We learn in the subsequent cases that Kirk works, in effect, on both fronts:

To handle the immediate situation, Trowbridge meets with Lesley and other women employees. Apparently at his suggestion, the Hampton Division orders the creation of an affirmative action committee to act as a legitimate (in the eyes of the company) sounding board for any future complaints. But will this work? Should Kirk rather than Trowbridge have met with Lesley? Should the meeting have been in a group setting rather than an individual setting? Is the situation beyond the talking stage? Perhaps a more immediate and dramatic step could have been taken, like the removal of the plant manager.

Removing Benson could have been a symbolic gesture to the women while at the same time overcoming a stumbling block to further affirmative action progress. The option of firing him, however, raises questions of fairness. If the company has never criticized Benson's handling of affirmative action matters in the past, is it now fair to fire him for that failure? Another option might be to transfer him to a new plant. He might prove to be an equal stumbling block in a new setting, in which case he could—after appropriate warnings—be fired. However, the new environment might afford Benson the opportunity to change, something that would be more difficult to do if he stayed at North Haven.

And was the possible effectiveness of the affirmative action committee blunted by the failure to appoint Susan Lesley to it? If she had been on the committee her responsibility would have shifted from criticizing the existing discrimination to helping to formulate a plan of improvement (co-optation).

For the long run, Kirk is seeking change by concentrating on the attitudes (sensitivity development programs) and behaviors (management incentive plan) of managers. Whether this will lead to long-range improvement remains to be seen. The problem is that Susan Lesley is seeking some immediate improvement. Her final letter [(D) case] indicates that she distrusts management solutions and is looking for quick signs of good faith and intentions. She is now prepared, she insists, to file suit. If the "it" was to keep Highland out of court, Kirk has apparently failed.

TEACHING PLAN

20 min.   1. What is Susan Lesley upset with?
          a. What types of practices does she charge exist at the plant?

| | b. What are the legal obligations and/or company policies vis-à-vis affirmative action that these practices violate? |
| *20 min.* | 2. What should Kirk do now? |

      a. What does John Robie mean by "fix it"? What is "it?"

      b. How should Kirk go about assessing the validity of Lesley's charges? What data can he turn to?

      c. Should Michael Benson be fired? Transferred?

      d. What can be done by February 14 to keep Lesley from carrying out step two? Should Kirk talk to her? Other women? Should somebody else meet with Lesley? In what form?

5 min.   3. Hand out and read (B) case.

10 min. 4. What do you think of Trowbridge's reaction?

5 min.   5. Hand out and read (C) case.

10 min. 6. What do you think of Hampton Division's affirmative action plan?

      a. How does it differ from the plan already in place?

      b. Will it satisfy Lesley? How?

      c. Will it improve the situation at North Haven in the long run? How?

      d. Should Lesley be appointed to the affirmative action committee? What are the risks in putting her on? In keeping her off?

5 min.   7. Hand out and read (D) case.

10 min. 8. Now how would you evaluate Kirk's response?

      a. What, if anything, should he have done differently?

      b. Is Lesley likely to sue?

5 min.   9. Summary lecturette on any or all of the following topics:

      a. EEO affirmative action, legal and social issues.

      b. Job posting—role in managing human resource flow and in meeting EEO standards.

      c. Managing change in corporate culture to reduce discrimination (see the Gery article).

NOTES

1. Gloria J. Gery, "Equal Opportunity—Planning and Managing the Process of Change," in Michael Beer and Bert Spector, eds., *Readings in Human Resource Management* (New York: Free Press, 1985).
2. Theodore M. Alfred, "Checkers or Choice in Manpower Management," *Harvard Business Review* (January–February 1967), pp. 157–167.

MEDICAL AND ENVIRONMENTAL
ELECTRONIC DEVICES CORPORATION
Teaching Note

A rapidly growing company is short of competent managers and engineers. What, if anything, can they do to assure a supply adequate to meet their growth expectations? The case helps demonstrate the relationship between corporate strategy, HR availability, and flow policies.

Perhaps more powerfully than in any previous case, "MEED" shows students the need for coordination between line managers and HR staff people in devising business strategies and planning HR policies that will work together rather than interfere with each other. Moreover, it raises the dilemmas HR managers face when they do not have the full commitment of line management.

ASSIGNMENT QUESTIONS

Students should read the (A) case and come to class prepared to discuss the following questions:

1. What are the problems in Medical and Environmental Electronic Devices Corporations (MEED's) Integrated Circuit Group (ICG)? What are the causes of those problems?
2. What actions should Barbara Hamlin recommend for ICG? In particular, what process for human resource flow planning should Hamlin recommend? What policies with respect to recruitment, education, and personnel development should she recommend?

CASE ANALYSIS

In October 1979 Barbara Hamlin was assigned the job of manager of human resource development and planning (HRDP) for the ICG of MEED. ICG was established to purchase, design, and manufacture semiconductor components. MEED's increasing need for semiconductors led to the ICG's rapid growth which, in turn, created a serious gap between needed managerial and engineering talent and supply. IC group manager Tom Douglas articulated the feeling that his group's main problem in the upcoming years would not be financial, technical, or product-related. Rather, it would be a problem in human resources. Barbara Hamlin, who reported directly to

ICG's director of personnel, was assigned the task of developing a human resource plan and presenting that plan to Douglas.

Case analysis can proceed by first looking at some of the human resource problems that existed within ICG, then at the underlying causes of those problems, and finally at possible solutions that consider the overall business strategy of MEED and ICG as well as HR needs and availability.

The Problems at ICG

ICG's problems can be seen as falling into three broad categories: shortage of human resources, stress and overload on existing personnel, and problems in performance.

1. Shortage of Human Resources. Managerial talent was clearly in short supply. Throughout ICG, managers held down two and three jobs, often operating in both supervisory and technical positions. Group manager Tom Douglas was a prime example. Kenny Lash, plant manager for the manufacturing subunit, stepped down because of "overwhelming obstacles," and took the position of manager of operations. Douglas added Lash's former job to his own. Subsequently, Lash resigned, and Douglas assumed *that* position as well. Thus, Douglas was attempting to fill three positions—group manager, plant manager, and operations manager—himself. Altogether, a total of 106 positions remained to be filled by ICG just to bring the ICG up to its authorized 1980 headcount.

Engineering talent was also in dangerously short supply. The national labor pool of properly trained electrical engineers was 2,000 and MEED, with its state-of-the-art technology, already employed 160 of them. Nationally, there were 20,000 electrical engineers graduating from college (of a total 57,000 graduating engineers) compared to a demand for 40,000 (up 40 percent from the previous year and in sharp contrast to the slack demand of the early 1970s).

2. Stress and Overload. Lash's decision to step down as plant manager, perhaps also his eventual resignation, was an indication of the extreme stress placed on ICG's overworked managerial force. The problem was a self-reinforcing one: managers were expected to do their own hiring, but often did not have the time to follow through, and jobs went unfilled, stretching them even further. This stretching of resources provided many employees with management opportunities they never otherwise would have received. But many felt overworked. And the 10 percent annual attrition rate (not high by industry standards, although it was expected to rise to 15 percent) may have been tied directly to that stress.

3. Performance Problems. In part attributable to the lack of know-how in project management, delays in delivery parts for assembly were leading to unrecoverable losses for MEED. The life cycle of devices in the semiconductor industry is quite short, and a week's delay could mean $100,000 in lost profit before taxes. The head of the advanced technology development group within ICG reported $2 million worth of design work on which production was currently being delayed.

There were other indications that performance was below par. Manufacturing expenses were running $11 million more than forecast. While industry yields (good chips as a percentage of chip starts) were running 71 percent, the relatively new plant in Jackson was running 65 percent. Altogether, ICG-produced components cost about twice as much as components bought from the outside.

Causes

Analysis can now move from seeing the problems and understanding their impact in costs and personal stress to an evaluation of the causes of those problems.

Business Strategy of Rapid Growth. The speed with which ICG was growing and was predicted to grow in the near future fueled all the other HR problems, adding both urgency and complications to them. MEED's sales, which grew more than 30 percent per year over the previous five years, topped $1 billion in 1979. The total number of employees that year was 24,900 and another 7,000 were expected to be hired in 1980.

About 25 percent of MEED's equipment cost was semiconductor components. Although MEED set up ICG with the goal of meeting vendor cost standards, ICG-produced components cost nearly 100 percent more than those available on the outside. They were currently supplying MEED with between 5 percent and 8 percent of its semiconductor components, and the ICG was expected to produce up to 20 percent of these parts eventually.

These facts signal two points:

1. ICG is not only a minor supplier of semiconductor parts, but was never intended to be a major supplier. Since the financial well-being of MEED apparently does not depend on ICG, then the group could well be expendable. The commercial viability of ICG is also questioned by the comment of George Constantine from advanced design (AD): "In fiscal year 1979 we spent $9.3 million to ship $2.5 million worth of products."
2. ICG is expected to grow rapidly in the upcoming years: 50 percent through 1981 and 35 percent per year over the next five years. The number of exempt personnel (where, we are told, the supply prob-

146

lem is most acute) in the advanced design, manufacturing, and materials subunits was expected to grow an average 66 percent over the next five years (from casebook Exhibit 16–2):

	1980	1981	1982	1983	1984	1985
Projected exempt total (three units)	122	195	310	496	815	1,504
Growth (%)		60	60	60	64	85

The growth projections indicate that ICG will face an increasingly severe HR problem in the upcoming years. The position of ICG within MEED indicates that the group's very survival may well depend on solving those HR problems.

No Human Resource Development Plan. The strategic business decision by MEED to encourage rapid growth by ICG has been made *before* Barbara Hamlin or anyone else was assigned the task of developing a human resource plan, rather than along with or after the development of such a plan. Will the human resources be available to meet the needs of such projected growth? There have been some preliminary attempts to "build relationships" with area colleges, mainly by providing funding to the colleges, that should lead to shortened on-the-job training time for area graduates who come to work for MEED. There is clear evidence that this is not nearly enough.

MEED's Culture. The culture that has been developed and promoted by MEED over the previous 20 years mitigates against careful human resource planning. "Rapid growth" is a key element of that culture, but so is informality and the lack of structure. MEED's managers express little faith in planning, and point to the company's history of remarkable growth in justifying that approach. Why change a good thing, they ask? The anticipated rapid growth of ICG in the absence of planning can also be justified as a "risk" worth taking even though it might end in failure. Such justification is circular, however, since the lack of planning is what might well lead to failure.

Another reason MEED's fast-and-loose culture creates problems is that it contrasts with the culture of traditional semiconductor companies which emphasize tight controls and a strong hierarchy. MEED's determination to impose its own culture on ICG could be either driving out or keeping away experienced semiconductor personnel.

At this point, it is possible to at least raise the question of whether MEED should be in the semiconductor business at all. MEED is currently buying between 92 and 95 percent of its semiconductor components from the outside, and the parts it is getting from ICG are not competitively priced. MEED's culture clashes dramatically with the semiconductor culture. Because MEED's culture mitigates so strongly against planning, the company appears to have created ICG without considering the implications, or even the need, for such an internal unit.

Recruitment. There was no formal recruitment for managers. It is assumed that engineers will move "up" into management (see section below on management talent). The cause of the recruitment problems for engineers is more complex. As mentioned earlier, competition for engineering talent had become quite intense by the late 1970s. Adding to the problem of finding qualified engineers among the relatively small supply was the fact that MEED was located in Michigan, far from the most concentrated center of engineering-oriented universities—California. Moving new college graduates and employed engineers to Michigan was a costly process for MEED ($5,000 in relocation costs, 30 percent salary raises to lure an experienced engineer). Additionally, many West Coast engineers simply did not want to move to Michigan. While the "growth potential" for engineers at MEED was considered a recruiting asset, the stresses and culture shock to many semiconductor people also created the potential for high turnover. Clearly, MEED's best bet lies in attracting qualified, new graduates from area colleges. While some attempts to build bridges between the company and area colleges has been attempted, there is little evidence that MEED's expenditures for donating new equipment to the colleges have aided the company's recruitment position appreciably.

Management Talent. ICG has no formal plan for recruiting MBAs in particular or managerial talent in general. It was assumed that engineers could be brought in and eventually (quickly, in many cases) move into managerial positions, since a "good" engineer would make a "good" manager. Tom Douglas is an example of an engineer (he came to MEED in 1962 as a systems engineer) who is not necessarily a good manager. He had no experience with semiconductors, a speciality which we know involves a very different culture than many other engineering tasks, before becoming Group head. As ICG head, he avoids regular meetings, preferring instead "informal" contacts. He assumed Kenny Lash's position as plant manager of the manufacturing subunit with a great deal of enthusiasm, but with absolutely no experience in running a plant. If Douglas is out of his depth in these two jobs, what will happen when he also assumes the role of operations manager, as he does at the conclusion of the (A) case?

Often, the movement from engineer to manager was disorderly, as engineers were simply saddled with such managerial tasks as budgeting and scheduling. The speed with which engineers and managers shifted assignments also virtually eliminated the possiblity of any systematic approach to performance appraisal. Even engineers who *might* have made good managers had a problem, since there were no managerial models. "People don't know what a good manager looks like," observes employee relations specialist Anne Scotti.

Solutions

Prior to reading the (B) case, students can be expected to make the following suggestions for action:

1. Fill some top management positions (ones that have been authorized but left unfilled) from the outside rather than from within. This should include one of the positions Tom Douglas is currently filling, plant manager of manufacturing. Hire people with manufacturing backgrounds to be plant managers. Les Hogan, manager for materials, may be the only one who understands management needs (his submit is the only one with a systematic performance appraisal system), and he is the only prospective plant manager inside ICG with a management background (see casebook Exhibit 16–6).

2. Step up college recruitment both for newly graduating engineers and for MBAs and other management potential types.

3. Develop a process for identifying, with the aid of line managers, the key manufacturing and technical positions that now or in the near future need to be filled, as well as future potential performers. A more rigorous performance appraisal system is required here.

It should also be noted that some attempts are being made to deal with MEED's problems within the materials and AD groups. Materials plant manager Les Hogan has divided the acquisition function into an operations group which focuses on the day-to-day production purchasing needs, and a strategic group which can engage in longer-range planning. He has further emphasized the need for planning by appointing a planning manager who, along with the managers of acquisition and testing, reports directly to him. Furthermore, a separate career path has been established for their buyers. In the past, buyers became operations supervisors or left the company. Now, with the additional option of moving into the strategic group, the turnover rate for buyers has been reduced dramatically.

The AD unit was also struggling with ways to overcome MEED's recruiting and staffing problems. Because of the cyclical nature of AD, the subunit went through numerous peaks and valleys (with annual budgets varying from $5 million to $2 million). In an attempt to smooth out those cycles, manager Dom Raffaelli shifted his emphasis from service to product development and drew up rolling five-year plans with particular emphasis on personnel needs. He initiated his own aggressive college relations program, emphasizing recruitment from Midwestern schools (where relocation costs and "culture shock" would be minimized). The computer-aided design group within the subunit set up a "recruiting machine" whereby certain managers were given recruitment responsibilities. A full-time recruiter was brought in from AD's personnel organization with responsibility for overseeing the process and keeping flow charts to make sure no likely prospects were simply forgotten (as apparently was happening elsewhere in the organization). One sign of AD's success in meeting their staffing problems was that attrition had been reduced from a quarterly rate of 17 percent to zero.

Line/Staff Relationship. MEED (B) offers students an important opportunity to evaluate the relationship between line managers (particularly group manager Tom Douglas) and HR staff specialists (particularly manager of HRPD Barbara Hamlin). Students can evaluate the specific ways in which Hamlin sought to manage that relationship. She made specific action recommendations that included having Douglas and his staff work together to identify and describe the key technical and mangerial jobs for the near future, identify internal candidates who might fill some of these positions, and establish a plan (including an improved performance appraisal system) that would help develop internal talent while committing the company to a systematic hiring program for filling in key gaps. However, Hamlin made no attempt to build a constituency for her proposals, and we already know that Douglas tends to shy away from formal, regular meetings (which would be required under Hamlin's proposals). Douglas rejected Hamlin's plan, apparently on two grounds:

1. Too much time and energy were required.
2. ICG had more immediate and important problems than those addressed by Hamlin.

It was obvious that Hamlin was one of the few managers in ICG with a long-range perspective.

Hamlin then worked to develop a broader commitment to HR planning, meeting personally and discussing problems with the various line managers. She was able to persuade Douglas and the line managers to constitute themselves as a "board of directors," meeting monthly to review the planning process, and offering important symbolic as well as real support to the idea that future HR planning is critical to the success of ICG. However, poor attendance at the November 1980 meeting (after six months of full attendance) led Hamlin to wonder whether Douglas's commitment is waning. These are typical problems faced by HR managers and line managers. Who is responsible for HRM? Can staff HRM specialists do the job without active involvement by line managers? How can line managers balance day-to-day pressures with long-term HRM needs?

TABLE 5-17

Elements of Human Resource Planning and Development

—Line managers need to pay attention to and be involved in the formulation of HRP policies.
—Managers should connect strategic business planning and HR planning.
—HRDP decisions should be derived out of interplay between general managers and staff specialists.
—Organizations should do regular external scanning to be aware of changes in the labor market, in individual and societal values, in government laws and regulations, and trends in education and training that will affect availability of talent.
—Organizations should create mechanisms to match individual and organizational needs.

Source: Edgar Schein, "Increasing Organizational Effectiveness Through Better Human Resource Planning and Development," in Michael Beer and Bert Spector, eds., *Readings in Human Resource Management* (New York: Free Press, 1985).

CONCLUSION

Edgar Schein[1] has suggested an approach to HRDP that brings together line managers and staff specialists in an effort to meet both organizational and individual needs. Table 5-17 summarizes his approach to such planning and Table 5-18 lists some specific approaches to matching organizational and individual needs.

TABLE 5-18

Improving Work Force Flow Planning and Development—
What Organizations Can Do

—Improve work force planning and forecasting system.
—Rethink cradle-to-grave philosophy—institute critical point reviews to decide on individual/organizational fit.
—Improve dissemination of career option information.
—Make available career counseling in connection with performance appraisal.
—Develop internal and external assessment centers.
   —Include career counseling programs.
—Support education and training for workers at all levels.
   —Make a yearly budget per person for education and training.
—Initiate job posting.
—Introduce special assignments and job rotation.
—Institute career development workshops.
—Introduce sabbaticals, flexible working hours, and encourage off-work activities.
—Make available flexible reward and promotional systems.
   —Make multiple career tracks available.
   —Make it easy for employees to switch careers.

TEACHING PLAN

20 min. 1. What are the problems in MEED's IC group? One approach to opening the discussion would be to ask: should MEED be in the semiconductor business? This will lead not only to a discussion of the problems facing the group, but also to an understanding of ICG's rather fragile position within MEED, and thus make it easier for them to see how the survival of the ICG could well depend on solving their HR problems.
   a. Shortage of human resources: managers and engineers
   b. Stress and overload on present personnel
   c. Delivery and overhead problems

20 min. 2. What are the causes of those problems?
   a. It is important to see how the corporate strategy, particularly the emphasis on fast growth in the absence of any short- and long-range understanding of human resource needs that will be brought about by that growth, or any plan for meeting those human resource needs has led to most of ICG's problems. Then the question should be asked: why has there been no planning?
   b. MEED's culture of quick growth coupled with distrust of planning leads to problems and conflicts with culture of semiconductor industry.
   c. Recruitment
      (1) No plan for recruiting managerial talent (MBAs or experienced managers)
      (2) Generally weak attempt to build relations with area colleges
      (3) Tight national market for engineering talent
      (4) Location of company in Michigan
   d. Lack of managerial talent and models
      (1) Do good engineers necessarily make good managers?
      (2) What are the advantages and disadvantages of such rapid employee mobility?
      (3) What's happened to performance appraisal at ICG?
      (4) Look at Tom Douglas and compare him to Les Hogan.

15 min. 3. What actions would you recommend for ICG?
   a. What is being done in the materials and AD subunits?
   b. Identify key needs for future: managerial and engineers. Who should be involved?
   c. Improve internal development: identify potential, strengthen PAS.
   d. Improve recruitment.
   e. Look at business strategy.
      (1) Does quick growth strategy for ICG need to be reevaluated?
      (2) Return to original question: should MEED be in the semiconductor business?

10 min.	4.	Hand out and read (B) case.
15 min.	5.	Evaluate Barbara Hamlin's actions.

     a. What do you think of her original proposals?

     b. Why were her proposals rejected by Douglas?

     c. Will the board of directors work to solve ICG's short- and long-term problems?

     d. What would you do now?

10 min.   6. Closing lecturette on HR flow systems

     a. Show the three main parts of a flow system—inflow, internal (through) flow, and outflow—and how they are modified or influenced by the needs of individual employees, the requirements of the organization, and societal institutions.

     b. What are the elements of flow planning and development?

       (1) Forecast future personnel needs—numbers and types.

       (2) Describe position requirements in terms of knowledge and skills required.

       (3) Develop data base on employees' knowledge, skills, and career goals:

         (a) Performance appraisals

         (b) Personnel development specialists or auditors

         (c) Self-report

         (d) Assessment centers

       (4) Develop a process for matching individual and organizational needs:

         (a) Centralized process—personnel department

         (b) Decentralized market-oriented process

         (c) Both

       (5) Accountability for development plans—follow-up

       (6) Involve managers in consensual process for identifying promotable individuals and reviewing the promoting process.

     c. What can organizations do to improve HR flow planning and development? (Review Table 5–18.)

NOTE

1. Edgar Schein, "Increasing Organizational Effectiveness Through Better Human Resource Planning and Development," in Michael Beer and Bert Spector, eds., *Readings in Human Resource Management* (New York: Free Press, 1985).

CHAPTER 6

Reward Systems

The objective of this section is to help students understand a major human resource management (HRM) task: the design and administration of reward systems. We want students to appreciate the difficulties of designing and implementing a reward system that achieves the dual objectives of perceived equity (internal and external) and motivation. Students often bring with them a bias in favor of using merit increases or bonuses to "drive" behavior. We want to make them more cautious about this bias, while appreciating the many conditions that must be met to make pay an effective motivator. The major issues dealt with in the rewards section include:

1. *External equity.* Students learn that the perception of external equity has a powerful bearing on how much rewards will satisfy employees, as well as how effective rewards will be in motivating the behavior most desired by the organization. Employees compare what they bring to and put into a job (input) with the rewards they receive from that job (output). They then compare their own input/output ratio with the input/output ratio of employees at other, comparable organizations. A perception of external inequity can lead to high turnover. Students learn something about job evaluation and salary surveys as tools for maintaining internal and external equity. We also teach that managers should not assume that a feeling of inequity is necessarily an indication that the company's salary structure is not competitive. It may simply indicate that an employee has outgrown his or her job. In the work systems section, which also deals with rewards, students will learn that rising expectations of employees that can occur in innovative work systems (which place new demands on employees and thus in-

crease their perception of what they are putting into their job) must be considered when managing a reward system ("Alcon Laboratories," "Megalith, Inc.–Hay Associates").

2. *Internal equity.* Students learn that employees also compare their input/output ratio with the ratio of other people within their own organization. Like external equity, the perception of internal equity can greatly enhance the ability of a reward system to enhance employee satisfaction and trust. Students also see that some tension may exist between the desire to achieve both internal and external equity. A job evaluation system that is intended to achieve external equity may or may not achieve the perception of internal equity depending on many factors, including the degree of trust and/or participation in devising and administering the system ("Megalith, Inc.–Hay Associates," "LEP Corporation").

3. *Pay as a motivator.* Students learn that, from an organization's point of view, rewards are intended to motivate certain types of behavior. But how well, and under what conditions, will rewards actually motivate employees? And is the behavior that is being motivated in fact the behavior that will lead to enhanced organizational effectiveness? Students also see that rewards can have indirect effects. Executive bonuses, for instance, can be used by an organization to encourage managers to set objectives with their subordinates, while a Scanlon plan can work, beyond whatever individual motivation it does or does not provide, to encourage cooperation between union and management ("Alcon Laboratories," "LEP Corporation," "First Federal Savings," "Dana Corporation").

4. *Level of aggregation.* Students learn that an important distinction between various pay-for-performance systems is the level at which performance is defined. We include cases on individual pay-for-performance such as merit pay and executive bonuses, as well as organizationwide performance. In deciding at which level to peg pay for performance, students learn that an organization must analyze carefully such questions as: how much independence or interdependence do various tasks require? What kind of behavior (individual competition or organizational cooperation) will increase organizational effectiveness? What kind of mix between a base salary and a bonus (either individual, group, or organization wide) can be offered that will enhance both employee satisfaction and organizational effectiveness ("LEP Corporation," "First Federal Savings," "Dana Corporation")?

Sequence of Cases

We are suggesting the following sequence of cases:

1. *Alcon Laboratories, Inc.* "Alcon Laboratories" opens the reward systems section by exploring the effectiveness of commission systems as

motivators. The case illustrates the need for fit between the reward system and the task. The case nicely spans the flow and reward system sections by demonstrating how these two HRM policy areas are interconnected, and how they both affect and are affected by the overall business strategy.

The immediate problem in the case is high turnover. In attempting to design an action plan for improving Alcon's retention rate, students must analyze what kind of business Alcon is in, and then look at some of their human resource policies—flow (recruitment, promotion, development), rewards (level of compensation, mix of salaries and commissions, the way commissions are calculated, promotions), and job design (what salespeople are expected to do)—and then determine the extent to which human resource policies are helping or hindering overall organizational effectiveness. Do the policies fit with each other? With the goals of the business?

"Alcon Laboratories" also touches on the issue of a psychological contract (in this case, the promise of quick upward mobility). Like "Nippon Steel Corporation" and "Webster Industries" before it, "Alcon Laboratories" also raises the question of the cost of breaking the psychological contract. Unlike those earlier cases, however, "Alcon Laboratories" demonstrates one of the costs—high turnover—and allows students to calculate in dollar terms exactly what this problem is costing the business. In fact, because diagnosis and action planning must take into account broadly defined HRM strategy and its relationship to corporate strategy, "Alcon Laboratories" offers an excellent opportunity for summarizing and pulling things together.

2. *Megalith, Inc.-Hay Associates.* If rewards are to motivate employees and help the organization perform successfully, they must meet a number of criteria. One of the most important of these criteria is that rewards must be perceived by employees as being equitable, and equity is defined both externally and internally. "First National Bank of Lake City" in the employee influence section and later "Alcon Laboratories" introduced the issue of external equity and demonstrated the problems that can, in part, be caused by external inequities. "Megalith, Inc.-Hay Associates" offers more sophisticated data on the same problem and asks students to evaluate whether, in fact, it is a problem in this particular case. It also introduces students to job evaluation as a system for maintaining external and internal equity and raises questions about such systems and how they must be managed, particularly the involvement of line management.

3. *LEP Corporation.* The case provides students with the details, principles, and mechanics of an individual merit pay system. It places students in the middle of many of the problems corporations encounter in designing and administering pay systems, particularly the problems of salary compression and motivation.

As seen in all the cases in the reward systems section, compensation techniques and controls can be developed to guide pay decisions. But management judgment is considered key in the implementation of any pay system.

4. *First Federal Savings.* Students first looked at commissions as part of an overall reward mix in "Alcon Laboratories, Inc.," and now return to the bonus issue on a management level. As holds true for any other form of reward, bonuses will help motivate certain kinds of behavior based on such variables as amount, frequency, mix with other rewards, and how they are tied to behavior. The firm must be sure that the behavior being motivated is the behavior sought (one of Alcon's problems). First Federal relied on the bonuses to help create a culture of entrepreneurialism.

Using rewards to help change the culture of an organization is a matter that will also come up in the next case, "Dana Corporation—The Richmond Camshaft Plant." At Dana, in fact, the specific details of the Scanlon plan may be somewhat less important than the fact that the plan itself gives union and management a reason, even an excuse, to work out a cooperative arrangement on any number of other business-related issues. Class discussion can raise the question of whether executive bonuses are an effective way of creating an entrepreneurial culture and what happens to both the culture and the reward system designed to reinforce that culture when the business environment shifts. The problems encountered by First Federal Savings with bonus systems are typical and may be explored here. They raise fundamental questions about the efficacy of bonus systems, and these should be brought out in the case discussion.

5. *Dana Corporation—The Richmond Camshaft Plant.* The question, once again, is how to motivate employees and what kind of behavior is being motivated by the compensation system. In this case, however, the incentive is not based on individual performance [as in "Alcon Laboratories" and "First Federal Savings," in which 50 percent is allocated on the basis of individual performance against management-by-objective (MBO) goals], but plant-wide performance.

The "Dana" case allows an analysis of the fit between the plant's task (requiring interdependence) and the organization-wide bonus system. More important, it also allows students to see how critical the process of introducing the plan and the culture of the plant are to its effectiveness. Can the plan succeed with effective supervision or without a manager committed to a philosophy of participation?

"Dana" is an important bridging case as well. The Scanlon plan affords union and management the opportunity to set aside, occasionally at least, their traditional adversarial relationship (such as we saw in "Bethoney Manufacturing") and work together on mutual problem solving. As such, "Dana" offers an alternative to the more traditional approaches to employee influence covered in the opening section of the course, and anticipates the corporate level ("General Motors and the United Auto Workers") and plant ("Sedalia Engine Plant") efforts to increase employee participation. Because the Scanlon plan necessitates participation and involvement, it hints at some of the critical attributes of innovative work systems described in both "Sedalia Engine Plant" and "General Motors and the United Auto Workers."

Supplementary Reading Assignments

The following supplementary reading assignments can be made from *Readings in Human Resource Management:*

TEXT MATERIAL	SUGGESTED READINGS
Chapter 5	Edward E. Lawler, "Determining Total Compensation: Strategic Issues"
"Megalith, Inc.–Hay Associates"	
"Alcon Laboratories, Inc."	David J. McLaughlin, "Reinforcing Corporate Strategy Through Executive Compensation"
"First Federal Savings"	
	Edward E. Lawler, "The Mythology of Management"
"LEP Corporation"	William J. Kearney, "Pay for Performance? Not Always"
"Dana Corporation—The Richmond Camshaft Plant"	James W. Driscoll, "Working Creatively with a Union: Lessons from the Scanlon Plan"

Supplementary Audiovisual Materials

"First Federal Savings"   A ten-minute interview with Gene Rice, the president, describing the company's response to the executive bonus crisis (available through Harvard Business School).

ALCON LABORATORIES, INC. (CONDENSED)
Teaching Note

The sales force of a small pharmaceutical company is experiencing high turnover. What are the causes of that turnover? What might be done about it? This case explores salary and compensation systems as motivators, the need for fit between tasks and reward systems and the interconnection between rewards and other human resource (HR) policies like recruitment and promotion.

ASSIGNMENT QUESTIONS

Students should read the case and come to class prepared to discuss the following questions:

1. What is the cost of the turnover experienced by Alcon's sales department?
2. Why is Alcon's sales department experiencing such high turnover and morale problems?
3. If you were Mr. Leone, what changes would you make in Alcon's HRM policies and practices, particularly in their reward systems?

CASE ANALYSIS

Alcon Laboratories was founded in 1947. In 10 years a sales force of 30 promoted the company's speciality—eye care products—and company sales totaled nearly $1 million. By 1965, Alcon's share of the domestic ophthalmological market was nearly 20 percent. Total sales for 1966 were $9.1 million. About $6 million of that was domestic sales of 33 products and a sales force of 70.

Alcon's marketing director (who also served as a vice-president) was Ed Schollmaier, a Harvard MBA. Reporting to Schollmaier were the director of market research, product managers, and George Leone, the national sales manager. To provide salespeople with the technical information demanded by doctors, Alcon maintained a medical department which engaged physicians doing clinical research to test and study new uses for Alcon products and responded to requests from marketing by providing technical data to support product claims—as well as a research and development (R&D) department. Both the medical and the R&D departments reported to one director—Dr. Earl Maxwell. Maxwell sat on a product committee along with

Copyright © 1984 by the President and Fellows of Harvard College. Harvard Business School teaching note 5-485-013.

Ed Schollmaier as well as the director of international operations and the president/chairman of the board.

The Sales Force

Below national sales manager George Leone were three sales levels: regional sales managers, district sales managers, and medical sales representatives. Broadly speaking, each of the 70 salespeople had two functions:

1. *Creating demand.* Calling on doctors, trying to get them to prescribe Alcon products.
2. *Distribution.* Getting the product to wholesalers, hospitals, and pharmacies.

Typically, a drug salesperson averaged 48 calls per week. Alcon salespeople typically started their day by driving 50 miles, waited up to 30 minutes to see a doctor, spent only 5 minutes with the doctor, and saw only five of nine doctors called on. They also averaged seeing one drug wholesaler and three retailers (about 15 minutes with each) per day.

The visit to the doctor was the key to the job. Once a month for five minutes, the salesperson was to "detail" to the doctor one primary product, one secondary product, and one "door handle" product (just mentioned on the way out). That brief visit would have to make a lasting impression (to be supported by journal advertising and direct mail promotions).

When calling on retail druggists, the salesperson would let the druggist know which products were currently being detailed or specially promoted. The salesperson could check the druggists' stock and usually wrote up orders themselves. The salesperson was also expected to spend time with the area wholesalers' purchasing agents to ensure that two months' supply of Alcon products were on hand (all sales were guaranteed, with the company agreeing to buy back products that were unsold). Salespeople were expected to spend the bulk of their time—75 percent, instructed George Leone—creating demand by visiting doctors. This represented a change, in 1964, from salespeople concentrating their efforts on distribution.[1] When doctors themselves were asked what they expected from a drug salesperson, the following characteristics were mentioned:

1. Pleasant and sincere, not pushy or demanding
2. Ability to provide up-to-date information on products, sizes, availability, and so forth; ability to answer doctor's questions; may be a "frustrated doctor"
3. Call frequently

Pharmacists placed a high premium on integrity and were particularly disturbed by high turnover among the sales force. Wholesalers, like doctors, reacted negatively to overly aggressive or pushy salespeople.

The Problem at Home

The immediate problem at Alcon is excessive rate of sales force turnover. In the fiscal year ending in 1966, the turnover rate among Alcon's 70-person sales force was 28 percent, as compared to an industrywide rate of 12.1 percent. And that 28 percent figure represented Alcon's *second-best* year since the decade began:

1961	35 percent
1962	27 percent
1963	35 percent
1964	42 percent
1965	34 percent
1966	28 percent

There are several dimensions to that turnover problem:

1. *Flow.* Alcon liked to hire MBAs, so it recruited for its sales force primarily from business schools (and secondarily from employment agencies). Newly hired personnel were given a four-week training program. There was a prevalent view among salespeople that Alcon presented excellent opportunities for advancement. George Leone and Ed Schollmaier provided highly visible symbols of the ability to rise from the sales force. Schollmaier, for instance, had moved from being a salesman with an MBA degree to the vice-presidency within five years. The company, however, had no immediate plan to expand the existing number (nine) of district sales managers.

There also seemed to be a noticeable lack of emphasis on development. The district sales managers (DSMs) were supposed to spend 75 percent of their time with their salespeople, providing any necessary additional training. DSMs were often "too busy" to carry out this training. The DSM is supposed to see the salespeople once a month, but often does not do that. The DSM does conduct an annual performance appraisal of the salespeople. Regional sales managers were supposed to train and develop DSMs. There is no evidence that this process is taking place. Regional sales managers (RSMs) spend most of their time working with George Leone, and there seems to be little direct contact between DSMs and RSMs. Part of the problem may be that three of the four RSMs are physically located in the central office, and the fourth is about to be moved to the central office.

2. *Compensation.* Salespeople at Alcon worked on salary plus commission. Salaries averaged $580 per month in 1966. Salespeople were eligible for raises once a year, and those raises could be up to one half of the previous year's commission. Alcon believed that their salaries were now competitive with the industry.

New salespeople were placed on commission after three months. Commissions were paid twice a year and based on 10 percent of increased sales after total expenses (car, motel, telephone, meals) had been deducted. Some managers complained that this system penalized unfairly salespeople with large territories. Total commissions paid to the 70 salespeople this year were $26,000, ranging from $0 to $1,500 per individual, and with 80 percent of the commissions going to 20 percent of the salespeople.

Alcon occasionally engaged in "distribution campaigns" during slow sales periods. During a recent campaign (May 1964), a Mexican vacation was awarded to a salesperson in each region. After that contest, however, some wholesalers shipped goods back to Alcon (in one winner's territory, returns exceeded sales for several months). Within nine months, three of the four contest winners quit Alcon.

The Turnover Problem

The heart of the case analysis should deal with *why* the turnover is taking place. Before turning to that question, however, students should be asked to look at two things: what are the functions of an Alcon salesperson, and what are the costs of Alcon's excessive turnover?

The Selling Job

Salespeople at Alcon enter into a "give-and-take" relationship with four parties—doctors, druggists, wholesalers, and the company itself—as summarized in Table 6-1.

TABLE 6-1
The Selling Job

	Doctor	Druggist	Wholesaler	Alcon
Salesperson gives	—Information on use and availability —Free samples	—Knowledge of possible prescriptions —Detail scheduling and promotions —Inventory assistant	—Turnover orders —Orders information —Retail ordering	—Sales —Growth —Client contact —Knowledge of doctors
Salesperson gets	—Professional affiliation and status —Feedback on products —Competitive information	—Information on doctors' responses —Competitive data —Sales	—Sales —Inventory data	—Promotional support —New product development —Pay —Security —Professional status

162

The Cost of Turnover

There are several ways to figure the recruitment cost component of Alcon's turnover problem. We know that in 1964 the average turnover for the drug industry among salespeople was 12.1 percent. We also know that Alcon's turnover for 1966 was 28 percent or 20 individuals, and that Alcon paid $7,612 (excluding salary) for selection, training, and supervising of each new salesperson. Probably a more telling figure than the 28 percent, however, would be the average turnover for the years 1961–1966 which was 33.5 percent. Minus the industry average of 12.1 percent, Alcon's turnover problem is 21.4 percent. Based on 1966's work force, that comes to 15 individuals times $7,612 equals $114,180. If that cost alone were eliminated, Alcon would be able to raise the salary of each salesperson an average of $1,631 and place them above the national average mean.

Perhaps more significant than even that figure is the cost in lost sales. Turnover means breaking relationships with doctors and pharmacists and starting all over again with new recruits. Most of those who left had been with Alcon less than two and a half years (79.5 percent). That meant they had just barely gotten to know their customers and would now be replaced by newcomers (a fact which, we are told, particularly irritated pharmacists). A dollar figure can be estimated for loss of profits. In total we have estimated that turnover costs the company as much as 8 percent of its after-tax profits.

Finally, the high turnover rate forced district sales managers to spend an inordinate amount of time on recruitment, distracting them from time that could be spent training and developing their sales people.

Reasons for the Turnover

Now that something is understood of the cost of the high turnover, students should then turn to the question of *why* it is taking place. There are several points that should be considered:

1. *Recruitment.* There is reason to question Alcon's recruitment policies. By seeking MBAs (a significant number came from Harvard as had Ed Schollmaier who started as an Alcon salesman), Alcon was bringing in people committed not to selling, but to rising in the managerial ranks. (Are management people recruiting in their own image?) This fact could create a number of problems.
    a. Selling to doctors requires a great deal of patience—waiting in doctors' offices, seeing only some of the doctors that are called upon. Patience is not necessarily a commodity associated with "fast-track" MBAs who would take a selling job only as a first quick step up the managerial ladder.

b. Despite Alcon's reputation for quick advancement, the facts of the case indicate that there is really little room for advancement. Thus, while its reputation may be able to attract MBAs, the reality of corporate life is likely to be disappointing and lead to turnover.

c. One of the major rewards of the job is the one-on-one dealings with doctors, and having doctors treat you with respect for your ability to converse intelligently on medical matters. An individual who enters the job with an interest in medicine is likely to find this intrinsic reward more satisfying than an MBA who is interested mainly in management.

2. *Promotions.* As mentioned above, the opportunities for advancement are much more limited than newly recruited salespeople have been led to believe. Thus, a psychological contract has been made and repeatedly broken. As one salesperson put it, "Alcon promises you the sky in terms of advancement and then they just don't come through." The advanced management program which salespeople attend also raises their expectations for promotion.

3. *Compensation.* Alcon's compensation problems have to do with both *what* people are paid and *how* they are paid.

The average earning for Alcon's salespeople in 1966 was $7,331 (base salary of $6,960—casebook Exhibit 17-5—plus average individual commission of $371). Since 80 percent of the commissions go to 20 percent of the salespeople, that means that 14 received an average commission of $1,500, while 56 received an average commission of $90. The industrywide total compensation data presented in casebook Exhibit 17-6 are for 1964 and cannot be compared directly to Alcon figures. But Alcon's 1966 figures would be well below the 50th percentile in 1964 terms.

Also, looking at Alcon's salaries (minus commissions) since 1962 shows that increases have been far less recently than in previous years:

Year	Increase over Previous Year (%)
1963	7
1964	9
1965	2
1966	3

There is reason to believe, then, that Alcon is not compensating its sales force well, either in comparison with previous years or the overall pharmaceutical industry.

Another problem is the structure of the compensation system. Three specific points can be made about that structure:

1. *Use of commission.* Is an individual commission an appropriate and effective reward for a drug salesperson? Commissions are meant to serve as motivators, particularly of short-term results and aggressive selling. But we are told over and over that "pushy" or "aggressive" salespeople are precisely what doctors and pharmacists do not like. Individual commissions may be particularly ineffective for selling drugs.

2. *Structure of commission.* Commissions are tied to increases in sales. But do Alcon salespeople really control those increases? Salespeople felt that increased sales depended a great deal on the development and introduction of new products and that Alcon was severely lagging behind in this area. Rewards can motivate behavior. But one of the prerequisites for motivating behavior is that rewards be tied to behavior that individuals can *control.*

Also, by deducting total expenses before figuring commissions, Alcon was penalizing salespeople with large regions who had to drive a great deal and stay overnight in motels.

3. *Special rewards.* The one described in the case—the Mexican vacation—seemed totally ineffective. Salespeople loaded orders during the campaign with unneeded merchandise, took the vacation, and then quit as Alcon was faced with buying back all the excess merchandise.

Organizations generally get the kind of behavior that is rewarded, or, at least, that is perceived by employees as being rewarded. So companies should take great care to make sure that the behavior being motivated by their rewards is in fact the behavior they wish to motivate.

4. *Job design.* There is reason to believe that some of the problems at Alcon come from incompatible tasks designed into the sales job. The job requires salespeople to call on doctors and this demands a relationship orientation. The job also requires salespeople to call on druggists which requires inventory management skills and only moderate relationship skills. Finally, the job requires salespeople to call on wholesalers and this requires inventory and business management skills. The last two tasks are more compatible with the MBA and management recruit. The first task requires a less aggressive and more relationship-oriented person. To align recruiting with the demands of the job may require redesigning the job so that different salespeople call on doctors and druggists/wholesalers.

5. *Organization structure.* There are too many levels in the organization with the DSM and RSM doing virtually the same job (see descriptions). Can one level be eliminated?

6. *Training.* The training program for new salespeople is not appropriately structured. Training in biology and products is best conducted at corporate headquarters where salespeople can be exposed to the corporation and loyalty can be built.

What Can Alcon Do?

The first step would be to change their recruitment policies. One doctor suggests that a good drug salesperson may be a "frustrated doctor." Instead of hunting for MBAs, perhaps Alcon should recruit among medical school dropouts. Moving onto college campuses with literature emphasizing a medical-related career might attract people who could not get into medical school. Alcon's near-exclusive recruitment of MBAs makes little sense.

Another change in the recruitment might be to bring in some older, experienced, well established salespeople. This could add some stability to the sales force, and provide good models for younger salespeople. Older salespeople would be less likely to come in looking mainly for promotion through the ranks and would likely stay with the company longer than younger ones.

Something must be done to readjust the assumption of promotability, to bring the psychological contract in line with reality. Recruiters should be more honest about the possibilities for promotion.

Training should be made more rigorous, with special emphasis on the particular approaches to selling demanded by doctors. There is clearly a need for more follow-up and on-the-job training, particularly for direct contact with DSMs. Salespeople now are too isolated from the company. One way to overcome this is to conduct product training (the first week) at corporate headquarters. Moreover, Alcon's Advanced Management Program might be best dropped or applied more selectively.

The compensation system needs to be changed. Whatever happens to the commissions, base salary should be raised, probably by $2,000. A high base salary might eliminate entirely the need for commissions. But if commissions are kept, some revisions can be made:

1. Eliminate the expense deductions from the calculations.
2. Change the base–commission mix. In 1966, Alcon's commission represented only 5 percent of total average earnings. Should that be raised, perhaps to 33 percent? How will that affect salespeople? Will it lead them to overly aggressive behavior? If this recommendation is to be followed, there certainly needs to be greater emphasis on training.
3. Change the mix, but also change the way the commission is figured. Perhaps base it on the number of visits rather than the volume of sales. Tie the commission to the behavior desired quantity and quality of doctor visits. As students grapple with what behavior is desired and how it might be measured, they will quickly see the difficulty inherent in designing a pay-for-performance system. Perhaps it is better after all to eliminate the commission system, particularly if the recruitment pattern changes in the way suggested above.

Alcon might consider redesigning the sales job. Medical school dropouts might be moved into a selling job that concentrates on detailing doctors. Management recruits (MBAs) might be assigned to call on druggists and wholesalers. This would align people and jobs thereby reducing turnover, but it might break the crucial link between calling on doctors and calling on druggists. The salesperson tells the druggist what doctors might order and occasionally writes up the order himself. The salesperson also checks to make sure the druggist has in stock what doctors will order. Students should be encouraged to be creative in designing two different jobs that still preserve this critical marketing link. For example, should salespeople who call on doctors be teamed with one person who calls on all druggists and wholesalers, thus preserving the coordination link through teamwork and communication? Do the benefits of lowered turnover outweigh the risks of lowered coordination between different levels of selling?

Finally, how might the structure be changed to reduce redundancy and cost without reducing opportunity for promotion, the reason it was created in the first place. Of course, if fewer MBAs are recruited, it will allow reducing management levels. If levels are reduced it may improve communication and training. But this can only be done if turnover is reduced thereby reducing the demand for management time to recruit. Students should see in this case the interrelationships between several HRM policy areas, HR flow, work systems, and rewards.

CONCLUSION

David McLaughlin[2] has suggested that no more than 10 percent of the top companies in the United States approach pay from a strategic business perspective. Although his article deals specifically with executive pay, there are some more general points that can be related to designing reward systems through the organizations. Among those points (summarized in Table 6–2) are:

TABLE 6–2
Reinforcing Strategy Through Compensation

Articulate distinctive personnel and reward implications of firm's unique business strategy.

Use not just pay but other rewards (benefits, bonuses, promotions, job design, and so forth) to reinforce strategy

Make sure policy tradeoffs in pay fit with other policy decisions:
    —Short- versus long-term orientation
    —Individual versus team orientation
    —Unit versus corporate orientation

Involve general managers in monitoring pay systems to determine whether pay systems reinforce strategy.

Source: David J. McLaughlin, "Reinforcing Corporate Strategy Through Executive Compensation," in Michael Beer and Bert Spector, eds., *Readings in Human Resource Management* (New York: Free Press, 1985).

1. Since each company has a unique business strategy, the distinctive personnel and compensation implications of that strategy should be articulated.
2. Use not just pay but other elements of compensation to reinforce strategy.
3. Strategic compensation decisions involve certain policy tradeoffs: short-term versus long-term orientation of pay mix, unit versus corporate orientation, individual versus team focus. Whatever policy decisions are made on these tradeoffs should be reflected and reinforced in other decisions that significantly impact organization: culture, control systems, information sharing, performance criteria.
4. Involve general managers in monitoring pay systems to determine whether systems reinforce strategy.

TEACHING PLAN

20 min.	1.	What is the cost of Alcon's turnover program?
30 min.	2.	What is the cause of Alcon's problems?
		a. Recruitment?
		b. Promotion?
		c. Compensation?
		d. Corporate support?
20 min.	3.	What are the characteristics of the Alcon job and how are Alcon's human resource policies encouraging or discouraging to those characteristics?
15 min.	4.	What can Alcon do now to correct its problem?
5 min.	5.	Closing lecturette: what are the important points of the case? (See Table 6–3.)

TABLE 6–3

Important Points About the Alcon Case

1. Case demonstrates the impact that the total package of human resource practices has on performance
2. Human resource policy mistakes can be costly
3. Case demonstrates the important linkage between human resource plans and basic business plans and strategy
4. Case demonstrates the need for congruence among the various components of human resource policy package
5. The design of a reward system needs to be based on an analysis of job characteristics
6. Case demonstrates the hazard of generalizing from one's own career experience to younger junior managers and professionals

NOTES

1. Numbers in the case indicate that net income dropped substantially when Alcon changed its emphasis from loading up the distribution channels to indirect selling through doctors, and picked up slightly in 1966. Net income grew 86 percent between 1962 and 1964, and only 9 percent between 1964 and 1966.
2. David J. McLaughlin, "Reinforcing Corporate Strategy Through Executive Compensation," in Michael Beer and Bert Spector, eds., *Readings in Human Resource Management* (New York: Free Press, 1985).

MEGALITH, INC.–HAY ASSOCIATES
Teaching Note

The senior vice-president of finance for Megalith, Inc. wants to give large pay increases to his top managers. Those increases would put his people over the tops of their ranges, but would also—so he believes—stem the flow of his best people out of the organization. He runs into conflict with the vice-president for human resources and the Hay system of job evaluation. The often difficult relationship between general managers and HR staff, first detailed in "MEED" and revisited here, exists in a great many organizations. In this case students can analyze the conflicting needs and goals of the two vice-presidents (finance and HR).

The case adds depth to students' understanding of the complexity of balancing internal and external equity, and deals with the role of personnel and job evaluations in maintaining equity. Students will learn some of the specifics of the Hay system and also learn that the tendency of managers to use pay as an explanation for most of their problems may be oversimplified.

"Megalith, Inc.–Hay Associates" introduces the important element of internal equity. Job evaluations as a way of determining salary range, and particularly the Hay system, are meant to offer managers a way of dealing with internal equity. In coming to understand a job evaluation system, students will assess both the strengths and weaknesses of such a system.

One of the traditional complaints about job evaluation systems is that they pay for the job rather than for the individual. In the work system section, students will encounter a company that has replaced entirely job evaluations with individual skill evaluations ("Sedalia Engine Plant").

This is a three-case series. the (A) case is assigned for preparation before class. The (B) and (C) cases are handed out in class.

ASSIGNMENT QUESTIONS

Students should read the (A) case and "Note on Job Evaluations" and come to class prepared to discuss the following questions:

1. Who is right in the argument between Boyd, the line manager, and Nicodemus, the vice-president for human resources, and why?
2. What are the benefits and problems of a job evaluation system?
3. Should Megalith be willing to allow for exceptions to their salary system or hold the line in accordance with the limits set by the job evaluation system?

CASE ANALYSIS

John Boyd, Megalith's vice-president for finance, and Frank Nicodemus, vice-president for human resources, are engaged in a debate that has been going on for over a year. Boyd would like to raise the salaries of his key managers by 25 percent. In one month he lost two of his best managers—half the team he had originally brought with him to the finance group—to jobs that paid higher salaries. Unless he can get more money, he is convinced, he will lose others.

Nicodemus explains that Boyd's people are at the top of their ranges. "To make exceptions to a well-grounded scale would be both hasty and rash," he explains. "I just can't compete," Boyd reports. "You've got us locked in with a pay schedule that looks competitive on the surface, but when the chips are down, it's a loser." Boyd is ready to ask Megalith's president, Allen Whitfield, to review the whole compensation system. Nicodemus suggests Boyd talk with Ed Rogers from the Hay Associates who has been hired to do a job evaluation study for Megalith.

When Boyd meets Rogers, he wonders whether the Hay system will be able to distinguish between talent and mediocrity. Rogers says that the data will show how Megalith's salaries compare across a broad industrial spectrum, but will not evaluate the talent of the individuals involved. He then explains to Boyd the three major areas on which the Hay Associates evaluate a job. (See Table 6-4.)

Megalith, Inc. has grown significantly since the end of World War II. In 1969—at the advice of a consulting firm that suggested Megalith beef up its central planning and control staff in order to meet the requirements of a large company—Whitfield asked Boyd to move from office products to finance. Between 1969 and 1975 the finance group grew from 110 to 630 employees. This "fast-track" growth enabled Boyd to attract a group of

---

TABLE 6-4
Three Areas of Hay Job Evaluation

1. Know-how
   a. Technical and practical knowledge
   b. Managerial knowledge
   c. Human relations skills needed to perform job
2. Problem-solving
   a. The thinking environment
   b. The thinking challenge of the job
3. Accountability
   a. Position's freedom to act
   b. Position's impact on end results
   c. Dollar magnitude of the area most clearly affected by the job.

TABLE 6–5
Rating of Top Management Jobs

Finance Group Positions	Total Points	Current Base Salary
Senior VP—finance	3,192	$90,000
Controller	1,976	59,000
General counsel	1,856	65,000
Treasurer*	1,988	54,000
VP—management information*	1,688	55,000

*These are the two positions that have just turned over.

"young stars" into his four top manager positions, and two have just resigned.

(B) Case—To Be Handed Out in Class

This case presents findings from the Hay Associates survey and suggests that Megalith's compensation structure as practiced in the finance group is not relatively low. The only individual rated below the "commendable" line on a total cash compensation package is Boyd himself.

A listing of total Hay points and base salary for Boyd and his four top managers shows a large gap between Boyd and his subordinates. (See Table 6–5.)

(C) Case—To Be Handed Out in Class

Data from the Hay Associates' climate survey (completed by 48 employees of the finance group: 7 top managers and 41 others) show that the top 7 managers rate their compensation system more "equitable, competitive, and related to performance" than about 70 percent of the thousands of people who have filled out this survey. They also perceive their work environment as relatively unchallenging, undynamic, not innovative, and constraining.

Is Pay the "Easy" Answer?

The evidence of the cases indicates that Boyd has grabbed onto pay as an explanation for his problem when, in fact, several others present themselves:

Slower Growth. Boyd was an entrepreneur who sought like-minded young people to enter onto his "fast track." By 1975, however, his group's rapid growth pace had ended.

Year	Increase in Employees (%)
1970	50
1971	57
1972	50
1973	31
1974	18
1975	5

His "young stars" were at the top of their promotion and salary ceilings. As such the three key rewards that they had been receiving—exciting, challenging, changing work; fast promotions and fast increases in pay—all disappeared. Two responded by leaving for line jobs, at least one of which was in a growth division.

Delegation of Authority

Boyd has had a difficult time delegating authority. The gap in the Hay point rating indicates that there is a good deal of responsibility that Boyd is keeping for himself rather than delegating to his subordinates. More delegation of authority and responsibility might make up for at least some of the loss of growth-related challenge.

Change in Organizational Realities

Some turnover may be inevitable, and not all turnover is bad. The young people Boyd originally attracted to his group fit well with the conditions of dynamic growth. Now, a new situation is established, and a new type of employee may be needed. Some turnover may actually help the process of fitting people and culture.

The Hay System

The case also answers some questions about the Hay system itself:

How Does It Work? Using the overall categories and subcategories listed above, the Hay system derives numerical indexes for each job in an organization. The Hay system offers a comparison between the organization's numbers and industrywide numbers to give the organization an idea of what the job is worth. The company can then build a range—high, low, and midpoint—around certain "benchmark" jobs.

Why Do Companies Use the Hay System? The Hay system adds "objectivity" to a difficult process. It also provides documentation about the worth of comparable jobs in other companies. This data base is one of its key values.

What Are the Weaknesses of the Hay System? It does not deal with equal pay for *comparable work;* does not rate individuals on the skills they possess, but only their job's characteristics; favors corporatewide consistency over local problem-solving; and, in this case, does not tell Boyd what his problem is, only what it isn't.

What Are the Alternatives to the Hay System or Any Other Job Evaluation System? The most common alternative in the United States is to base pay on a skill evaluation. This is thought to encourage the learning of new skills and allow flexibility in job rotation. There are drawbacks as well. Skills may be difficult to define and costly to measure. External equity will not be nearly as easy to deal with as under a system of job evaluations.

Equity

What is equity? Employees look at the relationship between the "input" to their jobs—seniority, education and training, job performance, skills and competence, the nature of the job itself—and the "output" from their jobs—value of total compensation system, pay for performance, intrinsic rewards, and nonpay extrinsic rewards. They compare that relationship to the input and output of other employees. When they look at employees at various levels within their own organization, they are looking at *internal equity.* When they look outside their organization at similar jobs, organizations, and professions or within their own geographic region, they are looking at *external equity.* (See Table 6–6 for summary.)

CONCLUSION

Students should be assigned "Note on Job Evaluations" in the text for a fuller discussion of job evaluations. Tale 6–7 summarizes the main steps in constructing a job evaluation system, while Table 6–8 identifies some of the main problems with the system. This case points to the interdependence of compensation with HR flow and work system issues. Lack of promotional opportunities or challenging work can easily be attributed by employees to pay. Pay might be increased but the problem would not be solved.

TABLE 6–6
Equity

Individual employee	?	Other employees
$\dfrac{\text{Input}}{\text{Output}}$	=	$\dfrac{\text{Input}}{\text{Output}}$

Input	Output
Seniority	Value of total compensation
Education and training	Pay for performance
Job performance	Intrinsic rewards
Skills and competence	Nonpay extrinsics
Nature of job	

Other employees

Employees in similar jobs, organizations, professions, type of work, geographic area

TEACHING PLAN

Before class discussion begins, you can make the issues raised by the case more immediate by opening with a statement like, "Whether you like the Hay system or not, once you leave here you will most likely be living under it."

20 min.   1. What is Boyd's problem and what should he do about it?
   a. Is Boyd's analysis of the problem correct?
   b. Why are Jackson and Arnold leaving? Here, students should begin to get beyond money to issues of job satisfaction, responsibility, and growth.
   c. Should Megalith be willing to make exceptions to their salary system, as Boyd suggests, or stay with an internally consistent system, as Nicodemus urges? Perhaps role-playing can be useful here, with "Boyd" and "Nicodemus" presenting their arguments to you, or another student as "Whitfield," while "Whitfield" presses them on their analysis.

TABLE 6–7
Job Evaluation

—Develop framework for rating value of jobs.
—Rate benchmark jobs.
—Rate all other jobs.
—Align all jobs against benchmark jobs.
—Adjust evaluations.
—Decide on range spread and spread between jobs.
—Conduct salary survey for benchmark jobs and other jobs.
—Readjust job relationships based on survey.

TABLE 6–8

Problems in Administering Job Evaluation Systems

—How to administer individual merit system within job evaluation system
  —Evaluating performance
  —Communicating decision
  —Deciding on increase or place in range
—Finding an effective and fair system and process for job evaluation
—Developing confidence and trust in the system and processes
—Accommodating the need for exceptions ("red circle jobs") to the system
—Salary compression
—External equity based on regular salary surveys
—Administering salaries to reflect adjustments

---

15 min.   2. What do you think of the Hay system?

        a. How does the Hay system work? This can be answered either by eliciting responses from the students based on their reading of the (A) case or by lecturing in the answer. There will likely be a good deal of confusion about how the Hay system works.

        b. What are the assumptions of a job evaluation system? What are its advantages and disadvantages?

        c. Why would a company use the Hay system?

10 min.   3. Now that you understand the Hay system, do you sympathize with Boyd or Nicodemus?

        a. Those students who agreed with Boyd about making exceptions for his young "stars" can now be pressed about how that would work. What would exceptions do to the job evaluation system? Why have a system if you are going to make exceptions?

        b. Those who agreed with Nicodemus can be pressed on what can be done to "save" Boyd's group. Isn't a system that allows for no exceptions too rigid? Isn't the loss of Jackson and Arnold evidence that the system is not working?

        c. What are the alternatives to job evaluation?

10 min.   4. Hand out "B" case

10 min.   5. What is your analysis of the situation now?

        a. Was Boyd correct in his emphasis on pay? Were Jackson's and Arnold's pay below their market value?

        b. What do you make of the total point ratings? What do they suggest about the way Boyd runs his group and the options that he has?

10 min.   6. Hand out the "C" case

10 min.   7. What do you make of the situation in the finance group?

        a. What does the Hay survey suggest are the problems in the finance group?

        b. What do you think of the management climate survey?

        c. If you were Whitfield, what would you say to Boyd and Nicodemus after reading the Hay Associates, findings?

5 min.   8. Closing lecturette summarizing main points of case.
   a. Main points of job evaluation system and why it is used
   b. Special advantages of the Hay system or some other national survey
   c. Emphasis on need to be aware of equity and the difficulty of dealing with equity, and the need to beware of using pay as a simple answer to more complex questions

LEP CORPORATION
Teaching Note

LEP employs an individual merit system designed to motivate and reward sustained superior performance over time. The case introduces a number of problems that face the company's advanced technology division and asks students to consider, as general managers of the division, how to use—or change—the pay system to help deal with those problems.

ASSIGNMENT QUESTIONS

Students should read the (A) case and come to class prepared to discuss the following questions:

1. What are the responsibilities of the general manager in the LEP salary system?
2. How does the operating manager apply merit pay principles to subordinates?
3. How do division and corporate staff monitor the application of the salary system and its impact on the corporation?
4. How does the salary system fit into the overall policies of the LEP Corporation?

CASE ANALYSIS

The case offers students an opportunity to understand in some detail and to analyze an attempt by a major American company to pay individuals for sustained, long-term performance; then to look at the role of the line manager in and the impact of a shifting environment on that pay policy. Analysis can start, then, with a discussion of the pay policies, and then turn to the matter of action alternatives in response to environmental and business pressures.

LEP'S PAY PLAN

The basic objective of LEP's pay plan is to attract, retain, and motivate above-average performers. To achieve that objective, the design of the plan rests on two main concepts: equity and individual merit.

Equity. LEP's pay system starts with a job evaluation and classification system similar to the one encountered in "Megalith, Inc.—Hay Associates." (Unlike Megalith, Inc., however, LEP conducts its own job evaluation rather than going outside to the Hay Associates.) LEP then conducts regular salary surveys (national surveys for exempt, local surveys for nonexempt) to insure that the company maintains "an average level of pay that is higher than the average level of pay for similar skills in other companies with which they compete in the marketplace."

The job evaluation and wage surveys are intended by LEP to ensure *equity* in the pay system. Lawler[1] has argued that, if a reward system is to have any motivational and satisfactional value, it must meet the criteria of perceived equity, both of internal and external equity. Internal equity has to do with the distribution of pay within the organization. Employees who feel that their pay level is at least equal to comparable (based on some judgment as to the input or contribution of the employee) employees within the organization will feel that internal equity has been achieved. As seen in "Megalith, Inc.—Hay Associates," job evaluation systems offer a method for "scientifically" or "objectively" judging just what the input or contribution of any job is. External equity means that employees perceive their pay level as at least being equal to the level of similar employees at comparable organizations (usually these are companies that recruit in the same labor market).

Once a company conducts a wage survey, it can choose from one of three options:

1. It can peg its pay at levels *less than* the competition. Such a policy runs the risk of leading to high turnover. Some companies—especially those that do not need to rely on highly trained or experienced workers—may decide that the savings from such a policy choice are worth the "risk" of relatively high turnover.
2. It can peg *to the average* wage of competitors. The company may then seek to satisfy (retain) employees through nonpay rewards like employment security, promotions, or perquisites, or intrinsic rewards like feedback, self-esteem, or autonomy.
3. It can peg its pay *above average*. Such a policy is intended to attract above-average performers. LEP has selected this third option (although it is worth noting that they pay above the average payer, not above the highest payer, so there will be employees in competing firms who are more highly paid).

Organizations should not assume that a combination of job evaluations and wages that meet the criteria of internal and external equity at one point in time will necessarily continue to achieve equity in the future. Pay systems require continuous and expert monitoring and revising. Wage surveys must be constantly updated (LEP conducts theirs annually), and jobs must be reevaluated for shifting content and responsibilities, especially if a company is involved in a rapidly changing field like high technology.

Merit Pay. LEP views individual merit as a significant part of their overall HRM policies which, they say, emphasize individuals, and their contribution to the organization. As John Taylor summarizes the company philosophy in the case (case book Exhibit 20–1): "LEP Corporation believes that rewarding individuals for their efforts and contributions to the business encourages employees to seek their highest level of productivity, promotes positive employee relations, and provides the company with the best return on its investment. This belief in merit is reflected in . . . other practices such as promotion from within and participation in selected developmental programs."

LEP's merit system consists of the following elements:

1. *Planning.* Using the established job descriptions as a guide, managers determine and then describe to employees their major responsibilities for the upcoming year. This becomes a performance plan, which is to be established in terms that are both measureable and understandable.

2. *Rating.* All employees are rated annually by their immediate supervisor on a scale of 1 to 4—"outstanding" to "satisfactory"—based on their performance against the established performance plan.

3. *Merit pay.* Salary ranges are constructed based on wage surveys, with "minimum" and "maximum" levels for each grade. The "minimum" level is intended to reflect the amount of wage it would take to attract somebody to the company with the minimum requirements for that job, while the "maximum" is intended to reflect what that job is ultimately worth to the company. It is worth noting that the spread between "minimum" and "maximum" is not consistent throughout the pay grades. Generally, the higher the grade, the greater the spread. Thus, there is a larger pay span for engineers than for clerical workers.

Merit raises are then allocated based on the spread of a particular job and the performance rating given the employee. The "merit increase guide" in casebook Exhibit 20–1 provides a sample for how merit increases will be awarded. For a starting employee at the "minimum" level of pay (the lowest quartile), a "satisfactory" rating will mean a 7 percent raise for the next 14 to 17 months. Starting employees with better ratings will both receive a greater percentage increase and have a shorter time to wait for their eligibility for their next pay increase. An "outstanding" starting employee will receive a 13 percent raise over only eight to ten months.

Several points are worth noting about this process:

a. As employees move from the lowest to the highest quartile of their job ranges (or, to put it another way, as employees approach the maximum rate for their job), the percent of increase becomes smaller, while the time between increases becomes longer. Some students may argue that this relative leveling-off as an employee moves up through the performance quartiles represents a disincentive to continue performing well. LEP rejects that argument, noting that at the highest level the dollar amount is greater, even if the percentage gets smaller. In addition, as an individual approaches the highest level of his or her job, there are likely to be other nonpay rewards such as promotions.

b. Although the issue comes up more directly later in the case [the (B) case], students may wonder if there is a suggested or forced curve to the rating of employees. (This might be especially true of students who are operating under some kind of a "forced" curve grading system.) The company denies the existence of a forced curve, but says there is a suggested distribution, and uses that distribution to help budget its wage costs.

c. The merit increase guide is only a suggested guide to managers. They are free to deviate from the guide in order to achieve "appropriate merit pay relationships" and ensure "consistency" in the criteria used for granting merit increases.

d. In addition to the pay increase, LEP employees will also receive a raise when their entire range is adjusted to survey data and forecasts of external wage trends. This is important, because it avoids the problem found in many companies where merit pay is the only increase. In times of inflation such merit increases are seen as less and less related to performance and more and more as an inflationary adjustment, creating cynicism about the merit system.

4. *Sustained performance.* The stated policy of the individualized merit plan is "to achieve significant pay differentials based on sustained performance over time." The merit increase guide is constructed to meet this policy goal. Note in the graph of the four quartiles that the pay gaps between the levels of performance *increase* over time. So, although two employees may start at the same point and their initial pay raises may be only 5 percent different, the employee who can sustain an "above-average" rating over time can earn 26 percent more than a "satisfactory" performer.

5. *Counseling.* Initiated either by the employee or the manager, counseling is considered to be a critical part of the merit pay system. Counseling is to take place throughout the performance period to review progress and discuss problems. For an employee who receives an "unsatisfactory" rating (and thus no merit increase), their managers will help them develop an improvement program and counsel them to help them improve performance.

6. *Review.* The recommendation for any merit increase must be approved by the next level manager. The supervisor communicates the rating and reviews the reasons for that rating as well as the amount of the merit increase to the affected employee.

In a recent article on pay and motivation, W. Clay Hamner argues that organizations can benefit from a well-defined and administered individual merit pay plan, but there are a great many problems in the implementation stage.[2] Among those he discusses are:

1. *Pay is not perceived as being related to job performance.* Part of the problem here is that the goals of the organization on which performance appraisals are based are either unclear, unrealistic, or unrelated to pay. Research has shown "that the more frequent the formal and informal reviews of performance and the more an individual is told about the reasons for an increase, the greater his preference for a merit increase system and the lower his preference for a seniority system." This regular feedback can also help avert the danger that merit pay will damage self-esteem when raises don't agree with a person's self-evaluation.

2. *Secrecy.* Because of the secrecy that so often surrounds merit increases (secrecy supported by compensation managers, in part because they would have a difficult time explaining the basis for many of their decisions), the direct relationship between pay and performance—if it exists—may be blocked from the view of managers.

3. *Trust in the system is low.* "A merit system will not be accepted and may not have the intended motivational effects if managers do not actively administer a performance appraisal system, practice good human relations, [and] explain the reasons for the increases. . . . The organization must provide an open climate with respect to pay and an environment where work and effort are valued." In a study of 184 organizations, only 72 percent had a written statement of the basic compensation policy, and about a third of those companies communicated those policies directly only to managers.

4. *Viewing money as the sole motivator.* Hamner agrees that compensation managers and organizations generally should place greater emphasis on the intrinsic rewards of work. He disagrees, however, with research conducted by E. L. Deci that paying people extra money for performing interesting tasks actually *decreases* their intrinsic motivation for performing that task (presumably by focusing their attention on the money rather than the intrinsic value of the task).[3] His own research has shown that combining intrinsic and extrinsic rewards can have an additive impact rather than a negative one.

Role of Line Managers. In reviewing the various stages of the merit pay system, students can identify the points at which line managers play a key role:

1. Keeping job descriptions up-to-date
2. Working with subordinates on performance plan
3. Counseling during the year on progress and development

4. Rating the performance of a subordinate and *explaining* that rating to the subordinate
5. Deciding on amount of merit increase and whether to stick with suggested model or alter it to maintain desired relationships
6. Explaining to subordinates how and why the merit increase was arrived at, including explaining the workings and rationale of the company's pay program
7. Reviewing merit pay increases with subordinate managers
8. The president of each division reviews annually proposals generated by the personnel staff on the development of ranges, merit increase guidelines, relationship of pay to other companies, and projected costs.

The manager–subordinate relationship is a critical interface in the system. The line manager must not only *evaluate,* but *communicate* reasons for that evaluation. The compensation system will live or die at this juncture. Will employees believe they are being paid equitably and fairly based on their performance? Managers must not only possess an in-depth knowledge of the pay system and the rationale behind it, but must also have interpersonal competencies in two-way communication and counseling. The role of managers in reviewing the merit increase decisions of subordinate managers should not be overlooked. It is at this stage that any tendency on the part of a manager either to overrate or underrate performance can be discovered and corrected [an issue brought up in the (D) case]. Not in the case is the fact that LEP provides every new line manager with 100 hours training in personnel and employee relations matters in their first year, and 40 hours a year after that.

Merit Pay and Internal Equity. Because of merit pay, two people on the same job with the same background and seniority may be getting significantly different pay. How can LEP maintain the perception of internal equity under such circumstances? For one thing, surveys indicate that employees, especially white-collar employees in U.S. companies, prefer some sort of pay-for-performance system. If employees perceive decisions about pay for performance to be valid and fair, they are likely to believe the system is equitable.

LEP believes that another important contributor to the perception of equity is *secrecy* (an issue which is not explicitly raised in the case but which can be brought into the discussion). What happens, for instance, if a subordinate approaches his or her manager and says, "You tell me I'm an outstanding performer. But I happen to know that Charlie, who does the same job, receives $500 more a week than I do. He told me so himself." The manager is not to discuss Charlie's pay (even if that manager knows that Charlie is not getting $500 more). Instead, that manager will say, "I'm not going to talk with you about what we pay Charlie. What I want to do is make sure you are being paid fairly and equitably based on your contribution to the company.'' Once again, the skill of that manager in explaining the rationale of the system and the individual rating of the questioning employee is critical.

The National Labor Relations Board recently had the opportunity to rule on the secrecy of a merit pay system in a large American company. That company had fired an employee for releasing to fellow employees secret documents concerning internal pay. The Board upheld both the company's action and their rationale for maintaining secrecy. The company, the Board said, ''does not prohibit employees from discussing their own wages or attempting to determine what others are paid. Rather, the [company] merely has chosen not to inform employees what it pays others.'' The company established, to the Board's satisfaction, a ''legitimate business justification'' for its policy of secrecy. Simply put, the company viewed secrecy as essential to the maintenance of internal equity: ''such a rule allows it to attract, motivate, and retain employees by allowing managers to reward employees on performance alone *without having to worry about creating dissatisfaction among other employees.''*[4]

Case Issues

The (A) case background on the advanced technology division and the company, details of the pay plan, and problems facing the division's new president, Dr. Richard Campbell.

Personnel Policies of Company

LEP is considered a leader in industry personnel policies with its emphasis on communication and manager–employee relations. Such policies are reflected within the division, which is nonunion, enjoys low attrition (3 percent annually), and has never resorted to a layoff.

Division Background

The advanced technology division, established in 1957, has enjoyed substantial profit and growth (annual growth rate of 8 to 10 percent). The size of the work force doubled between 1971 and 1981, but such rapid growth is now leveling off. The Division hired 500 new employees in 1980–1981, but did minimal hiring the following year.

In general, four challenges face the Division:

1. National recession, which is forcing internal belt tightening
2. Slower growth, which means less opportunity for advancement

3. Increased production pressures, which lead to greater emphasis on quality and reliability
4. New technology, which requires increased capital and revenue investments

Salary Program Review

According to company policy, in the third quarter of each year the personnel department of each division develops a salary plan for the upcoming year which includes such matters as the development of ranges, merit increase guidelines, relationship of pay to other companies, and projected costs. The plan is then submitted to the division's president for review and approval.

John Taylor, the division's manager of personnel, submitted the 1982 salary plan to Dr. Campbell with the following provisions:

1. It was predicted that the average salaries paid by other companies in LEP's wage survey would increase 9.1 percent in 1982.
2. To keep their leadership position, the division would increase salaries by an average of 9.5 percent. The average period between increases would be 11 months.
3. The projected costs of such increases will be $9.1 million.

Challenges and Concerns

In the process of reviewing this plan, Dr. Campbell learned from LEP headquarters that the competitive technical position of his division was eroding. To meet that challenge, a new technology planned for the Division would have to become operational two years earlier than originally scheduled. That speed-up would require the hiring of 100 engineers and 50 technicians and the transfer into the division of 100 employees from elsewhere in LEP. Campbell then asked Taylor to report on the impact of these and other environmental pressures on the pay program.

Taylor listed four main problems:

1. *Salary compression.* Hiring 100 new engineers in a national labor market where engineers were in heavy demand by American industry meant that attracting the best graduating engineers would require a starting salary that was equal to, if not greater than, the salaries received by engineers who had been with the division for several years. Hiring new engineers at inflated salaries could thus raise problems of internal equity.
2. *Dissatisfaction.* With inflation (11.2 percent) running well ahead of the rate of salary increase (9.5 percent), employees were expressing

185

dissatisfaction and some were calling for across the board cost-of-living adjustments.

3. *Transfers.* Bringing in 100 employees, some of whom were paid more than divisional counterparts simply because of the labor market from which they were coming, could raise problems of internal equity.

4. *Design specialists.* An external equity issue has been raised among the division's 30 design specialists. They are aware that a major employer in the area has granted their design specialists large increases two years in a row. Under the division's 1982 plan, their average rate of pay will be only slightly more than that of the competitors. Will design specialists, critical to the successful implementation of the new technology, be tempted to leave the division in upcoming years?

Campbell must consider alternatives and develop solutions while maintaining the integrity of the merit pay system.

(B) Case. Taylor proposes alternative measures for Campbell's consideration:

1. *Salary compression.* Concerning incoming engineers, Taylor proposed five alternatives. (Although the cost of these alternatives was not a major criterion, the estimated additional cost of each alternative—not given in the case—is provided here in parentheses.)
   a. Increase all engineers' rates in the same proportion as starting salary rates ($500,000)
   b. Constrain starting salaries (no additional cost)
   c. Make no change (no additional cost)
   d. Construct a model to maintain current engineers' salaries 5 percent ahead of those of new engineers ($225,000)
   e. The alternative selected by Campbell—a combination model which accelerates movement of engineers while maintaining the 5 percent ahead relationship ($171,000)

2. *Dissatisfaction.* Campbell directed stepped up training of managers and communications with employees to explain that, while cost of living is taken into account because of the salary survey, LEP does not pay based on the cost of labor.

3. *Transfers.* Higher-paid employees (because of labor market) would be transferred at their past salary, but would receive new increases based on local practices.

4. *Design specialists.* To meet the challenge, Campbell decided to exercise flexibility and ordered the use of a rating one step higher than the performance rating actually earned. This was to be only a temporary solution.

(C) Case. Campbell's solutions raised the projected costs of the pay plan from $9.1 million to $9.3 million. Three months later, he learns that the actual cost of the salary plan is running 9 percent above the project costs (a figure that could eventually reach $750,000). One of the main reasons for the overrun is that the performance rating distribution is running higher than expected (55 percent of employees are being rated "outstanding" or "above-average" performers, compared with the projected 51.5 percent). Campbell wonders again what actions he can take. Students can debate suggestions for a "forced" or "suggested" performance rating curve (or whether, in fact, the projection becomes a kind of suggested curve itself). Other action alternatives might include more emphasis on the review process by managers one level up, further education of managers, or no action.

CONCLUSION

This case raises many of the problems companies face on their own merit pay programs. Table 6–9 presents commonly identified barriers to the effective implementation of a merit pay program. Students can analyze the question: has LEP dealt effectively with each of these barriers? They should come out of the discussion realizing that there are no simple solutions to pay problems, that pay systems require persistent management to deal with inevitable problems, and that managers might learn to rely less on pay systems as a primary management tool.

TEACHING PLAN

10 min.   1. Ask students how many would prefer to work under an individual pay-for-performance plan of the type LEP has. Then

TABLE 6–9

Barriers to Effective Administration of Individual Merit Pay Program

1. Poor definition/measurement of performance
2. White-collar workers' pay tied to union contracts to avoid further unionization efforts
3. High inflation dilutes value of merit pay.
4. Managers are unwilling or unable to confront subordinates with poor performance; have not been trained in coaching and development.
5. Employees receive little or irregular feedback on performance.
6. Salaries of top executives are not tied to performance of company—negative "trickle-down" impact.
7. The company's concern is with satisfying employees rather than motivating them.
8. Secrecy blurs the relationship between pay and performance.
9. Line managers have little understanding of or participation in pay system.
10. Money is viewed as only motivator; there is little attention to other rewards, such as promotions, intrinsically rewarding tasks.

ask for feelings pro and con on individual pay-for-performance systems.

15 min.   2. What are the main elements of LEP's pay-for-performance
plan?
   a. What are the elements of the plan?
   b. What role do line managers play? Personnel staff?
   c. What are the objectives of the plan, and how well is it meeting those objectives?

10 min.   3. What are the various problems facing the pay plan, and what
should Campbell do about them?

Note: If the case is to be taught in a two-day sequence, the above discussions
should be expanded to cover the first class. Hand out the (B) case at the end of
class, and ask:

What is your evaluation of Campbell's actions? Do his actions deal adequately with the dissatisfaction among employees? Do you agree with
his decision on design specialists?
What else could he have done?

5 min.   4. Hand out and read (B) case.

10 min.   5. What is your evaluation of Campbell's actions?
   a. Will the pay system continue to satisfy advanced technology division employees?
   b. Will Campbell's decision to rate design specialists one step
higher than earned help the pay system meet current challenges? Will it undermine the long-run integrity of the system?
   c. What else could he have done?

5 min.   6. Hand out and read (C) case.

10 min.   7. What should Campbell do now?
   a. Do you agree with his decision to cut the budget by $1 mil-
lion? What about his staff's complaints that such an action
will demoralize employees?
   b. What alternative should he select for reducing the expendi-
tures and why?

5 min.   8. Hand out and read (D) case.

10 min.   9. What, if anything, should Campbell do about the "inflation"
of performance ratings?

10 min.   10. Closing lecturette on the advantages and disadvantages of individual pay-for-performance systems (Table 6–10) and prob-
lems of implementation (Table 6–9).

TABLE 6–10

Advantages and Disadvantages of Individual Pay for Performance

Pros	Cons
Most employees want to be paid for performance.	Depends on highly trained and competent managers
Can be a frequent, visible signal that organization is seeking good performance	May enhance competition rather than cooperation between employees.
Should help retain better-performing employees	Pay treatment (and the underlying performance ratings) may damage employees' self-esteem
"Forces" managers to make performance judgments and communicate them to subordinates	Assumes that valid discriminations can be made about the performance of employees who already constitute a select group

NOTES

1. E. E. Lawler, "Determining Total Compensation: Strategic Issues," in Michael Beer and Bert Spector, *Readings in Human Resource Management* (New York: Free Press, 1985).
2. W. Clay Hamner, "How to Ruin Motivation with Pay," in Richard B. Peterson et al., eds., *Readings in Systematic Management of Human Resource* (Reading, MA: Addison-Wesley, 1982), pp. 215–223.
3. See, for instance, E. L. Deci, "Effects of Externally Mediated Rewards on Intrinsic Motivation," *Journal of Personality and Social Psychology* 18 (1971), pp. 105–115; and "Intrinsic Motivation, Extrinsic Reinforcement, and Inequity," *Journal of Personality and Social Psychology* 22 (1972), pp. 113–120.
4. Bureau of National Affairs, *Daily Labor Report* No. 238, December 10, 1982.

FIRST FEDERAL SAVINGS
Teaching Note

In 1968 First Federal Savings initiated a system of executive bonuses along with a management-by-objective (MBO) system. An economic downturn in 1974 has prevented First Federal from achieving its projected growth rate and its president, Gene Rice, must decide whether to award bonuses for this year. Class discussion will raise questions about the impact of that decision on the future motivation of executives, about how First Federal Savings might redesign its executive bonus system to avoid such problems in the future, and more generally on how necessary executive bonuses are in stimulating effective executive performance.

ASSIGNMENT QUESTIONS

Students should read the (A) case and come to class prepared to discuss the following questions:

1. Should Gene Rice recommend a bonus for this year even if profits are less than projected?
2. What will be the impact of Gene's decision on the future motivation of his executives?
3. What is your evaluation of First Federal's bonus plan? How would you redesign it to avoid these problems in the future?
4. How important are bonus systems like the one at First Federal to stimulating effective managerial performance?

CASE ANALYSIS

In 1968 First Federal began both an MBO and a bonus program for top managers (branch managers and up). Both were aimed at changing the culture of First Federal from "ordinary" to "entrepreneurial."

First Federal's MBO System

The key elements of the MBO program are:

1. Each third quarter, the branch manager establishes financial and nonfinancial goals for the upcoming year.

2. That projection is reviewed by the regional manager, differences are negotiated, and consensus reached. Then the projection is forwarded to corporate headquarters.
3. These regional projections are worked into an annual profit plan for the company.
4. Each month, branch managers receive a computerized report on the financial performance of the branch compared against goals.

First Federal intended their MBO program to be a kind of participative, or at least negotiated, planning tool. "The MBO system was instituted as a planning tool for the future," says Gene Rice, "and the changes it would bring."

First Federal's Bonus Plan

The bonus plan is made up of the following elements:

1. The executive salary committee compares annual performance to the annual profit plan. Any profit above that plan's projection is then placed into a total bonus pool. Thus, if the annual profit plan projected a growth in profits of 15 percent, any actual growth *above* that 15 percent would be placed in the total bonus pool. If profits grew, but by only 11¼ percent (as happened at First Federal in 1974), there would be *no* bonus pool, and thus no individual bonuses.
2. Once—and if—the total bonus pool is established, a bonus is assigned to individual managers based on the following criteria:
   a. Half of the pool is allocated on the basis of salary as a percent of total salaries.
   b. Half is allocated on the basis of individual performance, using performance against MBO goals as a guideline.
   c. Individual bonuses are not to exceed 40 percent of base salary.

The System's Rationale

The purpose of the bonus plan is twofold. First, it is used to attract good performers. Almost half of the businesses in the United States have some form of bonus system for their top executives, so offering a bonus plan becomes something of a competitive necessity. In fact, Gene Rice has used the bonus system as a tool in recruitment, thus creating expectations for a bonus system and a bonus payoff.

Rice also sees the bonus as a key motivational tool that will "help make things happen." He believes that the way to get outstanding performance is to offer rewards of sizable amounts at frequent intervals. It is worth reviewing that link between rewards and the two outcomes that Gene intends: motivation and satisfaction (retention). According to E. E. Lawler's Expectancy Theory Model[1] employee behavior (effort) that leads to certain results that are rewarded by the organization leads to satisfaction. Employees will thus be motivated to continue to engage in such behavior. A direct relationship can exist between behavior and rewards such that efforts may be rewarded by the organization even if it does not lead to the desired results.

That direct relationship between behavior and rewards represents the action question raised by the case. The MBO system helped clarify the kind of behavior and effort that was expected out of managers. It then issued a projection—the profit plan—of what the results of such cumulative behavior would be: an increase in profits of 15 percent. But the external environment broke the linkage between behavior and results. Because saving accounts were being reduced due to changes in the housing market and the rising interest offered by short-term treasury bills, the company shifted its strategy from generating new mortages to developing more savings deposits. Gene admits that the company did a bad job selecting objectives: "We had been lulled to sleep by a fantastic growth rate and a good economy. In 1974 the market went to hell, and our targeted 15 percent increase in profit before tax was not realistic." So, despite what was apparently still excellent effort, the planned results were not achieved. Should Gene now say that, because that linkage is now broken (even though the problem is a changing environment and inability of corporate planners to take that into account when establishing corporate goals), the next linkage between results and rewards will also be broken? Or should he pay anyway, tying rewards to behavior (as indicated by the dotted line) rather than to results?

The action question comes down to this: the MBO program created the expectation on part of managers that if they behaved in a certain way, certain results (a 15 percent increase in profits) would occur, to be followed by the reward of an executive bonus. The environment, rather than individual behavior, broke that connection. To not pay a bonus would thus violate the *expectation* that certain behavior will eventually lead to a bonus (some managers, as we see in the case, have already "spent" their bonus money). Dissatisfaction may follow, and Gene is worried that motivation will be dampened, and some top performers may go elsewhere. But if a bonus is paid on the basis of behavior rather than results, what was the meaning of the formula in the first place? Will managers become less concerned with results in future years?

There are several specific problems that relate to the way First Federal has constructed its bonus plan:

1. *Trigger mechanism.* No bonus is paid unless the projected growth is reached. Even a growth rate of 14 percent this year would result in

no bonus being paid. As one new First Federal manager noted, "What would bother me is if we hit 75 percent of our corporate profit objective [which is, in fact, what happened] and we got zero reward. The company is still making millions, and we should get part of the pie."

2. *Level of performance.* Under the First Federal plan, although half the bonus is allocated on the basis of individual performance, the payment of a bonus is triggered entirely by *corporate* performance. As vice-president Bill Blodgett notes, "In a bad economy the company may not meet its profit objectives, but I could have a number of branches that are meeting or exceeding their office objectives. How do I tell them that there is no bonus this year?"

3. *Link between bonus and MBO.* As noted earlier, the MBO system is meant as a *planning* tool; the bonus as a *motivating* tool. But are the two compatible? Will difficulties in the bonus scheme undermine the usefulness of the MBO system as a planning device? Any suggestion to decouple the two, however, should be accompanied by an alternative suggestion as to what to pay bonuses on? Profits? If so, should it be on company or branch profits? Individual performance (such as we saw at LEP Corporation)? If so, what will the bonus pool consist of? Will bonuses be paid on individual effort even if there is no profit?

In addition to these points, there are some more general concerns about executive bonuses that this case can help students address:

1. *Short-term emphasis.* Bonuses are typically based on performance over a 6- to 12-month period. Such bonuses can result in managers hesitating to make decisions that are good for the long-term effectiveness of the organization but may result in short-term losses of profit. As Ray Walker, a branch manager at First Federal, says, in order to meet the new corporate strategy concerning savings, "I hired six new tellers, and the cost of these six tellers has placed me way over my expense budget. I know it, and my boss knows it, but I do not expect to have my bonus penalized for being over budget." If Ray does not receive a bonus this year, will he be encouraged the following year to make decisions that may not be compatible with long-term strategic goals, but will help maximize short-run profits?

As noted in casebook Exhibit 21-3, J. C. Penney addressed this issue in 1971 when it coupled its cash bonus based on annual performance with a stock bonus based on results over a three-year period.

2. *Motivation.* A pervasive assumption in the case is that bonuses are what motivates managers. "The bonus tells me how much management appreciates my work," says Ray Walker. "If Gene Rice pays [a bonus] this year [even though profit goals were not met], I might not be so concerned about meeting my financial objectives next year," adds Harry Turner. And

without a bonus, Bill Blodgett wonders, "How do I motivate them [branch managers] next year?" Such comments provide the opportunity to discuss the question of what motivates people, in this case upper-level managers, to work? If Ray Walker is to be believed, it isn't so much the money as the display of corporate appreciation for his effort. But are there other less risky and perhaps less costly ways of showing appreciation? Will they be as effective? Do students believe that managers will lose their concern with financial objectives in the absence of a bonus based on achieving those objectives? Is Bill Blodgett's assessment of how to motivate branch managers accurate, or is he using bonuses as a "crutch," an "easy" way to seek motivation without paying enough attention to maximizing the intrinsic rewards of the job? What will happen to the culture of First Federal if the company were suddenly to deemphasize or discontinue executive bonuses?

There are no simple answers to such questions, of course. Some students may conclude that executive bonuses are useful mainly to attract and retain good people. Others will insist that they are the best, perhaps even the only, way to motivate hard-driving managers like Harry Turner.

Action Planning

Students can develop an action plan both for the short- and long-run. The immediate question that must be answered is, should Gene pay a bonus this year, and what will the long-run impact of that decision be? This question can usually be counted on to stimulate controversy. The longer-run question is how, or if, to alter the system for the future? A short film of Gene Rice explaining the actions he and the company took can be shown to students, or they can simply be told what happened.

Audiovisual Material

In the brief taped interview with Gene Rice, we learn that in 1974 profits reached only 75 percent of projections, but Gene paid a bonus of 75 percent of the previous year's bonuses. (This information is also provided in the (B) case, which can be used in place of the audiovisual material.) "Even though our plan did not call for a payment of a bonus," Gene explained, "we decided that we did have a psychological contract with those people." The bonus plan was thereafter restructured to be paid on the basis of earnings compared with First Federal's top 20 competitors. Company policy officially downplayed the implicit promise of a bonus by saying, "It is also recommended that . . . management and personnel department representatives *do not* promise or imply, in conversation with present or prospective employees, the probability of a bonus." No bonus was paid between 1975

194

and 1977. And although senior management continued to encourage the practice of MBOs, it is no longer formally tied to the bonus plan.

Gene's conclusion from all this is that, while he likes the idea of an executive bonus in theory, they are exceedingly difficult to construct and administer, especially over the long run. To maintain their integrity and employee support, bonus plans must be reevaluated and renegotiated with regularity.

CONCLUSION

Table 6–11 can be used to review some of the key steps in designing and administering a bonus plan. Students can also be assigned the article by William Kearney on the various barriers organizations often encounter in pay-for-performance systems.[2] Although most American managers say they believe in pay for performance, Kearney says, there is evidence that the concept is often not used. A survey of *Fortune* 500 companies showed that 42 percent used no formal performance appraisal system for professional and technical employees, while 41 percent used single-rate compensation systems for blue-collar workers, so that wage increases would not be based on individual performance but on general increases or job promotions. Other surveys add further evidence by indicating that at top management levels, company size (measured by sales volume) is the primary factor in de-

TABLE 6–11
Bonus Plan Guidelines

1. Cash bonus plans are useful in many but not all firms depending on such factors as the following:

PRO-BONUS FACTORS	ANTI-BONUS FACTORS
Short-term measureable results	Long-term, hard-to-measure results
Growth stage of product cycle	Mature stage of product cycle
Aggressive image desired	Conservative image desired
Few local uncertainties forcing time-consuming renegotiations	Many local uncertainties forcing renegotiations

2. Different companies need different kinds of bonus plans. In tailoring bonus plans match:
   Interdependent managers—Group bonus plan
   Independent managers—Individual bonus plan
3. No plan can be expected to last forever—keep an escape clause.
4. All bonus plans generate considerable managerial "toil and trouble."
5. In cyclical businesses—anchor bonus pool on industry indicators.
6. Do not hesitate to discuss the real problems of keeping a bonus plan realistic with the key managers involved.
7. Consider whether the benefits of a bonus plan outweigh the problems and costs of administration.

termining managerial pay, and that pay differentials are then built downward to determine wages of lower-level executives.

Kearney then identifies what he considers the various barriers to the construction of a pay-for-performance system:

1. *Pay policies that tie compensation in some way to competitive wages.* When top executives think about pay "policy," they usually think in terms of, "How will our company's pay stack up against the opposition?" A 1975 survey of 480 companies showed that 6 percent of the companies opted for a leadership position (wages 5 to 10 percent above those prevailing in their area of operation); 23 percent set wages above competitors, but not on the cutting edge; about half set pay to be competitive; and a little less than 20 percent intentionally lagged behind competitors by at least 10 percent.
2. *Measuring merit.* The problem here is twofold. First, instruments of measurement are often of unknown validity. Second, many managers simply feel uncomfortable providing their subordinates with negative feedback about their performance.
3. *Union contracts.* These define pay for covered workers, and really determine pay for many noncovered workers (as companies like Bethlehem and Honeywell seek to avoid unionization drives among white-collar workers).
4. *Inflation.* Cost-of living adjustments (COLAs) in union contracts have led to large increases in nonunion pay which either deflate the value of merit pay (an issue also raised in the "LEP Corporation" case) or reduce the amount of money available for merit pay.

TEACHING PLAN

30 min.
1. Should Gene Rice pay a bonus if growth does not reach 15 percent?
   a. Take a vote, and then ask students to defend their position.
   b. If they say "yes," ask:
      (1) What will impact be on the future?
      (2) How should he determine the bonus pool?
   c. If they say "no," ask:
      (1) Will motivation be hurt next year?
      (2) What would you say to somebody like Harry Turner or Ray Walker to explain why he wasn't getting a bonus? Perhaps role-playing can be used at this point.

20 min.
2. What are the elements of First Federal's bonus plan?
   a. What is the MBO system and what is its purpose?
   b. How does the bonus work and what are its advantages?
   c. What are the advantages and disadvantages of coupling the two?

15 min.	3. What are the advantages and disadvantages of the bonus plan for First Federal?

<table>
<tr><td>15 min.</td><td>3. What are the advantages and disadvantages of the bonus plan for First Federal?
  a. Does it motivate managers? How and why?
  b. Does it help create an entrepreneurial culture?
  c. What are the alternatives to achieve these ends, if any?</td></tr>
<tr><td>15 min.</td><td>4. How would you address the bonus plan for the future?
  a. Decouple it from MBO? Based on what then?
  b. Eliminate trigger mechanism? How would pool be established and under what conditions would bonus be paid? Or, tie trigger mechanism to the relative performance of First Federal Savings when compared with others (the solution they chose).
  c. Revise formula? How?
  d. Eliminate bonuses? What would impact be?
  e. Do better environmental scanning? But how would uncertainty be built into formula?</td></tr>
<tr><td>10 min.</td><td>5. Show videotape and/or hand out (B) case. Do you agree with Gene's actions and conclusions about executive bonuses?</td></tr>
</table>

NOTES

1. E. E. Lawler, *Pay and Organization Development* (Reading, MA: Addison-Wesley, 1981), pp. 20–23.
2. William J. Kearney, "Pay for Performance? Not Always," in Michael Beer and Bert Spector, eds., *Readings in Human Resource Management* (New York: Free Press, 1985).

DANA CORPORATION—THE RICHMOND CAMSHAFT PLANT
Teaching Note

Due to a serious economic downturn, Dana's Richmond (Indiana) plant has not awarded a Scanlon bonus for seven months. Plant manager Ronald Cooke, who is interested both in starting up new production and maintaining the plant's superior production quality, wonders how he can motivate employees with an incentive plan that is paying no bonus. The (A) case consists entirely of a brochure given to employees by the company explaining the background and mechanics of the Scanlon plan. The (B) case describes the product and the processes of the plant, and the historical development of the use of the Scanlon plan at Richmond.

Class discussion should raise the issue of organization-wide incentives, as compared with individual and even group incentive schemes. It should also focus on some of the Scanlon plan's implications for work system design: involvement, feedback, identity, and participation. The Scanlon plan can be viewed, in fact, not so much as a motivator in the traditional Skinnerian sense, but rather as a way of installing a participative management system in a union-organized plant. This case is a bridge into the work systems section of the course that follows.

ASSIGNMENT QUESTIONS

Students should read the (A) and (B) cases and come to class prepared to discuss the following questions:

1. What is the Scanlon plan? How does it work? What are the assumptions behind it? How effective has it been at the camshaft plant?
2. Examine in some detail how the Scanlon plan was introduced at the camshaft plant. Was this process effective? What do you consider to be the aspects of the process that were most effective?
3. If you were Ron Cooke, would you recommend to other plant managers that they adopt the Scanlon plan? If yes, under what circumstances and how? If no, why not?

CASE ANALYSIS

The Toledo-based Dana Corporation has traditionally served three principal marketplaces: original equipment for cars and trucks, replacement parts, and industrial components. By 1970, the market for passenger car equipment (universal joints, frames, and axles) had dwindled to 20 percent of sales. Two years later, 40 percent of Dana's sales came from supplying these same parts to truck makers (mainly Ford and General Motors [GM]). Under the leadership of Rene McPherson (1972–1979), Dana prospered nicely because of their truck business despite the automobile recession. Under McPherson sales more than tripled (to $2.76 billion), earnings-per-share grew at an annual rate of 15 percent, and productivity-per-employee more than doubled. McPherson also transformed Dana from a highly centralized organization to one where most decisions were made at the plant level. He demonstrated a willingness to try almost anything (throwing out time clocks, putting nonexempt workers on salary, introducing productivity bonuses, a generous employee stock participation program, a stated policy of "continued employment for all Dana people") to increase productivity. He also attempted to ensure benevolence in the workplace by maintaining a good relationship with the United Auto Workers (UAW), promoting from within, maintaining an in-house university for employee training, and offering a generous employee stock-participation plan (70 percent of Dana employees are stockholders).

In 1979 McPherson left Dana to become Dean of the Stanford Business School. His replacement, Gerald Mitchell, carried on McPherson's commitment to a benevolent workplace, as well as Dana's stated philosophy of "continued employment for all Dana people." However, that same year, the bottom fell out of the truck market. For fiscal 1980 Dana's earnings dropped 40 percent from the previous year. Productivity was down as well. "Continued employment" gave way to the termination of nearly one-third of Dana's 29,000 U.S. work force.

At the Richmond plant 1980 sales dropped 28 percent from 1979 levels, profit fell 38 percent, and return on sales sagged 15 percent. The plant went from 220 employees to 165.

The Richmond Plant

Started in 1971, the Richmond plant manufactured camshafts for large machinery. Workers were represented by the UAW and there had been no strike since the plant began operations. The plant makes camshafts to order to customer specifications (mostly for large agricultural and construction machinery). It is a batch operation with a fairly standard flow between stations. The plant sees itself as divided into four main groups:

1. *Stations 2 (the first manufacturing station) through 6.* Turning and machining soft, unhardened forgings with relatively low tolerance.
2. *Stations 7–16.* Hardening, drilling, and straightening operations.
3. *Stations 17–20.* Closer-tolerance grinding on hardened steel.
4. *Stations 21–24.* Miscellaneous finishing steps, inspection, and shipping.

In groups 1 and 3 accurate, speedy machine setup and monitoring of tool wear are most important. The process in groups 2 and 4 include many operations that are hand controlled. Operations such as hardening and annealing are essentially process-controlled steps. Quality control is the responsibility of each operator down the line, plus an inspector who makes random checks at each station.

The Scanlon Plan

Created by Joseph Scanlon, a steelworker and local union officer, in the 1930 as a way of assuring productivity and profitability through management–labor cooperation, the Scanlon plan began receiving serious academic consideration after World War II when Douglas McGregor invited Scanlon to join the Massachusetts Institute of Technology (MIT) faculty. The plan has received a good deal of attention in more recent years from managers concerned with stagnating labor productivity.

Before looking at the specifics of the Scanlon plan, some general observations can be made about how pay can be tied to performance. The following chart indicates the three levels upon which pay for performance can be based:

Individual Performance	Group Performance	Organization-wide Performance
Merit system	Productivity incentive	Profit-sharing
Piece rate	Cost-effectiveness	Productivity sharing
Executive bonus		(Scanlon plan)

1. *Individual incentive.* At first glance, the individual incentive would seem to meet the critical criterion for reward-motivating behavior. The reward is tied directly to behavior that individuals can control: their own performance. Such a plan, however, fails to take into account the interdependence between employees in a complex organization. Organizational effectiveness is based on employee cooperation much more frequently than is realized. Thus, an incentive system tied directly to individual performance may result in dysfunction (competitive rather than cooperative) behavior.
2. *Group incentive.* To avoid setting individual employees in competition against themselves and, ultimately, the company, some organizations may adopt a group plan. The steel industry, for instance, often pays a productivity incentive to small work groups. Paying for group behavior may encourage cooperative behavior on the part of individuals within the group. On the other hand, such a plan might

foster harmful competition between groups that are, in fact, dependent on each other for such things as good performance and, as is particularly true in the case of the Richmond plant, quality control.

3. *Organization-wide incentive.* In addition to reinforcing team work and cooperative behavior *between* groups, such a plan is designed to focus attention on cost savings, encourage employees at all levels of the organization to offer new ideas, and motivate employees to "work smarter."

The matter of motivation is an important one. In a large organization individual employees may feel that their behavior will have little impact on the organization-wide performance that is being rewarded. This might interfere with the link between behavior and performance that is being rewarded, a link which is necessary for rewards to motivate behavior. How can a scheme like the Scanlon plan, then, be said to motivate individual behavior? The question can be dealt with in two parts:

1. *Symbolic motivation.* An organization-wide scheme signals to all employees in a symbolic way that certain kinds of cooperative and mutually beneficial behavior is perceived by management as leading to the kind of performance that will, in management's view, enhance organizational effectiveness. There is an important linkage between individual cooperative behavior and effectiveness, even if that linkage is not immediately obvious. An organization-wide plan can work in a symbolic way to enhance the perception of a linkage between behavior and the type of performance that will be rewarded.

2. *More than an individual motivator.* Because such plans often involve communicating financial and other business data through all levels of the organization, they can help overcome the gulfs created by a highly bureaucratic structure and call forth a new degree of trust and interdependence between management and labor. In a union setting, an organization-wide plan like the Scanlon plan can allow, even encourage, a new willingness to talk and work together, and a greater degree of mutual commitment. The Scanlon plan allows union leaders the political leeway to cooperate with management without being accused of "selling out" workers.

The Dana Corporation first tried the Scanlon plan at a Canadian plant in 1969. In 1973 the UAW agreed to support Dana plants that voted in a Scanlon plan (that was the same year that UAW signed a letter of agreement with the Big Three automakers for a joint commitment to quality of work life programs), and Dana agreed to provide consultants for any interested plant. By 1975, ten Dana units had adopted the Scanlon plan, and when Leo Henken became plant manager at Richmond that June, he began to consider the plan as a possible way of improving the plant's generally poor performance. The Richmond plant constantly ran behind on orders. There was a high degree of distrust between union and management, and productivity was poor. The work force was paid on a day rate and Henken balked at their suggestions for individual or even group incentives. Fred Lesieur, a colleague of Joseph Scanlon's, was brought in as a conultant and within a year, a memorandum of understanding was prepared calling for an employee vote on the Scanlon plan. Since widespread support from all interest groups within the plant was considered a prerequisite for the successful introduction of the plan, Henken insisted that 75 percent approval would be needed for implementation (it received 77 percent support).

The Scanlon plan, as implemented at Richmond, would follow these steps:

1. Employees provide suggestions to improve productivity through improvements in such things as operating methods, machinery and equipment, or paperwork.
2. Suggestions go to one of eight *production committees* made up of the supervisor (committee chairperson) and two elected employee representatives from that production unit.
   a. Committee may reject suggestion or call for further investigation.
   b. May accept and put into operation suggestions costing less than $200 (later raised to $300).
   c. May approve suggestions costing more than $200 ($300), and pass them on to screening committee.
   d. May pass along disputed suggestions to screening committee.
3. Suggestions are reviewed by *screening committee,* made up of five employees elected from production committees, four management representatives appointed by plant manager, plus the plant manager.
   a. Committee screens suggestions passed on by production committees.
   b. Reviews calculations of monthly bonus made by plant management.
   c. Bargaining and safety issues kept separate from Scanlon plan discussions; does not replace grievance structure.
4. Increases in productivity or other savings in labor costs will generate monthly bonus expressed as percentage of such individual's gross monthly income.
   a. Basis of calculation is ratio of total payroll costs to sales value of production (or labor costs per $1.00 sales value of product).
   b. Sales value is adjusted by plant management for returns, increases, or decreases in inventory.

5. *Example:* using Richmond's initial base ratio of 37 percent (or 37¢ for each $1.00 sales value):

Sales value of production	$700,000
Allowed payroll at 37% (or 37% of sales value)	259,000
Actual payroll	215,000
Scanlon bonus pool	44,000
25% set aside for reserve*	11,000
Bonus balance	33,000
Company share—25%†	8,250
Employee share—75%‡	24,750
Participating payroll	210,000
Bonus % (employee share/participating payroll)	11.79%

*If the actual payroll exceeds the allowed payroll, the resulting deficit is charged against the reserve. All money remaining in the reserve is distributed once a year: 25% to the company, 75% to employees.

†Company is given bonus share because it supplies money needed to make improvements.

‡Actual payroll *minus* payroll for employees on paid nonworking days (vacation, holidays, jury duty, and so forth) or on job less than 60 days.

6. Substantial changes in conditions such as wages, sales volume, pricing, product mix, subcontracting, introduction of new technology, and so forth, may necessitate a change in the base ratio to be made by plant management.
7. How will bonus affect individual employee? Example:

Name	Total Hours Worked	Overtime Hours	Hourly Rate	Total Pay	Bonus (%)	Bonus	Total Earnings
J. Doe	190	30	$5.00	$1,230	11.79*	$145.02	$1,375.02

*From above example.

In addition to the financial incentive tied to organization-wide labor savings, and the interlocking system of joint worker–management committees, there is a third less formal but equally important aspect of the Scanlon plan, according to James W. Driscoll.[1] It is "a philosophy of participative management. It rests on what Douglas McGregor called the Theory Y assumptions about human motivation . . . all workers are capable of self-directed effort toward organizational goals provided their work gives them the opportunity for taking responsibility for their actions and using their abilities. Furthermore, with workers recognized as a professional resource, the primary task of management is to tap their ideas in order to increase production.''

The new structure introduced to an organization by the Scanlon plan serves to facilitate certain kinds of behavior which, in turn, may lead to changes in attitude as depicted in Table 6–12.

Scanlon Plan Implementation

Until 1980 the Richmond plant increased its profitability each year. The profit pattern followed almost precisely sales volume (see casebook Exhibit 23–2), so it is possible that the Scanlon plan had little direct impact on the plant's profits. The plant experienced four plant managers between the tenures of Leo Henken and Ronald Cooke, and that frequent turnover probably served to disrupt the fragile growth of trust and commitment somewhat. Not all labor–management suspicion was eliminated with the introduction of the Plan. Some employees felt that management was manipulating its computation of sales value and participating payroll. Others complained that allotments under the plan either exacerbated already existing internal inequities (because every employee receives the same percentage bonus, those employees with higher wages received more money; thus the bonus adds to the existing perceptions of internal inequities) or created new ones (some employees felt that not every employee deserved an equal share of the bonus based on their individual performance).

Still, most agreed that cooperation and communication among employees at all levels was increasing. The average Scanlon bonus percentage for the four Scanlon years (see casebook Exhibit 23–8) was 6.65 percent (fluctuating between 1.17 and 3.7 percent) and the average bonus per employee per year was $1,031.50 (between $1,995 and $575).

Now as the plant, and the entire corporation is in a downturn, no Scanlon bonus has been paid for seven months, and the prospects are that none would be paid for the remainder of the year. Ron Cooke's interest in the Scanlon plan was secondary to his desire to start up new camshaft models and to maintain quality. He understood that productivity was falling, in part, because employees either consciously or unconsciously were trading bonuses for jobs. Although he was not happy with what this decline in productivity was doing to current profits, he was even more worried about the establishment of bad work habits which would become ingrained and hard to remove once volume increased.

Cooke was not nearly so committed to the Scanlon plan, or as adamantly opposed to individual or group incentive plans, as had been Leo Henken. He wonders, as the case ends, whether now is the time to change the Scanlon plan or whether he would recommend such a plan to other plant

TABLE 6–12

Scanlon Plan Facilitates Changes in Behavior and Attitudes

Key Individuals	New Structure Under the Plan	Facilitated Behavior	Likely Change in Attitude
Managers	Meetings with representatives elected to discuss production issues	Open communication	
	Meetings and discussions with top plant management	Participative management style	Theory Y assumptions about human behavior
	Possibility of worker representative bypassing first-line supervisors	Influence based on task-relevant information	Respect, liking for union head
	Meeting with union head in nonadversarial settings	Problem-solving with union head	
Union leaders	Screening committee meetings	Discussion of market-based and technological problems	Understanding of long-run problems facing the organization
		Problem-solving rather than bargaining	Respect for management
Workers	Solicitation for suggestions on behalf of organizational objectives	Discussion of organizational issues	Involvement with work
	Election of representatives to tackle new range of problems		Commitment to organization and union
	Receipt of bonus based on organization-wide effort	Cooperation with peers and other work groups	Liking and respect for management and union leaders
	Observation of union leaders and managers meeting in nonadversarial setting		

managers. In asking whether to drop the plan, two points should be considered:

1. The Scanlon plan was a successful vehicle for introducing participative management into the plant. While the Scanlon plan is certainly not the only way to introduce participative management, it is the way that worked at Richmond, and there is no reason to think it will not continue to motivate, in the broadest sense, the kind of cooperative behavior the plant will need after the turnaround or that might even help the plant achieve a turnaround.

2. There is some question whether the plan motivates individual behavior in the strict Skinnerian sense in the first place. Therefore, the fact that bad work habits are developing is not necessarily a sign of the plan's failure. It could be, for instance, that Cooke needs to improve the level of the plant's first-line supervisors. There is some indication that there are problems in this area.

CONCLUSION

Table 6–13 summarizes the conditions necessary for successful implementation of the Scanlon plan, while Table 6–14 lists some of the benefits to be derived.

TEACHING PLAN

10 min.   1. Lecturette on Scanlon plan. How does it work? Or ask a student to explain how the plan works.

TABLE 6–13
Conditions for Success of Scanlon Plan

—Union–management dialogue
—Third-party facilitator to guide process, help build openness and trust
—Education of workers and management
—Participation and mutual influence in determining formula
—Worker commitment to plan—vote
—An effective committee structure for participation in finding improvement opportunities
—Effective supervisors and managers
  —Demanding of people
  —Good at planning
  —Skillful in involving people
—Workers who are skilled technically and interpersonally
—A culture of collaboration

TABLE 6-14

When the Scanlon Plan Works

—Coordination, teamwork, and sharing of knowledge are enhanced.
—Social needs are recognized through participation.
—Attention is focused on cost savings not just quantity of production.
—Acceptance of change is greater.
—Workers demand more efficient management and better planning.
—Workers try to reduce overtime, work smarter not harder.
—Workers produce ideas as well as effort.
—More flexible and better union–management relations come to exist.
—The union is strengthened because it is responsible for better work situation and pay.

30 min.   2. What do you like or not like about the plan? Ask students to express what they see as the pros and cons of the Scanlon plan. Make sure they articulate why the points they mention will either help or hurt the plant.

This is an example of some of the responses you might get:

PROS	CONS
Corporation committed	Not working/no bonuses
Workers committed to plant well-being	No incentive
Better labor relations	Plan too complex for workers to understand
Better communications	Cooke not committed to Scanlon plan
Adjustable to technology	No clear link between individual performance and reward
Provides incentive for support personnel	Layoffs have nullified benefits of plan

30 min.   3. Should Ron Cooke change Scanlon plan?
     a. What are his alternatives? Relate to the plant's technology and task.
       (1) Individual incentive: advantages and disadvantages
       (2) Group incentive: advantages and disadvantages
     b. Is the Scanlon plan really responsible for downturn in productivity? Are work habits deteriorating? If they are, what can Ron do about them short of changing the bonus system?
     c. What will happen to participative management if the system is altered or abandoned?

10 min.   4. What can a successful Scanlon plan do for you as a (future) manager?

10 min.   5. Summary
     a. Scanlon plan motivates in a symbolic way, allows for a new way for managers, workers, and union leaders to interact.
     b. Important points about Scanlon plan (see Table 6–15).

TABLE 6-15

Important Points About Scanlon Plan

—Incentives are hard to maintain because so many outside forces work to break link between bonus and performance.

—Plan has *symbolic* as well as incentive importance.

—Not everyone's behavior will change.

—System must evolve—needs regular updating.

—System triggers need for different management and supervisory skills.

—Plan is excellent device for economic education of employees.

—Culture more important than techniques, and different techniques can lead to same culture.

—Changed culture provides *intrinsic* rewards to supplement bonus.

—Implementation of plan is assisted by education and *informed choice*.

—Innovative HRM plans do not guarantee competitive health in the marketplace.

NOTE

1. James W. Driscoll, "Working Creatively with a Union: Lessons from the Scanlon Plan," in Michael Beer and Bert Spector, eds., *Readings in Human Resource Management* (New York: Free Press, 1985).

CHAPTER 7

Work Systems

The objective of the work systems section is to help students understand a fourth and final human resource management (HRM) task: designing jobs, technology, supervisory practices, and complementary human resource policies that increase the coincidence of interest between employees and employers. We opened the course by highlighting the differing interests of various stakeholder groups, the potential for conflict between those stakeholder groups, and the costs of that resulting conflict. We can now look at the impact that work system design has on the relationship between stakeholder groups within the organization and at the potential of work system design for either exacerbating differences in interests or building a greater coincidence of interests. While no work system can totally eliminate conflict, its design can help determine how conflict will be handled and the resulting costs—or even benefits—of that conflict to the organization. Our goal is not to take a normative position on work systems. Rather, it is to point out alternative approaches which move away from total reliance on bureaucratic mechanisms by incorporating market and clan mechanisms (see Chapter 7 of the casebook). Among the major issues raised by the cases in this section are:

1. *Job design.* Students learn about problems associated with traditional job design and about innovations in job design on a plant level which involve semiautonomous work teams and "whole-task" jobs. Students also learn about job design innovations in the office

where market and clan mechanisms were included in the job design to achieve awareness of and commitment to the overall good of the enterprise. Students also see the impact on individual employees, and the resulting effect on organizational effectiveness, of both traditional and enriched job design ("New Technology and Job Design in a Phone Company," "Kalamazoo Plant," "Sedalia Engine Plant," "Office Technology, Inc.").

2. *Coincidence of Interests*. Students learn about a trend in work design of planned innovations designed to enlarge the coincidence of interests between employees and employers. Greater cooperation between employees and employers can be achieved in both union and nonunion settings. Students also learn that there are inherent differences between various stakeholders in an organization. Through its work system, an organization can attempt to manage those differences and thus reduce conflict, but even work systems that promote coincidence of interests do not eliminate conflict between employers and employees over pay and other matters ("Sedalia Engine Plant," "Office Technology, Inc.").

3. *Change strategy*. Students learn that when an organization changes and attempts to institutionalize a work system, the process can be long and involved. They see the barriers to change that can exist inside an organization, supervisors' traditional assumptions about managing, short-term production pressures, and the forces for and against change in the organization's environment. They also learn about the manner in which change might be managed and institutionalized ("Office Technology, Inc.").

Sequence of Cases

We suggest the following sequence of cases:

1. *New Technology and Job Design in a Phone Company*. This case opens the work systems section of the text by providing students with the opportunity to participate in an exercise of job design. The exercise can generate a student discussion of criteria for effective job design as it might be applied specifically to the development of new work technology and more generally to the design and redesign of other jobs students will encounter in the following cases.

2. *Kalamazoo Plant Parts Division*. The case introduces students to a "traditional" (model A) work system, and to some of the problems that may arise under such a system, especially at the level of first-line supervision: the critical interface at which management and the work force meet

directly. The issue was visited briefly earlier in the course in "Bethoney Manufacturing." We will revisit the question of the critical role of the first-line supervisor and alternative ways of defining that role in "Sedalia Engine Plant." In "Office Technology, Inc." students will be able to compare directly the differing approaches of two first-line supervisors and look at the impact of their approaches on the work force. "Kalamazoo" also provides an opportunity to raise the question of what motivates people to work. The assumptions, both explicit and implicit, concerning motivation at Kalamazoo vary dramatically from those made at Sedalia Engine Plant.

3. *Sedalia Engine Plant.* This case offers an opportunity to pull together every section of HRM while concentrating on the details of the work system. Surrounding the basic matter of how to design jobs is a concern for employee influence (an elaborate governance structure has been established by management, and a union is attempting to organize the workers); human resource flow (one possible conclusion of the case is that not enough attention has been paid to flow issues, since the special dynamics of a high-commitment work situation may require recruitment, training, and promotion policies significantly different from a more traditional setting like the Kalamazoo plant); and reward systems (external and internal equity problems, skill rather than job-based evaluations, lack of hierarchically based prerogatives, an all-salaried work force, participation in design and administration of the pay system).

4. *Office Technology, Inc.* This case continues our exploration of work systems by focusing on the operation of two work groups. The laboratory and medical products (LMP) group functions as a semiautonomous work team. While students first encountered work teams in "Sedalia Engine Plant," they will now have the opportunity to analyze a specific team in far greater detail. They will need to understand in some detail, the content and design of the job itself, as well as other mechanisms—supervision, selection and training, adaptability to new technology, and so forth—that support that work system. By providing the same kind of details on the original equipment manufacturer (OEM) group, which is organized along much more traditional model A lines, students have an opportunity to compare the two groups along all the various dimensions that make up a work system. They can also make judgments concerning the outcomes of the two contrasting work system designs. Most importantly, the case raises questions of implementation and the possible roadblocks to change: questions that will also be addressed, but on a broader scope, in "General Motors and the United Auto Workers." Students will be able to plan an approach to changing the OEM work systems and will be able to examine problems encountered by OEM's management in moving to a "team approach."

Audiovisual Materials

Instructors may wish to consider the following audiovisual materials to supplement or accompany cases in the work systems section:

1. "Clockwork." A 25-minute documentary on the application of Frederick Taylor's Scientific Management system to time-and-motion studies and assembly line production. Can be used to accompany "Kalamazoo Plant Parts Division."
2. "Loose Bolts." A 33-minute documentary focuses on "blue-collar blues" as experienced by assembly line workers at General Motors' Lordstown plant in the early 1970s. Can be used to supplement "Kalamazoo Plant Parts Division" and "Sedalia Engine Plant" as well as to accompany "General Motors and the United Auto Workers" in Chapter 7.
3. "Changing Work." A 40-minute documentary film which follows a group of Detroit assembly-line workers on a tour of a Saab–Scania factory which has redesigned jobs around semiautonomous work teams. Can be used to accompany or supplement "Kalamazoo Plant Parts Division," "Sedalia Engine Plant," and "Office Technology, Inc." as well as to accompany "General Motors and the United Auto Workers" in Chapter 7.
4. "Why Work?" This two-part documentary (each part is 20 minutes long) offers a critical view of worker participation experiments in the United States and Europe (part 1) and European responses to unemployment which seek to promote greater work place democracy (part 2). Can be used to supplement "Sedalia Engine Plant" and "Office Technology, Inc." as well as "General Motors and the United Auto Workers" in Chapter 7.
5. "Managing in a High-Commitment Work System." This 16-minute videotape offers the view of two managers at Sedalia Engine (Danny Gobel, the current plant manager, and St. Claire, the first plant manager) and a corporate president on the special challenges involved in managing a high-commitment work system. To be used with "Sedalia Engine Plant."
6. "Office Technology, Inc." Two 15-minute videotapes are available to accompany this case. The first is of the laboratory and medical products (LMP) group (which operates as an autonomous work group). It reveals rich detail about supervision, work practice, relationships, and means for recruitment training and socialization. The second tape is of two groups in OEM after the change to an organization based on semiautonomous groups. Problems resulting from the change are revealed. These raise many questions about implementing work system change.

Supplementary Reading Assignments

The following supplementary readings can be assigned from *Readings in Human Resource Management:*

TEXT MATERIAL	SUGGESTED READINGS
Chapter 6	John Simmons and William Mares,
"Kalamazoo Plant Parts Division"	"The Plum and the Lash"
"New Technology and Job Design in a Phone Company"	Richard E. Walton, "Social Choice in the Development of Advance Information Technology"
"Sedalia Engine Plant"	Richard E. Walton, "Work Innovations in the United States"
	Rosabeth Moss Kanter, "Dilemmas of Managing Participation"
"Office Technology, Inc."	J. Richard Hackman, "Work Redesign for Organization Development"

NEW TECHNOLOGY AND JOB DESIGN IN A PHONE COMPANY
Teaching Note

In the late 1970s, a phone company decided to automate a major portion of its customer repair system. The automation significantly affected the job of the repair service answerers (RSAs) and was plagued by high worker dissatisfaction, poor interunit coordination, and, most troubling of all, growing customer dissatisfaction. Students can use this case as an exercise in developing principles of job design and applying those principles to the development and introduction of new work technology.

ASSIGNMENT QUESTION

Students should read the (A) case and come to class prepared to discuss the following question:

1. What aspects of the job and work environment of the RSAs in the new answering center are different from the repair clerk positions in the local bureaus and probably are contributing to work dissatisfaction and other negative symptoms in the answering centers?

CASE ANALYSIS

The first task students have is to analyze the repair clerk job as it existed prior to automation and then to analyze the RSA task after automation. Following such an analysis they can begin to examine the critical differences and the possible negative consequences of those differences.

Repair Clerk Job Before Automation

Students can easily determine that the repair clerk job prior to automation consisted of at least six key components:

1. Talks to customers
2. Trouble-shooter—manually tests service
3. Schedules repairs
4. Talks to repair supervisors
5. Does customer-initiated follow-up
6. Files and assists other personnel

As such, repair clerks deal with at least three key groups:

1. Customers
2. Repair supervisors
3. Other repair clerks

Also, because repair bureaus service particular geographical areas, the repair clerks have a certain area identity; they can become quite familiar with the area they are servicing.

RSA Job After Automation

The phone company has introduced a technological change—on-line computers—with the goal of making the customer repair operation more efficient. There are three components of that efficiency goal:

1. Reducing time taken to process requests
2. Reducing the number of required clerks
3. Reducing supervisory time required to manage the answering task through consolidation

Once they understand the goals of the change, students can look at how the *job* has been changed.

1. RSAs have been moved physically from local bureaus to a centralized answering center. The local identity of the job has been lost.
2. Phone calls that come into the center will be automatically routed to any available desk. Thus, the chances for follow-up with customers have been minimized.
3. Physically, the room of 100 RSAs has been set up in a rigid format. RSAs have been tied down to their terminals with the opportunity for interaction with other personnel minimized. With a clock and two supervisors in front of them and with the automatic routing of calls to any desk, RSAs may feel that they have become interchangeable parts of a technology that has come to dominate their jobs.
4. The job has become more repetitive (routine) than before. While the repair clerks were trouble shooters who questioned customers and initiated manual tests, RSAs "precisely" elicit information, probably by following some strict format, and record details on their video display rather than in writing. And instead of conducting tests and looking for trouble, they now initiate automatic tests. Another part of the task that has become more routine is the scheduling. While the older repair clerks made tentative commitments for completing repairs, the RSAs now follow a "prescribed guideline."
5. Loss of on-the-job interaction. The physical layout of the room has cut back considerably on the possibilities for interpersonal interac-

tions. But there is more. Under the old system, there was direct contact between the repair clerks and the repair people, since the clerks physically handed repair orders to the supervisor of the repair people. Now, it is the RSA supervisors who deal directly with the repair operators. Furthermore, the RSAs and the repair operations are separated organizationally. Each now reports to company headquarters through a different chain of command. There are also separate unions for the RSAs and repair people.

6. Finally, there is little or no chance of follow-up. The repair clerks could see a customer complaint through from the initial complaint to conclusion. Under the new system, customers are assigned randomly to RSAs, so the chances of them dealing with the same customers on a follow-up basis are slim.

Job Design Problems

Clearly, the efficiency goals of the phone company are not being met. They are saving neither time nor money, and the quality of service is deteriorating. Students can, as part of the discussion, be asked, *what* the RSAs will say is "wrong" about their new jobs, and they will likely come up with most, if not all, of the problems surfaced through interviews with RSAs in the (B) case. When students are asked *why* such negative impacts are occurring, they can begin to develop their own theories about job design. What are the critical factors of a job and what are their predictable outcomes? Instructors might suggest that students use the five core job dimensions of Hachman and Oldham that are discussed in the text—skill variety, task identity, task significance, autonomy, and feedback—to analyze the old and new jobs. They can see that on each of the five key dimensions—skill variety, task identity, significance, autonomy, and feedback—the jobs have been *un*enriched. In this framework, students can be asked what the outcomes will be in terms of both critical psychological states and personal and work outcomes. It is probably best, however, not to impose this particular framework too early. Rather, allow the class to create and develop its own theory about the critical aspects of a job and the impact of those characteristics on both the people and the organization. Once they gain such "ownership" over a theory of job design, they can apply those theories to all the future cases in the work system section.

CONCLUSION

There are three key learnings that can be derived from this exercise:

1. The exercise offers students yet another opportunity to learn one of the key lessons of the HRM course; that organizational effective-

ness and employee well-being are interrelated. In the long run, there is a coincidence of interests between employees and their organization. It would be naive to assume that there will not be some conflicts between the goals of the two stakeholder groups, at least in the short run. But over time, the aims of the two can become largely, if not entirely, compatible as improved human outcomes will ultimately have a positive impact on organizational performance. The central task in the work system policy area is to explore and increase the potential areas of overlapping interests while containing the costs of occasional inevitable conflicts of interest.

2. While there is a tendency to think that technology can enforce certain work system decisions on organizations, managers can and do make important decisions as to the application of new technology and the impact that technology will have on work systems. Students may be assigned Walton's article[1] in which he suggests the important variables affected by managerial choices whether those choices are implicit or explicit:

   a. Applications of new technology sometime narrow the scope of jobs and sometime broaden the scope.
   b. Choices about how new technology will be employed may emphasize the individual nature of task performance or promote the interdependent nature of the work of groups of employees.
   c. Choices may change the focus of decision-making toward centralization or decentralization, with further implications for the steepness of the hierarchy.
   d. Choices may create performance measurement systems that emphasize learning and self-control or surveillance and hierarchical control.
   e. Choices may lead to the transfer of certain work functions from the unionized work force to supervisory or professional groups, or they may provide developmental opportunities for the workers.
   f. Choices can increase the flexibility of work schedules to accommodate human preferences or they can decrease flexibility and introduce shift work.
   g. Managerial choices can contribute to social isolation, or they can have the opposite effect.

3. Walton further argues that most of the choices regarding the above outcomes are made randomly and implicitly, rather than through a planned, strategic process. The final point of the exercise is to ask the students: Why is this so? Why is it that better planing often does not occur? Students' experience in the exercise has shown them that job design is not some mysterious or unfathomable process better left to specialists. They *can* predict the outcomes of work system choices. By recalling their own work experiences and empathizing

with the people going through the change process described in the case, they can predict both *what* many of the outcomes will be and *why* they came about. Why then does careful planning and consideration of the long-run impact *not* take place? There is, of course, no single answer to this question. Students can, however, be expected to point to the dividing line between the "planners" and the "doers," to the difficulty of measuring the costs of poor work system choices in terms that can be weighed against other benefits (assumptions about cost improvements deriving from improved productivity and reduced work force needs in this case, for example).

TEACHING PLAN

Instructors should turn to "Assignment for New Technology and Job Design in a Phone Company" for more details on how to conduct this exercise.

NOTE

1. Richard E. Walton, "Social Choice in the Development of New Information Technology," in Michael Beer and Bert Spector, eds., *Readings in Human Resource Management* (New York: Free Press, 1985).

ASSIGNMENT FOR NEW TECHNOLOGY AND JOB DESIGN IN A PHONE COMPANY

Objective

The objective of this case is to generate discussions of criteria for effective job design and how such criteria might be applied during the development of new work technology.

This assignment was prepared by Richard E. Walton.

Copyright © 1982 by the President and Fellows of Harvard College. Harvard Business School case 9-483-075.

This case may not be reproduced. Separate copies for classroom and other use should be ordered from HBS Case Services, Harvard Business School, Boston, MA 02163. An order form with information on how to order cases will be found at the back of this manual.

Schedule

Step 1 (15 Minutes). Form groups. Please read the (A) case individually and then discuss the following:

1. What aspects of the jobs and work environment of the RSAs in the new answering center are different from the repair clerk positions in the local bureaus and probably are contributing to work dissatisfaction and other negative symptoms in the answering centers? You may utilize the attached worksheet.

Step 2 (30 Minutes). The (B) case will be distributed to your groups. It reports on the results of interviews with answering service personnel and their managers. Please peruse it quickly and then discuss the following:

1. How many of the consequences did you anticipate on the basis of the (A) case?
2. What additional information would have been useful to you?
3. Could the negative effects have been reversed or minimized, if there had been a timely effort to do so, without sacrificing the basic technical and economic advantages offered by advanced information technology?
4. Should management attempt to deal with these issues? When? Before or after the system is implemented? How?
5. What would you see as your responsibility to this type of case if you were a union official?

Step 3 (30 Minutes). We will reconvene in general session and continue the discussion. We will not require formal reports by groups.

Worksheet

What aspects of work technology, job design, and work procedures have potential relevance for the quality of work life (QWL) for personnel who receive subscriber complaints?

How do they differ between the earlier bureaus and the new centers?

Aspects of Job Situation	Clerk in Repair Bureau	Representative in Answering Center (RSA)
1.		
2.		

Continued

Aspects of Job Situation	Clerk in Repair Bureau	Representative in Answering Center (RSA)
3.		
4.		
5.		
6.		
7.		
8.		
9.		
10.		

KALAMAZOO PLANT PARTS DIVISION—ACME MOTORS
Teaching Note

Acme Motors' Kalamazoo plant is faced with a critical problem of dissatisfaction and high turnover among their first-line supervisors. The turnover rate ran about 50 percent in 1978, with about half of those leaving their positions voluntarily and the rest being asked to leave after "failing." With increasing pressure to reduce costs and increase productivity, plant manager Rich Howards has given Bob Moore, supervisor of salaried personnel (industrial relations department) a month to provide him with recommendations for reducing the turnover problem. The case not only allows an examination of the first-line supervisor's job in a traditional plant. It also allows an analysis of the effects of the total work system, particularly supervision and union–management relations, on worker attitudes and motivation.

ASSIGNMENT QUESTIONS

Students should read the case and come to class prepared to discuss the following questions:

1. How do first-line supervisors at Kalamazoo feel about their jobs and why?
2. What is the relationship between first-line supervisors and other groups within the plant: general supervisors and superintendents, top management, labor relations, the unions, workers, each other?
3. What action plan should Bob Moore recommend?

CASE ANALYSIS

Case analysis can proceed by students asking a number of questions: how do first-line supervisors feel about their jobs? What are the consequences of those feelings? What are the elements of the Kalamazoo work system that contribute to those feelings? What action steps might be taken to help overcome the problem?

How Do First-Line Supervisors Feel?

From a combination of exit interviews and an employee attitude survey, Bob Moore concluded that the "morale problem" among first-line supervisors was composed of the following elements:

1. They feel *unequipped for the job*. One first-line supervisor com-

plained that he was placed on the job without any training and given no coaching once he got there. He was effectively left alone on the job without having the required skills and competencies.

2. There is *little discretion* in dealing with employees. The same first-line supervisor noted that the general supervisor simply imposed his will by telling him how employees were to be "controlled."

3. Moore concluded that *"lack of recognition"* was a critical part of the dissatisfaction. First-line supervisors feel that "no one is paying attention to them—just putting demands on them."

4. First-line supervisors feel *alienated from the plant*. First-line supervisors feel that poor communication has cut them off from the rest of the plant, including their own general supervisors.

5. They feel *betrayed by labor relations* people who are "selling out" to the union by making deals and "giving the plant away." Part of this frustration has to do with their belief that their authority is constantly under challenge by workers and the union, and is then undermined by deals made by superintendents and labor relations people.

6. *Career frustration*. At least some of the first-line supervisors (about 40 percent of those hired in the production department in 1978 were college graduates) must have felt frustrated by their low potential for advancement. Although almost all of the general supervisor and superintendent positions at Kalamazoo were filled from within the plant, the quite typical pyramid structure (167 first-line supervisors, 31 general supervisors, and 10 superintendents) of the plant meant that 4 of 5 first-line supervisors had reached the peak of their career progression within the plant.

What Are the Consequences of Those Feelings?

Dissatisfaction and high turnover are the most obvious consequences of their feelings of frustration and alienation. As a result, almost half of the first-line supervisors are new and inexperienced. This problem will certainly reduce Rich Howard's chances of making his plant more cost-efficient and productive. But these frustrations will also have an impact on the attitudes and behavior of those first-line supervisors who remain on the job, affecting their relationships downward with their employees and upward with top management.

First-line supervisors apparently see their relationship both with the workers and the union as totally adversarial: one side wins at the expense of the other. This view leads to a psychology of "revenge," where confrontation and "beating" the local contract are viewed as integral, even positive aspects of the job of being a first-line supervisor. Such an attitude almost certainly leads to distrust, alienation, and bitterness on the part of supervised employees. It is not surprising, therefore, that when a discipline decision of a first-line supervisor is reversed by labor relations, the employees gloat over their perceived victories ("laughing at him, waving a check for lost time in the supervisor's face"). Such a reaction, in turn, reinforces the view on the part of the first-line supervisors that they are engaged in a constant battle over authority.

Union leaders, for their part, complain that first-line supervisors fail to treat employees "like human beings," and upper management agrees with that assessment. As a consequence, upper management holds first-line supervisors in low esteem, believing them to have little real potential for advancement. That belief likely has its own set of consequences. Upper management seeks to hire more college graduates. Upper management cuts out training programs for first-line supervisors to save money. Those actions may be a consequence of the problems, but they also exacerbate the problem. Frustration over lack of advancement opportunity and proper training is enhanced. The problems spiral and cause further problems. The manner in which first-line supervisors behave is both a *consequence* of problems in the Kalamazoo work system and a *cause* of further problems.

What Are the Elements of the Kalamazoo Work System that Contribute to Those Problems?

Training. The complaint of supervisors about the lack of adequate training is apparently justified. Moore says that many of them are placed on the line after only a few hours training: "The general supervisors expect them to just walk in and hit it." The problem, says Moore, is that general supervisors "don't have the time to spend" training first-line supervisors. But there are only five first-line supervisors for every general supervisor, so it is possible that there is an opportunity for on-the-job training by general supervisors that is not being taken advantage of. Furthermore, there is apparently no effort to promote networking among first-line supervisors themselves: having experienced supervisors coach inexperienced ones, or having college graduates help those with less formal education. There is no incentive, either through pay (raises are based entirely on longevity) or benefits like time off or tuition rebates for supervisors to seek training on their own. Moore did institute an innovative training program in 1978. But it was only accessible to college graduates, could handle only two supervisors at a time, and involved only one month of training. As limited as the program might have been, even it was cut out of the 1979 budget.

The consequences of this lack of training are serious. Supervisors feel frustrated by their lack of preparedness. Much of their job is a mystery to them: how to fill out a time sheet, how to handle a grievance. They know little or nothing about the terms of the local contract, and thus feel disadvantaged in their relationship with apparently better-trained union representatives. Finally, this lack of training results in little or no real understanding of how the rest of the organization works: including departments like industrial engineering (IE) which have such a critical impact on their own job (IE, for instance, establishes the performance standards for supervisors). Such lack of knowledge makes commitment to the total organization difficult, and enhances feelings of frustration and alienation. As part of the "vicious cycle," it also reinforces top management's notion that first-line supervisors have little potential for anything other than failure.

Recruitment. Although "interpersonal skills" is listed as one of the three primary dimensions of evaluating applicants for the job, there is little evidence that such interpersonal skills as ability to communicate, ability to delegate, ability to work well with others, and so forth are given much weight. Interpersonal skills within the plant means ability to be tough and to control workers. In the screening process, the emphasis instead seems to be on the task and on short-term results.

Listed number one among the criteria for selecting new superintendents outside of the plant is "desire for a career in manufacturing." As the plant management moves to increase the number of supervisors recruited from the outside, they will presumably attract more people who share advancement as a primary goal. But since advancement opportunities are so limited, such a policy can lead to even more frustration and turnover.

Evaluation. First-line supervisors are evaluated annually. Five criteria—budget performance, labor control, housekeeping, absenteeism, and training—are formally included. Training, apparently, is never considered at all, and, in fact, the key criteria are controlling workers, keeping the number of grievances down, and "running back" (meeting quality and labor cost standards). Standards are set elsewhere. First-line supervisors have little or no expertise in the handling of grievances, and when they do handle them their decisions are often reversed by labor relations people who then do not bother to explain their reasons to the supervisors. Thus, the only factor of evaluation over which supervisors seem to have much influence is "control" of workers. And with the adversarial norms of the plant (more on this below), that means getting tough. But getting tough is obviously not seen as an indicator of advancement potential, so a management development package is rarely kept on first-line supervisors.

Communication. Much of the alienation felt by supervisors is due to the almost total lack of communication from other groups within the plant. Other departments operate according to their own priorities, and seem unresponsive and unsupportive of first-line supervisors. On this point, there is also evidence that supervisors themselves show little competency in dealing with other departments: "You used to be able to pick up a phone and *make engineering jump*." Labor relations admits to doing a poor job communicating with first-line supervisors. They are told virtually nothing about the process of contract negotiations or the content of the resulting contract. When labor relations makes a decision or reverses one, first-line supervisors are more likely to hear of it from the union or the affected employee than from labor relations people. The reasons for such decisions are never explained. It is not surprising, therefore, that first-line supervisors are confused and frustrated when such a decision is made.

Norms of the Plant. The industrial relations view (as articulated by Bob Moore) that workers are not to be trusted and are engaged in a constant battle with management over authority sets the norms of the plant and affects the behavior of the plant's supervisory force. "If the hourlys feel they can get away with something," says Moore, "they'll do it." Other comments show how this attitude is reflected among supervisors and superintendents: workers are constantly trying to "stick it" to their supervisors and the company. The work ethic is declining. Workers are motivated "not by this Maslow stuff"—presumably meaning that management dismisses the notion that workers will be motivated to the extent that the work environment meets their "higher-level" needs for esteem, autonomy, and self-realization[1]—but by confronting people, being unpleasant and aggressive, showing intestinal fortitude, seeking revenge, and beating the agreement.

The Job Itself. An important point not to be overlooked is that the job itself is an extremely difficult and demanding one. In addition, the Kalamazoo plant is not alone in having difficulty deciding just what the position should be. Is it a dead-end job, to be used as a reward for hourly workers? Is it a first step on the way to a career in upper management to be filled by people with developmental potential? Right now, the Kalamazoo plant management seems to be recruiting with the second definition in mind, then treating the job in accordance with the first definition.

The problem of defining the job, then filling the position with the right people is certainly not unique to Kalamazoo, or even to traditional, model A plants. As will be seen in "Sedalia Engine Plant," an innovative, model B plant can also have difficulty deciding whom to recruit and how to satisfy (retain) first-line supervisors.

Summary. Marvin Dunnett[2] has identified certain critical dimensions of effective leadership performance of traditional supervisory roles. It is possible to look at how the work system at the Kalamazoo plant places restraints on many of the important dimensions of effective supervisory leadership (see Table 7–1).

TABLE 7-1

Effective Supervision

Critical Dimensions of Effective Leadership Performance in Traditional Supervisory Roles*	Work System Constraints on Effective Supervision at Kalamazoo Plant
Know-how. Supervisor keeps thoroughly informed of organizational needs and keeps up-to-date technically.	Little pretraining and no on-the-job training; no communication with other departments keeps supervisors uninformed with little or no up-to-date knowledge.
Responsibility. Supervisor is ready and able to accept personal responsibility for actions.	Supervisors feel out of control, have low authority, are responsible and accountable only for "controlling" workers
Wisdom. Supervisor exhibits informed commitment and loyalty to organizational goals, policies, and practices.	Lack of communication, training, and consulting with others leads to supervisors who are uninformed about company goals and either ignorant of or resentful toward policies and practices.
Empathy. Supervisor shows personal concern and understanding for other people.	Norm of confrontation and distrust makes empathy difficult
Communication. Supervisor communicates effectively, thoroughly, and accurately.	No mechanisms for communication; norm of secrecy: hoarding rather than sharing information
Training. Supervisor determines subordinates' training needs and institutes program to meet them.	No incentives through pay, culture, or performance evaluation for supervisors to undertake training
Coordination. Supervisor negotiates with and cooperates with other organizational units for optimal use of all resources in meeting organizational goals.	No coordination between supervisors and other departments
Innovation. Supervisors develop and apply innovative procedures to accomplish organizational goals.	Supervisors feel general supervisors allow no leeway or flexibility
Delegation. Supervisor assigns tasks to others and monitors performance.	No encouragement, incentive, training, or norm for sharing power or delegating authority

Source: Marvin Dunnett, cited in Richard E. Walton and Leonard A. Schlesinger, "Do Supervisors Thrive in Participative Work Systems?," *Organizational Dynamics* (Winter 1979), pp. 25–38.

Action Plan

Walton and Schlesinger[3] presented the successful strategy of one company seeking to address the supervisory issues that can be used as a model for action at the Kalamazoo plant:

1. *Recruitment and selection.* Company deliberately strives to achieve a mix of skills, backgrounds, ages, and educational experiences in the first-line supervisory force. A sizable number of college graduates can be recruited for the job on a short-term (one to three years) basis, complemented by a contingent of individuals promoted up-from-the-floor and outside recruitment of individuals with extensive manufacturing background. Such a policy has three goals.
   a. It ensures continuing technical and managerial skills at the base of the managerial hierarchy.
   b. Such a policy provides a high-level managerial personnel with an in-depth understanding of and appreciation for the problems of the first-line supervisor and the hourly work force.
   c. By fostering formal and informal interaction among first-line supervisors, it promotes the exchange of individual skills and competencies—for example, assigning a supervisor with extensive manufacturing experience to help a new college-educated supervisor in learning the technology, and assigning a new college-educated supervisor to help the experienced supervisor in writing reports and conducting meetings.
2. *Training.* All first-line supervisors are provided with extensive formal and on-the-job training in human resource skills—performance appraisal, problem-solving, communication, and so on—as well as education in the manufacturing process; the company provides new supervisors with an 8- to 12-week training period that allows them to gain in-depth knowledge of the work system and personnel throughout parts of the organization without the pressure of meeting daily production demands.
3. *Performance appraisal.* The company seeks appraisal feedback from subordinates, peers, and superiors, and the results are reflected in both salary and the career development system.
4. *Evaluation.* Specific 6- and 12-month benchmarks are set for performance in such areas as training of subordinates and the attainment and use of interpersonal skills, with regular meetings between first-line supervisors and general supervisors to discuss progress and growth.
5. *Communication.* There are continued regular meetings with salaried work force, but representatives of line management and staff rather than industrial relations personnel are brought in to discuss common issues, problems, concerns, and so forth; off-site meetings

227

are held with all first-line supervisors to address issues of personal and general concern; temporary, problem-solving task forces are formed between supervisors, representatives of the union, and labor relations people to defuse growing distrust and suspicion and to open channels of communication.

CONCLUSION

"Kalamazoo Plant Parts Division" offers students an opportunity to use the first-line supervisor issue to bridge ahead to future cases that describe high-commitment, model B alternatives to Kalamazoo's traditional work system. A feature common to a great many new plants opening in the United States (not just the ones described in the cases) is an attempt to redefine the role of first-line supervisor.[4] The first-line supervisors at the Sedalia Engine Plant, for instance, are called "team advisors." Their duties differ considerably from those of the first-line supervisors at Kalamazoo. They are responsible for the training of individual team members under them, and the development of a mature, self-managing, well-functioning team. They also act as team builders, communicators, trainees, and occasional fill-ins, but not as autocratic overseers or tough "controllers" as at the Kalamazoo plant. A similar redefinition took place at General Motors' Livonia plant. There, the first-line supervisors are called "team coordinators," and sit in on all team meetings, share information with the team, and work with an assistant coordinator—an hourly worker elected by the team—to solve team problems. Applicants all go through an assessment center "to determine their suitability for the newly defined foreman's role."

If the first-line supervisors' role is to be redefined as an integrator, team builder, communicator, conflict-resolver, priority-setter, and diagnostician,[5] careful consideration should be given to recruiting, developing, appraising, and placing supervisors with greater competencies in behavioral skills. Interviews by hourly workers, for instance, can help render judgments about an individual's ability to share influence, communicate, and fit in with the existing work system. An assessment center may be used to understand better developmental needs in relation to behavioral issues. Appraisals based in part on employee attitudes and surveys can help signal clearly to supervisors what is expected of them in terms of subordinate relations. Pay systems can either reward the acquisition of new skills or block such changes by continuing to reward old behaviors.

Scientific Management and Model A Plants

"The Kalamazoo Parts Plant" offers students an opportunity to step back from the particular problems of the case and address the broader matter of what a work system is, and what the assumptions are that underlie a work system. To supplement the case, students can be assigned "The Plum and the Lash" by John Simmons and William Mares.[6] As a traditionally organized and managed plant, Kalamazoo can be used as the basis for a brief discussion of the theories of Frederick Taylor and the type of organization that flows from those theories. An understanding of the history behind the traditional model A work system will help illuminate the contrasting Model B system that students will encounter in "Sedalia Engine Plant."

Frederick Winslow Taylor was a mechanical engineer who formulated a system, while working at the Midvale Steel Company, for measuring individual tasks in the work place. This process, which he termed Scientific Management, sought precise, scientifically derived definitions of how jobs would be best accomplished. Each job was subdivided into its smallest constituent parts, then timed, measured, and defined.

Taylorism also involved a philosophy of management that included, but went beyond, these "scientific" measurements. The task of planning and directing every job, down to its most minute detail, was assigned to management alone. All aspects of planning and controlling work were directed exclusively by management toward the goal of achieving maximum productivity. Workers would simply fit into this system and do what they were told.

But Scientific Management represented more than just a way of ordering workers to perform certain precisely defined functions. It also represented a kind of bargain with workers. Speaking at the newly created Harvard Business School in 1909, Taylor defined the role of management in dealing with workers as threefold:

1. Holding a plum for them to climb after.
2. Cracking the whip over them, with an occasional touch of the lash.
3. Working shoulder to shoulder with them, pushing hard in the same direction, and all the while teaching, guiding, and helping them.

The "plum" to which Taylor referred was high wages: an increase of between 30 and 100 percent over the average pay was his recommendation. Such generous monetary reward would make workers compliant to the system: "If you are a high-priced man, you will do exactly as this man tells you, from morning till night. . . . And what's more, no back talk." Management's unilateral attempts to pay high wages in return for absolute obedience to the functioning of the assembly line perhaps reached its peak with Henry Ford's $5 a day wage in the 1920s.

What happened to the philosophy of Scientific Management with the increased power of unions in the 1930s and beyond? There were some union critics who objected particularly to the notion that workers should have no control in deciding *how* to do a job. The Editor of the *International Molders' Union Journal* wrote:

> The one great asset of the wage worker has been his crafts-manship. . . . The really essential element in it is not manual skills and dexterity, but something

stored up in the mind of the worker. This something is partly the intimate knowledge of the character and usage of the tools, materials, and processes of the craft which . . . has enabled the worker to organize and force better terms from the employers. . . . The greatest blow that could be delivered against unionism and the organized workers would be the separation of craft knowledge from craft skill.

Despite such critical commentaries, the mainstream response of organized labor was to accept rather than challenge the assumptions of Scientific Management, particularly the precise and limited definition of jobs. A combination of factors—the philosophy and experience of powerful labor leaders like Samuel Gompers, the power of management, and the attitudes of workers themselves—led American unions to accept the resulting division of labor and to use collective bargaining to fatten the wage "plum" and to widen control over job opportunities and definitions by negotiating detailed wage schedules tied to particular jobs. The Kalamazoo plant represents the bargain between management and union—tight and narrow job classifications, high wages, and a well-defined dichotomy between management and workers—and some of the problems that can result.

Shoshana Zuboff has attempted to place the employee–employer relationship in an historical context by showing how changes in the environment—ranging from the Industrial Revolution to Scientific Management and more recently economic expansion—have brought about new theories of work motivation which have, in turn, affected managerial choices concerning work system design.[7] Her arguments are summarized in Table 7–2.

TEACHING PLAN

20 min.　1. What should Bob Moore recommend to Rich Howards to correct the problem among first-line supervisors? Allow students to make specific suggestions, but be sure to push them to see the constraints imposed by the work system itself. For example,

　　a. Improve communications with labor relations, BUT there will still be adversarial union–management relations.

　　b. Recruit *more* college graduates, BUT won't that lead to increased frustration over career progress? Recruit *fewer* college graduates, BUT where will future superintendents come from?

　　c. Improve supervisory training, BUT won't culture of plant that says supervisors have little potential and workers are out to "stick it" to company get in the way of any real change?

10 min.　2. Once some of the constraints of the work system are identified (save the details for later), you can move to a discussion of the specific problems by asking students to identify what are the problems at the Kalamazoo plant.

TABLE 7-2
Shifting Work System Design Choices

Historic Developments	Environmental Change	New Theories of Work Motivation	Managerial Choices Regarding Work Design
Industrial Revolution (19th century)	Industrialization, but considerable craft/self-employment Considerable social mobility within industrial firms Protestantism	*Protestant Work Ethic* —Individual effort —Working harder equals being better person —Rewards for achievement	Centralized supervision Standard work scheduled BUT Continuity with craft tradition —Considerable autonomy in organizing and executing tasks
Scientific Management and the rationalization of production (early 20th century)	Growth in size of business More dependency on machinery Decline of agriculture, self-employment, craft tradition Increased need for standardization	*Economic/Rational Work Ethic* —Work for economic benefits, improved standard of living —Steady employment	Emphasis on efficiency and obedience —Subdivision of labor —Close supervision —Increased hierarchical control
Economic expansion (mid-20th century)	Legitimacy of collective bargaining Formalization of adversarial relations—"The less work the better" Loss of intrinsic work rewards Abundance satisfies workers' basic needs Increasing educational level of workers	*The "Self" Work Ethic* —Mayo's worker as psychological self whose motivation depends on fulfillment of social and emotional needs	Coordinate work design (how workers relate to each other, performance measurement, rewards, authority, and status distribution, career paths) to provide challenge, mutual influence, and interesting work with less emphasis on competition.

Source: Shoshana Zuboff, "The Work Ethic and Work Organization," in Michael Beer and Bert Spector, eds., *Readings in Human Resource Management* (New York: Free Press, 1985).

a. Costs

b. Quality

c. Low morale and turnover among supervisors

d. High frustration and alienation among supervisors

20 min.   3. Move more specifically to first-line supervisors by asking: why is morale so low and frustration so high among first-line supervisors?

a. Underequipped for job

b. Little discretion dealing with employees

c. Career frustration

d. Feel alienated and betrayed by plant (upper management, staff, labor relations).

30 min.   4. What is causing all these problems? Discussion can now move into a more detailed analysis of the work system.

a. Poor training

b. Recruitment doesn't fit with job

c. First-line supervisors evaluated on matters beyond their control

d. Communications within plant

e. Adversarial norms within plant

f. Assumptions about what motivates people to work (use Table 7-1 for summary.)

10 min.   5. Closing lecturette—introduce model A and B work systems, give some historical background on model A systems and reasons why various innovations that students will be seeing in upcoming cases (autonomous work teams, job enrichment, redefined supervisory jobs, reduction of supervisory levels, joint union–management committees, concern with QWL) are being attempted.

NOTES

1. For a discussion of Maslow's theories of motivation, as well as other theories, see Michael Beer, *Organization Change and Development: A Systems View* (Santa Monica, CA: Goodyear Publishing, 1980), pp. 30, 168–172.
2. Cited in Richard E. Walton and Leonard A. Schlessinger, "Do Supervisors Thrive in Participative Work Systems?" *Organizational Dynamics* (Winter 1979), pp. 25–38.
3. Walton and Schlesinger, "Do Supervisors Thrive in Participative Work Systems?"
4. E. E. Lawler, *Pay and Organization Development* (Reading, MA: Addison-Wesley, 1981).
5. This definition is suggested by Leonard A. Schlesinger and Barry Oshry, "Quality of Work Life and the Manager: Muddle in the Middle," Harvard Business School Working Paper no. 83–06 (July 1982).

6. In Michael Beer and Bert Spector, eds., *Readings in Human Resource Management* (New York: Free Press, 1985).

7. Shoshana Zuboff, "The Work Ethic and Work Organization," in Michael Beer and Bert Spector, eds., *Readings in Human Resource Management* (New York: Free Press, 1985).

SEDALIA ENGINE PLANT
Teaching Note

"Kalamazoo Plant" showed students the elements of a traditional work system. "Sedalia Engine Plant" presents a contrasting approach to work systems based on a distinct and powerful philosophy about work and employee motivation. This philosophy governs virtually every aspect of the operation and differs in almost every specific from the work system at Kalamazoo.

At the core, job design must be made to be harmonious with the other human resource elements. In fact, the term "work systems" is meant to go beyond job design and include supervision, technology, the competence of people, cooperation and other personnel policies and practices.

As the (A) case ends, new plant manager Danney Goble must face a series of problems—heavy turnover of top management, a severe economic downturn, dissatisfaction with compensation, problems with the team advisor concept, and discipline—and seek solutions consistent with Sedalia's philosophy and work system. The (B) case describes Goble's actions. If the case is to be taught in one day, the (B) case can simply be given to students at the end of class. If "Sedalia" is to be used in a two-class sequence as we recommend, the (B) case can be handed out at the end of class and assigned for the following day.

The purpose of this case is to present students with a work system design that increasingly is being applied in part or whole by many corporations. Students should learn about the positive impact of such work systems on commitment, competence, congruence, and cost, but they should also learn about the special problems of managing these systems.

ASSIGNMENT QUESTIONS

Students should read the (A) case and come to class prepared to discuss the following questions.

1. What are the philosophy and assumptions that guide the work system at Sedalia? What are the key design elements and how do they reflect those assumptions?
2. What is your evaluation of the Sedalia Engine Plant's approach to management? What are the assets? What risks and special problems does it present?
3. What should Goble do about the problems facing the plant at the end of the case, particularly the leadership transition problems, the

compensation issues, business downturn, discipline problems, team advisor problems, and union organizing?

If cases are to be used in a two-class sequence, the following questions can be assigned in preparing for discussion of the (B) case:

1. Evaluate Goble's actions in regards to leadership, the layoffs, the discipline problem, and compensation.
2. What problems still face the plant at the end of the (B) case, and what should Goble do about them?
3. What are the special skills and demands of working in a place like Sedalia? What special management competencies does it seem to call for?
4. What is your evaluation of SEP? How would you like to be part of the management there?

CASE ANALYSIS

When American Diesel opened their Sedalia plant in 1974 they allowed the new plant manager, Donald St. Clair, and his organizing team time to design and install a highly participative style of management with innovations in work design, compensation systems, governance, and organizational structure. Five years later, St. Clair has left and Danney Goble must step in. Confronting Goble are a number of problems relating to heavy turnover among top management and a severe economic downturn. There is a seeming lack of trust in the new leadership and a growing sense of dissatisfaction with the compensation system. The (B) case examines the manner in which Danney Goble handled his first year as plant manager.

When St. Clair and his organizing team drew up the blueprint for SEP, they attempted to design a work system that integrated the various elements of human resource management—employee influence, flow, job design, and rewards—under a powerful overriding philosophy. Analysis of the case should start with an examination of that philosophy and how that philosophy informs the various elements of the human resource system design at SEP, particularly employee influence, flow, rewards, and job design.

SEP's Philosophy

The document developed by the original organizing team (Exhibit 26–1 in the casebook) identifies the four key building blocks of the organization as *excellence, trust, growth*, and *equity*. Table 7–3 presents the philosophical assumptions that underlie the document and SEP's organization.

TABLE 7-3
Key Assumptions of SEP Work System

---

1. People *want* to work hard, perform well, learn new skills, and be involved in decision-making that affects their jobs.
2. Creative talents are widely distributed at *all* levels of the organization.
3. The job atmosphere can unleash a powerful work ethic still extant in most employees.
4. It is important to limit the size of business units so that managers personally know their employees.
5. Participation can lead to quality decisions and commitment.
6. If people have high expectations, they will work hard to make those expectations come true.
7. Employee influence, including due process, can be provided without a union.

Case discussion should identify these various assumptions and allow time for debate on their validity.

St. Clair and his team then moved to build these assumptions into the organizational design.

Employee Influence

SEP's operation organization is divided into five levels: plant manager, directors, business managers, team advisors, and team members (Figure 7-1).

As Table 7-3 indicates, there was an attempt made to give at least some of the directors responsibility for *both* manufacturing and support functions. Each business also contained its own support personnel, organized into teams just like the manufacturing personnel.

Additionally, there was a governance structure that included the elected board of representatives (BOR) and the plant operating team (POT) made up of the plant manager and his directors. Thus, employee influence was dealt with through a number of formal and informal mechanisms.

1. Governance structures, including POT (charged with giving a general sense of direction to the plant) and BOR (20 representatives elected from all the plant's businesses and support teams, acts as a forum or sounding board for SEP employees)
2. "Fireside chats" started by St. Clair and continued by Goble as an informal safety valve
3. Norm of openness
4. Frequency of meetings, for example, daily team meetings
5. Limit of 200 to 300 individuals in business unit to develop close ties between business managers, advisors, and members
6. Great deal of top-down and bottom-up communication
7. Numerous task forces to deal with specific plant problem

FIGURE 7-1
SEP's Operating Organization

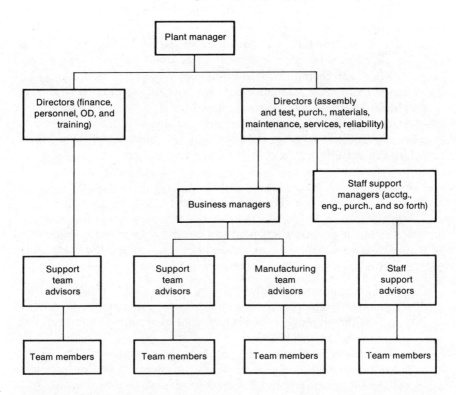

It was hoped that such influence mechanisms would reduce the likelihood of employees supporting a unionization drive, but more importantly that they would provide a means for giving employees a voice in plant affairs.

When Goble became plant manager in the fall of 1979, he found a number of problems with the organizational and governance structures. St. Clair had systematically bypassed many of his directors in the early stages of the plant's operations and worked directly with the business managers. Goble felt a need [(B) case], particularly in light of the growing size of the plant, to disentangle himself from the day-to-day operations of the businesses. He wanted his business managers to operate more freely in that regard, while he and his directors (POT) took more responsibility for the overall functions of the plant. Some business managers apparently resented what they saw as a loss of power. Goble learned late of the problem, but felt that it had been ironed out through informal discussions.

The main complaints about the governance structure came from nonexempt manufacturing team representatives who felt they were underrepresented on BOR. (There is also a hint of dissention between nonexempt support and nonexempt manufacturing personnel.) It is also possible to wonder whether Goble was too quick to go to ad hoc groups [economic review group (ERG) for the compensation crisis, the special task group to evaluate the corrective action process] rather than working through established groups like BOR. The failure of the union to attract much attention, however, was taken by some plant leaders as a sign that employees were, by and large, satisfied with their amount of influence.

Finally, there is the intangible but clearly significant matter of the role of a "charismatic" leader. To what extent did employees depend on their close relationship to St. Clair to satisfy their need for influence, and to what extent could Goble satisfy that need through a stronger use of the organizational structure itself?

Human Resources

Not as much attention was paid to flow as to some other elements of SEP's work system. Still, the matter was not ignored and did create some problems. Consider the following points:

1. All new nonexempt employees were put through a 13-session orientation program. There was some concern, expressed by St. Clair as well as the employees themselves, that expectations had been built up too high by these sessions.
2. There was a problem getting people to serve as advisors, SEP's first-line supervisors (compare to similar problems caused by somewhat different reasons at the Kalamazoo plant). Those promoted from the teams did not seem to be working well, often complaining of dull work and long hours. SEP had trouble attracting qualified people from the outside. Traditional first-line supervisors might have shied away because the job at SEP did not include their traditional authoritarian power (the advisors were more "facilitators" than "foremen"). Others might have stayed away because the job was seen as a dead-end one.
3. The management of human resource flow from top SEP management ranks into other American Diesel assignments had its pluses and minuses. On the plus side, American Diesel was attempting to spread SEP's managers throughout their system in order to spread this new organizational philosophy. On the minus side, 15 of the top 25 managers left at about the same time, and their departures coincided with the changeover from St. Clair to Goble. This sudden shift probably damaged the trust level so important to SEP's operations. Perhaps enriched, innovative work systems inherently seek strong, consistent leadership, and a company engaging in such innovation should reevaluate its traditional flow policies.

The issue of recruiting employees at the lowest level of the organization—the team member—does not come up directly in the case. Nonetheless, students often bring up the matter of a need for "fit" or "conformity" between the values of the work system and the values of the people who come to work for Sedalia. As can be learned from discussions of the pay system, SEP pays well in relationship to the rest of the Sedalia community, so they have little trouble attracting potential employees. Since the case was written, the plant has given thought to the need for some prescreening, especially around the issue of values. A videotape has since been developed in which potential employees are told in rather blunt terms by current employees of the special strains inherent in a high-commitment system (quite similar to the discussion in the case of stress). Recruits will then, at least it is hoped, select themselves out of the hiring process if they do not fit.

SEP's top management candidly admits that there is a similar need for some degree of conformity, especially around values, of management-level recruits. The special skills of managing in a setting where *process* is as important as *content* can be learned, they believe, over a 6- to 12-month period (that may be a somewhat optimistic estimation, depending on the experiences of the individual). But they must accept the basic values and assumptions of Sedalia. Otherwise, they will have great difficulty and may have to be encouraged to leave.

A number of scholars have noted that failure to give due attention to the culture of an organization and the demands of its work system and to the implications of that assessment for the types of people needed can actually increase conflict, turnover, and resistence. While many sophisticated screening techniques such as psychological tests, assessment procedures, and computer-reactive tests exist, they are often calibrated statistically against narrow criteria of traditionally defined job performance. A recent survey of new developments in preemployment testing concluded, in fact, that while a number of companies are interested in the possibility of looking at values as well as skills among recruits, little real movement has taken place in this area. Perhaps as matters like values, culture, and fit become increasingly important to organizations, they will seek new recruitment procedures, some of which—assessment centers, group interviews, self-screening—students have been introduced to in this course, as ways of seeking cultural fit.

Job Design

The assumption underlying the way jobs are designed at Sedalia is that jobs that allow employees to experience achievement, responsibility, advancement, recognition, and growth in competence will increase motivation.[1] Hackman and Oldham[2] have refined that approach to motivation by identifying the specific core functions of a job that can be said to be motivators:

1. Skill variety
2. Task identity
3. Task significance
4. Autonomy
5. Feedback

An examination of the design of work for nonexempts at Sedalia shows how that design significantly impacts on each of these five core dimensions:

1. *Skill variety.* By requiring all members of a team to learn how to set up, operate, and maintain their equipment, and to perform housekeeping tasks, Sedalia has increased the variety of activities, skills, and talents required of employees.
2. *Task identity.* Except on the assembly line, teams are organized around "whole" tasks like manufacturing pistons, piston rings, and flywheels so that all team members are involved in the completion of an identifiable piece of work. Even on the assembly line, groups of workers are held responsible for successful assembly of some subpart of the total assembly process with buffer stock separating the segments of the assembly line.
3. *Task significance.* With the emphasis on team work and interdependence, team members can experience the impact of their individual contribution on others and on the organization. By providing teams with details on cost-per-piece performance, management also provides team members the opportunity to understand how they have contributed to meeting plant goals.
4. *Autonomy.* While plant management sets general goals (cost and monthly output goals), each team has substantial discretion in determining specific improvement goals and how these goals will be met. Individual autonomy is enhanced further by the elimination of time clocks, with each team responsible for scheduling.
5. *Feedback.* Through the elaborate cost-per-piece accounting system, team members obtain clear and direct information about their performance. Individual performance is reviewed annually by the team advisor and peers.

With the enrichment of these characteristics, say Hackman and Oldham, employees will experience meaningfulness of work, responsibility, and knowledge of results. The predicted outcomes—high internal work motivation, high-quality work performance, and high work satisfaction—seem to apply to the Sedalia plant and have been shown to manifest themselves in practice through reduced absenteeism and turnover, and improvements in productivity and quality, and those improvements have been sustained over time.

A problem in this job design faced by SEP was that some teams matured faster than others (the organization development [OD] director estimates that only 25 percent of teams are truly mature). Those teams that are mature become virtually self-managing, while less-mature teams depend more on team advisor for direction, training, housekeeping, evaluation, and discipline. Advisors were often seen by team members as an important obstacle to achieving maturity. Some placed pressure on team members to stay on their manufacturing assignments rather than attend to vertical tasks. One team, the cambox team, apparently matured faster than their advisor. Following serious quality problems, team members went around their advisor to redesign the entire team.

Rewards

Consistent with its rather flat organizational structure, SEP eliminated many of the reward differentials that traditionally exist in a plant: there are no status symbols (special parking places or eating facilities, for instance) and both exempt and nonexempt (a distinction demanded by law) employees are paid by salary. Nonexempt employees can take time off during the week, but are expected to make up that missed time. The most important aspect of the compensation structure is that it is skill-based rather than job-based. Some important points about a skill-based system are summarized in Table 7–4.

The five-level, nonexempt, skill-based salaries were at first tied to wage levels in the Sedalia community. That was changed in 1977 when pay levels were more or less tied to union-negotiated wages in Beacon. The given reason for the change was that Sedalia's economy was depressed and wages

TABLE 7–4
Important Points in Skill-Based Pay System

1. People-based rather than job-based
2. Opportunities
   a. Job rotation
   b. Encourages learning new skills
3. Potential problems
   a. People will reach top of skill level—then what?
   b. Calls for large investment (time and money) in training
   c. External equity
      (1) To whom will employees compare themselves?
      (2) Rising expectations
      (3) Cost of measurement
      (4) Validity of measurement
      (5) Skill acquisition versus performance
   d. Administration
      (1) Who will measure skills?

tended to be low. Unspoken was the desire to remove another possible reason to support unionization.

The rewards system at SEP has caused some specific problems which are dealt with in the cases:

1. Any real evaluation of skills has all but disappeared (there is some disagreement on the extent to which it has disappeared), and promotions to the next higher skill level and associated raises are occurring almost without exception. Therefore, they are, in effect, based on seniority. There is no evidence, however, that the acquisition of new skills is not continuing, motivated most likely by peer pressure more than the threat of failing a skill test.

2. Problems of both external (what level of worker at Beacon, with its traditional job design, will SEP workers look to for comparison?) and internal (team members versus skilled tradespeople) equity, arising mainly out of the problem of rising expectations.

3. How much participation to allow in designing reward system? St. Clair believes that self-interest is too dominant in the area of pay to allow for extensive participation: "Compensation is one of those areas I don't think should be too participatory. I tried to keep people informed about what we were doing, but me and my directors made final decisions ourselves. Seeking too much participation on compensation issues can get you in trouble" (from videotape, "Managing in a High-Commitment Work System"). There is evidence that self-interest has intervened with the intended functioning of peer evaluation. Some team members are reluctant to oppose openly the awarding of a skill-based increment to a fellow member. As one team member says, "Nobody wants to stand up at a meeting and say so-and-so shouldn't get a raise this year. If you do that, what's going to happen to you when it's time for your raise to be considered?" As will be seen in the (B) case, Goble favors more participation than St. Clair in the matter of pay. The issue is one that will probably create some debate and disagreement among students, just as it has between St. Clair and Goble.

4. As more nonexempt workers reach the fifth (top) skill level, how will the compensation system motivate them to acquire new skills, and will it keep them satisfied with their pay when it has plateaued?

Case Problem

At the conclusion of the (A) case, there are certain specific problems with which Danney Goble must deal. Any action plan must be carefully considered, however, so that it either fits or reinforces SEP's culture *or* consciously and purposefully changes parts of the culture that need changing.

1. *Leadership turnover.* There is little Goble can do about the large turnover in SEP's top management ranks. But what, if anything,

can or should he do about the perceived differences in leadership style between himself and St. Clair?

2. *Corrective action process.* Teams were having difficulty with disciplinary problems (fighting, sleeping on the job, absenteeism), and the corrective action process (informal counseling by team members and advisor) seemed to offer little help.

3. *Economic downturn.* With engine orders falling off dramatically, Goble faces the possibility of layoffs (20 workers, or 4 percent).

4. *Nonexempt worker compensation.* Layoffs at the Beacon plant have, because of the compensation tie-in, led to smaller than expected raises for most nonexempts, while the small group of skilled trades people have received considerably larger raises. Goble must consider:
   a. Whether to stick with the old compensation formula
   b. If and when to open up the formula to a complete review and possible overhaul
   c. How much participation should be allowed in that process, and how that participation should be managed

5. *Union.* The independent Machine Workers of America, who represent Beacon's employees, have started an organizing campaign in Sedalia.

The following actions are then described in the (B) case:

1. *Leadership turnover.* Goble feels that, because the plant has grown and matured, the organizational chart should be adhered to more closely, particularly the roles of directors and business manager. St. Clair has raised a question about this approach (*not* in the case) that should be considered: will stricter adherence to rules and charts interfere with flexibility and innovation?

2. *Corrective action process.* A new performance improvement process has been designed which keeps disciplinary matters within the teams, but offers increased training and support. Likewise, the specific problem of absenteeism will be dealt with by offering teams more data, but keeping the decision about how to act *within* the team (a proposal to impose from above a specific definition of "excess absenteeism" was rejected).

3. *Economic downturn.* Through a series of measures (swing teams, cutbacks in contract help, voluntary one-month layoffs), SEP avoided the massive layoffs of the Beacon plant (there were no layoffs at SEP). Throughout the crisis, Goble shared all financial information with team members. While there is some question as to whether he tooted his own horn enough ("It was great . . . and the whole thing was St. Clair's idea"), his handling of the situation seemed to have built a great deal of trust in his leadership.

4. *Nonexempt compensation.* Goble stuck with the old formula and seriously underestimated the emotional importance of internal and external equity. Perhaps, more important, he overestimated the coincidence of interests between workers and management on compensation matters. He then set up a special task force, ERG, and carefully insisted that ERG constituted not a collective bargaining agency, but an advisory board. Goble was generally pleased with the results. ERG's proposals showed the rising expectations of SEP's workers who now wanted fourth-level workers to be compared with some Beacon employees with 15 or 20 years experience.

There are several compensation questions left unanswered at the end of the (B) case:

   a. How can these rising expectations be managed?
   b. Will the plant have to move to some sort of a gain-sharing plan?
   c. Can skills evaluations be made more rigorous? Should they be?
   d. How can the skill-based pay system be extended to offer continual growth for those at the fifth level?

5. *Union.* The union drew little support, but the question is raised of what will happen if POT rejects ERG's compensation proposals?

CONCLUSION

Any well-designed work system can be seen as working on three levels: design techniques, work culture ideals, and intended results.[3] The specific elements of each are indicated in the table below, and SEP's work system can be judged on the basis of how well it meets each of these intended outcome levels (see Table 7–5).

The principles reflected in the above three-level work improvement structure are summarized in Table 7–6.

What are the important lessons of the case?

1. Philosophy and values can be a powerful part of a work design system.
2. There is a trend in the design of work toward self-conscious innovations to enlarge coincidence of interests between employer and employee.
3. SEP is an example of encouraging and managing cooperation within organization:
   a. HRM can enlarge and exploit potential integration of interests.
   b. SEP shows potential danger of ignoring inherent conflicts.
4. Managing participation requires a new set of skills. Participative work design will require managers to be more skilled in[4]:
   a. Selecting and training subordinates who can successfully fit into such a system

TABLE 7-5
Three Levels of Work System

Level I: Design Techniques

—Job design	—Pay	—Supervisors' role
—Training	—Performance feedback	—Goal-setting
—Communication	—Employment stability	—Status symbols
—Leadership patterns	policies	

Level II: Work Culture Ideals

—High skill levels and flexibility in using them	—Identification with product, process, and total business viewpoint
—Influence by expertise and information rather than position	—Mutual influence
—Responsiveness	—Trust
—Egalitarian climate	—Joint problem-solving
—Equity	—Openness

Level III: Intended Results

FOR BUSINESS	FOR QUALITY OF WORK LIFE
—Low costs	—Self-esteem
—Quick delivery	—Economic well-being
—High-quality products	—Security
—Low absenteeism	
—Equipment utilization	

Source: Richard E. Walton, "Work Innovations in the United States," in Michael Beer and Bert Spector, eds., *Readings in Human Resource Management* (New York: Free Press, 1985).

    b. Designing and running meetings

    c. Dealing with conflicts between strong individuals and groups

    d. Influencing and negotiating from a lower power base than in a traditional system

5. Work design involves trade-offs between individual and business needs, but proper choices can strengthen *both* sets of needs.

TABLE 7-6
Principles of Work System

1. Commitment to results, pragmatism in selecting techniques to achieve results
2. Test all hypotheses about enhancing human experience at work—no universal set of principles and priorities regarding QWL.
3. Most techniques affect business and human results *indirectly*, affecting organizational *climate* first.
4. Designing work structure requires attention to two sets of goals: business results *and* QWL.
5. Techniques of work design—rewards, division of labor, performance reporting, status symbols—should be internally consistent.

Source: Richard E. Walton, "Work Innovations in the United States," in Michael Beer and Bert Spector, eds., *Readings in Human Resource Management* (New York: Free Press, 1985).

Audiovisual Material

Instructors who intend to use the available videotape, "Managing in a High-Commitment Work System," should know that Richard Allison is the undisguised name of "Donald St. Clair" and Craig Colburn is the undisguised name of "Danney Goble." The tape opens with their discussion of the handling of the compensation crisis as summarized in the (B) case (Allison/St. Clair believes too much participation was allowed; Colburn/Goble believes that was about the right amount of participation) and then features a discussion about the special stresses, opportunities, and skills required of managing in a high-commitment work system such as the one featured in "Sedalia Engine Plant." The videotape closes with a brief discussion by the president of American Diesel (from an address delivered at the Harvard Business School) on the "proper" and "improper" ways business schools tend to train future managers.

TEACHING PLAN

Day 1—(A) Case

10 min. 1. To involve students in the discussion, a poll can be taken on whether students would like to manage in such a setting as SEP and their reasons for that choice. A similar poll can be conducted at the end of the discussion, and students who have changed their minds can explain why.

Instructors can then move either to the specific design elements of SEP and then to the general philosophy and assumptions that underlie that philosophy, or vice versa. This plan will move to the specific first and then to general, but points two and three can be reversed.

25 min. 2. What are the key design elements and how do they reflect these assumptions?

30 min. 3. What are the philosophy and assumptions that guide the work system design at SEP? Discussion should go beyond the four "key building blocks"—trust, growth, excellence, equity—to the operational assumptions about people and work (see p. 236).

   a. Employee influence
      (1) Governance structure (BOR) meant to supply influence to all employees, particularly nonexempt (in lieu of union)
      (2) Importance of leadership—St. Clair
      (3) Fireside chats
      (4) Task force
      (5) Participation in team decisions about day-to-day activities

(6) Self-policing on disciplinary problems

(7) Can appeal to plant manager

b. Flow

    (1) Orientation and training

    (2) Initial management team stayed together through start-up and early period of plant operations.

c. Rewards

    (1) Peer evaluation

    (2) All-salaried pay system, lack of status symbols adds to equity

    (3) Skills evaluation—people rather than job-based, opportunities for flexibility and problems

d. Job design

    (1) Semiautonomous teams responsible for operating, maintenance, and administrative tasks

    (2) Team advisor concept

    (3) Organization structure integrates manufacturing and support functions under one manager.

    (4) Extensive cost-per-piece information system.

25 min.   4. What specific problems does Goble face at the end of the case, and what can be done about them? Students should be pushed to be specific about what they want to do to solve the problem and how they intend to do it.

a. Leadership turnover

b. Corrective action process

c. Economic downturn (What do students plan to do if they do not want to lay off workers?)

d. Nonexempt worker compensation (A lot of time can be spent on this very difficult and sensitive problem.)

e. Union

Day 2—(B) Case

30 min.   1. Evaluate Danney Goble's action.

a. Strengthening of POT and relations with business managers (Was Goble right to change his relationship with business managers?)

b. No layoffs—sharing of information (Was too much information shared?)

c. Corrective action (Is this adequate?)

d. Compensation (Too much participation? What are the dangers?)

e. What is the prospect for unionization? Can work innovations like this be installed in a union setting? If a union did get in what would be the effects?

15 min.   2. What are the special stresses of working at SEP as a team member and as a manager? What is the source of the stress? What

	special skills and competencies would be required to work there?
15 min.	3. Show videotape of St. Clair and Goble and president of company talking about Sedalia Engine Plant and philosophy of management.
30 min.	4. What is your evaluation of SEP?

    a. How would *you* like to manage in a setting like Sedalia? What do you think would be the advantages and disadvantages of working there?

    b. What is SEP's outlook for the future? What problems might it face in the near future? The long run? Will their philosophy be an asset or a liability? How is this type of work system vulnerable?

    d. What problems would you see in spreading the work design system features of Sedalia to other new plants the company might build? Which design elements would you change?

One-Class Design

Those instructors who wish to teach SEP in one class rather than two might concentrate on questions 1, 2, and 3 of day 1, show the videotape, then go to question 4 of day 2.

NOTES

1. F. L. Herzberg, B. Manser, and B. Snyderman, *The Motivation to Work* (New York: John Wiley & Sons, 1959).
2. J. R. Hackman and Greg R. Oldham, *Work Redesign* (Reading, MA: Addison-Wesley, 1980).
3. Richard E. Walton, "Work Innovations in the United States," in Michael Beer and Bert Spector, eds., *Readings in Human Resource Management* (New York: Free Press, 1985).
4. Adapted from Edgar H. Schein, "Increasing Organizational Effectiveness Through Better Resource Planning and Development," in Michael Beer and Bert Spector, eds., *Readings in Human Resource Management* (New York: Free Press, 1985).

OFFICE TECHNOLOGY, INC.
Teaching Note

Faced with the responsibility of standardizing the order administration (OA) system for all product lines within OTI's scientific markets group, Robert Dorr uses the opportunity to think carefully about what approach to work system design he would want to apply across all OA groups. The OEM group and the laboratory and medical products (LMP) group provide quite different approaches to organizing work and workers, and the managers of each of these groups believes their approach is the "right" one for all OA groups. When no consensus can be reached on a uniform work system, Dorr decides on semiautonomous work teams, announces that decision to the board, and leads discussions about how to implement the team concept.

The purpose of this case is to continue examining how work systems may be changed in the office to incorporate high-commitment principles. At the same time, this case introduces students to the problems of changing a work system from a traditional (model A) system to a high-commitment system (model B). Finally, the videotapes of the two work groups provide an in-depth exposure to autonomous work group issues.

ASSIGNMENT QUESTIONS

Students should read the (A) case and come to class prepared to discuss the following questions:

1. What are the elements of the LMP work system and what are the elements of the OEM work system?
2. How would you compare the results (outcomes) of the two groups?
3. How would you evaluate Dorr's decision to adopt the team concept? What are the roadblocks to implementing that concept?

CASE ANALYSIS

Before moving to a discussion of possible action alternatives for Robert Dorr, students should possess a thorough understanding of the basic OA task, of how the two groups—OEM and LMP—function, of what conditions are necessary to make them work, and of the outcomes of the two groups. Another necessary element for students to have is an understanding of the larger organization: its structures and culture. A key element in the debate over which of the two alternative work group structures to adopt involves the question of which fits better into the overall structure and culture of the organization. It also involves personal values; those of the managers in OEM (Everhart and Hancock) and those of the students.

The Organization

Office Technology, Inc. (OTI) is a computer and word processing systems manufacturer and supplier. In 1979 OTI's revenues were $1.4 billion, with profits of $144 million. Their sales and net income had quadrupled in the previous five years. At the time of the case, OTI employed 35,000 people, all of whom were nonunion.

Prior to 1978 OTI was comprised of 14 separate and autonomous operating groups. In an effort to increase control and decrease intergroup competition, OTI created three "supergroups" in 1978, of which the scientific markets group was one. Robert Dorr was the administrative manager of that group. The scientific markets group in turn, was made up of five products groups, each of which had its own OA group. Three of the groups—engineering products, education products, and government products—were located at OTI's Menlo Park facility, where Robert Dorr maintained his own office, and were managed by John Haley. The other two groups—OEM and LMP—were located together at Los Altos, about an hour's drive from Menlo Park.

Since OEM and LMP are the two groups upon which the case concentrates, students should understand exactly what their reporting relationships are. Figure 7–2 presents those relationships as they stood at the time of the events in the case. But students should understand that Dorr has decided to change that reporting relationship. He has informed both Tim Everhart and

FIGURE 7–2
Los Altos OA Organization

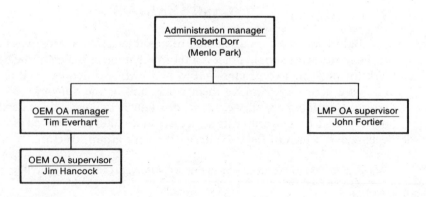

250

TABLE 7-7
Sequence of OA Tasks

1. Distribution—get orders from computer and place in folders*
2. Administrative editing—edit orders to see that they meet all requirements—most complex step (30 minutes)
3. Data entering—enter order data into computer (15 to 30 minutes)
4. Scheduling—schedule order for delivery based on manufacturing capacity and materials availability (15 minutes)
5. Booking and acknowledgment—notify headquarters and field office of order

*Although not stated in the case, this task takes about 20 minutes.

John Fortier that "sometime in the future" Tim would be made manager of both OA groups at Los Altos (a position comparable to Jim Haley's at Menlo Park) with John reporting to Tim rather than to Dorr.

OTI Culture

The case allows students to identify two key elements of the OTI culture: people-orientation and encouragement of individual entrepreneurship. The culture seems to reflect the personal values and philosophy of OTI's president, James Ingalls: "I believe that the worker always knows more about his job than his boss. And as the company becomes larger, our challenge is to see that we don't stifle our people."

The OA Task

At the core of the analysis of the two work systems is an understanding of the task itself. The case presents a sequence of tasks that is common to all OA groups. Those steps, along with the estimated time required to complete each step, are summarized in Table 7-7. The case also presents the four core OA jobs, summarized in Table 7-8.

TABLE 7-8
Profile of OEM and LMP Groups

Work Group Characteristics	OEM	LMP
No. nonsupervisory personnel	20	9
No. new orders received per quarter	2,500	2,000
Average no. changes per order	2.5	4
Average order size	$50,000	$30,000
Order range	$10,000–$200,000	$1,000–$1,000,000
Average no. days to process order	5	9

The first important difference between the two groups is in how the task itself is accomplished. While the two groups differ in both size and in number and amount of orders received (Table 7–8 offers a brief profile of the two groups derived from the case), they still have the same task to perform. The way in which they organize the task is quite different.

In OEM, workers are assigned to a specific step in the sequence. Once they perform that step, they place the completed order in a slot, then pick up a new order from another slot. Any problems with an order (pricing errors, customer changes) are given to supervisors for handling. Problems of material availability or manufacturing schedules are also handled by supervisors.

By contrast, while the nature of the LMP task is much the same, the way in which the task is organized is quite different. The group itself has developed a computer program that automatically performs step 3 (data entry) and even performs much of the editing. The remaining tasks—including negotiating directly with manufacturing and materials personnel, dealing directly with product line representatives, and handling problems encountered at any phase—are performed by members of the group themselves rather than by supervisors.

Outcomes

Referring to Table 7–8, it can seen that the OEM group processes more orders of a higher average size and in less time than does the LMP group. LMP, on the other hand, processes more complex orders (judging from the average number of changes per order) that can be five times larger than an OEM order with fewer people. The four day difference in average time needed to process an order needs to be considered against the fact that the "time lag between scheduling [done by the OA group] and filling [done by the product line] an order, even when materials are available, can stretch anywhere from *two to nine months*." Both groups, we are told, perform well during the "absolute mayhem" of the regular—and apparently uncorrectable—end-of-the-quarter crunch. The difference is in attitude: OEM people complain about the "toll" of the crunches, while an LMP person sees the crunch as an exciting (and "fun") challenge.

That difference in attitude gets at another set of outcomes, and students should be pressed to see that there are many facets to the outcomes of any HRM policy. Turnover is an outcome that needs to be considered. Of course, different organizations will assign different weights to the cost of their turnover; depending on such variables as difficulty and cost of recruitment, selection, and training, and the need for experienced workers. In this case, there is a marked difference between both rates of turnover and attitudes toward turnover on the part of the two managers. Almost *all* OEM personnel, we are told, leave the group after only six months to a year; and fully 50 percent of those leave, Tim Everhart acknowledges, "just to get away from OEM." LMP, by contrast, has lost two employees in two years; both for non-work-related issues (an 11 percent annual turnover rate compared to a 95 percent annual turnover rate for OEM).

Tim is apparently not dissatisfied with the high turnover in his group. There are a great many other potential hires, he believes, who will be attracted to OTI for a variety of reasons, so finding and selecting replacements will be an easy process. The need for experienced workers, furthermore, is minimal, since OA employees in the OEM group have little autonomy, responsibility, or variety as part of their tasks. As will be discussed in greater detail in the section below on selection, LMP's selection process is more complex, involving a great deal of the supervisor's time. It can be assumed that a need to select a large number of new hires in LMP would be viewed as a considerable burden and cost by John Fortier.

The outcomes in terms of commitment also vary widely between the two groups. OEM personnel, we are told, have little understanding of or respect for other parts of the OTI organization, especially management. LMP personnel, on the other hand, feel committed, recognized, and rewarded.

Other Elements of the Work System

An important lesson from the case is that the manner in which jobs are designed comprises only a part of the overall work system. "OTI" (A) gives students the opportunity to examine, in some detail, the conditions that affect the way the two work groups function.

Supervisory Attitudes. The difference in the attitudes of Tim Everhart and John Fortier (summarized, using their own quotes, in Table 7–9) is

TABLE 7–9
Contrasting Supervisory Attitudes

Tim Everhart	John Fortier
Job is "babysitting."	"In my career at OTI I've worked with a lot of autocrats. . . . My goal in life is to . . . do things different."
"Hourly people . . . are not paid to make decisions."	"I rolled up my sleeves and I went out on the floor and said 'I want you to teach me how to process an order.' "
"My faith in human nature isn't exactly what you would call positive."	"I told them [LMP personnel] if they would tell me what was really wrong . . . we would change it . . . if we could."
"If you give people an inch, they'll take a mile. It's human nature."	

striking. John Hancock, the supervisor under Tim, seems somewhat ambivalent, although he strongly sides with Tim in the September 24th debate.

As seen in the summary of comments, the differences between Tim and John are in both attitude and style. Tim is rather aloof, spending most of his time in his office, waiting for problems to be brought to him. John, although his office is also physically separated from his group, has worked side-by-side with his employees: learning from them and building a close, trusting, and even personal relationship with them. John has nurtured a "helping" norm within the group by giving people responsibility for making both individual and group decisions. He encourages the group to hold weekly team meetings without him, and allows them to schedule any extra work on their own. The job design itself demands a degree of flexibility and cooperation on the part of LMP employees missing from the OEM group.

Clearly, the organization of the two groups reflects the values and styles of the two managers. The problem that Dorr will have to address if he should decide to adopt the team approach for all OA groups is that Tim's supervisory style would not be conducive to the delegation of authority and responsibility or the nurturing of a helping norm. Not only might Tim have difficulty creating and sustaining a teamwork culture in OEM, but he will soon also be the responsible manager for LMP as well.

Selection. The issue of building some sensitivity for the culture of an organization into the selection process was discussed in some detail in the "Sedalia Engine Plant" teaching note. Students can now see the sensitivity operationalized in OEM and LMP. Tim Everhart has little reason to devise an elaborate selection process, due to both the nature of the OEM tasks and the rate of turnover. For the same reasons—little turnover and a great deal of task flexibility and responsibility—John Fortier pays close attention to the selection process. He spends hours interviewing candidates, looking not only at their technical skills but also at their ability to fit into the work group culture. He defines those attributes as:

—"A positive frame of mind"
—"Potential for creative thought"
—"Ability to take the ball and run with it"
—"Good attitude concerning cooperation"

While Tim generally recruits new hires from outside the organization, John has taken his replacements from inside; presumably in order to have people in his group who already understand the OTI culture.

Appraisals. Performance appraisals in OEM involve a rather formal process in which the supervisor and the employee fill out an evaluation form every six months and meet together to discuss the results and discrepancies. In contrast, John Fortier meets once a week with his LMP employees to provide and receive feedback on performance. As formal appraisal time approaches, the dialogue becomes more focused. As a result, performance feedback is more regular and frequent, while the formal appraisal "contained no surprises" for the appraisee. As discussed in the "SEP" teaching note, feedback is one of the five core job functions that Hackman and Oldham have identified as motivators. Moreover, John Fortier's approach approximates more closely the guidelines for performance appraisal discussed in connection with the "Colonial Food Services" case and summarized in the "Note on Performance Appraisal."

Rewards. It is clear from the comments in the case that, due to job design and supervisory styles, LMP personnel find greater intrinsic rewards in their jobs than do OEM personnel, and also feel rewarded and recognized by the organization. Pay policies are, of course, standard across groups; with wage ranges assigned to jobs and individuals moved within a range largely according to performance. But while pay policies may be the same, there is a likelihood that attitudes toward pay differ across groups. Particularly where pay for performance is involved, research has indicated that the more frequent are the formal and informal reviews of performance, the greater an individual's preference for a merit increase system (as compared with a seniority system) will be.[1] Because LMP personnel receive weekly performance feedback, while OEM personnel receive appraisals once every six months, satisfaction with performance based increases is likely to be higher in LMP.

Development. Although Tim Everhart hopes that his people will be highly regarded throughout OTI, he sees little opportunity for advancement *within* the function: "There is just no career path in OA." John Fortier takes the opposite position, emphasizing to his personnel the opportunity for growth and development within OA. John also spends time educating his people about the role of OA in the entire organization (an education reinforced through experience by direct contact with field and product line people), while OEM people developed only a "narrow understanding" of the larger organization. It is not surprising that half the people who left OEM did so because they were looking for growth opportunities, while LMP people apparently found opportunities for growth within the group.

Action Planning

The divergent positions of Tim Everhart and John Fortier on work structures are clearly spelled out at the September 25th meeting (see Table 7-10). The Menlo Park groups present a third alternative: work organized mainly on production line basis, but with some OA personnel receiving special training in problem-solving.

TABLE 7–10

Views on Work Systems

Tim Everhart	John Fortier
Product Line	*Team Approach*
—In order to meet goals of *standardization and efficiency*, a *pipeline organization* needed with each individual performing a *single function*, as *little identification* or specialization by product line as possible, with *all* problem-solving being done by supervisors.	—Emphasizes need and desirability for individuals to perform *multiple tasks*, becoming involved with *problem-solving*, familiar with a particular product line, able to *identify* with product line people.

In analyzing Robert Dorr's actions, students can start by asking two questions:

1. Dorr was asked to develop a uniform order processing system, and used this mandate as a springboard for reexamining the structure of the work itself. Students can debate whether he was well advised in doing so.
2. Should Dorr have imposed a work system on the groups, as he did at the end of the case? Can new values, attitudes, and style be imposed upon Tim (or upon John should Dorr decide in favor of the OEM approach)? Instead of imposing a decision, should he have waited for Tim to be moved over both LMP and OEM, thus allowing the groups to evolve naturally? What would the costs and gains of either approach have been?

Students should be pressed on these issues as they attempt to offer action suggestions.

After debating the relative merits of Dorr's decision for standardization and his desire to impose a decision, students can analyze the relative merits of the two work systems, discussing such issues as job design, supporting conditions, and outcomes. However, the emphasis will be on how to introduce the "team concept." Then, students can be asked what roadblocks Dorr would face in implementing the team concept:

1. *Tim Everhart will manage both groups, but is he committed to the concept?* One action suggestion would be to delay Tim's promotion, but students need to weigh the possible outcomes of that action in terms of Tim's attitudes. Students might also suggest special training for Tim, Jim Hancock, and OA employees; perhaps using John Fortier and LMP personnel as trainers. Students can be pressed here to identify what such training would consist of.
2. *Selection and appraisal.* Should OEM continue to select and appraise as they have done in the past, or should they change their

methods of selection and appraisal to conform to LMP? Is Jim Hancock capable of making the same judgments about the ability of people to fit into a team culture as John Fortier can? Should some other method(s) be employed to help insure fit with the team culture? Team interviews? Peer evaluation?

3. *Supervisory selection and appraisal.* Special consideration should be given to how supervisors are selected and appraised in the future. Building off previous discussions on the "Kalamazoo Plant" and "SEP" cases, students can be pressed to suggest specific selection and evaluation criteria for future supervisors.

4. *Structural changes.* Prior to Tim's reassignment, there are two managers specifically assigned to the 20 OEM people; now there will be just a supervisor. Is one supervisor for a group of 20 people that accounts for 40 percent of the scientific markets group's overall revenue enough? Should further structural changes be made? Perhaps adding another layer of OEM management or splitting the OEM personnel between two supervisors? Obviously the number of supervisors required will depend on the job design concept. If a team approach is chosen, one supervisor should be sufficient.

5. *Staffing assignments.* Should we assume that Jim Hancock and John Fortier will remain in OEM and LMP, respectively? Can their assignments be switched to allow John to help build the team concept in OEM and Jim to learn from LMP personnel? Remember, Jim has worked in a more "democratic" atmosphere before coming to OEM and reports that such an environment "worked much better."

6. *Job design.* Students can be pressed to say precisely how they would reorganize the work in OEM and what, if anything, they would change in the current job descriptions. This discussion will be the longest and most detailed. It should include a discussion of how work teams would be organized in OEM, around regions (geographic regions was OTI's choice), client product line groups, plants that will manufacture the product.

7. *Oversight of the process.* How will the employees in OEM participate in an effort to move to the "team concept?" How will they make sure that the process, once it is put in place, continues to work smoothly or will they suggest appropriate mid-course corrections? The person responsible for this should be Robert Dorr. But will his physical distance from the Los Altos facility hamper his ability to spot oversights? Does it make sense to move his office to Los Altos to be right on top of the largest and biggest-revenue OA group? What would be the impact of such a move on Menlo Park? What consulting resources will be needed by OEM from John Fortier and/or organization development specialists?

The Change Itself

OTI (B) provides a quick overview of the approximately two-year period that followed the September 24th meeting. The case can be used either to analyze the implementation and change process, or to be handed out at the end of class to inform students of the events (depending on whether a one- or two-class design is planned).

The primary events, as recounted in the (B) case, are summarized in Table 7–11. If classroom discussion affords the opportunity to analyze implementation and change procedures, important questions can be raised about each step of the change process:

1. *Dorr's unilateral decision to change.* If this point has not been touched on in previous discussions, it should come up now.
2. *Tim Everhart's "conversion."* Tim's conversion to "giving people total responsibility for their work and for solving their own problems" seems rather sudden and dramatic. Students may question the sincerity of such a conversion (perhaps attributing Everhart's motive to "getting on board" rather than real understanding). On the other hand, students may wonder whether his conversion is too

TABLE 7–11
Chronology of the Change Process in OA

September 1979
—Dorr decides to organize all OA groups into work teams. After one-on-one meeting with outside consultant, Tim Everhart "sees the light" and supports team approach.
—Tim Everhart and Jim Hancock receive training on managing a team, with John Fortier serving as a resource.
—Robert Dorr heavily involved in implementing change at Menlo Park.

February 1980
—Implementation schedule for OEM change delayed.
—All OA staff at Los Altos given training through cases and team-building exercises.
—OEM personnel told to reorganize into four- and five-member regional teams with each team developing its own procedures for administrative orders.

April 1980
—Implementation schedule for OEM change delayed again.
—Robert Dorr resigns from OTI.

September 1980
—Changes implemented at Los Altos:
—Tim Everhart made manager of two groups.
—Jim Hancock's and John Fortier's positions upgraded to manager.
—Jim Hancock hires new OEM supervisor.
—"Contribution to team" added to performance appraisal.

September 1980
—John Fortier leaves OA.

extreme ("giving people *total responsibility*") and will lead to unrealistically high expectations on Tim's part, as well as on the part of OA personnel whom Tim will later help train. The problems that this creates later can be seen in the videotape of the OEM group and Jim Hancock.

3. *Training*. Students may question whether the training procedures were adequate. We know little about the training of Everhart and Hancock, but learn more details on the staff training. Cases and team-building exercises seem somewhat abstract and removed from the "real world" of OA. Apparently, no "real-world" exercises were used in which people dealt with real, occurring OA issues and problems in the presence of trained facilitators. There is evidence, presented by both employees and Tim, that by the time OEM people moved into teams they possessed a low level of interpersonal and problem-solving skills.

4. *Delays in implementation*. These constant delays, justified by Tim on the basis of changes occurring in the product line organization, may have signaled to employees a lack of true confidence on Tim's part in the ability of team members to deal with uncertainties and solve problems.

5. *Organization of regional teams*. The manner in which this decision was implemented can be faulted on two grounds. First, after telling people they would be able to select their own team co-members and raising expectations that it would be a thoughtful process, Tim suddenly gave people the order to divide up into teams. Second, within OEM there was ironically no standardized procedure set. Each team developed its own procedures. That decision may have undermined, to some extent, identification and cooperation between teams, and added particular stress to the handling of the "special projects" described at the end of the case.

6. *Robert Dorr's resignation*. It was apparent that Dorr was a very "hands-on" manager who gave most of his attention to the Menlo Park operation, where his own office was located. That same kind of direct pressure and facilitation may have been of great help to the Los Altos groups. Although the change process is in place when he leaves the company, his absence creates a gap in terms of who will nurture the process along, a gap that is apparently not filled at the end of the case.

7. *Follow-up facilitation*. A dramatic change process like the one OEM is undertaking will almost always require a great deal of careful and *sustained* attention. Once Dorr has left, the sustained attention is apparently lacking. There is no follow-up training or continued monitoring of the system. No internal consulting help is provided by the personnel department.

8. *Hiring a new supervisor.* Students can wonder whether Jim Hancock possesed a sufficiently sophisticated understanding of the dynamics of autonomous work groups to be able to make a proper supervisory choice. Tim says the new supervisor is great at facilitation and feedback, but students may again wonder at Tim's sophistication in making such judgments. The case does not say whether the new supervisor came from inside or outside the company (she came from outside), but the question can be asked whether it might have been wise to hire a supervisor from within the groups, especially from the LMP group. There are indications in the videotape of the OEM group that the new supervisor did not have the skills to manage the team concept.

The case closes with a discussion of special projects, and the negative impact those projects were having on morale. These special projects were handled on a national rather than a regional basis. Special project teams would thus be required to deal with all regional OEM teams. The fact that the OEM group had no standardized administrative procedures made the relationship between special project teams and regional teams difficult and confusing. Also, students can discuss the problems, as well as the opportunities, of making internal changes at a time when the external environment is changing so rapidly. In this case, the business is growing rapidly. In the following case, "General Motors and the United Auto Workers," change is also taking place in the midst of a rapidly changing environment, this time one of decline. Most companies do not have the opportunity of utilizing "slack time"—as seen in the "Sedalia Engine Plant" case—to plan and implement changes.

Audiovisual Material

Two videotapes are available to supplement the case material. In "Office Technology, Inc.: The LMP Group," members of the LMP group discuss the generally positive experience of working as a semiautonomous team. In "Office Technology, Inc.: The OEM Group," members of that group discuss their general disillusionment with the experience. The tape closes with a brief discussion by Jim Hancock. Hancock has been named OEM manager and has hired a new supervisor, Joy Caldwell, for the OEM Group. Both he and the group discuss that new supervisor as well as their frustrations with the "special projects," the progress the group has made, and the continued unhappiness of the group members.

We have provided an alternative teaching plan for instructors wishing to use these two videotapes.

TEACHING PLAN

One-Day Teaching Plan

15 min.   1. Evaluate Dorr's decision to impose a standardized work system on OA groups. You can start by asking students to vote on whether they agree or disagree with Dorr's unilateral decision, and give the reasons why. This discussion should bring up two specific questions:
   a. Should Dorr have sought a uniform work system across the OA groups? Why or why not?
   b. Can or should new work systems be imposed unilaterally? What alternatives did Dorr have?

30 min.   2. Prior to Dorr's decision, how was work organized in the two groups, what were the mechanisms that supported the work systems in each—job design, organization and work group culture, supervisory attitudes and style, recruitment and selection, performance appraisal, pay, and so forth—and what were the outcomes, both financial and nonfinancial, from these alternative work systems?

15 min.   3. What roadblocks should Dorr anticipate in the implementation of his decision, and how should he deal with those roadblocks?
   a. Are Tim Everhart and Jim Hancock committed?
   b. Do selection and appraisal systems need to be reconsidered?
   c. How will work be organized in OEM?
   d. Who will supervise OEM?
   e. Who will oversee change effort?

10 min   4. Hand out and read (B) case.

15 min.   5. Evaluate Dorr's implementation of the change.
   a. Dorr's decision to standardize organizations
   b. Dorr's unilateral decision to impose type of work organization
   c. Tim Everhart's conversion
   d. Adequacy of training
   e. Organization of regional teams
   f. Impact of Dorr's and Fortier's leaving
   g. Follow-up of change effort

5 min.   6. Instructor gives lecturette on managing changes in work system design.[2]

Two-Day Teaching Plan

Day 1
15 min.   1. Evaluate Dorr's decision to impose a standardized work system on the OA groups.

15 min.	2. View LMP videotape.
30 min.	3. How was work organized in the LMP group, what were the mechanisms that supported that work system, and what were the outcomes of that work system?
30 min.	4. What roadblocks should Dorr anticipate in the implementation of his decision, and how should he deal with those roadblocks?
	5. Hand out the (B) case at the end of class.

Day 2

15 min.	1. View OEM tape
45 min.	2. What are the problems faced by OEM? What are the mechanisms that support this group's work organization and how well are they working? What is your evaluation of Hancock as a manager? Why is OEM having problems making the transition to the team concept? How might those problems have been anticipated and dealt with?
20 min.	3. What generalizations can you make about the problems in managing work system changes toward high commitment (model B)? What are the implications for companies that seek to move in this direction?
10 min.	4. Instructor gives lecturette on managing changes in work system design.

NOTES

1. Michael Beer and Gloria Gery, "Pay Systems Preferences and Their Correlates." Paper presented at the American Psychological Association Convention, San Francisco, 1968.
2. See Michael Beer, *Organization Change and Development: A Systems View*, (Santa Monica, CA: Goodyear Publishing, 1980), pp. 168–174; and Richard J. Hackman, "Work Redesigns for Organization Development," in Michael Beer and Bert Spector, eds., *Readings in Human Resource Management* (New York-Free Press, 1985).

CHAPTER 8

Integrating Human Resources

The objective of this section is to get students to see that the four human resource management (HRM) policy areas are interrelated and can be viewed as part of a company's human resource *system*. Internal consistency between all four policy areas is needed to provide clear signals to people about the behavior that is expected and will be rewarded. Inconsistency can not only preclude such clear signals; it can also reduce the effectiveness of a policy in one of the four areas. William Ouchi's bureaucracy/market/clan framework is introduced as a way to help students understand how fit patterns have developed in companies over the years and in response to shifting environment pressures. This section introduces the problem of managing human resources on a companywide basis. In contrast to "Office Technology, Inc." (OTI) or "Sedalia Engine Plant" (SEP), where innovative human resource policies and practices are introduced in a department and plant, in this section students can examine the problems of corporatewide changes at General Motors just as they can examine innovative human resource policies initiated by founders at Hewlett-Packard and People Express. Moreover, how unions may be involved in change is introduced in the General Motors (GM)–United Auto Workers (UAW) case. The following key issues are dealt with:

1. *The need for fit.* Students learn, once again, that the various elements of the human resource system must fit together. Cases in the work system section began to raise the theme that innovations in job design must also be accompanied by changes in all other HRM policy areas: influence mechanisms, pay, screening, supervision, pro-

motions, and so forth ("Sedalia Engine Plant," "Office Technology, Inc."). Two of the cases in this section, "People Express" and "Human Resources at Hewlett-Packard," show students organizations that have attempted from the very beginning to build HRM policies that were consistent not only with each other but also with the business strategy being pursued by the organizations. "General Motors and the United Auto Workers" demonstrates an attempt to reshape an already existent human resource system.

2. *The power of philosophy.* Students see again that the assumptions of leaders (Stephen Fuller at General Motors, Irving Bluestone at the United Auto Workers, Don Burr at People Express, Bill Hewlett and David Packard at Hewlett-Packard) about people and about the role of the enterprise in society can have a powerful impact on the design of an HRM system.

3. *Long-run institutional development perspective.* Students see that internal consistency between HRM policies will create a strong and pervasive culture which will work to develop employees, in the present and in the future. The employees will accept those values and will develop certain skills and competencies consistent with the assumptions of the organization about the capacities and motivation of people at work. Moreover, students are introduced to the problems of managing a corporate transformation or sustaining innovative HRM policies over a long time.

Sequence of Cases

We suggest the following sequence of cases:

1. *General Motors and the United Auto Workers.* This case opens the chapter on integrating HRM by pulling together many elements of an HRM system: (1) *employee influence*, in which the company and the union attempt to move toward a cooperative relationship and to institutionalize that relationship; (2) a *flow* policy in which training and promotions are designed by GM to enhance the company's commitment to quality of work life (QWL) programs; (3) *reward systems* that (at the Livonia plant particularly) emphasize growth, flexibility, and teamwork; (4) *work systems* that emphasize employee involvement and in some cases the team concept of an SEP; (5) *QWL* which, broadly defined, involves a well-integrated, internally consistent approach to HRM.

Perhaps the most important contribution made by the case is that it deals in some detail with the issue of *change*. Like "Bethoney Manufacturing" and "Office Technology, Inc.," "General Motors and the United Auto Workers" allows students to analyze the process of change. Like "Bethoney Manufacturing," "Alcon Laboratories," and "Kalamazoo," this case demonstrates how failures in HRM can have a direct, negative impact on the company's performance. "Sedalia Engine Plant" deals with a new and nonunion plant; "Kalamazoo" deals with an old unionized plant. "General Motors and the United Auto Workers" deals with an old and established corporation attempting to change from adversarialism to collaboration with their union. "Bethoney Manufacturing" showed one way (a power strategy), by no means the only or best way, to create such an atmosphere for change. "Dana Corporation" showed a way to institutionalize union–management cooperation through a reward system. In "General Motors and the United Auto Workers," the change is institutionalized from the corporate level down to the shop floor, with union and management working together through a whole array of HRM policies.

2. *People Express.* This case continues the integrative section by providing a detailed example of a company that *started* with an integrative HRM system (as opposed to a company like General Motors which is attempting to change the manner in which they manage human resources in response to various environmental pressures, People Express is a company in which the business strategy is largely driven by its HRM strategy in general, and particularly by the belief of its founder in high-commitment work systems. As such, "People Express" also serves to reemphasize the important point which first emerged in "Sedalia Engine Plant": the values of top managers and/or founders play a key role in determining how people in organizations will be managed.

3. *Human Resources at Hewlett-Packard.* This case offers students an opportunity to analyze policies and practices in all four policy areas. Many of the specific HRM system elements encountered in this case will have been introduced in previous cases: emphasis on building trust and equalizing power ("General Motors and the United Auto Workers," "Sedalia Engine Plant"), semiautonomous work teams ("Office Technology, Inc.," "Sedalia Engine Plant"), and clan-type relationships based on shared norms and employment security ("Nippon Steel Corporation"). This case, however, provides a detailed example of a more fully integrated, corporatewide culture than the previous ones. Also, unlike the U.S. examples encountered previously in the course, this is a company not trying to create a new way of managing its human resources or to change its work environment, but rather one in which the norms about how people in the organization are to be managed, and the policies to support these norms, were established practically from the beginning by founders with a strong set of values and beliefs. More than any previous case, "Human Resources at Hewlett-Packard" allows students to examine the relationship between a company's HRM policies and its business strategy and financing policies. Finally, the case allows students to examine how long the HRM approach at Hewlett-Packard (HP) can be sustained given the retirement of the founders, the growth of the firm, and the new competitive environment in computers.

Audiovisual Material

The following films, mentioned in the work systems chapter, may also be considered to supplement or accompany the material in this chapter, particularly "General Motors and the United Auto Workers":

1. "Loose Bolts"
2. "Changing Work"
3. "Why Work?"

Supplementary Reading Assignments

The following supplementary reading assignments can be made from Readings in Human Resource Management:

TEXT MATERIAL	SUGGESTED READING
Chapter 7	*Business Week*, "The New Industrial Relations"
"General Motors and the United Auto Workers"	Rosabeth Kanter, "Organization Change, Affirmative Action, and the Quality of Work Life"
	David C. Ewing, "The Endless Wave"
	Daniel Quinn Mills, "Reforming the U.S. System of Collective Bargaining"
	Edward E. Lawler and John A. Drexler, Jr., "Dynamics of Establishing Cooperative Quality of Worklife Projects"
"People Express" "Human Resources at Hewlett-Packard"	Fred K. Foulkes, "How Top Nonunion Companies Manage Employees"

GENERAL MOTORS AND THE UNITED AUTO WORKERS
Teaching Note

In 1973 General Motors (GM) and the United Auto Workers (UAW) agreed to work together on a quality of work life (QWL) committee. This case focuses on human resource management (HRM) systems at a corporate level and in a setting with a long tradition of union–management conflict.[1] The case offers students an understanding of how such a commitment was achieved and managed, and suggests both the potential advantages and possible problems raised by such factors as the severe downturn in the U.S. automobile industry in 1980 and the predicted introduction of robotics into American automobile plants. The case closes with a proposed experiment at a new GM plant (Cadillac–Livonia) that will, if GM and the UAW approve the particulars, go far beyond any previous QWL program.

ASSIGNMENT QUESTIONS

Students should read the case and come to class prepared to discuss the following questions:

1. What is QWL at General Motors?
2. How was acceptance of QWL by GM and UAW leaders brought about? What were the mechanisms of change? Who were the key people?
3. Can QWL continue to be effective in the future?

Note: As part of this assignment students can be asked to read *A Note on the 1982 Auto Negotiations* and asked to prepare question 3 in light of that note. A copy of the note can be found in Appendix II of this manual.

CASE ANALYSIS

The first question to be asked of the case is why GM became so concerned with QWL in the first place. The following reasons (summarized in Table 8–1) can be derived from the case.

1. *Human resource failures of the late 1960s.* The numbers seem to speak for themselves. Between 1965 and 1969 absenteeism rose 50 percent, turnover soared 72 percent, the number of grievances climbed 38 percent, and disciplinary layoffs rose 44 percent. By 1969 employees absent without excuse on Mondays and Fridays of-

TABLE 8-1
Why Concern with QWL at GM?

—Income as percentage of sales fell from 10 percent in 1960s to 6.8 percent in 1971.
—Absenteeism up 50 percent from 1965 to 1969.
—Turnover up 72 percent between 1965 and 1969.
—Number of grievances up 38 percent between 1965 and 1969.
—Disciplinary layoffs up 44 percent between 1965 and 1969.
—"Lordstown syndrome"—1971

ten reached 20 percent. Alienation of the assembly line worker is certainly not a new phenomenon (C. R. Walker and R. H. Guest produced a classic study in 1952 entitled *The Man on the Assembly Line*).[2] And it is not easy to determine whether the above figures are a sign of increasing alienation or simply workers finding new forms of expressing their long-felt alienation. In any event, things have changed on the assembly line, and the case suggests several possible reasons behind that change:

a. The new, younger assembly line workers are better educated than their predecessors, a fact which could either increase their alienation or increase their willingness and ability to express that alienation.

b. Various social movements of the 1960s have had an impact on workers. The "counterculture," civil rights movement, and experiences connected with the war in Vietnam may have worked to undermine a traditional willingness to yield to authority figures.

c. A local union president suggests that children of plant workers who have vowed never to work on an assembly line find themselves working in plants nonetheless. They are disillusioned and resentful.

d. Former GM vice-president Earl Bramblett suggests that rising wages ($134.60 average per week in 1969) have created an affluence and abundance among workers that allows them to put less effort and time into their work.

e. The quoted statement of a young Lordstown worker ("Why do I work four days a week? Because I can't live on what I make in three") may well be apochryphal, but it is often cited to indicate the decline of the American work ethic. It might also be used to suggest the increasing affluence of automobile workers.

f. Despite increased educational levels, the company was still treating workers as an extension of the assembly line. Dutch Landen, director of organizational research and development (OR&D), suggests that GM had failed to some extent by assuming that workers were motivated entirely by the desire for more money, thus ignoring their potentials and abilities for participation. Of course this assumption was fed by workers' willingness to accept poor working conditions and low involvement for higher and higher wage settlements and by management's willingness to create this psychological contract.

g. Implicitly, it can be assumed that the UAW, like GM, had overlooked the problem of alienation among the work force. It should be remembered that, at Lordstown, the young rebellious workers directed as much of their anger against aloof union officials as against the corporation.

2. *Human resource impact on the bottom line.* Despite a record level of profits in 1971, income as a percentage of sales was off considerably:

	Net Sales (in Billions of Dollars)	Income (% of Sales)	Payroll (% of Sales)
1965	21	10.3	26.3
1966	20	8.9	27.8
1967	20	8.1	28.1
1968	23	7.6	28.7
1969	24	7.0	28.5
1970	19	3.2	33.4
1971	28	6.8	28.4
1972	30	7.1	28.5
1973	35	6.7	28.8
1974	32	3.0	31.0
1975	36	3.5	28.1
1976	47	6.2	27.4
1977	55	6.1	27.8
1978	63	5.5	27.2
1979	66	4.4	28.4
1980	58	(1.3)	30.8

Many in the corporation felt that the problem was caused by poor performance on the part of employees.

3. *The Lordstown syndrome.* Lordstown, with its production rate nearly twice that of older GM plants, became a nationally known symbol of disaffection among young workers, of what the press was increasingly referring to as "blue-collar blues." GM officials rejected the view that something different was taking place at Lordstown (as did UAW leaders), but there is no denying the power of Lordstown as a symbol. BY 1971 there were some leaders in both GM (Landen) and the UAW (Irving Bluestone) who were already

calling for a movement toward more participation on the part of workers. Lordstown probably helped them sell their ideas to their own governing bodies.

4. *The oil crisis.* If Lordstown helped get the notion of QWL going, the oil crisis of the early 1970s added urgency. As seen in the chart above, income as a percentage of sales plummeted in 1974 (and has never reached pre-1974 levels), while payroll as a percentage of sales remained rather constant. The need to enable employees to "work smarter" was becoming more apparent.

5. *Foreign competition.* If the gasoline crisis added urgency in the mid-1970s, the impact of foreign competition fueled even more GM's drive to turn its work force into a competitive advantage by unleashing more of its potential talent. GM posted a loss in 1980 of $763 million,[3] while payroll as a percentage of sales increased from 28 to 31 percent. Japan particularly increased its share of the U.S. market, in part because Japanese companies enjoyed a net cost advantage of anywhere from $1,000 to $1,700 per car over U.S. cars, in part because of the perception among U.S. consumers that foreign-made cars were of superior quality to domestically manufactured ones,[4] and in part because dramatic increases in fuel prices made smaller, lighter, fuel-efficient Japanese cars attractive to consumers.

Objectives of QWL

It is important to note that while the goals sought by union and management from QWL may, at times, have overlapped, they were not entirely congruent. First, what were the objectives of QWL for the company? Not necessarily in order of importance, a list derived from the case could include:

1. *Survival.* It is probably an exaggeration to say that GM faced a "life-or-death" situation in the 1970s. However, declining profits and increased foreign competition seriously altered the complexion of the American automobile industry, and convinced GM executives that they faced a "shake-up situation." Some executives also believed that QWL gave GM an important competitive advantage.

2. *Productivity/quality.* Here is where that competitive advantage came in. Because company use of the term "productivity" translated for union members directly into "speed-up," the term itself was not officially used at top management levels when discussing QWL with the union (although local plant managers did not hesitate to talk openly about their hope that QWL would increase productivity). Still, Steve Fuller and others saw

improved productivity as an "interesting" and important by-product of QWL.

By reducing alienation and its side effects (absenteeism, which leads to shifting, unstable job assignments, little attention to quality, and so forth) and increasing the commitment of the workers to the final product, GM also hoped to improve the quality of their products. Improved quality would also provide a competitive advantage, especially against Japanese cars.

3. *Nonunion plants.* As GM placed new plants throughout the South and introduced QWL into them, UAW officials believed that the company saw in QWL another possible objective: to produce a "union-free environment." GM denies that such was their intent.

4. *Welfare of employees.* Whether QWL actually improved productivity or the quality of the final product, Steve Fuller insisted that GM should support it because it was "right." Workers should be allowed to make decisions about their work environment.

5. *Increased influence on the shop floor.* It can be inferred that GM feared its loss of control and influence over workers. Alienation, frustration, boredom, and anger had apparently built a wall between the company and its workers which could not be torn down by relatively generous pay settlements. There were specific cases [General Motors Automotive Division's (GMAD) Lordstown and Fisher Body's Fleetwood where the fifth floor, supposedly dominated by "communists," was seemingly out of the control of both union and management] where communication between workers and management had broken down almost completely. Since QWL is a *joint* commitment, a successful program would, GM hoped, reintroduce the company into the workers' lives on a positive note.

What about the UAW? What did they hope to gain from QWL?

1. *Industrial democracy.* Unlike GM executives, Irv Bluestone saw QWL as part of a larger struggle for industrial democracy, by which he meant not only the right to bargain collectively but also the right to assume responsibility over the management of work and even, to some extent, the entire enterprise. Because he hoped blue-collar workers would share responsibility as a *right* rather than a privilege, Bluestone insisted that QWL at GM be the joint venture of both union and management. Unless the union is involved at all levels as an equal partner, QWL would be viewed as old-fashioned paternalism and rejected by workers, or certainly by union officials. Any job enrichment program that is bestowed upon workers unilaterally by management, however well meaning, can, Bluestone warned, be just as easily shelved.[5] Just as GM executives purposefully played down the productivity angle of QWL, so, too, did Bluestone mute his discussion of industrial democracy.

2. *Well-being of workers.* Bluestone also insisted that workers, who were treated as full-fledged citizens outside of the work place should not be forced to give up those rights once they entered the plant. Their heads as well as their bodies should be viewed as valuable assets.

3. *Economic survival.* Layoffs followed the downturn in the automobile market. QWL was touted, by union officials as well as management people, as a way of improving America's competitive position against the Japanese because of the presumed positive impact it would have on quality. Simply put, QWL could, the UAW hoped, help save jobs.

4. *Institutional growth.* With the UAW sharing the QWL driver's seat, noticeable improvements in the lot of workers could be attributed directly to union officials. Such efforts, union leaders hoped, could at least help overcome the growing alienation workers were feeling toward their union.

Managing Change

One of the most important aspects of the case is its discussion of the process of change, as both union and management move from a traditional adversarial relationship to one that emphasizes cooperation and mutually beneficial goals. (The chronology of the change process is summarized in Table 8–2.) The case then allows students to ask the question: how do you produce systemwide change in a large corporation?

Champions for Change. Any change needs forceful and respected leaders who will guide it through the inevitable resistance. While people like Dutch Landen and Howard Carlson worked within GM's OR&D department in the late 1960s to instill a new management attitude, they could be dismissed rather easily by more traditional labor relations people. They had no real clout over the people who controlled human resource policies: George Morris and his traditionally oriented labor relations staff. But following the upheavals of Lordstown and the resulting attention on blue-collar blues, as well as a 21 percent dip in net sales and an even more serious drop in income as a percentage of sales (from 7.0 to 3.2 percent) in 1970, GM separated its personnel staff from the labor relations staff. Steve Fuller was brought in from the Harvard Business School and immediately announced himself, to the press as well as to GM executives, as the "champion" of improvements in job satisfaction.

Likewise, Irv Bluestone became the QWL champion within the UAW, where, at the beginning of his crusade, he was virtually alone in his endorsement of QWL.[6] His reputation throughout the union as well as his elevation

TABLE 8-2

Chronology of QWL at GM

1968	GM/Institute for Social Research (ISR) job satisfaction survey
1970	Irv Bluestone becomes VP of UAW in charge of GM division; asks for joint union–management QWL agreement
	Job improvements initiated at GMAD Lakewood (GA)
	67–day strike at GM
1971	Lordstown (OH) strike
	GM splits personnel department into separate personnel and labor relations departments; hires Stephen Fuller to head personnel
	Job improvements initiated at GMAD Tarrytown (NY)
1972	Detroit truck plant "stall-build" experiment
1973	Joint GM–UAW committee to improve the quality of work life created
1975	First national GM–UAW QWL conference
1976	GM develops QWL survey
	GM agrees to remain neutral in all future representational elections
1978	UAW sponsors QWL conference at Tarrytown
1979	GMAD Oklahoma City plant opens—representational election centers on QWL
	GM agrees to automatic UAW recognition in all future plants
1980	Al Warren, QWL supporter, becomes GM's VP for labor relations
	GM begins training program for all new supervisors teaching QWL values
	Irv Bluestone first UAW official to address GM Executive Council on QWL
	Bluestone and Horner retire from UAW
1981	GM reports loss for 1980 of $763 million
	GM and UAW approve QWL plans at Cadillac's new Livonia (MI) plant

in 1971 to head the UAW's GM division allowed him to begin to convince skeptics that QWL would not necessarily mean a sellout of hard-fought collective bargaining victories.

Champions Line Up Support and Make Converts. Both Fuller and Bluestone proved adept at managing change in such a way that converts were made and lined up behind their own QWL commitment. Fuller either oversaw or initiated a number of steps that were designed to promote QWL within GM: the increasing use of QWL surveys, QWL "show-and-tell" conferences at which plant managers were given the opportunity to convince other plant managers of the benefits of QWL, and a corporatewide training program begun in 1975 and expanded over the years to instill QWL values in all levels of management. At the beginning, when support for QWL within GM was weakest, Fuller carefully insisted that participation in QWL programs be strictly voluntary. That changed in 1979 when James MacDonald mandated at least some type of QWL program for all GM plants. After years of behind-the-scenes politicking, Fuller also managed to get "one of his own" (Al Warren) appointed to replace George Morris on the labor relations side. The QWL victory within GM was, at least for the time, complete.

Within the UAW, Bluestone had to take care that local union sensibilities were not stepped upon by national leadership, and that QWL was not seen as a sell-out of union militancy. The 1973 letter of understanding (see casework Exhibit 28-2) was the first important symbol that QWL meant an equal partnership between management and union. With George Morris's signature on that letter, Bluestone could, and did, virtually ignore Morris's real opposition to QWL and begin selling the concept to both national union executives and local leadership. He then promulgated the six iron-clad "laws," the other indispensable symbol of QWL for the union, to assure locals that they would not be giving up any "rights." He and his staff worked carefully and slowly with local unions. Instead of ignoring the politics inherent in any local action setting, Bluestone used those politics to his advantage by insisting that support for QWL strengthened chances for reelection. He also cleverly used symbols such as Tarrytown (often transporting local leaders to Tarrytown to see for themselves) to convince still skeptical union members (Jim Adams of Fleetwood, for instance) that QWL did not mean simply "getting in bed" with management.

Vague, Normative Goals Rather Than Specific, Well-Defined Programs. One of the most striking aspects of the change process at GM was the lack of a well-defined, specific goal or definition for QWL. Bluestone had some general notion as to where he wanted QWL to lead, as did Fuller, Landen, and other leaders. Since these notions did not overlap entirely, any precise statement of goals could have jeopardized a joint agreement at the earliest stages. Certainly, neither side had a well-defined vision of precisely what a GM plant would look like after a QWL program was installed. So, instead of imposing a specific program from "above" (GM corporate headquarters and Solidarity House), each local plant and union was allowed to work out their own statement of philosophy (see casebook Exhibit 28-3), as well as their own program. Even as QWL moved from a voluntary to a mandatory commitment within GM, there was still no attempt to impose specifics on a plant. In addition to allowing the maximum of flexibility and innovation, such a normative approach allowed, indeed almost forced, a feeling of "ownership" by plant and union leadership over whatever programs were initiated under the QWL banner.

Parallel Structures. Labor-management committees on QWL at corporate, division and plant level offered a forum for dialogue in a more cooperative environment away from the adversarial environment of collective bargaining. Such parallel committee structures seem to be a critical part of most changes in union–management relations. Integrative problem-solving occurs in these forums while distributive bargaining occurs in collective bargaining.

Concessions. Because of the traditional adversarial relationship that existed between GM and the UAW, both sides had to make certain concessions to assure support from the other side. First, the union. Despite the stated opposition of Bluestone and other national leaders to a linkage between QWL and improved productivity, local UAW officials allowed and even encouraged discussions by management of ways to improve productivity (at Livonia, for instance) as long as those discussions included the union as an equal partner. At Livonia the UAW also allowed a pay system (pay-for-knowledge) that deviated significantly from the classification system of the national contract. They also allowed the Cadillac division to use a transfer policy designed to weed out union members not interested in working under such a system despite seniority. There is also some indication that GM's commitment to QWL has led to a more benign attitude on the part of at least some union officials toward the introduction of robotics. The UAW official quoted in the case as saying that robots replace only the worst jobs and may help save the industry is, in fact, the international service representative for Livonia, where several robots are already in place.

For its part, GM made several concessions, one of which was the careful avoidance of any open linkage between QWL and productivity, at least at the national level. Another was its decision to not fight union representation at its new plants. In 1976 George Morris attached a letter to the national contract in which he stated, "In situations where the UAW seeks to organize employees not presently represented by a union, General Motors management will neither discourage nor encourage the union's efforts in organizing production and maintenance employees traditionally represented by the union elsewhere in General Motors, but will observe a posture of neutrality in these matters." At the next bargaining session (1979) GM agreed to a concession that virtually assured automatic representation for the UAW in all new plants: union workers in existing plants would be given preferential treatment when staffing new plants. Students can be asked two questions concerning GM's concessions on "automatic recognition": did the company give away too much long-term currency for short-term problems without the help and cooperation of the union?

Living Symbols. The change process in GM featured the development of innovative, leading-edge plants like Lakewood, Tarrytown, and Livonia. These plants were then held up as models to the management and union leaders. Through visits and the transfer of people from these plants to older, less-advanced plants, the QWL approach was spread.

What Is QWL at GM?

While there was a purposeful effort to define QWL only in broad, general terms, it was eventually translated into specific programs at the local level. The case describes a wide range of QWL projects. While by no means an exhaustive list, some of the following examples are described in the case:

1. Special training courses for first-line supervisors to encourage a more open attitude in dealing with subordinates (Lakewood, Hyatt Bearing)
2. Quality circles, transactional analysis, and Transcendental Meditation courses for employees
3. Hourly workers participate in redesign of work areas during model changeover and introduction of new function (Lakewood, Tarrytown, Chevrolet–Bay City)
4. Worker task forces to reduce absenteeism, improve quality, and increase production (Oldsmobile division)
5. Allowing mechanics to make inspections and necessary corrections on their own work (Buick division)
6. Two- to three-day QWL workshops for all employees to emphasize the aims of QWL and the skills of communication, team building, and cooperation (all plants with QWL after 1973 agreement)
7. The most extensive experiment described in the case is the Livonia plant. Now approved by the UAW and GM are the following QWL innovations:
   a. Elimination of special privileges, dress codes for management
   b. All hourly workers organized in business teams; involved in production, quality control, material handling, daily job placement and rotation, housekeeping, and safety
   c. A three-step "pay-for-knowledge" system that replaced the elaborate multistepped classification system negotiated into the national contract.
   d. First-line supervisors, now called "team coordinators," expected to act as "facilitators," while the traditional level of general foreman has been abolished

Results of QWL

The question must be asked: how successful has QWL been? There is little hard evidence to indicate that it has led to increased productivity and improved quality. The case does suggest some of the following positive results (summarized in Table 8–3):

1. *Fisher Body–Fleetwood.* Absenteeism down from 18 to 8 percent; grievances down from 5,000 to 69; costs used to run 134 percent of sales, now in black; quality audit has moved from worst in division to best
2. *Buick Plant 81.* Absenteeism down from 9 to 0.7 percent

TABLE 8-3
Preliminary Readings on QWL Projects

Fisher Body–Fleetwood
—Absenteeism down from 18 to 8 percent
—Grievances down from about 5,000 to 69
—Costs used to run 134 percent of sales price; now in black
—Quality audit from worst to number 1

Chevrolet–Bay City
—Savings of 16 cents per engine from new diesel engine push rods

Buick Plant 81
—Absenteeism down from 9 to 0.7 percent

GMC
—Number of early local plant settlements:
 —1 in 1970
 —2 in 1973
 —18 in 1976
 —54 in 1979 (42 with joint QWL committees)

3. *GMC.* The number of local plants that have come to an agreement prior to the termination of a national contract has risen from 1 in 1970 to 2 in 1973, 18 in 1976, and 54 (42 of which had joint QWL committees) in 1979.

4. *Chevrolet–Bay City.* The case provides a specific example of cost savings generated directly by worker participation, under the QWL banner, during remodeling for a changeover to new production of a diesel engine push rod. The estimated investment for new machinery and equipment of $349,000 was eliminated entirely with suggestions for innovative uses of current equipment. The general superintendent estimated that overall savings to the company from worker-generated suggestions came to 16 cents per engine.

The Future

The case includes a discussion of some of the problems that may face QWL at GM in the near future (economic downturn, robotics, differing philosophies, and so forth. One of the more interesting questions raised implicitly rather than explicitly by the case is whether the UAW's QWL effort indicates a new direction for the American labor movement, a direction away from exclusive emphasis on bread-and-butter issues to more intangible matters.

The percentage of the work force that is unionized has been declining in recent years (from 35.5 in 1945 to 30 percent in 1960 and 26.6 percent in

1978). While the reasons for this decline are many,[7] the fact of the decline may lead some union leaders to reconsider their traditional, almost exclusive bread-and-butter approach to workers. As the American economy expanded, unions emphasized a demand for a larger slice of the economic pie for their members. The fact that this pie is shrinking may force those same leaders to look elsewhere for an appeal to workers.

While this is seen dramatically in the case of Chrysler, the automobile industry is not alone in winning wage concessions from unions. Some other recent examples include:

1. *Uniroyal*. Almost 6,000 members of the United Rubber Workers union accepted wage and benefit concessions totaling $9.9 million.
2. *Firestone*. Some 1,450 employees at the Memphis, Tennessee plant agreed to cost concessions and job restructuring, allowing Firestone to schedule regular Saturday and Sunday shifts with no premium pay.
3. *Armour*. The United Food and Commercial Workers Union agreed to an increase in production line speed in order to save a slaughterhouse plant in Hereford, Texas.
4. *Conrail*. The United Transportation Workers Union has granted reduction in train crew sizes and approved special work rules to help attract business. The Milwaukee Road and the Boston & Maine have also won such concessions.

Declining appeal and wage concessions are only two of the reasons union leaders may follow the lead of the UAW. Michael Beer and James Driscoll have suggested a change of strategy for unions that moves them away from exclusive emphasis on such traditional areas of concern as fair payment, secure employment, and fair treatment to less tangible issues such as increased decision-making responsibility, improved relations with supervisors, and more interesting jobs that may find a greater appeal among today's workers.[8] The president of the CWA, Glenn Watts, believes that now is the time for unions to grab hold of the QWL issue: "For many years there have been problems we were not able to take care of. Our members were expressing concern about things that went beyond wages and benefits. They complained about what they called job pressures; morale was at a low ebb."

Even the traditionally bread-and-butter-oriented Teamsters are beginning to wonder whether joint union–management efforts to improve the QWL might not be worth looking into. "Unions have got to play a different role," explained an officer of the Teamsters' Honeywell local in Minneapolis. "The view that participative management is manipulative is old thinking. Most people want to work. If you try to beat the system, time drags. It's easier to work."

Not all union opposition has evaporated. An August 1981 issue of *Labor Notes* contained a "Special Report" on QWL in which the prevailing

278

tone was decidedly negative. The general secretary of the independent United Electrical Workers (representatives of GE workers in Lynn, Massachusetts), explains his union's opposition this way: "We should reject participation in any of these employer-generated groups which bypass our regular union structure with the goal of—by use of advanced psychological techniques—brainwashing workers into making suggestions that will result in speed-up, combination of jobs, downgrading, and layoffs." This position, though, is not really so different from Irv Bluestone's reasons for opposing the imposition of QWL in GM's southern, nonunion plants. Still, it is apparently too soon to tell whether the UAW is pioneering a new direction for the American trade union movement. But, there is no question that QWL concepts are being applied in many large corporations like Bethlehem Steel, Honeywell, and Goodyear Tire to name only a few. Management at least sees these approaches as critical to competitiveness in the 1980s and 1990s.

TEACHING PLAN

Option A

25 min. 1. What *is* QWL at General Motors? Allow students to engage in rather free-wheeling discussions of what the various elements of QWL at GM are. Some responses might include:
   a. Improve HRM
   b. Not precisely defined
   c. Done at local level—allows participation, local ownership
   d. Industrial democracy—giving workers piece of decision-making process
   e. Cooperation between union and management
   f. Generating employee satisfaction
   g. Meetings (experience-based exercises)
   h. Not a program, but an embodiment of values about "labor and management"
   i. Generating employee satisfaction
   j. Treating employees differently, and getting more out of them
   k. Improving productivity
      Include a discussion of whether management and union means the same thing by QWL, and what problems might be created if different meanings are held.

20 min. 2. What are some of the mechanisms that make up QWL?
   a. Special training courses
   b. Quality circles
   c. Business teams
   d. Pay for knowledge

e. Worker participation in design of plant
f. Emphasis on "whole" tasks
g. Worker task forces on absenteeism, improved quality, production
h. Business teams for workers, emphasis on communication, teamwork
i. Elimination of some special privileges for management
j. Elimination of general foreman

15 min.   3. How was the change to QWL managed? Implications for managing changes like this in other corporations? What are the key principles we can derive for managing change?

a. Within company
(1) Steve Fuller became "champion"
(2) Reorganization of labor relations staff
(3) QWL surveys
(4) QWL "show-and-tell" conferences
(5) Corporate training program
(6) Gradual move from voluntary to mandatory participation
(7) Concession of neutrality in new plants (did they give away too much?)
(8) Vague, normative goal for QWL (is it time now for the company to assert more specific goals?)

b. Within union?
(1) Bluestone became "champion"
(2) Insistence of "joint" letter
(3) Iron-clad "laws"
(4) Reliance on local unions
(5) Use of Tarrytown as symbol

20 min.   4. What is or should be the future of QWL at GM?

a. If "Note on the 1982 Auto Negotiations" is assigned, ask whether QWL and demands for concessions are compatible, and evaluate GM's handling of those negotiations.
b. What does GM and the UAW have to gain/lose in the current economic environment by their continued commitment to QWL? What changes, if any, should be made in QWL as GM enters a new period of recovery and growth?

10 min.   5. Closing lecturette—what are the important points of the case? (See Table 8–4 for summary.)

a. Shows clearly the linkage between human resource policies and business performance; how economic pressures forced a large corporation to address fundamental human resource questions
b. Like any other approach to management, QWL reflects a philosophy, some basic assumptions about human nature, and why and how people work; philosophy can be a powerful tool.
c. QWL is an attempt to provide influence for workers outside of the traditional collective bargaining domain.

TABLE 8-4

Important Points of Case

—Linkage between HRM policies and business performance
—Philosophy can be powerful tool.
—QWL is attempt to provide influence outside of collective bargaining.
—Human resource data (QWL surveys) can be used to help judge performance of managers and health of organization
—Enlarging areas of joint union–management responsibility raises questions about management prerogatives.
—QWL usually does not involve technology of job design innovations.
—Importance of leaders (Landen and Fuller for GM; Bluestone and Horner for UAW)
—Some conflicts inevitable—QWL attempts to exploit mutual interest while allowing collective bargaining to deal with distributive issues.

      d. Shows attempt to gather human resource data (QWL surveys) in order to judge the performance of managers as well as the health of the organization.

      e. Does QWL mean giving up traditional management prerogatives or enlarging the ares of joint union–management responsibility?

      f. Most innovations at GM do *not* involve innovations in job design to this point in time.

      g. Important role of leaders (Fuller and Bluestone)

      h. Some conflicts between various stakeholder groups are inevitable. QWL does not ignore these conflicts. Rather, it attempts to exploit overlapping areas of agreement and mutual interest while allowing the collective bargaining process to iron out differences.

Option B

25 min.   1. What really is the QWL effort at GM?
      a. Why is GM management supporting QWL?
        (1) Human resource failings of the late 1960s, symbolized by Lordstown
        (2) Human resource impact on the "bottom line"
        (3) Economic pressures—oil crisis, foreign competition, declining performance, declining quality
        (4) Welfare of workers
        (5) Seeking a "union-free" environment
      b. Why did some UAW leaders support QWL?
        (1) Industrial democracy
        (2) Well-being of workers
        (3) Economic survival
        (4) Promote institutional growth
25 min.   2. What tactics have been used by the company to bring about the

desired change? By the union? Evaluate the effectiveness of those tactics.

15 min.   3. As the relevant company officials, would you go ahead with the Livonia plant? As the relevant union officials? Why or why not? What problems would you anticipate?

15 min.   4. Are QWL and demand for concessions compatible? Why or why not? Discuss "Note on 1982 Auto Negotiations" here.)

10 min.   5. Closing lecturette—what are the important points of the case?

NOTES

1. For a brief historical overview of labor relations at GM, see "Conflict and Consensus at General Motors, 1900–1979," Harvard Case Services, no. 9-376-170.
2. *The Man on the Assembly Line* (Cambridge, MA: Harvard University Press, 1952).
3. The U.S. automobile industry as a whole reported a combined loss of over $4 billion.
4. Compare the results of a 1977 (Roper) poll and a 1981 (*New York Times*/CBS) poll in which Americans were asked about the quality of Japanese cars:

	1977 (%)	1981 (%)
Better quality than U.S. cars	18	34
About the same quality as U.S. cars	30	30
Not as good quality as U.S. cars	32	22
Don't know	20	14

5. Communication Workers of America (CWA), which has recently written a QWL provision into its contract with American Telephone and Telegraph (AT&T), echoes Bluestone's sentiments. Says CWA President Glenn Watts, "I don't believe QWL can work successfully without a union. Otherwise, bosses never give up the idea of being a boss. Mutual respect doesn't come from altruism on the part of the boss, but from authority and power centered in both groups."
6. For a profile of Bluestone, see Michael Maccoby, *The Leader* (New York: Simon and Schuster, 1981).
7. For a fuller discussion, see Bert Spector, "Note on Why Employees Join Unions," in Michael Beer and Bert Spector, eds., *Readings in Human Resource Management* (New York: Free Press, 1985).
8. See Michael Beer and James Driscoll, "Strategies for Change" in J.R. Hackman and J.L. Suttle, eds., *Improving Life at Work: Behavioral Science Approaches to Organizational Change* (Santa Monica, CA: Goodyear, 1977), pp. 403–406.

PEOPLE EXPRESS
Teaching Note

INTRODUCTION

People Express was a young (1½-year-old) airline, begun after that industry was deregulated in order to stimulate competition. Taking full advantage of the letter and the intent of the airline deregulation act, People's managing officers set out to provide cut-rate air travel and demonstrate a "better" way to run an airline. A year after its maiden flight, People Express employed a work force of 1,200, was flying 17 airplanes, served 13 cities, and showed a profit, one of the few airlines in the United States to do so at that time (Spring 1982).

ASSIGNMENT QUESTIONS

Students should read the case and come to class prepared to discuss the following questions:

1. What *is* the People Express concept?
2. What accounts for People Express's performance to date? What have been the key business decisions and success factors?

PURPOSE OF THE CASE

This case is intended principally as an illustration of (1) a company whose fundamental business strategy *is largely driven* (versus *supported*) by its human resource strategy and (2) a service business application of a high-commitment work system.

For People Express, the "people" policies are not less important than the cost, marketing, and overall business strategies. Don Burr, People Express's founder and chief executive officer (CEO), claims that "the people thing drives everything else" and that his mission in founding the airline was "to create a work environment in which people can do their best."

The case documents the interrelationships (particularly strong in a labor-intensive business) between human resource practices and virtually ev-

This teaching note was prepared by Debra Whitestone and Leonard A. Schlesinger.

erything else in the business. It can quite effectively be used therefore as an integrative case in a general or HRM curriculum.

The case has the added value of throwing into sharp relief the often fuzzy connection between a company's dominant philosophy and its management practices. Because People's operating philosophy is articulated so explicitly, and because its leaders have consciously and deliberately attempted to keep their policies and practices consistent with that philosophy, the case naturally leads to an evaluation of the company's success by its own philosophical criteria. This, in turn, suggests a consideration of the connection between *any* organization's philosophy and its business success.

MAJOR LEARNING OBJECTIVES OF THE CASE

1. To examine the unusual situation of a company's philosophy and human resource strategy which drives versus supports its business strategy and to learn how such a company operationalizes its beliefs
2. To better understand the interdependent relationships between an organization's human resources strategies and its marketing, finance, and other business strategies
3. To explore the ramifications of People Express's priorities, strategies, and practices for the health and performance of the organization
4. To suggest an expanded set of criteria for assessing organizational success to include human ("soft") as well as financial measures
5. To identify major factors contributing to a high level of commitment and productivity in an organization
6. To examine the mechanisms by which a new company entering a deregulated industry (has) rapidly become a major competitive force
7. To anticipate (and propose preventive measures) for the long-term problems of rapid growth in a labor-intensive business

ANALYTICAL NOTES

What *is* the People Express concept?

What accounts for People Express's performance to date? Key business decisions and success factors?

A short answer to these earlier-stated assignment questions can be found in a comment by one of the managing officers: "If you look for one or two key factors, you miss the point." A full answer must include reference to business decisions which proved correct, the policies, strategies, and practices which constitute the People Express concept, and the work culture.

Key Business Decisions

The key business decisions include (not necessarily in order of importance):

1. Locating at the underutilized Newark airport, which was accessible to New York, the world's biggest air travel market, and an alternative to the two major New York airports
2. Going public for start-up funds, which enabled much stronger than usual entry into the market (17 purchased planes flying 12 routes in the first year)
3. A rapid, creative response to the Professional Air Traffic Controllers Union (PATCO) strike which had drastically reduced People Express's landing slots, particularly at Newark, thereby threatening the company's viability. [The response entailed developing several new, longer-haul routes between medium-sized northern cities (for example, Buffalo) and three Florida airports other than Miami. Longer-haul flights meant fewer landings, and smaller airports meant less competition for landing slots.]

Key Policies, Strategies, Practices: People, Marketing, Cost

While the case follows the sequence of the Morgan Stanley prospectus—marketing, cost, *then* people, it is "the people thing" which, according to just about everyone inside the company, forms the foundation on which the company is built. This note starts with people: A good class discussion could probably result from either direction.

People Express—Key Characteristics. Ownership, self-management, and broad-based participation. This is the crux of the People Express strategy—the sharing of ownership, profits, and responsibilities. All full-time, permanent employees own stock, are managers, and have a promise of job security for the life of the company.

1. *Minimal hierarchy.* The organizational structure is relatively flat—three levels of management (and pay) are cited in the case: (1) managing officers; (2) general managers; and (3) customer service managers (CSM), flight managers, maintenance managers. There were no supervisors, no "support" staff. There was a de facto another level of employee—"sales representatives" (reservations operators) but both the individuals and the situation in the reservations area were considered temporary. Since the case was written, a fourth official management level has been added—team manager, and Burr has considered combining the top two levels into one.

285

2. *Broad, multifunction job descriptions of universal cross-utilization and rotation.* No one did the same work all the time. Everyone is expected to be capable of performing many functions and to be available for filling any of those functions if needed. Almost everyone is expected to assume line (flight-related) as well as staff (business) responsibilities. This is seen as minimizing the size of the work force and maximizing the challenge, variety, and learning potential.
3. *Work teams.* Almost everyone, including top management belongs to at least one team and effective teamwork is highly valued. This requires and promotes interpersonal competence, for example, communication, problem-solving, decision-making skills.
4. *Rigorous hiring process and intensive training.* Recruits are screened meticulously to select those bright, energetic, creative, flexible, egalitarian types most likely to do well and contribute most to People Express's culture. On average, one in a hundred applicants was hired during the airline's early history and those hired are trained extensively.

Marketing Strategy. Definition of air travel as a commodity product and People Express as a basic, cut-rate, no-nonsense reliable brand of that product. Key characteristics of the marketing strategy included:

a. Very frequent, convenient flight schedule on every route
b. Multiple routes from the outset
c. Entertaining advertising campaign, pitched to the "smart" portion of the air traveler market
d. Memorable, up-beat, in-flight atmosphere created by unusually smart, sensitive, high-energy flight crews

Cost Structure. The key here is that management, that is, everyone, was committed to looking for every possible way to do things more simply and efficiently while preserving safety, quality, and spirit. Major cost-minimizing factors included the following:

1. *Economical aircraft.* People Express chose fuel-efficient Boeing 737s, purchased them in bulk for price advantage, redesigned them to improve space utilization, and kept each plan flying over ten hours per day.
2. *Lean, hard-working work force.* Here, the assumption was that with smart use of better (i.e., brighter, more creative, more dedicated) people, fewer were needed than most airlines employed. With a smaller work force, labor costs could be kept down. While most salaries and benefits were competitive, high executive salaries and consultant fees were kept to a minimum.

3. *Simple, low-cost facilities.* Both the major terminal and company headquarters were located at the least luxurious, cheapest part of an expensive airport. All offices, even Burr's, were shared and on-ground flight-related transactions were streamlined (for example, ticketing was done in-flight) which kept space needs to a minimum.
4. *Unbundled costs.* Basic transportation costs were separated from convenience costs, for example, food, baggage handling. The latter were optional for a fee added to the ticket price.

Interrelationships Among Key Success Factors

Human Resource Practices and Key Business Decisions, Strategies. It is the people strategy and culture that fostered the high commitment and high performance that rendered the other business strategies viable and profitable.

People Express's low fares were largely dependent on low labor costs, that is, lean staffing. Maintaining safety, service quality, and a pleasant travel atmosphere with fewer than normal staff required the hiring of bright, versatile, flexible people. Using them intelligently (cross-utilization) and providing incentives and rewards for hard work were also essential.

Offering frequent flight schedules in each of several routes and rapid establishment of new markets required that People's work force be dedicated to the company, and willing to work long hours and sacrifice personal schedules to the needs of the company.

To reap profits while keeping fares low, People sought to maximize efficiency. Again, commitment, cooperation, and intelligence were key factors, along with quality assurance. The self-management concept, the work team structure, and personal responsibility of ownership fostered undefensive problem identification. Creative problem-solving also provided tangible rewards for cost containment, ownership, and sharing. (Managers continually chose to forego luxuries, for example, decorating their offices, in the hope of seeing the savings in their bonus check.)

Even the success of major business decisions was at least partly related to People Express's people. It was the management team's airline experience, and commitment to an innovative management vision that persuaded investors to buy stock in the airline before it even had one airplane. The purchase of a whole fleet of planes would not have rendered such financial benefits if the company had been unable to gear up fast enough to begin flying each plane upon delivery.

People's selection process for and insistence on employee flexibility, together with the intense personal interest shown by manager–owners, has made it possible for the company to "turn on a dime." This capability has been tested and reinforced several times now, as the company has responded with seemingly miraculous success to external emergencies (for example, the PATCO strike) and self-made ones (for example, purchasing 17 versus 3 planes). Indeed, doing the impossible—breaking records—has become a tradition at People Express, an integral part of the company identity, and an important source of nostalgia and pride.

Is People Express a Successful Company? It is too early to determine if People Express will succeed in the long run, given the volatile character of the airline industry since deregulation. However, the traditional numeric indicators of airline success show that People Express was succeeding as of its second year of operation, mid-1982, when the case was written.

The following indicators appear in the case:

- —*Net profits.* Three million dollars as of mid-1982; one of only five U.S. airlines to show any profit at that time
- —*Revenue.* Nearly $200 million
- —*Return-on-revenue.* 15.3 percent (second highest in the industry)
- —*Market.* Over 3 million passengers. Substantial increases (over 100 percent on some routes) in overall market size in cities serviced by People, since People Express's entrance.
- —*Costs.* Lowest costs per seat mile of any airline (5.2 cents compared to 9.4 cents industry average)
- —*Productivity of aircraft.* 10.36 hours per day per plane as compared to 7.06 industry average
- —*Employee.* 1.52 of .62 revenue passenger miles per employee. (See Exhibits 30–5 and 30–6, pp. 777–778 and p. 779 of casebook, for more information.)

The case suggests that there are also human and philosophical criteria by which organizational success must be evaluated.

People Express's general philosophy, as Burr states it, is that "people can be trusted to do a good job." Unstated but implied is the tenet that wealth ought to be shared with those who create it. Beyond these fundamental beliefs, the company is committed to following six precepts (note the sequence):

1. Service, commitment to growth of People Express
2. Best provider of air transportation
3. Highest quality of management
4. Role model (for other airlines and other businesses)
5. Simplicity
6. Maximization of profits

The case presents evidence of both success and problems in the human sphere. A brief climate description, sample individual stories, and a reference to generally positive climate survey results all indicate considerable personal growth and satisfaction of managers (that is, full-time, permanent employees). Most of People's managers, along with being exhausted and overworked, felt they were learning more, having more fun, and making more money faster than they could almost anywhere else. As of June 1983 the average CSM with one-year tenure owned nearly $50,000 worth of stock!

People Express is not without problems, however. As Don Burr himself pointed out to the casewriter, "This place isn't Nirvana and I'm not God—we're only about 50 percent successful so far in the people sphere."

There is evidence that trouble is already brewing in this "paradise," and we can infer that if certain matters go unchecked, additional problems will emerge.

Problems already in evidence include:

—*Chronic staffing shortfall.* Due to People Express's rapid growth and its selective, time-consuming, recruiting practices hiring hasn't kept up with staffing needs. As of August 1982 the shortfall was approximately 200.

—*Widespread fatigue and illness.* Due to long hours and pressure imposed by rapid growth and understaffing.

—*Staff (versus line) tasks and systems were suffering.* Since flight-related jobs must be covered, understaffing means many staff jobs were being done only partially, slowly, or not at all, for example, recruiting, accounting (including accounts receivable), team-building training for flight managers. In a similar vein, many structures, systems, and policies had not been fully implemented: for example, governance, staff–line rotations, appraisals.

—*Reservations area.* Is becoming a ghetto of sorts, staffed with over 400 "temporary" workers, some reemployed several times for over a year, hired, managed, and compensated very differently from the real (that is, permanent) People employees.

Other problems were resulting from People Express's success: for instance, telephone lines were chronically overloaded, resulting in annoyance, customer inconvenience, and loss of some prospective passengers. The bank of available telephone lines at Newark Airport was insufficient and the telephone company had not been able to keep up with People Express's demands for more lines (information not in case).

—*Declining morale.* Though still generally high, satisfaction was decreasing and frustration increasing. According to the attitude survey, top management was starting to be seen as less accessible, less supportive, less consultative, or less communicative than at the outset.

Most of the above could be attributed to Burr's decision to build the business faster and bigger than the management structure and systems. Other problems, while perhaps aggravated by the growth rate, were more related to the nature of People policies and the resulting climate, as well as decisions to trade short-term against long-term efficiencies (for example, staffing with rotating generalists versus stable specialists).

Long-Term Concerns: What Must People Watch For as It Matures and Grows?

—Can the abundant enthusiasm and energy present during the start-up phase be maintained over time? Aren't people bound to get tired, burned out, less apt to pitch in for every crisis?
—While the work force was small (under 100), the feeling of community was perpetuated by relative ease of interaction, preference for oral, face-to-face communication, frequent meetings, an open-door policy, and quarterly financial meetings which doubled as company-wide celebrations. Many employees had moved from Houston, but their People Express colleagues had little time to meet or socialize with anyone outside the company. Once the work force is too big to fit in one ballroom, other mechanisms will have to be found to maintain the feeling of community. Communications could become strained and more formalized. As access to the top managers becomes necessarily more cumbersome, additional incentives and aids will be needed for lower-level managers to make original suggestions, voice concerns, and so on.
—As start-up and first-year members gain experience and seniority, there is likely to be a demand for further differentiation, e.g., of status rewards. Within the existing flat structure and egalitarian policies, integrating newcomers with old-timers so that all continue to be excited and enthusiastic will be a special challenge.
—On another front, how will People Express maintain its competitive edge if the larger airlines begin competing seriously with low fares and cost reductions?

TEACHING STRATEGY

1. *Introduction.* the role and importance of a company's human resource policies and practices vis-à-vis key business strategies. The influence of a leader's fundamental beliefs about human nature, the organization's culture, and all business practices.
2. *Exposition of People Express's concept.* Philosophy, strategies
3. *Discussion of People Express's success.* Is it successful? Yes? No? How? Why? Make sure to get to personal and organizational, financial, and cultural indexes.

4. *Prognosis*—short term. Begin to discuss/debate whether People Express can continue to succeed. Hand out first update for class to read. Ask what students think now? (Update shows continued rapid expansion *and* profits.)
5. *Long-term*. Concerns, cautions, preventive measures. Pass out or summarize update (see Appendix II), focus on innovative solutions and factors contributing to such innovation.
6. If time, discuss applications elsewhere.

Summarize by suggesting questions and speculating regarding possible results of such applications.

RECOMMENDED READINGS

—Larry Greiner, "Evolution and Revolution as Organizations Grow, *Harvard Business Review*, July/August 1972.
—Richard Walton, R. Miles, and J. Kimberly "Establishing and Maintaining High Commitment Work Systems, " in *The Organizational Life-Cycle Issues in the Creation, Transportation, and Decline of Organizations* (San Francisco: Jossey-Bass, 1980), pp. 208–290.

HUMAN RESOURCES AT HEWLETT-PACKARD
Teaching Note

This case provides an overview of all the human resource policies and practices applied by Hewlett-Packard (H-P). We recommend this as a closing case.

ASSIGNMENT QUESTIONS

Students should read the case and come to class prepared to discuss the following questions:

1. Would you want to work for H-P? Why or why not?
2. What is the H-P Way? What is the mix of business policies and practices that supports their approach to managing people?
3. Can H-P continue to apply its HRM approach as the company grows and moves into new businesses, or will it have trouble adapting to a changing competitive environment?

CASE ANALYSIS

The case allows students to see a company that has started with a strong philosophy about how people in organizations should be managed ("Early in the history of the company, while thinking about how a company like this should be managed," said cofounder Dave Packard, "I kept getting back to one concept: if we could simply get everybody to agree on what our objectives were and to understand what we were trying to do, then we could turn everybody loose and they would move along in a common direction") and a business strategy that complements the company's human resource management (HRM) approach. (It is not clear which, business strategy or human resource philosophy, came first.) The case allows students to identify the elements of the H-P philosophy (HRM policies and business strategy) and to see how these various elements fit with each other. Finally, they can make some judgments on the results of that system.

The H-P Way

Although there is some talk in the case about the "fuzziness" or ambiguity of the H-P Way [like quality of work life (QWL), at General Motors (GM)], it is possible to identify some key elements of that philosophy:

1. *Participative management* demanding individual *entrepreneurship* while emphasizing *common purposes* and *teamwork*
2. Belief that it is easier to maintain autonomy in *small work units*
3. Emphasis on *goal setting* through participation (negotiation) and shared data
4. *Emphasis on process* rather than content ("heavier attention than in other companies is paid to the *way* things are 'done' ")
5. The expectation that *those who can contribute will be actively sought out*

It is important to note that H-P had no separate personnel department until 1957, so the assumption about how people should be managed as well as the policies based on those assumptions came from the company's founders and early general managers.

The H-P Way has clearly become a dominant company culture. So the concept of corporate culture can be introduced into the class discussions. Defined variously as shared beliefs and assumptions about what behavior is expected, shared beliefs and values about how to do things, and a system of informal rules that spell out how people are *to behave most of the time*[1] culture exists in every organization. There is extensive talk throughout the case about what those beliefs and assumptions about behavior are in H-P. For example:

—"It's basically a faith in people."
—"There's just sort of a feeling . . . of how people are to be treated."
—"Managers had better get off their chairs and go out and get in touch with people."
—"You can't mess with the process."

There is also talk about the socialization process wherein new employees are taught the culture. "New people with bad attitudes quickly learn that it's not acceptable to be that way at H-P." One of the most important mechanisms for teaching that culture (what distinguishes "good" from "bad" attitudes) is the story-telling: stories about Dave Packard's intolerance for poor quality or H-P's decision to reduce pay and work hours rather than lay off employees during a recession. Such stories serve both to present models of management behavior and to reinforce the company's philosophical commitment to its people. The informality of the office space and the "beer bust" parties further the feeling of equity and trust, and the belief that all employees have something significant to contribute to the company. In 1973 a more formal training program, "Working at H-P," was established to insure the passing along of the culture, values, and methods instilled by the company founders. *All* new employees go through this training.

It is likely that students will not respond entirely favorably to the H-P culture, particularly to its apparent emphasis on conformity and fit. There are some employees in the case, in fact, who complain about this emphasis and see the process of teaching and passing along the culture as "indoctrination." The case acknowledges that there can be a fine line between encouraging individuality, while insisting that all employees fit in with the same culture. In discussing organizations that emphasize clan-type relationships, William Ouchi[2] has noted the tendency of such organizations to emphasize conformity and to produce a homogeneous group of employees and managers. Students can air their personal feelings regarding the balance between individuality and "fitting in."

Human Resource Elements

Students can look at policies and practices in all HRM areas to see how they impact on the four C's (commitment, competence, costs, and congruence).

Employee Influence. Part of the attempt to create an open, trusting environment at H-P relates to the assumption that employees should have the ability to influence any decision over which they have some expertise and which will affect their job. The case makes clear that such influence is based on knowledge and job rather than hierarchical ranking, and that such influence is exercised not as a veto power, but rather as the ability to have input into decisions.

There is no union at H-P and no contractually obligated influence mechanisms. Neither are there the management-initiated but nonetheless formal quasilegislative mechanisms that we saw at the Sedalia Engine Plant. The company's personnel manual does specify that supervisors are expected to create and maintain a culture of openness that guarantees any employee the "right" of access to any other. Other practices augment this policy of openness:

1. Socializing across hierarchical levels around common coffee breaks, beer busts
2. Frequent plantwide meetings
3. The physical closeness and lack of formality of the office layout
4. A loudspeaker system used by company executives to communicate with employees
5. "Management by walking around"—getting managers out of their offices to seek contact with and input from their employees
6. The norm of openness communicated by example through meetings and parties
7. Attitude surveys of the kind discussed in the case

Human Resource Flow. The various flow policies of H-P make up one of the critical elements of the way the company manages its human resources, and employment security rests at the heart of the policy area. The assumption that people will be hired for life encourages careful consideration of a number of other flow practices. For example,

1. *Hiring.* To ensure that the company is getting the "right" people, there is a great deal of emphasis in the hiring process on adaptability, growth potential, and fit. Many companies make use of sophisticated screening techniques such as psychological testing, assessment procedures, and computer-reactive tests in their hiring process. Such techniques are often calibrated statistically against narrow criteria of job performance. H-P, on the other hand, explicitly downplays such testing in the hiring process. "We don't hire somebody for specific short-term skills." Instead, they pay attention to the culture of the organization and to the implications of that cultural assessment for the type of people needed. Will they "fit in"? Do they seem to have the potential to develop throughout their careers? Do they have or will they be able to develop initiative and self-motivation?

In an earlier case, "General Motors and the United Auto Workers," we noted attention being given to cultural fit in the hiring of supervisors for their high commitment Livonia plant:

> Foreman or general foremen from any Cadillac plant interested in working at Livonia would participate in a two-day training program prior to making application. If they were still interested, they would go through an assessment center *to determine their suitability for the newly defined foreman's role.* [emphasis added]

H-P seeks cultural fit by relying more heavily on interviewing than on testing.

2. *Promotion.* H-P develops and promotes its managers from within. The elaborate socialization procedures described earlier work to ensure that all managers will understand and accept the H-P culture. Promotions and frequent lateral moves across functions and divisions help create managers who are generalists and seeks to encourage integration across functions and divisions. Questions about the true extent of that integration will be raised below.

3. *Reward systems.* In keeping with the cultural norm of openness, all reward policies—as well as an individual's wage curve—are known to employees. Since 1940 all employees have been on the same profit-sharing and stock option plan. Furthermore, the work force is all salaried, and every employee has flexible hours with no time clocks. These reward policies serve to reinforce the notion of equitable treatment of employees, since they do not vary by hierarchical level.

Individual pay is based largely on "sustained performance." A forced curve helps identify exceptional and poor performers. The emphasis on individual performance is enhanced further by the policy that performance adjustments are not to be governed by budget limits; while the emphasis on development is underlined by the evaluation of "sustained" as opposed to short-term performance.

4. *Work systems.* The key elements of H-P's work system are relatively small working units with a good deal of autonomy and accountability, and, for individual employees, participative goal setting based on a management-by-objectives (MBO) system. The policy regarding small operating units, as well as the assumptions upon which that policy is based, is clearly stated: "The division . . . is an integrated, self-sustaining organization with a great deal of independence. The aim is to create a working atmosphere that encourages solving problems as close as possible to the level where the problems occur. To that end, H-P has striven to keep [divisions] relatively small and well defined." (There were some 40 divisions at the time the case was written.) The practices that sustain the autonomy and accountability of the divisions and that keep them relatively small are:

1. Divisions are created for new products that can be profitable or when old divisions become too big.
2. To ensure autonomy, no product area becomes a division until it contains all the necessary functions: research and development (R&D), manufacturing, marketing, quality assurance, finance, and personnel.
3. Corporate staff is kept small to avoid interference with the autonomy of divisional functions.
4. Divisions are measured by the financial results of their products adjusted for worldwide activity. The division's profit-and-loss statement then becomes the basis for allocation of R&D funding. There is a loosely negotiated transfer pricing system, a market mechanism that keeps divisions in touch with an internal and external market.

On an individual level, the MBO system allows participation in and commitment to organizational goals. Both short- and long-term organizational goals are communicated to employees who are then expected to have a good deal of influence in planning their own objectives for meeting the goals of their units. There is a good deal of research to indicate that goal setting can motivate employees and lead to improvements in productivity, an improvement which does not differ significantly whether those goals are reached in a participative way or whether those goals are assigned (provided the assigned goals are understandable and acceptable).[3] There is good reason to think that H-P's work system has helped create a highly committed work force. The results of one survey cited in the case show that identification with the company runs 25 percent higher at H-P than the national norm.

Business Strategy

If, as mentioned earlier, the business strategy of H-P fits their HRM policies, class discussion should be able to identify the elements of that strategy and the specific impact of that strategy on the HRM policies. Employment security, and the resultant nurturing of a strong company culture, is dependent on the business strategy of slow, steady growth and stability. A number of specific business policies work to keep price and margins steady, ensure consistency in volume and profits, and allow stable employment practices and the maintenance of the culture:

1. Emphasis on technological innovation and leadership rather than volume (on R&D rather than marketing) helps to avoid dramatic swings in the business caused by the market. Modest-sized markets allows H-P to keep its business units small.
2. Avoiding contract business helps ensure stability.
3. Avoiding low introductory pricing to gain market share allows for slow growth and long-term development.
4. No forward pricing helps ensure steady margins and reduces business risks later on. The result is business stability that supports a full-employment policy.
5. Avoiding tailoring products to specific customers and emphasizing standardized products also helps serve to even out employment demand.
6. "Pay-as-you-go" internal financing avoids rapid growth on borrowed money and the accompanying risks. It insulates the company from Wall Street pressures for quarterly earnings.

A question that can be asked of this business strategy, and the HRM policies, one raised in the assignment questions, is just how adaptable does it leave the company to shifts in the external environment? An H-P vice-president is quoted as saying, "This is designed as an adaptive company." But is it? Students may wonder, for instance, how well H-P can adapt for competition in the computer systems and personal computer business. Such businesses require a high degree of coordination across many divisions, and that coordination may be hampered in H-P by the strong emphasis on divisional autonomy. Likewise, these highly competitive markets call for marketing skills traditionally de-emphasized at H-P. If the company recruits marketing specialists, will they be rejected by the strong R&D-oriented culture, or will the culture change?

The following update, not included in the case, can be presented to students as evidence that these are very real problems for H-P[4]:

By 1982 H-P's growth into computer systems was becoming hampered by a lack of coordination. Such products require a degree of compatibility, timely development, and product line rationality that far exceeds the integration required for H-P's traditional offerings of test and measurement instruments. Different H-P divisions found themselves offering new computer systems products, like a new graphic printer, that would be incompatible with other H-P products made by other divisions available in the same market. Computers are now H-P's dominant product, in 1982 yielding approximately $2 billion of a total $4.25 billion in sales. But the firm is losing market share in the fastest growing areas of the systems businesses, areas that create important footholds for later growth. Market share in medium-sized business computers has dropped from 10 percent of a $2.86 billion market in 1980, to 8 percent of a $5.88 billion market in 1982. Market share in personal computers has dropped from 9 percent of a $745 million market in 1980 to 7 percent of a $2.25 billion market in 1982. H-P president John Young notes that, "Becoming a computer company has had a dramatic effect on our company . . . [my biggest challenge] is to orchestrate the divisions and provide a strategic glue and direction for the computer efforts, while keeping the work units small."

Thus, students can see the conflicts (interdivisional lack of coordination) and costs (loss of market share) as well as the impact on competencies (high in technological innovation but low in marketing) and commitment (high) of H-P's HRM policies and the complementary business strategy that the company has pursued over the years.

TEACHING PLAN

15 min.   1. Would you like to work at H-P? Students can be asked to vote and state their reasons for and against.

30 min.   2. What is the H-P Way? (Have students list and discuss the various policies and practices.)
   a. Culture and philosophy
   b. Influence mechanisms
   c. Recruitment and promotion
   d. Rewards
   e. Work system

15 min.   3. What business policies support the H-P Way?
   a. Importance of technological innovation rather than volume; leads to steady employment demands
   b. Avoid contract business; leads to employment stability
   c. Maintain modest markets; leads to small business units
   d. Emphasize standardization, leads to stable demand
   e. Pay-as-you-go financing precludes pressure for quarterly earnings from Wall Street. One senior executive told us, "We don't pay attention to Wall Street."

20 min.   4. Will the H-P Way interfere with the company's ability to compete in rapidly changing markets?
   a. Division autonomy can cause poor integration.
   b. High commitment and consensus management can lead to homogeneous but not adaptable work force.
   c. Will going into the computer business, particularly personal computers, make it difficult to sustain the H-P way? Should HRM considerations lead to a decision not to enter the personal computer market?

10 min.   5. Closing lecture on need for integration and fit between HRM policies and business strategy, and difficulty of achieving such a fit pattern in old companies versus instituting patterns at founding of company, as at H-P. Difficulty of sustaining an H-P culture over time.

NOTES

1. N. Marguiles and A. P. O. Raia, *Conceptual Foundations of Organizational Development* (New York: McGraw-Hill, 1978); William Ouchi and R. L. Price, "Hierarchies, Clans, and Theory Z: A New Perspective on Organization Development," *Organizational Dynamics* 7 (1978), pp. 25–44; Terrence E. Deal and Allan A. Kennedy, *Corporate Cultures: The Rites and Rituals of Corporate Life* (Reading, MA: Addison-Wesley, 1982).
2. William Ouchi, *Theory Z: How American Business Can Meet the Japanese Challenge* (Reading, MA: Addison-Wesley, 1981).
3. E. A. Locke, "Toward a Theory of Task Motivation and Incentives," *Human Performance* 3 (1968), pp. 157–189; John M. Ivanevich, "Different Goal-Setting Treatments and Their Effects on Performance and Job Satisfaction," *Academy of Management Journal* 20 (September 1977), pp. 406–419; Gary P. Latham and Garry A. Yukl, "Effects of Assigned and Participative Goal-Setting on Performance and Job Satisfaction," *Journal of Applied Psychology* 61 (April 1976), pp. 166–171; John M. Ivanevich, "Effects of Goal-Setting on Performance and Job Satisfaction," *Journal of Applied Psychology* 61 (October 1976), pp. 605–612.
4. "Can John Young Redesign Hewlett-Packard?" *Business Week*, December 6, 1982, pp. 72–78. We have occasionally distributed copies of this article to the class.

Information on Ordering Audiovisual Material

"Between a Rock and a Hard Place"
  (16 mm color—59 minutes)

First Run Feature
Shelby Fox
144 Bleecker Street
New York, NY 10012
(212) 673-6881

"Close the gate—88" (16 mm color—
  25 minutes)

Department of Education
United Steelworkers of America
Five Gateway Center
Pittsburgh, PA 15222
(412) 562-2400

"Flight 52"

Modern Talking Picture Services
230 Boylston Street
Chestnut Hill, MA 02164

"Harlan County, U.S.A." (16 mm
  color—90 minutes)

Almi Cinema 5
1500 Broadway
New York, NY 10036

"Loose Bolts" (16 mm color—
  33 minutes)

Red Ball Films
P.O. Box 315
Franklin Lake, NY 07417
(201) 891-8240

"Clockwork" (16 mm color—
  25 minutes)
"Why Work?" Parts 1 and 2 (16 mm
  color—60 minutes)
"Changing Work" (16 mm color—
  40 minutes)
"The Wilmar 8" (16 mm color—
  50 minutes)
"Taylor Chain" (16 mm color—
  30 minutes)

California Newsreel
630 Natoma Street
San Francisco, CA 94103
(415) 621-6196

The following videotapes can be ordered through Harvard Case Services (use order form supplied at the end of this manual). Purchase price is $75 for educational institutions and $150 for companies:

"Colonial Food Services Company: Performance Appraisal Interview" (40 minutes—no. 9-884-018)

"Managing in a High-Commitment Work System" (16 minutes—no. 9-884-022)

"Office Technology, Inc.: Members of the LMP Group" (15 minutes—no. 9-884-012)

"Office Technology, Inc.: Members of the OEM Group" (15 minutes—no. 9-884-013)

APPENDIX II

Supplementary Cases

BETHONEY MANUFACTURING (C)

In the spring of 1980, Arn Nelson looked back over the past two and a half years at Bethoney's Farmington Plant G and thought of the way things had changed. Since the settlement of a three-month strike in 1977, the atmosphere at Plant G had become more relaxed and cooperative. A relationship of mutual trust was beginning to form between management and union leadership. The foremen were working more effectively with hourly employees. Plant G's performance against division standards had improved (see Exhibit 1). It seemed like everything about Plant G was better than it had been three years earlier.

Nelson had only one objective at the end of the 103-day strike. He wanted the plant back in operation quickly and did not want tensions between people to prolong the start-up time. He even gave the foremen specific instructions on how to act towards the returning workers. One foreman remembered Arn's directions: "Arn instructed the foremen after the strike not to be vindictive. The job at hand was to get the plant running again. We were to be fair and firm."

Workers' attitudes after the strike were dramatically different than before it. One observer commented on them:

> The people acted meek. They were eager to get the plant running. It was a kind of paradise. Everyone felt a sense of accomplishment getting it going again. The first reunion of foremen and workers was one of welcoming.
>
> After the strike there was very little absenteeism. There was an attitude of "we" rather than "I" and "you." Foremen had been back at machine jobs during the strike, so they were more aware of the problems of operators. They could relate better to their situations.

Once the plant was in full operation after the strike, Jim Riley, manager of organizational development for the Glass Division, began working with production superintendent Tom Anderson and Arn Nelson on increasing the plant foremen's competence. A values survey administered a few months before the strike [see case (B)] indicated that the foremen were con-

This case was prepared by Amy Johnson, Research Assistant, and revised by Bert A. Spector, under the supervision of Lecturer Michael Beer as a basis for class discussion rather than to illustrate either effective or ineffective handling of an administrative situation.

formists and liked to know clearly what was expected of them. As Jim Riley said,

> On the survey the most characteristic thing I found was that basically they (foremen) were perfect supervisors (subordinates) for an authoritarian type of manager. As long as somebody told these people what to do and how far to do it and when it was done, they worked effectively.

However, Tom Anderson's style of supervising the foremen was to expect them to act autonomously and take responsibility for their own decisions. One of the first things Anderson and Riley worked on was communicating clear performance standards to the foremen. Sheets were designed to show a foreman how he was doing in production, housekeeping, safety, and other performance areas. A schedule of two 4-hour meetings a month between foremen and Anderson was set up. At the first of these meetings, Jim Riley led a workshop on "Elements of Foremanship." From that point, Tom Anderson took over, training the foremen in supervisory and administrative skills. Eventually the topics covered were expanded to include discussions of plant performance and economics affecting the plant.

Not only did the foremen perform more competently because of these meetings, but plant objectives were communicated to the hourly workers as well. The addition of some clerical personnel allowed the foremen to spend more time on the plant floor, and the workers benefited from the increased contact.

One of Nelson's priorities was improving the way the workers viewed themselves in relation to Bethoney. He felt that the dirty condition of the plant contributed to the workers' feeling that they were treated like second-class citizens. Nelson was determined to reverse this perception by treating the workers like first-class citizens, beginning with their work environment.

Realizing that work in a glass plant could only be improved to a point, Nelson and Jim Riley looked for other ways to improve attitudes. Olsen's theory was, "If we can't make the job more glamorous, maybe we can make people feel better about themselves and the place they work." Riley's values survey had revealed that the people had "tribalistic" tendencies and needed a sense of community, and this led to the idea of sponsoring sports leagues. The first experiment was with a company-sponsored golf league. When this was positively received, Nelson tried leagues for other sports. He gave hourly employees the responsibility for organizing teams, competitions, and activities, and he provided the funding. Soon there were softball teams, basketball teams, bowling leagues, and a running club.

These sports leagues did not appeal to every employee, however. Some felt that if they did not participate in sports, they were being cheated because more money was being spent on the participants than on them. Others claimed that people participating in the leagues were treated preferentially: "If you golf or run around here, they don't put you to work."

In addition to his sports program, Nelson instituted tuition reimbursement for workers attending college. He even brought a professor from Farmington College to the plant to teach a class every week. Nelson estimated that Bethoney paid $15,000 to $20,000 per semester in tuition.

While Nelson worked on improving attitudes, plant engineer Larry Johnson worked steadily on improving machine maintenance. Under his direction the maintenance department established a reputation of being reliable and competent. Not only did the machines run more smoothly, but production personnel learned that they could depend on the promises of the maintenance department.

Roger Atkins was another key actor in improving the plant. After the strike, Atkins replaced Russell Waters as employee relations manager for Farmington Operations. He established a reputation for being absolutely trustworthy and fair. While he was sympathetic to the workers' situation, he never compromised management's position. In the months following the strike he spent many hours on the plant floor, developing personal relationships with hourly employees and foremen. For most workers, this was more contact with management than they ever had. This went a long way to defuse tensions between labor and management.

Roger Atkins had worked with Arn Nelson in the Riverton plant for a few years before coming to Farmington. They had a good relationship and worked well together. As the hourly employees grew to trust Atkins, he was able to improve Nelson's image in their eyes as well.

Jim Riley's values survey had indicated that nearly one third of Plant G employees, many of them union officers, had a high interest in plant management. He and Nelson wanted to give them a voice in decisions affecting them. They initiated a program to bring a participative management approach to the plant. This was intended to allow foremen, union leaders and workers to meet together and work on common concerns. The first step was to expose union leadership to participative management techniques. They took them to a seminar conducted by Scott Myers, whose theme was that mutual sacrifice and cooperation between union and management can be to the best benefit of both sides. The reaction of the union committee was generally positive. The next step was to give the same seminar to the foremen.

The foremen were interested in what they learned from Myers, but had some reservations. Some feared that the people they now supervised would prove to be smarter than they were if given a chance to express themselves. Others were insecure about conducting meetings with employees. Most foremen adopted the attitude of waiting to see how things turned out before fully committing themselves to Myers's participative approach.

The third step in the program was to have Myers talk to union stewards and foremen at the same time. This was to occur after contract negotiations in a the summer of 1980.

Meanwhile, the top levels of the union, the president and the union committee, were working more and more effectively with plant management. Bob Graham, former vice-president, was elected president of the local in 1978, and he set about to administer the contract fairly and accurately. Newly elected members of the union committee were more sympathetic to the company's needs. Nelson's reputation for honesty and fairness won the committee's respect and trust. Though never free from confrontations, union relations became workable.

Now Nelson looked to the future. He knew that according to the Bethoney pattern, he would *not* be manager of Plant G for many years longer. He hoped that the improvements which had begun at Plant G would continue. One hourly employee, remembering the management transition in 1974 when Nelson had come to Plant G, was not optimistic:

> Take Arn for example. He came here about five years ago. No one liked him at first and everyone had to adjust to a change. So by the end of five years, things are going pretty well. He's learned to talk to the people; he knows how the plant runs. He goes away and someone has to start from scratch. They are all gung-ho and they are going to make all these wonderful changes but they forget about the 500 people out there and what they are used to. Anytime you make a big change, there's some problems.

But Nelson had a more immediate concern. Contract negotiations would begin in June. The cost of living clause was likely to be the biggest issue again, but no one believed that any issue would be important enough to cause another strike. Arn Nelson was confident that a reasonable agreement would be reached without any of the bitter feelings that existed three years earlier, unless some unforeseen event occurred.

BETHONEY MANUFACTURING (C)

EXHIBIT 1

The performance of plants in Bethoney's Glass Division was measured by deviation from standards. Following are some of the key indicators of the performance of Plant G.

	1974	1975	1976	1977	1978	1979	1980***
OSHA Injuries per 100 Employees							
U.S. manufacturing	12	12	13	13	13	—	—
Bethoney	7	7	8	7	10	10	—
Glass division	8	10	6	6	7	7	—
Plant G	10	13	11	11	12	7	6
Shop Expense Controllables							
Ratio of actual controllable* production expenses to budget production expenses	.99	1.13	1.10	.97	1.05	.95	.89
Plant Expense Controllables							
Ratio of actual controllable** plant expenses to budget plant expenses	1.19	1.05	1.04	.94	1.01	.98	.88
Direct Material Usage Index							
Ratio of direct material usage divided by standard material usage	1.04	1.05	1.04	1.04	1.05	1.03	1.01
Direct Labor Usage Index							
Ratio of direct labor usage divided by standard labor usage	1.13	1.08	1.04	1.02	.97	1.02	.91
Shop Total Variation (% variation from standard)							
Actual usage of direct labor, direct material, direct expense (electricity, gas), and indirect expense, divided by the standard for production	3%	4%	1%	2%	2%	1%	(1%)

Abbreviations: OSHA, Occupational Safety and Health Act.

*Controllable shop expenses include overtime salary, labor premiums, special labor, that is, cleaning, maintenance labor and materials, personal expenses, and the like. Shop expenses are directly related to production.

**Controllable plant expenses include office supplies, purchased services such as telephone and postage, labor and materials for building maintenance, and so on.

***April year to date.

THE COAL STRIKE OF 1977/1978 (B)

White House Pressure

On the morning of Friday, February 24, 1978, President Carter summoned the chief executives of five major coal producers to the White House to discuss the stalled coal negotiations. The company chairmen called were Edgar Speer (U.S. Steel), Howard Blauvelt (Continental Oil, parent of Consolidation Coal), Nicholas Camicia (Pittston Coal), Lewis Foy (Bethlehem Steel), and George Stinson (National Steel).

Other high government executives attended this meeting with President Carter. These included Vice-President Mondale, Labor Secretary Marshall, Energy Secretary Schlesinger, and Federation Mediation and Conciliation Service (FMCS) Director Horwitz. Robert Strauss, Special Trade Representative and a key figure in discussions of steel import quotas and reference point steel pricing, was also involved.

President Carter had scheduled time on national television at nine o'clock that evening to discuss the coal situation. It was made clear that if a settlement was not reached by that afternoon, Carter would denounce the coal operators and begin the mine seizure process.

As Speer departed the White House he commented, "I think I can guarantee some kind of contract."

Second Settlement Reached

At 7:10 P.M., Carter announced that a "negotiated settlement" had been reached. Carter added that he had been prepared to take "drastic steps . . . if the negotiating process had failed." He appealed to the miners directly for ratification. He also announced plans for a Presidential commission to "find answers to the basic questions of health, safety and stable productivity" in the coal industry. He thanked those who "made the collective bargaining process work."

Although the United Mine Workers (UMW) Bargaining Council had not been consulted, Arnold Miller said the council had voted acceptance of

This case was prepared by Richard O. von Werssowetz, Associate Fellow, under the direction of Professor D. Quinn Mills, as a basis for class discussion rather than to illustrate either effective or ineffective handling of an administrative situation.

the provisions used in this latest agreement Wednesday night. This meant that this agreement would be submitted to the rank and file membership for a ratification vote. The vote was expected to take about ten days. This second contract agreement reached (Exhibit 1) was based on the provisions of the Pittsburgh and Midway (P&M) settlement but included some additional features:

—Wages would be increased $2.40 over three years if maximum cost of living assessments (COLA's) of $.30 were reached.
—A $100 payment would be made to each miner following a return to work.
—Health benefits would be guaranteed. However, the health and death benefits would be provided by individual employer plans. Deductibles of up to $750 per family would be charged to the miners. Eye care was added.
—The employers would set up a $5 million trust to reimburse miners for deductibles and coinsurance payments made between July 1, 1977 and December 5, 1977 (the last day before the strike).
—Pension checks omitted during the strike would be paid.
—Revisions would be made to speed up the settlement of grievances.
—Instigators of wildcat strikes would be disciplined. Miners who simply honored pickets specifically could not be penalized.
—A standardized absentee program was required.
—No changes were made to 1974 provisions governing shift determinations or days of work.

Asked what he thought of the final settlement offer, Nicholas Camicia said:

We certainly don't feel good about it. We agreed to it only because the country is in bad shape. We felt we just had to do it for the good of the country.

The UMW immediately began a program to win the miners' approval of the contract. Several hundred miners assembled in Washington to be briefed on the agreement. These union officials would then hold district briefings, to be followed by meetings of individual locals. A $40,000 advertising campaign was initiated. Miller would appear in some of the radio and television broadcasts. Others would feature country singer Johnny Paycheck whose hit song, "You Can Take This Job and Shove It" was popular in coal country.

On February 26, two days after the agreement, miners rejected the P&M settlement by a 2-to-1 margin. Marshall discounted the rejection as merely an attempt to win a better contract (the BCOA's). He noted that the Bargaining Council had accepted the P&M agreement by a vote of 25 to 13. Marshall said the vote "reflects the local union leadership . . . you would expect that would be some indication of the ability of that agreement to succeed.''

As the contract was discussed around the country, some observers noted it may have inadvertently created a "professional picket." Miners could not be punished for crossing a picket line. If someone were hired to picket, wildcat strikes could continue to occur with no penalties. (Presumably the picket could not legally be forced to disclose who hired him.)

With voting scheduled to begin on the weekend of March 4, Marshall indicated that the Carter Administration was prepared to take immediate steps to end the strike if the contract were rejected. Rejection did seem possible due to widespread reports of miners' dissatisfaction. Two of the most controversial issues were the penalties for instigators of wildcats and the new deductibles under the health insurance plans (Exhibit 2). Miller told the press that failure of the members to ratify the proposed contract could mean the end of the union. He said the union would be left bankrupt and that nationwide bargaining between the union and the industry could be destroyed.

Carter Invokes Taft-Hartley As Second Settlement Rejected

The UMW membership rejected the proposed contract by more than a 2-to-1 margin in voting March 3, 4, and 5.

Amid growing public clamor to take action, President Carter invoked the Taft-Hartley Act. (In the next week's Gallup Polls, the President's rating went up substantially.) President Carter declared that continuation of this strike could cause more than a million workers to be laid off within a month. Carter directed Attorney General Bell to seek a court injunction ordering the miners to return to work for 80 days. Three arbitrators were appointed to the fact-finding board of inquiry, which was required as the first step to seeking a court-ordered end to the strike.

In an unusual move, the petition for injunctive relief would request payment of individuals ordered back to work under the proposed wage rates. Normally rates paid under the expired contract would continue. This was done to serve as an incentive to miners to honor a back-to-work order.

The Bituminous Coal Operators Association (BCOA) called on the UMW to establish a new bargaining team "that enjoys the confidence of the membership and that can assure BCOA negotiators and the nation that any new contract recommended by that team will be acceptable to the membership.''

The board of inquiry held hearings on March 6 and then on March 8. At these hearings UMW vice-president Sam Church called use of the Taft-Hartley act "one-sided." Church told the board, "There is no national shortage of coal, only an allocation problem." He noted government reports which indicated that nearly 3 million tons of coal had been exported since the strike had begun and that coal stockpiles at oven-coke plants had actually increased during the same period. Church said:

> If there were a shortage of metallurgical coal for the steel companies, this strike would have been settled weeks ago.

Another union witness also disputed the claims that a national emergency existed:

> There is a big difference between the luxury in which some Americans are used to living, and the danger to the national health and safety. Stores closing early, theaters showing only one feature, heat turned down a few degrees, and slight curtailments of electricity to office buildings and factories is a great deal different from a true national emergency.

In a statement outside the hearings, the UMW outlined five major issues which were still in "serious dispute": the medical deductibles; the continued disparity in pensions under the two plans; a new method of accruing pension credit; the right to fire instigators of wildcats; and cancellation of "freedom of choice" in choosing vacation time (two floating vacation days had been combined with the Christmas holidays).

The BCOA presented its case to the public using full-page newspaper advertisements. The ads argued that the concentration of pressure and criticism on the BCOA was unfair, and that the UMW was unbending. They warned that "irresponsible conduct" should not be rewarded (Exhibit 3).

Temporary Back-to-Work Court Order

On March 9, the Board of Inquiry reported that the dispute had "reached a critical impasse." It said the dispute must be settled "as expeditiously as possible . . . in the national interest." President Carter immediately authorized application for a back-to-work order. A temporary restraining order was issued by the U.S. District Court ordering the miners to return to work Monday, March 13. March 17 was set as the date to consider a permanent injunction.

Under the restraining order, the UMW could not be punished if individual members made decisions to stay home in defiance of their leader's requests. However, the restraining order specifically prohibited anyone from picketing or otherwise interfering with miners who attempted to return to work. (This provision was felt by some to have a bigger impact on non-UMW operations. UMW miners had picketed many such sites and caused them to close. Many expected that removal of the pickets would result in greatly increased production of non-UMW-mined coal. There were widespread doubts that the Carter Administration would actively seek to enforce the order at UMW sites.)

Bargaining between the UMW and BCOA was scheduled to reopen March 10 in compliance with the court order. Federal mediators were not asked to participate. Both sides were reported to be anxious to resume because the government had declared an "impasse." Either side could legally break away from national negotiations and bargain on an individual company basis. There was apparent agreement that such a move would ruin the collective bargaining structure and result in many more disputes in the future.

On that March 9, two coal executives who had started their careers digging coal in the pits were walking back to BCOA headquarters together after lunch. "Hell, Nick," said Stonie Barker, President of Island Creek Coal Company (the fourth largest producer) to Nicholas Camicia. "Let's go over and see the union boys and talk this thing over." Both Barker and Camicia had growing doubts about the government's handling of the coal crisis. As Barker had put it:

> If you want to ask your boss for something, you don't send somebody else in to see him. We've got to eyeball these guys and cut a deal.

After a telephone call to UMW headquarters they started over to seek a new agreement.

THE COAL STRIKE OF 1977/1978 (B)

EXHIBIT 1

UMW-Prepared Summary and Explanation of Proposed 1978 National
Bituminous Coal Wage Agreement
(Agreement announced February 24, 1978)

HIGHLIGHTS OF IMPROVEMENTS IN PROPOSED NATIONAL BITUMINOUS COAL WAGE AGREEMENT OF 1978

WAGES

—A wage increase of $1.00 an hour immediately.
—A raise of 40¢ an hour, plus 30% an hour in COLA, in both the second and third years of the contract. (The same COLA clause that was a part of the 1974 contract is included in this contract, beginning in the second year.) Under the wage agreement, the average UMWA miner will earn an additional $12,000 during the life of the contract. The average miner, without overtime, will earn $5,000 a year more in the third year of the contract than he did in 1977.
—A $100.00 allowance will be paid to each miner in the first paycheck following a return to work.

HEALTH BENEFITS

—The 1950 Health Fund will continue, with a 75% increased in royalties. Benefits will be GUARANTEED.
—Guaranteed health benefits, with limited deductions, for the life of the contract for working miners.
—Employers will set up a special 5 million dollar fund to reimburse members for health-care costs resulting from the July, 1977, reduction in benefits.
—Eye-care coverage is provided for active and retired miners.

PENSIONS

—Payment in full of all pensions that were not paid as a result of the strike.
—An increase of $25.00 a month in pensions for those retired under the 1974 Funds.
—Those retired under the 1950 Pension Funds will have their pensions increased to $275.00, with the black-lung differential eliminated.
—The minimum disability pension is increased to $137.50
—Future pensions will be increased by $1.00 a month for each year of service for those retiring after the effective date of the Agreement (new pension levels are listed in the contract).
—The 1950 and 1974 Pension Trusts are continued as in the 1974 contract, and are GUARANTEED.

SICK AND ACCIDENT BENEFITS

—Sickness and accident benefits are increased from $100.00 a week to $150.00 a week during the course of the contract.

DEATH BENEFITS

—Retroactive death benefits will be paid for those who passed away since the benefits were cancelled.
—Life insurance benefits for working miners are increased to $12,000, plus an additional $12,000 in the event of accidental death or dismemberment.

ADDITIONAL TIME OFF

—An additional company-paid day off, combined with the floating days, will give all miners Christmas vacation extending from Christmas Eve until January 2, regardless of length of service with their Employer.
—Graduated vacations take effect a year earlier, in the sixth year of service.

PLUS

—Clothing allowance, to be paid in the first paycheck following a return to work, is increased to $100.00 a year this year and $125.00 a year thereafter.
—Shift differentials are improved from 15¢ to 20¢ an hour on the afternoon shift and from 20¢ to 30¢ an hour on the midnight shift.
—Major improvements in the grievance procedure will bring quicker action on grievances.
—Bereavement coverage is extended to stepchildren.
—Management is now bound by an absenteeism policy that is strictly controlled by the contract.

IN ADDITION

The UMWA beat back a number of demands by management. Because of this:
—No miner will be fined or disciplined for honoring a picket line.
—There will be no scheduled Sunday work.
—Royalty fees will continue to be paid to the Funds on purchased coal processed through union-operated facilities.
—There are no payback provisions.
—No change in starting times.
—No change in downward or lateral bidding.
—No probationary period.

NOTE

This contract received a two-to-one approval by the UMWA Bargaining Council.

EXHIBIT 1 (*continued*)

ARTICLE BY ARTICLE SUMMARY
AND EXPLANATION OF PROPOSED
1978 NATIONAL BITUMINOUS COAL WAGE AGREEMENT

Article I—ENABLING CLAUSE

No change from 1974 Contract.

Article IA—SCOPE AND COVERAGE

No change from 1974 Contract.

Article II—WORK FORCE STABILITY AND INDUSTRY DEVELOPMENT

This is a new Article, Section (a) provides that employees who picket or actively cause an unauthorized work stoppage may be disciplined. Section (a) also specifically states that miners who honor picket lines will not be disciplined.

Section (b) is a union proposal which standardizes and guarantees a reasonable absentee program through the contract.

Section (c) establishes a Joint Union–Industry Development Committee to study problems in the coal industry.

Article III—HEALTH AND SAFETY

There are only minor changes and clarifications in Article III. Members of the Health and Safety Committee must attend training sessions on a regular basis and will be paid at time and one-half rates for attending such sessions for hours beyond their regular shift. The Safety Committee will be paid for two meetings a month with management. In the future, members of the Safety Committee must have three years mining experience unless the mine is less than three years old.

The clothing allowance has been increased to $100 for 1978 and $125 for 1979 and 1980.

Article IV—WAGES AND HOURS

Hourly wages are increased by $1.00 during the first year of the contract; 10¢ during the second year; and 40¢ during the third year. These are across-the-board increases and apply equally to all employees. COLA is in addition to these wages. If inflation continues at the present rate, wages plus COLA will reach the levels shown below at the end of the third year.

Grade	Deep (8 hr. day)	Strip (7½ hr. day)	Preparation Plant (7½ hr. day)
5	$84.52	$82.12	
4	$81.28	$77.40	$76.22
3	$78.34	$74.76	$74.45
2	$76.56	$72.69	$72.40
1	$75.98	$72.10	$71.82

Article V—HELPERS

No change from 1974 Contract.

Article VI—SHIFTS AND SHIFT DIFFERENTIALS

The differential for the afternoon shift has increased from 15¢ to 20¢ and the differential for the midnight shift has increased from 20¢ to 30¢ per hour.

Article VII—MINE COMMUNICATION COMMITTEES

No change from 1974 Contract.

Article VIII—STARTING TIME

No change from 1974 Contract.

Article IX—ALLOWANCES

Stepchildren are now covered under bereavement pay. In addition, a $100 catch-up allowance will be made to each employee when he returns to work.

Article X—COST-OF-LIVING ADJUSTMENT

The same COLA formula as in the 1974 contract will be applicable beginning with the second year of the Agreement. There is a 30¢ cap for the second year and a 30¢ cap for the third year of the contract. This means there is a possibility of an additional 60¢ per hour on top of the wage increases provided under Article IV.

Article XI—SICKNESS AND ACCIDENT BENEFITS

Sickness and accident benefits will be $120 per week for the first year; $130 during the second year; and $150 during the last year of the Agreement.

Article XII—HOLIDAYS

No change from 1974 Contract.

Article XIII—REGULAR VACATION

There will be three vacation periods instead of the two provided under the 1974 Agreement.

The two floating vacation days under the 1974 contract have been deleted. These two days, plus one new paid day off, will be combined with the three Christmas holidays to provide for a Christmas shutdown period. All employees will now receive six days pay for nine days off beginning with Christmas Eve and ending January 2nd. There is no qualifying period and all employees will receive the full amount of pay regardless of how long they have worked for the Employer.

EXHIBIT 1 (*continued*)
Article XIV—GRADUATED VACATION

The schedule has been dropped from seven years to six years. This means that approximately 70% of all UMWA members will receive an additional paid day off.

Article XV—CHECKOFF

No change from 1974 Contract.

Article XVI—TRAINING

The only substantive change in this Article is that the 90-day period under Section (f) has been changed to 45 working days. The eight-hour yearly retraining under Section (c) will be done in not less than 2-hour increments.

Article XVII—SENIORITY

No substantive change. Panel members will now be allowed by Contract to update their layoff forms once each year.

Article XVIII—TONNAGE RATES AND HAND LOADING

No change from 1974 Contract.

Article XIX—CLASSIFICATION

No change from 1974 Contract.

Article XX—HEALTH AND RETIREMENT BENEFITS

The 1950 Benefit and 1950 Pension Funds

These funds will be continued as under the 1974 Contract. The benefits under these funds will be GUARANTEED. In addition, there will be an increase in the pensions for the 1950s retirees, and the Black Lung differential will be eliminated by the end of the contract. Pension checks missed during the strike will be paid retroactively. A special fund will be set up to reimburse the 1950 pensioners for deductibles and co-insurance payments that they made between July 1, 1977 and December 5, 1977. Although there will be deductibles for medical care, coverage for vision care has been added under the 1950 Benefit Plans. Royalties into the 1950 Funds will increase by approximately 70%. Death benefits for pensioners who died since the strike began will be paid.

The 1974 Pension Trust

This fund will continue as in the 1974 contract with a $25.00 raise for regular pensioners and a $12.50 raise for minimum disability pensioners. For working miners the pension schedule has been increased $1.00 per month per year of service. Benefits under the 1974 Pension Plan are GUARANTEED.

The 1974 Benefit Trust

This Fund will continue, but only for the purpose of providing health care benefits for two groups of miners:

1) Miners retired under the 1974 Pension Plan whose last Employer has gone out of business or goes out of business in the future.
2) Any miner who retires after the effective date of this Agreement whose Employer subsequently goes out of business.

The benefits provided under the 1974 Benefit Trust, including vision care, are the same as the benefits provided under the 1950 Benefit Trust. In addition, active miners and 1974 pensioners will be reimbursed for deductibles and co-insurance payments that they made between July 1, 1977 and December 5, 1977.

New Individual Employer Benefit Plans

As of the effective date of this Agreement, each Employer will provide and guarantee health and death benefits for all his working miners and 1974 pensioners. These benefits will be the same as under the 1974 Contract with the exception of certain deductibles. Eye care will now be provided and working miners will be covered by life insurance of $12,000 plus an additional $12,000 in the event of accidental death for any reason.

The Contract provides that an Employer may at his option continue to provide health benefits to his employees and 1974 pensions through the 1974 Benefit Trust until June 1, 1978, at which time the Employer must convert to an Individual Employer Benefit Plan.

Article XXI—SURFACE MINES

No substantive change from the 1974 Contract.

Article XXII—MISCELLANEOUS

No substantive change from the 1974 Contract.

Article XXIII—SETTLEMENT OF DISPUTES

This Article has undergone major revisions in order to speed up settlement of grievances. The new contract provides for District arbitrators, a shortening of the waiting period under the steps of the grievance procedure, a requirement that arbitrators render decisions within 30 days and a provision that grievances settled at the first step will not constitute a precedent. The Arbitration Review Board will be continued (See Memorandum of Understanding at the end of the Contract) but in a greatly modified form. There will be no Board—only a Chief Umpire—and he will hear only two kinds of cases: 1) those involving conflicting arbitrator's decisions or cases in conflict with prior ARB decisions, and 2) cases involving a substantial contractual issue.

Cases under the 1974 Contract pending before the ARB will be handled by a Special Umpire but the decisions will not be binding on the 1978 Contract.

EXHIBIT 1 (*continued*)

Article XXIV—DISCHARGE PROCEDURES

No change from 1974 Contract.

Article XXV—DISCRIMINATION PROHIBITED

No change from 1974 Contract.

Article XXVI—DISTRICT AGREEMENTS

No change from 1974 Contract.

Article XXVII—MAINTAIN INTEGRITY OF CONTRACT AND RESORT TO COURTS

No change from 1974 Contract.

Article XXVIII—SEVERABILITY CLAUSE

No change from 1974 Contract.

Article XXIX—RATIFICATION AND TERMINATION OF THIS AGREEMENT

This is a three-year contract and will expire thirty-six months from the date of ratification. In the event there is an economic strike when the Contract terminates in 1981, the Employers will pay health care premiums for one month and then deduct it from miners pay checks after they return to work. If the strike lasts more than one month, each employee will be entitled to continue his health care coverage by paying the premium himself.

Source: Reprinted by permission from *Daily Labor Report*, published 1978 by The Bureau of National Affairs, Inc., Washington, D.C.

THE COAL STRIKE OF 1977/1978 (B)

EXHIBIT 2

Coal agreement doomed

SIMON FAHEY

Lord Finchley tried to mend the elec-
tric light himself.
It struck him dead:
And serve him right!
It is the business of the wealthy man
To give employment to the artisan.

The writer Hillaire Belloc made that harsh assertion on morals in labor relations at the turn of the century. And while many of us would quarrel with the quality of justice meted out to Lord Finchley, as an observation of the way things are, the poem is a truism. To wit, we tamper with the working-man's lot only at great peril to our own well-being. And if that working man happens to be a coal miner, we can count on getting it back doubly hard.

Last week you and I became involved, involuntarily, in the coal dispute in the person of our President. As each day of the week passed, with no movement by either side in the dispute, we assumed that the President and his emissaries were working diligently to nudge each side closer to an agreement. In terms of the national economy the stakes were high; even higher for individual households and businesses in the Midwest.

But we didn't worry, you and I, because we, with the President, had all the trump cards remaining. We had Taft-Hartley, the possibility of legislation enabling seizure of the mines and binding arbitration. But best of all, we had the bully-boys of the various federal agencies leashed, growling and visible in the wings. In brief, we, through our leader, could knock some sense into, some intransigence out of, the heads of the disputants in order to achieve a fair and equitable settlement.

On Feb. 24, with Carter's announcement of a settlement "along the lines of . . ." the Pittsburgh and Midway agreement, we breathed easier. We shouldn't have.

The Bituminous Coal Operators Association and President Carter are trying to finesse the miners. It won't work. The settlement contains all of these points the owners want and virtually nothing for the miners. The new pact would take away the miners' free medical care card and replace it with an insurance contract with a $500 deductible. The new pact would, for the first time, allow the owners to suspend or dismiss "instigators" of wildcat strikes. The new pact would limit cost-of-living allowances to 30 cents per hour after the second and third years—a figure that doesn't cover half of our current, and relatively mild, inflation.

In brief, the new pact is a blueprint for disaster. As desperate as they may be, a majority of the miners are not going to ratify a settlement which threatens to destroy their union, takes away important first-dollar medical coverage and leaves them with no more purchasing power at the end of the contract period.

Then what? Brownouts, plant closings, Detroit's assembly lines idle and a ripple effect triggering the Recession of '78. And whether it's Taft-Hartley or seizure that ultimately gets the coal out of the ground, there is sure to be violence with the former or a serious dislocation of our economic system with the first peacetime seizure of private plant assets.

The BCOA managers deserve to be paddled, fraternity-style, by the presidents of Fortune's 500 for giving management a bad name. They, the owners, thought to exploit the lack of national UMW leadership and wound up raping the union in full public view. And all of us deserve at least a slap on the wrist for electing a President who couldn't discern the gross injustice in an agreement he was made to shill for.

Still, there is time for us to avoid Lord Finchley's fate, or at least to be burned less severely. Give the miners their free medical

EXHIBIT 2 (*continued*)

care—it's little enough for such debilitating work. Give the miners their real cost-of-living increases and the agreed-upon wages and let those increased costs be passed on to us through the conduit BCOA. As to stability in the coal fields, as long as mining remains a perilous occupation there will be wildcat strikes.

Finally, if, in the unlikely event that the miners, desperate and down-and-out, should ratify the current settlement, we should gird ourselves for increasing troubles from the coalfields with a concommitant reduction of the role that coal was to have played in our energy crisis. And gird ourselves too, for that time in the future when the young men, forged into leaders during this strike, return in the next to hold our collective hand to the fire.

Simon Fahey is a freelance writer.

Source: The Boston Globe, March 4, 1978. Reprinted by permission of the author.

THE COAL STRIKE OF 1977/1978 (B)

EXHIBIT 3
An Open Letter to: The American People, The Congress, The President

Labor negotiations between the United Mine Workers of America and the Bituminous Coal Operators' Association are receiving much attention from all segments of American society. Understandably, as concern has mounted, leaders from government, labor, and business have become increasingly vocal in their demands for a solution to the present coal strike. Unfortunately, however, the American public has not received any accurate account of what occurred in negotiations.

Until now the Bituminous Coal Operators have refrained from publicly commenting on either the substance or the status of the negotiations, our desire being to not do anything which might upset the delicate process of settlement. But with the rejection of our tentative agreement, we feel we must now set the record straight.

* * *

On February 6, 1978, after long months of bargaining, the Bituminous Coal Operators' Association reached an agreement with the United Mine Workers' bargaining team. The Union obtained a contract which it then described publicly as *"the best Agreement negotiated in any major industry in the past two years."* The first "Agreement" would have been very costly to the operators and coal consumers.

The terms of the Agreement provided for:

—Wage increases totaling $2.35 per hour over the next three years. The increase would result in a daily wage rate alone in excess of $80.00 for the average miner. (On top of this would be shift differential, overtime, holiday, and vacation pay.)
—A $100.00 special bonus payable to each miner upon his return to work;
—A clothing allowance increase to $125.00

by the beginning of the second year of the Agreement;
—A 33% increase in shift differential pay for miners working afternoon shifts, and a 50% increase in shift differential pay for miners working the midnight shift;
—Establishment of a special $5,000,000.00 fund to help reimburse miners for health bills incurred by them as a result of decreased health benefits which resulted from underfunding of their health plan due to illegal strikes during the term of the last agreement;
—Retroactive death benefits for the family of any miner who died during the strike which commenced at the expiration of the last agreement;
—Restored and guaranteed health insurance benefits;
—Guaranteed advancement of health and life insurance premiums for the first 30 days of any valid economic strike called at the expiration of the new Agreement;
—A new eye care program providing specified coverage for eye examinations, lenses, and frames;
—Establishment of increased life insurance benefits plus increased benefits for accidental death or dismemberment;
—Increased pensions covering even retired miners;
—Increased sickness and accident benefits;
—A Christmas shutdown period from Christmas Eve through New Year's Day; and
—Increased graduated vacation and one additional vacation day.

The employment cost resulting from the package of wages and benefits agreed to by the companies would have exceeded $35,000.00 per year per miner by the end of the contract.

In trade for all of these increases in pay and

EXHIBIT 3 (*continued*)

benefits, the operators received improvements in the contract designed to support productivity and stabilize the work force.

As *we are all aware*, the agreement reached with the Union's bargaining team on February 6, 1978, was rejected by the UMWA Bargaining Council. As a result of that rejection, it became apparent that future negotiations with the UMWA would be worthwhile only if the dissident factions of the Bargaining Council were represented in the face-to-face negotiations. BCOA representatives therefore insisted on that change in any new discussions.

Negotiations resumed, this time at the White House with members of the UMWA Bargaining Council present; and the UMWA's list of demands simply expanded. BCOA offered to submit all unresolved bargaining issues to binding arbitration by an impartial panel, but the Union categorically rejected our offer.

It must be remembered that the negotiations in the White House began *after* the original UMWA bargaining team had reached an "agreement" with the BCOA; *after* the UMWA president had stated that the agreement was "the best Agreement negotiated in any major industry in the past two years"; *after* the Secretary of Labor had said that the agreement was "a fair contract, genuinely good for both parties"; *after* Administration officials volunteered that their only concern was that the agreement was "very, very expensive"; and *after* the operators had made costly concessions in order to obtain the assurances of uninterrupted work during the agreement's term.

The agreement had been repudiated by the Bargaining Council; but we soon learned that not all bets were off. Instead, only the UMWA's promises were negated—the promises of BCOA were now deemed to be the *minimum* upon which the UMWA would build.

Under enormous pressures, BCOA gave in one-by-one on most of those hard-earned improvements to which the Union, in return for its rich package, had previously agreed.

But the UMWA gave up nothing from the "agreement" which its bargaining team had accepted two weeks earlier. Instead, it demanded and ultimately received an effective wage increase beyond what had been negotiated in that first "agreement." But still the Union is not satisfied.

* * *

The UMWA holds the nation hostage with threats of devastating losses of power. UMWA members have openly told the American people that "we may freeze, but you will freeze with us." Such threats, though they display remarkable insensitivity, might be tolerable if they were backed only by a legal strike. But even this is not the case. For although the UMWA represents only about half of the nation's coal miners, it has, through violence and intimidation, virtually stopped all movement of coal. It has denied the right to work to nonunion miners—miners who have not come to work to replace union miners, miners who are not "scabs," but men who have worked for years for nonunionized coal companies. Moreover, lost in recent weeks has been the memory of why the nation's coal stockpiles have been too low to weather the current strike: Those low stockpiles are the direct result of a widespread wildcat strike engaged in by UMWA members for 10 weeks in 1977, *during the term of the last labor agreement*.

Now the Union has rejected a contract which contained language intended to cure a problem which has plagued the industry and harmed the nation's energy goals—the problem of wildcat strikes.

During the three-year term of the last coal agreement, BCOA companies suffered over 8,900 illegal wildcat strikes which resulted in a loss of over 45 million man hours and lost production of over 62 million tons of coal. Miners themselves lost over 350 million dollars in wages; and their own welfare and pension funds lost in excess of 110 million dollars in royalties and contributions (which, ironically, BCOA is not asked to make up as an additional cost of settlement). Wildcat UMWA strikes during the term of the last labor agreement caused BCOA companies to lose the equivalent of 1/4 ton of coal for every man, woman, and child in the entire United States. Throughout the term of the last contract, mine after mine was shut down by UMWA pickets. Repeatedly, mine shutdowns dominoed as roving bands of pickets carried their disputes to neighboring mines. Violence and threats of violence by UMWA members were commonplace.

We emphasize that we are *not* talking here about economic strikes such as the strike currently in progress. The BCOA does *not* seek to require miners to relinquish their right to engage in a legal strike. Nor are we talking about situations where miners validly leave their jobs for legitimate safety reasons. Rather, our purpose was and is in halting wildcat strikes—strikes in disregard of the UMWA's contractual commitments and in violation of national labor policy. The dockets of federal courts across the country have been swollen with thousands of suits over such strikes; legions of contempt citations issued against UMWA locals and districts present a sad commentary on the impunity with which such strikes are called. History has shown contracts with the UMWA to be unique in one respect—they are the *only* labor contracts in the United States regularly flouted by union members.

Moreover, we are *not* talking about all mine workers. *We continue to believe that the majority of mine workers desire to work without these interruptions which are also costly to them; but we just as readily appreciate the psychology of mob action and the demonstrated potential for violence which flows from a union's total failure to curb the illegal acts of a few of its members.*

Against this background, the operators would have been unbelievably derelict not to insist on a contract which would support and stabilize work schedules in the coalfields. Ironically, at great cost we have sought only what one would normally expect as the automatic result of entering into a contract—namely, that the other party will perform its part of the bargain.

We as coal operators recognize a duty to the American people to do everything possible to bring an end to the present strike. We recognize the harmful effects of the strike on lives and property. *But we also recognize the very real possibility that the extortionary conduct of some miners will not end with the signing of a new agreement unless that agreement provides a mechanism for dealing with that same illegal conduct during the term of the agreement.*

In reporting on provisions which were to become part of the Labor Management Relations Act of 1947, the Senate Committee on Labor and Public Welfare commented:

If unions can break agreements with relative impunity, then such agreements do not tend to stabilize industrial relations. The execution of an agreement does not by itself promote industrial peace. The chief advantage which an employer can reasonably expect from a collective labor agreement is assurance of uninterrupted operation during the term of the agreement. *Without some effective method of assuring freedom from economic warfare for the term of the agreement, there is little reason* why an employer would desire to sign such a contract. (Senate Report No. 105, 80th Cong., 1st Sess 16.)

Yet ironically, from some quarters pressure and criticism continue to be concentrated against the BCOA, without recognition of any obligation on the part of the United Mine Workers. Some speak of seizure of the mines, never even mentioning the possibility of seizure of the Union. Some talk of the Taft-Hartley Act, but fail to recognize the significance of their own forecasts that the Union members will probably refuse to abide by any lawful order to return to work. Some label the operators "inflexible," yet berate our offers to submit to binding arbitration. Some attempt to place the onus of settlement solely on the BCOA, yet fail to grasp the basis of the Mine Workers' refusal to submit disputed issues to impartial arbitration.

We ask for a measure of reason and objectivity, especially by those privileged to represent the American people. The pressured settlement has already sacrificed many important energy goals. It has also broken the President's call for wage–price moderation. Surely it is not too much to ask merely for a reasonable assurance of labor peace during the term of the next labor agreement.

We reached an agreement with the UMWA negotiating committee—but that agreement was rejected by the UMWA Bargaining

EXHIBIT 3 (*continued*)

Council. So we reached another agreement with the Bargaining Council—now that, too, has been rejected. The responsibility for ending the coalfield chaos must now pass to the UMWA and its membership.

* * *

The Bituminous Coal Operators have leaned over backwards to end the strike. All of us must now support lawful efforts to work without rewarding irresponsible conduct.

Source: Reprinted by permission of the Bituminous Coal Operators' Association, Inc.

THE COAL STRIKE OF 1977/1978 (C)

Camicia and Barker's spur-of-the-moment overture to the UMW resulted in reopened coal negotiations February 9, 1978. First they sought a new union negotiating team without success. (Reportedly, the three anti-Miller district presidents offered to resign if Miller would, but were refused.) In return, the union objected to the continued participation of some earlier BCOA negotiators, particularly Johnston and Brown. Johnston was dropped as a member of the BCOA team.

After three days of bargaining, the negotiations recessed March 12 to allow the United Mine Workers (UMW) to consider the latest Bituminous Coal Operators Association (BCOA) proposal. The BCOA was willing to make a number of improvements to the second "agreement" in return for inclusion of a productivity bonus incentive program. (The UMW had opposed such incentive plans in the past, citing fears of endangering safety.)

Among the features of the new proposal were sharp reductions in health plan deductibles. Pension payments under the 1950 plan would be raised to lower the gap between payments under it and the 1974 plan. Disciplinary actions taken against instigators of wildcat strikes would be subject to possible reversal by arbitrators. The two floating vacation days would be restored.

On March 13, most union miners ignored the court order to return to work. According to the BCOA, "fewer than 100 striking miners complied."

On March 14, the third tentative contract agreement was announced by Miller and Camicia. The agreement incorporated the BCOA concessions offered March 12, but did not include the productivity incentive plan. Provisions which would have allowed operators to dismiss leaders of wildcat strikes were dropped.

On March 16, the Bargaining Council voted to accept the new proposal, 22 to 17. The council vote was taken at the Labor Department after miners protesting invocation of the Taft-Hartley Act blocked union headquarters. The council set March 24 as the single day for members to vote on ratification of the contract. Some union officials felt that spreading the voting for the second agreement over three days had influenced the outcome of the previous ratification vote.

This case was prepared by Richard O. von Werssowetz, Associate Fellow, under the direction of Professor D. Quinn Mills, as the basis for class discussion rather than to illustrate either effective or ineffective handling of an administrative situation.

The District Court refused government requests to extend the temporary back-to-work injunction which expired March 17. The court ruled that the evidence did not prove that a national emergency existed and scheduled a hearing March 29 on the request for the full 80-day injunction. In denying the request for extension of the temporary order, the court noted that the government had made no effort to enforce it with contempt-of-court citations.

There was a strong sense of victory in many coal mining areas. One coal miners' song related how the miners had had to beat the utilities and the government before they beat the owners. The long strike had exhausted the utilities' stockpiles of coal. The government-supported second agreement had been rejected and the back-to-work order ignored. The miners felt that without the backing of the utilities and the government, the owners were exposed. Once they had exposed the owners, the miners had won.

The UMW prepared no summary of this third agreement for distribution as they had for the second agreement. Copies of the full agreement were given to the miners as the proposed contract was discussed. No advertising was planned as it was felt that the campaign for the last agreement was counterproductive.

On March 24, UMW members ratified the third agreement, 57 to 43 percent. Miller signed the contract the next day officially ending the 110-day strike as of 12:01 A.M., Monday, March 27. The mines remained closed by pickets of construction workers awaiting settlement and ratification of a contract with the Association of Bituminous Contractors (ABC). By April 4, the ABC contract had been ratified and the miners returned to work.

On May 30, President Carter named West Virginia governor Jay Rockefeller to be chairman of the President's Commission on the Coal Industry. The commission was to report to Carter within a year. Rockefeller had been an active behind-the-scenes participant throughout the coal negotiations.

In August the UMW announced that a constitutional convention would be held in September 1979. The agenda of the convention was not disclosed.

After a prolonged discussion, the Carter Administration agreed in November to release data to Congress concerning the possible increase in unemployment that might have been caused by a longer coal strike. Despite some government assertions of possibly up to 3.5 million unemployed made in March, Labor Department reports only indicated 27,000 affected. A debate ensued about the past likelihood of a "national emergency" caused by the strike.

In May 1979, utilities regulators in a number of jurisdictions found that coal produced by captive mines owned by utilities companies frequently cost more than independently mined coal. Some utilities were suspected of using the captive-coal operations to artificially increase profits in nonregulated areas of their business, thereby circumventing the regulatory process. Utilities' representatives noted that the price of coal fluctuates as a commodity. These representatives argued that captive mines were needed to assure long-term supplies.

In late May 1979, Consolidation Coal, the second largest U.S. producer, announced its withdrawal from the BCOA and that it would bargain independently with the UMW in 1981.

THE COAL STRIKE OF 1977/1978 (C)

EXHIBIT 1
Cost of UMW Labor Contract

	1974 Agreement	1978 Agreement	1974 Agreement 12/5/77	1978 Agreement 3/27/78	3/27/79	3/27/80
Average per day rate for underground miners	$\frac{34 \times \$60.86}{227}$	$\frac{37 \times \$69.14}{224}$	$ 53.74	$ 68.14	71.34	74.54
COLA ($.80/hr. × 8 hrs.)			6.40		2.40	4.80
Shift differential (1)			.72	1.00	1.00	1.00
Straight time per day cost			$ 60.86	$ 69.14	74.74	80.34
Overtime (1 hour @ time and ½ rate)			$ 11.41	$ 12.96	14.01	15.06
Total per day wage			$ 72.27	$ 82.10	88.75	95.40
Cost of nonworking days (2)			9.12	11.42	12.35	13.27
Protective clothing	$\frac{\$75}{227}$	$\frac{\$100}{224}$	.33	.45	.56	.56
Reporting allowance		$\frac{224 \text{ days} \times 3 \text{ yrs.}}{224}$	—	.15	.15	.15
Per hour welfare fund (3)	9 hrs. × $1.54	9 hrs. × $1.65	13.86	14.85	14.94	14.85
1974 benefit trust make-up (4)			—	.04	.04	.04
Workmen's compensation	18% × $72.27	18% × $82.10	13.01	14.78	15.98	17.17
Unemployment compensation	$\frac{3.4\% \times \$4,200}{227 \text{ days}}$ $\frac{\$110.76}{227 \text{ days}}$	$\frac{4.9\% \times \$6,000}{224 \text{ days}}$ $\frac{\$134.04}{224 \text{ days}}$	.63	1.31	1.31	1.31
Sickness & accident insurance			.49	.60	.60	.60
Black lung	8.41% × $72.27	8.41% × $82.10	6.08	6.90	7.46	8.02
FICA	5.85% × $72.27	6.05% × $82.10	4.23	4.97	5.37	5.77
Total per man day cost			$120.02	$137.57	$147.51	$157.14
Per ton welfare fund			$ .82	$ 1.385	$ 1.385	$ 1.385

(1) Shift differential

Assumes 45% day shift, 40% second shift, 15% third shift.

(2) Nonworking days

	1974 Agreement	1978 Agreement
Days in year	365	365
Saturdays & Sundays	104	104
Regular vacation	10	10
Holidays	10	10
Floating vacation	2	4
Graduated vacation (assumes 12 yr. service)	6	7
Sick days	5	5
Safety seminar	1	1
Available workdays	227	224

(3) Per hour welfare fund

Assumes 1974 benefit trust can be funded for $.88 per man-hour as per 1974 Agreement

(4) 1974 benefit trust make-up

$.165 per man per hour for first month of agreement

$.165 × 9 hrs/day × 18.67 days/mo. = $.04 per man-day

224 days/yr. × 3 yrs.

	Per Ton Cost		
	Labor Cost	Per Ton Welfare	Per Ton Cost
6 tons/man-day	$2.925	+ $ .565	– $3.49
8 tons/man-day	2.194	+ .565	– 2.76
10 tons/man-day	1.755	+ .565	– 2.32
12 tons/man-day	1.463	+ .565	– 2.03
14 tons/man-day	1.254	+ .565	– 1.82
16 tons/man-day	1.097	+ .565	– 1.66
18 tons/man-day	.975	+ .565	– 1.54
20 tons/man-day	.878	+ .565	– 1.44

Source: Endowment Management and Research Corporation.

WORKERS' COUNCILS: HOBBEMA & VAN RIJN, N.V. (B)

During the evening of December 10, Dirk van Berkel and his colleagues on the management board took stock of the situation and reached several decisions. To counteract the possibility that the Central Workers' Council was reaching a decision without any feeling of responsibility for the outcome, it was agreed that before the meeting of the elected members, scheduled for the next afternoon, van Berkel would inform them that management would regard negative advice from the Council as a veto.

The management board also considered the idea that many of the difficulties had occurred because he had never had any face-to-face contact with the Amersfoort workers' council. He and his colleagues agreed that he should meet with them as soon as possible. This was arranged by having Jan Sonneveldt suggest to his council that they discuss the situation with van Berkel. Members of the council accepted this suggestion and a meeting was arranged for the morning of December 11 in Amersfoort.

Finally, the management board agreed that in the meeting with the Amersfoort council, van Berkel should attempt to explore the possibility of a compromise built on a partial sale. It was agreed that a retention of a 49 percent interest was out of the question, and that a 20 percent interest was most suitable. However, Dirk van Berkel was authorized to accept a deal based on Hobbema & van Rijn retaining, for a relatively short period of years, a 40 percent interest in the division. It was understood, of course, that if such a compromise were reached, it would have to be approved by the Board of Directors.

This case was prepared by Professor Dwight R. Ladd with the generous help of a company which wishes to remain anonymous. It is intended to provide a basis for classroom discussion rather than to illustrate either effective or ineffective handling of an administrative situation. This case has been revised and edited by Bert Spector, Research Associate, under the direction of Michael Beer, Lecturer, Harvard Business School, with the permission of IMEDE.

WORKERS' COUNCILS:
HOBBEMA & VAN RIJN, N.V. (C)

December 11: Amersfoort Council Offers Proposal

Dirk van Berkel met with the Amersfoort workers' council on the morning of December 11, and was immediately met with an ultimatum that the workers would go on strike if the sale of the division were approved. After this initial hostile outburst, van Berkel referred to the suggestion of a partial sale which had been included in the council's report to management. He explained that the 51 percent sale proposed in the report would not interest management because the result would really be a joint venture rather than a sale. However, he did indicate that Hobbema & van Rijn would consider retaining a smaller participation and after some discussion back and forth a 60 percent sale with the remaining 40 percent to be sold in equal annual installments over five years beginning in 1977 was proposed by van Berkel.

The Amersfoort council countered this with qualifications that the sale of the additional 8 percent in any year could be made only if the Amersfoort Division (not the whole of the purchasing company) had operated at a profit, and that Hobbema & van Rijn could sell to a third party only after five years and only if the purchaser had not used his option. Finally, the Amersfoort council insisted that the new company agree to maintain labor conditions on the same basis as those held under Hobbema & van Rijn.

A written statement was prepared in which van Berkel agreed to try to get approval from the board of directors for this agreement, and if the Board approved, the council agreed to give a positive advice to management. The meeting ended with the signing of this agreement about half an hour after it began.

December 12: Central Workers' Council Gives Its Advice

Because the Amersfoort members of the Central Workers' Council were unable to reach company headquarters in time for the afternoon meet-

This case was prepared by Professor Dwight R. Ladd with the generous help of a company which wishes to remain anonymous. It is intended to provide a basis for classroom discussion rather than to illustrate either effective or ineffective handling of an administrative situation. This case has been revised and edited by Bert Spector, Research Associate, under the direction of Michael Beer, Lecturer, Harvard Business School, with the permission of IMEDE.

ing of that group, it was postponed until the morning of December 12. However, during the afternoon of the 11th, van Berkel met informally with the other members and told them that their negative advice would be considered as a veto.

WORKERS' COUNCILS:
HOBBEMA & VAN RIJN, N.V. (D)

Dirk van Berkel did not have an entirely easy time selling the compromise to his Board of Directors. Opposition came especially from the chairman and from one other member. Two objections were raised. The first was that Hobbema & van Rijn was somewhat at the mercy of the purchaser who could shift all of his unprofitable business to the Amersfoort plant. The second was that for accounting purposes, the 40 percent interest should really be written down to a very nominal value, an action which would wipe out a substantial proportion of 1974 reported profits. However, after considerable discussion, the Board approved the terms of the sale.

Van Berkel Evaluates the Events

In reviewing the development of the Amersfoort situation, van Berkel felt that, on balance, the result was beneficial for all concerned, and better than it would have been if management had handled it alone. He believed that the results provided better protection for the Amersfoort personnel. Within Hobbema & van Rijn, he believed that employees' morale was fostered because employees felt that they had not been manipulated; that they had fought for a voice in decision making and had an impact on a decision which directly affected them. He agreed that in a purely financial sense, Hobbema & van Rijn would probably have been better off with a straight unencumbered sale, but that this was more than offset by the other factors mentioned above.

He also felt that the affair had left some scars that probably could have been avoided. He asserted that he should have intervened personally with the Amersfoort council before feelings had become so aroused. He did observe that his slowness in intervening was partly attributable to a deficiency in the law governing workers' councils. Some of the difficulty might have been avoided if there were legal provisions for combining the two councils

This case was prepared by Professor Dwight R. Ladd with the generous help of a company which wishes to remain anonymous. It is intended to provide a basis for classroom discussion rather than to illustrate either effective or ineffective handling of an administrative situation. This case has been revised and edited by Bert Spector, Research Associate, under the direction of Michael Beer, Lecturer, Harvard Business School, with the permission of IMEDE.

in such cases. This would have kept him in touch with the local council, and possibly have diminished the rivalry between the two councils.

On the morning of December 12, the Central Workers' Council met to decide on its advice to management. At the beginning of the meeting they were informed by van Berkel about the 60-40 compromise plan. The Council had previously arranged to have expert opinion from the manager and controller of the Amersfoort Division and from the controller of Hobbema & van Rijn. These men were questioned both about the sale in general and about the 60-40 arrangement. After due deliberation, the Council voted to give management advice approving the sale on the 60-40 basis.

WORKERS' COUNCILS: HOBBEMA & VAN RIJN, N.V. (E)

On March 11, 1975, Dirk van Berkel received a telephone call from the purchaser of the company's Amersfoort Division. The purchaser explained that because of the general deterioration of business conditions in the early part of 1975 which had weakened his markets and because of inability to make reasonable financing arrangements, he would be unable to go through with the planned purchase. While there was some doubt about the legality of the purchaser's position, the management board decided not to press the issue, and proceeded to arrange meetings with the Central Workers' Council and the workers' council of the Amersfoort Division to inform them of the change. The first meeting was with the Amersfoort council.

Van Berkel approached this meeting with a good deal of trepidation, because it had turned out that the bases for the Council's earlier objections to the sale had been proven to be quite sound. He was quite prepared to be met with, "We told you so!" However, the Council's response was quite different. The immediate conclusion of the members was that "we"—by which they meant workers *and* top management—"have been cheated by that bastard." They observed that even with the guarantees agreed to by the proposed purchaser, they would have been in a difficult position had the sale gone through quickly. Thus they were pleased with the delay resulting from the lengthy Council consideration.

Following this initial burst of enthusiasm, the Amersfoort council submitted a list of questions to management about the future. The prime concern, of course, was whether management would immediately look for another buyer. Because of the poor results of the Amersfoort Division, management had said repeatedly in the controversy over the sale, that to keep the division within Hobbema & van Rijn would require a good deal of cleaning up—including the elimination of a number of jobs. The Amersfoort workers' council understood this, but were concerned that management's purpose in cleaning up would simply be to make the division a more attractive purchase. Eventually management agreed not to sell the division for five years without the consent of the Workers' Council. In return, the

This case was prepared by Professor Dwight R. Ladd with the generous help of a company which wishes to remain anonymous. It is intended to provide a basis for classroom discussion rather than to illustrate either effective or ineffective handling of an administrative situation. This case has been revised and edited by Bert Spector, Research Associate, under the direction of Michael Beer, Lecturer, Harvard Business School, with the permission of IMEDE.

Council agreed to cooperate in the necessary clean-up of the operation, an agreement which included acceptance of management's refusal to put any ceiling on the number of jobs to be eliminated. In effect, management bought the cooperation of the workers in a major job-eliminating reorganization by agreeing to sell only with the latter's approval. A number of other matters regarding the operation of Amersfoort Division were also included in this agreement which was, in effect, approved by both workers' councils, in April.

After this rather unexpected denouncement, van Berkel still felt that, on the whole, the Amersfoort affair had been a positive experience for Hobbema, particularly as it affected the company's relationship with its workers.

WEBSTER INDUSTRIES (B)

In October 1975 Webster Industries found it necessary to reduce its managerial personnel by 20 percent. Bob Carter, manufacturing manager of the company's Fabrics Division, was charged with making a 15 percent reduction in his department.[1] This case describes how that reduction was accomplished and its impact upon the department.

THE PROCESS

Bob Carter described the sequence of events as they occurred on Monday, October 20, 1975:

> After discussing Cecil Stevens's memorandum on performance appraisal, we formulated our approach. This was around noon. We broke for lunch before beginning implementation of our plans. During lunch someone remarked that production superintendent Russell Brown, who was scheduled to be demoted, had the longest managerial tenure in the department and probably would be able to provide invaluable input.
>
> We all agreed that Russ was an example of the Peter Principle, that he had been an excellent plant manager before being promoted to production superintendent. We decided to offer him a demotion to a plant manager position. After lunch I made the offer to Russ who—to my surprise—expressed shock *and* relief. It was as if he had wanted the burden lifted. Russ also agreed to participate in our deliberations.
>
> I guess you can describe what we did later in four steps: (1) reorganization, (2) staffing of new organization, (3) a second review of personnel, and (4) an upgrading review. We decided that we would do what was best for the business. Our thinking was centered around three basic questions: What are our departmental objectives and tasks? How do we have to go about accomplishing these objectives and tasks? What positions are needed to accomplish these tasks and objectives? Based on our answers to these questions, we reorganized the department. Among other actions, this involved the closing of one apparel plant

[1]"Webster Industries (A)," HBS Case Services No. 476–110, contains background data, a description of Carter's reaction to his assignment, and Steven's memorandum.

Assistant Professor R. Roosevelt Thomas, Jr., prepared this case as a basis for class discussion rather than to illustrate either effective or ineffective handling of an administrative situation. All names and places have been disguised.

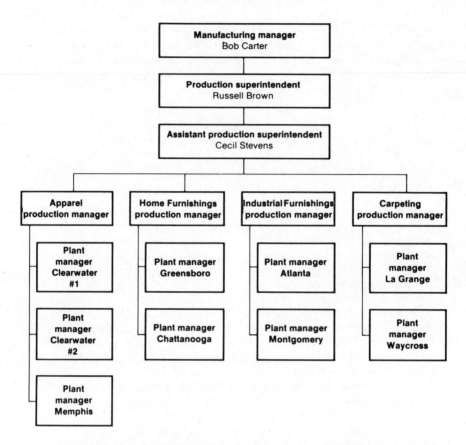

FIGURE A

Old Fabrics Division Organization Chart

and the elimination of the home furnishings production manager position. The home furnishings plants were made the responsibility of the industrial furnishings production manager (see *Figures A and B*).

After the reorganization, we wanted to staff the positions with the best possible people. Here, we called in Jack Bryant and his audit data. He served as a useful check on our perceptions. Typically, an individual's name would come up and we would all voice our opinions. It was a time of truth telling. I feel that the input was realistic and fair. Where our perceptions did not jibe with his audit data, Jack would quickly let us know. Between the audit data and our comments, I think we got some good assessments. PAS [Performance Appraisal System] data, where available, was thrown in by Jack; however, little weight was given to it. We just did not trust it.

During the staffing the basic issue was, Who is the best person for this position? Decisions were based on assessments of individuals' performance *and*

New Fabrics Division Organization Chart

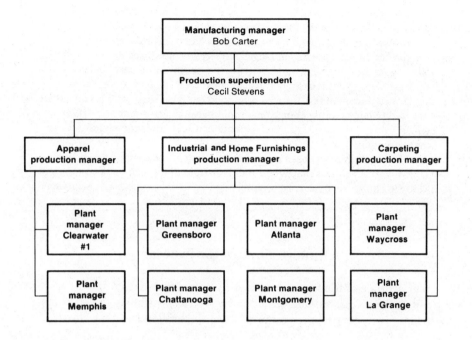

potential. It is difficult for me to say which received the greater weight. What was clear, however, was that an individual with both performance and potential was better off than one with either of the two. After staffing the positions, the excess employees were our prime candidates for separation. We referred to this as our excess list.

The excess list was reviewed. We wanted to make certain to the extent possible that we did not release anyone better than the people we were keeping. Again, Jack was very helpful. We did make several changes, especially where an excess individual was broad enough to qualify for more than one position. At this point our tentative list was 5 over our reduction guideline of 43.

Before finalizing the list I asked Jack to learn who was available from the other divisions. From Jack's list we identified seven people superior to individuals we were proposing to retain. We added to our reduction list accordingly and made offers to the seven former employees of our sister divisions. Our final list was composed of 55 names.

Because of our long working hours—until 10 P.M. on Monday and Tuesday nights—I was able to present our list at 2 P.M. on Wednesday to the other divisional managers. They disagreed with 3 of our recommendations; consequently, our final list was down to 53. In addition, 6 individuals were demoted to the weekly payroll.

I am finding it difficult to describe the trauma we experienced. What I have told you sounds too cold. It does not capture the intense sensitivity we had to human pain and suffering. One case in particular comes to mind.

We terminated a plant engineer. Ray Pearson, who had been with Webster 23 years and was 52 years old. He had three children—one of whom was just entering law school. Though his performance had been unsatisfactory for at least the last 10 years, he was not given any negative feedback until the fall of 1974. Concerned that he would be paying for the sins of his past managers, we really agonized over his case. Because we all knew Ray and had worked with him in various community settings, we found our decision to be especially difficult. But we had no other choice, he simply was not performing. Abe [Webster's president] reluctantly agreed with our action. Unfortunately, Ray's case was not unique.

The community has been very understanding of the company's position. Generally, the feeling is that Webster did the right thing. Abe did a good job of presenting our case. Drastic action was required to preserve our financial integrity.

Attitudes Toward the Process

The attitude of the top manufacturing managers was that the process had not been perfect, but had been done as well as possible—"given human frailties." Cecil Stevens, the new production superintendent remarked:

We did the best we could under the circumstances. I would have liked more time; I did not like the "rush-rush" atmosphere. We let some *good* people go. My guess is that 75 percent of those released were at least satisfactory employees. My misgivings about the process have been somewhat mitigated by the success that some former employees have experienced in getting new jobs at significantly higher pay.

When put in a situation like we were, one eventually begins to play God. And even to believe eventually that he is God. During the process a feeling of doing the right thing had prevailed. After all, God does not make mistakes. After the fact, however, we realized that we were still mortals and that mortal decisions had been made. Nevertheless, I do feel that the department is much, much stronger than before. We came out of it well.

The apparel production manager who participated in the process offered these thoughts:

My belief in the rightness of the macro-decision made it easier for me to participate in the micro-decision making. My greatest concern was that too many people had to pay for the mistakes of their managers. These employees either had no business being in their positions, or no inkling of their relative standing in terms of performance and potential. Also, there were too many instances of individuals having been retained long after they had ceased to be effective. All of this represented poor management of performance.

Impact of the Reduction in Work Force

The most frequently cited impact was the shattering of the Webster belief structure. Bob Carter considered this shattering to be a very important point:

> The Webster employee had been laboring under the assumption that "if I make it past my tenth year and remain loyal to the company, the company will take care of me." This was the basic premise of the belief structure that was shattered by the large reduction.
>
> A belief structure is what you believe even in the absence of supporting evidence. It is what keeps you going. And it is necessary—just to get out of bed each morning. Our task as managers is to foster the development of a replacement that will be supportive of the company. We want to reinforce those beliefs supportive of the company and discourage those that would be dysfunctional.
>
> If we were to encourage the belief that loyal individuals will be safe for life, we would be dishonest—for this simply is not true. It cannot be true. Loyalty is important and will be returned in kind, but it is not all encompassing. Employees cannot expect absolute loyalty; neither can the company. To do so would be destructive and incongruent with business realities.
>
> In addition to the loyalty belief, the expectation of continuous, unparalleled growth was shattered. To me this is not disastrous. For this expectation to have continued to prosper would have been destructive. We now must work toward a realistic and functional belief structure.

A production engineer and a quality control specialist were among those commenting on the effects of this shattering experience.

Production engineer. Whatever the company had with its employees before the reduction rift is gone. Consider my case. I looked around and saw men and women with twice my years of service being dismissed, men and women with children entering college and graduate school, men and women with all kinds of advanced degrees, men and women who never had worked for any other company. My conclusion? It could happen to me! My sheer sense of loyalty to the corporation used to make me do things beyond the call of duty. The loyalty I had has been greatly reduced. I am gravely concerned for my family and myself. When I reach 45 or 50, the company may kick me out. I saw good people with years of service go out the door. This signaled to me that Webster is no longer a "cradle to the grave" organization. I would like to feel reasonably comfortable that if I am doing a good job, I am safe. I would like some assurance that if I should peak out after a good career, I will be working here as long as I am doing my job well. The reduction did not give me that assurance. I saw the dismissal of individuals who had leveled off, *but who were doing fully satisfactory work in their position.* Does this company have a place for a good, solid performing, "peaked-out," middle-aged employee? I once thought it did, but now I am no longer certain.

Quality control specialist. The reduction has resulted in growing uncertainty, anxiety, and cynicism. Morale is low. Webster gave the individuals who survived no hope of promotions and, indeed, demoted several managers. On top of this, the company established a salary freeze. Those of us who remain are concerned that the company will not admit its mistakes. For example, in several cases Webster dismissed the wrong people but refused to rehire them. There is also a general belief—rightly or wrongly—that everybody terminated got more money in their new jobs. Many survivors are now beginning to wonder just how well off they are here at Webster. Cynicism toward personnel policies and practices is unbelievably high. A sign reading "Up your MBO and all that" was placed on one of the bulletin boards.

Most of the manufacturing managerial personnel agreed with Carter that the reduction and the shattering of the belief structure were positive factors. One plant manager in particular saw the shattering of the belief structure as beneficial:

I think maybe many of us were getting too comfortable. I am really a firm believer than an employee should not get too secure, but ought to always be a little afraid of losing his or her job. Employees should never get *too* comfortable—either because of seniority or performance. This holds for everybody! Security leads to performance below potential. I've seen it happen. People start arriving late in the morning and leaving early in the evening. Of course, uncertainty should not be carried to the extreme. A person should not have to come to work uncertain as to whether he or she will have a job at the day's end. However, some uncertainty is definitely in order.

The most frequent question asked by terminated employees was, "Why me?" This was especially true if he or she had a record of good performance or had received few formal appraisals. In several instances, separated employees reportedly were told in essence, "There was a meeting and your name came up on the list. I'm sorry, but I do not know any more." What most disturbed those terminated was their inability to place the dismissals in a performance context. Unable to relate their separation to poor performance, many concluded that other factors were involved—for example, politics, membership in the right groups, or the ability to keep selling oneself.

Reportedly, wives felt betrayed by the dismissals of their husbands. One manager commented: "Wives were much more bitter than their separated husbands. A typical reaction was, "Here we go again. After all you have done for the company, this [separation] is the thanks you get. And this is the thanks I get for being a camp follower."

Despite their puzzlement over the reduction decision-making process, terminated employees and their families were happy with the services provided by the Human Resources Division. In effect, the division became an outplacement center offering a number of services: training in the writing of resumes; circulation of job information; arrangement of carpools to Atlanta for visits with regional and national recruiters; and location of facilities for headhunters who wanted to recruit in Clearwater. Most of the released employees gave Webster an "A" in the area of "services rendered after termination." One individual reported, "I got more from personnel after I was separated than when I was employed."

Performance Appraisal

The common denominator underlying the various reactions to the reduction in force was a strong feeling that "something had to be done about performance appraisal." This sentiment was pervasive at all levels of the organization. Abe Webster spoke on the topic at the monthly meeting of divisional vice-presidents:

> The fact that many individuals terminated did not know where they stood in their managers' eyes reflected poor managerial practice. My position is that every Webster employee has a right to know where he or she stands and to be helped in his or her development. Managers must develop the capability of telling the employee "how it is." If he or she is doing well, the manager should communicate his satisfaction. Similarly, if the individual is doing poorly, the manager should make it known. The employee should be told, "If you do not do (a)——(b)——(c)——and (d)——, you will be asked to leave." We owe it to our people—especially the young people we bring on board—to give them honest and clear feedback and assistance.

Mark Webster, chairman of the company's board, concurred with his son Abe except that he believed the individual should always be given hope, so that he or she would remain motivated. Abe was in agreement with the psychology of his father's perspective, but he thought that it could lead to some poor decisions. He felt that motivational considerations should be handled separately from the feedback process. His position was, "the truth should be told."

There was some opinion at Webster that managerial resistance to the performance appraisal system (PAS) stemmed from concerns about its design. In particular, some complained about tying salary to performance ratings. The contention was that this link encouraged managers to play games in order to get top salary adjustments for their people. On the other hand, the human resources division staff argued that each manager was allotted a certain amount for salary adjustments in total and was expected to adhere to his or her allotment. Consequently, the opportunity for playing games was considerably reduced.

Another complaint was that the system was so complex that it often was misused. One example cited was the Performance Profile. Reports were plentiful that the Profile, though not designed for comparative purposes, was being used to rank employees.

345

Jasper Calhoun, a personnel auditor who was involved in the designing of PAS, believed the problem to be external to the system:

> Our managers simply are not cold-blooded enough. . . . [*pause*] I guess *objective* is a better word than *cold-blooded*. Right? . . . [*pause*] In any event our managers are not objective enough to tell an individual how he or she is doing. We're going to have to squeeze the managers to get them to use PAS. Our young people deserve to be told how they are doing and how they can improve.
>
> We need a monitoring system that will ensure usage. Monitoring could be done by keeping track of each manager's percentage of completions and the extent to which he or she follows through on recommendations from the Human Resources Division. The monitoring system also could be used to track the promotions process to ensure that promotions are based on appraisals. To work, the monitoring system must have *teeth*! There should be some punishment for failure to use PAS.
>
> The danger of such a monitoring system is that the manager will feel so controlled that PAS will be viewed more as an imposition from above than as a potentially useful tool. I firmly believe that PAS—like any performance appraisal system—is a necessary tool for fulfillment of managerial responsibility.

Carter's New Task

Approximately two weeks after the reduction, Ike Davis—head of the Fabrics Division—approached Carter about attaining 100 percent utilization of PAS. Davis informed Carter that the Human Resources Division was soliciting suggestions as to how full utilization might be realized. Reportedly, they were open to recommendations on design changes and implementation strategy. Davis wanted Carter to represent the Fabrics Division at an off-site brainstorming session the following week. The purpose of the meeting would be to formulate an implementation plan for PAS.

ASSESSING MANAGERIAL TALENT AT AT&T (B)

WALTER JACKSON'S RESULTS

Walter Jackson first came to the Bell System in 1970 on an exchange program from Western Electric. His first job was a level 3 line position in the plant department. Eighteen months later he was transferred to a similar position in marketing. Subsequently he was transferred back to the plant as district manager, the position he held when he was sent to AMPA. Five months after participating in the assessment program Jackson was promoted to general personnel supervisor, a level 4 staff position. According to Jackson the promotion was, at least in part, due to the overall *good rating* he received in Atlanta. Walt Jackson discussed his feelings before, during, and after AMPA and his opinions about the entire assessment process.

"For some time I've been familiar with the assessment process. When I heard I was nominated, I was flattered but didn't think much about it. I heard from my boss that I'd be going about 3 weeks before the program, put it on my calendar, and that was it. I was confident in myself. I thought it would be some kind of challenge but wasn't at all uncomfortable. I figured that the results of the process would either support data about me that had already been acquired from my on-the-job performance or would raise some questions. I wasn't expecting a promotion and wasn't really striving for one, so for me it was no big event.

"Once I got to Atlanta, though, my feelings changed a bit. It was stressful. There were people in my group who were also being assessed who were very anxious. They felt it could make or break them. It was a very competitive situation. There was some camaraderie but overall, it was competitive. As we got involved in the exercises it became very obvious that everyone was there to do well for themselves. The exercises were stimulating and I think they were valid measures of certain skills. The people there, assessors and assessees, were top notch.

"The group exercises were challenging. The investment problem was a good one for me. I felt I performed well on that one. I wasn't pleased with my performance however on the Riverview exercise. I struggled with

This case was prepared by Emily Stein, Research Assistant, under the supervision of Michael Beer, Lecturer, as a basis for class discussion rather than to illustrate either effective or ineffective handling of an administrative situation.

whether to say what I thought they wanted me to say or whether to say what I wanted to say. I tried to do a little of both and as a result it was a muddled mess. One thing I didn't like was all those paper and pencil and psychological tests. While doing those I got the feeling that this was an experiment for my level of management and that I was a guinea pig being observed every step of the way. During that part of it I kept thinking that if I had a choice I wouldn't go through with it. There was no choice though and I was there to participate so I did. I'm not convinced that those kinds of tests have much value.

"After the program, on my very own, although I tried not to, I couldn't help but evaluate my own performance. I thought at that time I'd done pretty well. However, my feelings of confidence came and went. Even though I thought I'd done well I wasn't quite sure I knew what the assessors had been looking for. I picked up signals from the people in my group and from some of the assessors that I had done well but I really wasn't sure. I really had no idea about the kind of feedback I'd receive. Two weeks later when the psychologist from Atlanta came to give me feedback he said that, in fact, I had done well. He told me that the *good rating* was 2nd from the top and that not too many people had earned such a high rating. Needless to say I was pleased. He said on the positive side, that I seemed very aware and well read. He also said I seemed to have high interpersonal skills. On the negative side he said I came across with very little motivation for advancement, and if my other strengths hadn't been there that I wouldn't have gotten such a good rating because of this. To tell the truth that surprised me a bit. But, I know myself pretty well and when I thought about it I realized that at this point in my life, I'm 45, promotion wasn't that important to me. I work hard but I don't need a promotion to let me know I'm good. I have a lot of outside interests, some real restate for instance, and I get a lot of gratification there. My job with the Bell System is only one part of my life. The psychologist also said, on the negative side, that I'm too demanding of myself and of others sometimes and ought to let up. He also said that I tend to be too cautious when making decisions and suggested I try to be more spontaneous. He didn't really have specific developmental recommendations for me. He said that I should just behave like I always behave because it seems to be working pretty well. After that meeting I felt pretty good. I didn't think a promotion was imminent but I definitely felt I was in the running.

"On the whole I feel that AMPA is a pretty good measure of certain skills but I'm not convinced that it really can predict how you do on the job in the day-to-day work environment. I don't think any assessment process can measure or predict that. In my company I feel that assessment is just one tool used to make decisions about promotions and that's good. But in other companies it seems to have more weight, I think that is wrong. There were people in my program for instance who I found out didn't do well at all. Maybe it's because they weren't capable but maybe it's because they were so wound up about it they couldn't do well, or really didn't want to be there. For those people, negative assessment results were devastating. They felt as if their value as individuals was diminished. As we left, some people were very depressed and were talking about resigning. That's just not right. From my understanding everyone who was sent to AMPA was viewed as competent on the job. If the assessment process ruins a career or someone's self-image that's just not right.''

ASSESSING MANAGERIAL TALENT AT AT&T (C)

DONNA LAWRENCE'S RESULTS

When Donna Lawrence graduated from college in 1970 with an engineering degree she joined AT&T as a level 1 engineer in the network department. Subsequently she was promoted to a level 2 engineer and was responsible for long-range planning and cost analysis. When she was sent to AMPA she held a level 3 district level manager position. Donna discussed her feelings about participating in the assessment program, her experience at AMPA, and her feelings about her feedback and the *"moderate" rating* she received:

"When I heard my boss had nominated me to attend AMPA I was flattered and anxious. Several years ago I had attended a lower level assessment program and knew basically what to expect. Although I had done very well there and was promoted, I was still very anxious about AMPA. I was sure my competition would be much tougher. I envisioned polished MBA types with enthusiasm, energy, and real management potential. I was certain it was a do or die situation. I learned I'd be going to Atlanta about 1 month before I went; my anxiety built up steadily during that month.

"When I got to Atlanta my fears were confirmed. The first night a bunch of the assessees went to dinner and I distinctly remember one woman in our group who set the tone by talking about what a cut-throat experience we'd be going through and she wanted us all to know she wasn't planning on giving anyone any support and suggested that we all look out for ourselves. She stunned a lot of us and intimidated me but finally a couple of us told her we didn't think it had to be a back-biting session but if she were going to back-bite us we'd be sure to back-bite her. That sort of set the tone for our group. It turned out to be very competitive and there was little camaraderie. There were subgroups formed of people who had similar reactions to that first encounter with 'back-biter.' I was with a group of about six who met for drinks and dinner and shared experiences, albeit reservedly under the theory that mutual support was as appropriate at AMPA as it is in life. That added to my anxiety. As anxious as I was though, I wasn't as bad

This case was prepared by Emily Stein, Research Assistant, under the supervision of Michael Beer, Lecturer, as a basis for class discussion rather than to illustrate either effective or ineffective handling of an administrative situation.

as some. Some people were afraid that if they didn't 'pass' they'd have to quit their job because they couldn't bear the embarrassment of having gone through assessment without a promotion. To be honest I guess I did feel some of that pressure too. . . . During the program I really had no idea of how I was doing. On some exercises I thought I'd done very well when in fact I didn't do well at all. In other aspects of the program I was sure I'd done poorly but in fact, I'd done well. On the group exercises specifically I could feel I didn't participate enough. When I did speak I wasn't speaking clearly, intelligibly, I was disorganized, distracted and still very anxious. Maybe that was because the back-biter was in my group. She really did intimidate me. I think I performed better on the paper and pencil tests. I guess I felt less anxious on those activities than during the group exercises themselves.

"As I left the center I was exhausted, relieved, numb, and had grave doubts about how I'd done. I finally got feedback at an off-site meeting with a psychologist from Atlanta. True, he was very skillful in the way he presented it. He started out by telling me the good things, then the bad things, then he gave me the bottom line overall rating. That was clever of him because if he'd given me the rating first I probably wouldn't have heard the rest. Anyway, he told me I was intelligent and very charming. He really stressed the intelligence aspect and that was great. Then he mentioned that my written communication skills were poor and that I was lacking in administrative abilities. He recommended I get an MBA to build up my areas of weakness or at least take some kind of English composition course. At the time I felt that the feedback was odd. Part of my job involves writing letters for my boss. I've never had any complaints about them, they always go through. That made me think that part of the assessment was inaccurate. No one has ever complained about my writing before so I was surprised by that part of the feedback. The psychologist also told me that I have received a *moderate rating*. He explained that the rating was one of the higher ones given in my group. I felt very upbeat when I left that meeting. It took me several weeks to get over how intelligent I was!

"When I look back on the assessment experience, in a way, I feel intruded. In one sense, I think in my case, the program measured how I reacted to anxiety rather than how capable I might be as a level 5 manager. In all my years working, I have never been put in as pressure filled a situation as I had been in Atlanta. I also felt the group exercises were more game-playing than anything else. When you are in a work environment you know who you're dealing with; why they are there; and for the most part you are all working for a common goal. At work, people are more concerned about their reputations as fair and honest people. At the assessment center it's a group of short-term strategists, with diverse motives; that just isn't like work. I don't think the exercises meant that much. For me the paper-and-pencil tests were more constructive than the exercises. When I think about how I did personally I can't help but think that the program put unrealistic time limits on me which just muddled my thinking. Also the back-stabber really intimidated me. That really made me too anxious to perform the way I really can perform. One other thing, when I think of the feedback I got I question their conclusions. No other source in my life had given me the kind of feedback they did, so I can't help but question it. I have some real questions too about the developmental recommendations. They make me feel intruded upon more than anything else. I'm too busy to take a course or get an MBA right now, to be honest I just don't want to now. I wonder what that will mean for my future here.''

HIGHLAND PRODUCTS, INC. (B)

March 11, 1980

TO: Mr. J.A. Robie
     Mr. Raymond S. Kirk
     Mr. George D. Wickes
     cc: M.R. Benson
         A.T. Kraft

Early in February, you received a letter from a Hampton North Haven employee, Susan Lesley. The thrust of her letter was that women were being discriminated against in terms of promotional opportunities and equal pay for equal work.

During the week of February 25, at the request of Ray Kirk, I interviewed Ms. Lesley as well as ten other female employees, at the North Haven facilities. Ms. Lesley has an additional 20 to 25 female employees for me to interview and these interviews will take place the week of March 17. Almost all of those interviewed indicated their frustration with their inability to get into the better paying jobs, and they feel that it's because they are women and not because they have less qualifications than the males. I feel that some of our practices—unintentionally, I believe—do impact negatively on promotional opportunities for women. I will make some recommendations as to how this can be overcome after I complete my round of interviews.

This case was prepared by Richard O. von Werssowetz, Associate Fellow, under the direction of Michael Beer, Lecturer, as the basis for class discussion rather than to illustrate either effective or ineffective handling of an administrative situation.

I have not found any evidence that would suggest unequal pay for equal work.

Ms. Lesley is dedicated to opening up opportunities
for women. She is articulate, well read or advised
as to equal opportunities for women, and does have
a following. She feels she was discriminated against
a short time ago when she applied for a buyer's job
in the purchasing department that was eventually
given to a male who possessed a college degree and
some years of experience in purchasing with another
company prior to joining Highland Products. She indicated that she might file an individual action relative to this particular situation and that she understood her "statute of limitations" would run out on
March 10. I personally do not think she has much
of a case in this specific situation.

My intentions are to conclude this inquiry and make
some recommendations to Hampton management by
the middle of April. Ms. Lesley is aware of this
timetable, but has not indicated when, if ever, she
would proceed with "Step 2" outlined in her letter.
Her Step 2 was to prepare letters for mailing to
"members of the Board of Directors," "The President of the United States," and 35 other individuals,
government agencies, newspapers, local politicians,
and so forth.

Daniel Trowbridge
Corporate Director
    of Salaried Personnel

HIGHLAND PRODUCTS, INC. (C)

On May 14, 1980, a new affirmative action program was announced for Hampton Division. The provisions are shown below.

Hampton Division
Affirmative Action Program

1. Conduct awareness/sensitivity development program for all levels of supervision
2. Post salaried job openings in conspicuous places so that all salaried and hourly workers have awareness and chance to advance based on qualifications. Level of jobs to be posted will be determined, but will include exempt positions.
   a. Posted jobs must realistically reflect responsibilities and qualifications for the given job.
   b. Lateral move practices will be defined on posting.
   c. The posted description of a job will correspond to the job description and/or the position classification record (PCR).
3. Maintain a skills inventory on all salaried and hourly employees, update annually, and develop an interviewing skills training program that will be conducted for all supervisors
4. Establish an affirmative action committee at each unit where number of employees would necessitate it. Each committee will have division personnel office representation.
5. Establish demanding goals for disciplines determined to be underrepresented by minorities and females, and these will be reviewed quarterly at a Hampton management staff meeting
6. Establish a divisionwide "Speak Up" communication system
7. Establish a division budget to fund adequately the above programs and other such programs that are introduced that will contribute to the upward mobility of minorities and females within Hampton Division

This case was prepared by Richard O. von Werssowetz, Associate Fellow, under the direction of Michael Beer, Lecturer, as the basis for class discussion rather than to illustrate either effective or ineffective handling of an administrative situation.

Copyright © 1981 by the President and Fellows of Harvard College. Harvard Business School case 9-481-161.

8. Establish the attainment of the above affirmative action objectives as a primary consideration when awarding payments under Management Incentive Plan

The above program is not developed to minimize other affirmative action responsibilities (that is, Vietnam Era veterans, handicapped, and so forth).

HIGHLAND PRODUCTS, INC. (D)

In late August 1980, Ray Kirk opened a copy of another letter from Susan Lesley:

August 12, 1980

To: Daniel Trowbridge
cc: John A. Robie
      Raymond S. Kirk
      George D. Wilkes
      [Eleven members of HPI Board of Directors]
      Arthur T. Kraft
      File

CORPORATE POLICY ON EQUAL OPPORTUNITY

Re: My letter of February 7, 1980

I have been trying to assimilate the many things that
we discussed yesterday, hoping that I hadn't heard
another delay of action. But I can't uncover or find
any signs of progress being made in the mire that exists here. I also checked when I came in this morning to see if there was a motto inscribed over the
door saying "Abandon hope, all women who enter
here." No matter how hard you strive, to tell me
that there is progress being made, when you look at
the scoreboard, we are still not on it; even though
we had qualified women that could have gone into
many job openings (even supervisory) within the last

This case was prepared by Richard O. von Werssowetz, Associate Fellow, under the direction
of Michael Beer, Lecturer, as the basis for class discussion rather than to illustrate either effective or ineffective handling of an administrative situation.

six months, we were not afforded the opportunities.
Blatant discrimination is practiced here, and you
now have proof. I'm not sure whether this makes a
difference to the Corporation; although I'm sure it
makes a difference to the company's women. Which
ever way that you choose to look at it, Highland
Products still remains a mighty fortress of inequality. When will Corporate attempt to redress this
shocking imbalance? When will you make the effort
to utilize our energies and talents? How do we overcome the obstacles placed before us, when they
are a brick wall? How much longer must we try to
climb unclimbable obstacles and see through blind-
ing smoke screens?

Men run Highland Products, Women aren't the
better half—they're the other half. But in Highland
Products they're the missing half!

Six months ago I wrote a letter to the Corporate
leaders of Highland Products asking for help, and
six months later I can still say that we are still being
subjected to the same treatment, with the same devastating results.

Women are hired into sex-segregated job classifications, and into jobs which are not in the line of
progression to higher paying positions. It also remains that the rate of growth with respect to promotions is not the same for women as for the men, and
that the preprequisites for higher jobs are not uni-
formly applied. So knowing that this has gone on,
how much longer can you delay action? Action delayed is still justice denied!

With the establishment of the new Affirmative
Action Plan, there was a glimmer of hope. But needless to say, that hope quickly died when the advisory
committee chosen was hand picked by the same people
who were aware of the problems here and allowed the

discriminating practices to grow and flourish. We have a committee made up of management to represent the oppressed. If we are trying to change the system, you can't start by making a mockery of it! Before we can start to have reform, we must first have abolishment of past practices. Many of the committee members lack the visual literacy to ever acknowledge what the problem is. I was told that Corporate had clout to prevent such happenings as this, but as I see it, you are still putting your seal of approval on the happenings here.

The time for pacification is over. We will no longer settle for promises, we want promotions and opportunities. Promises are easily made, it's keeping them that is difficult. In other words, the word MEN now stands for MAKE EQUALITY NOW!

In our closing comments yesterday, I told you that in August, I was through trying to change the system from within. This has become a practice in futility! Therefore, we will be filing suits against, Highland Products North Haven, Highland Products, Incorporated, the State of Connecticut, and the United States Federal Government.

In turning this problem over to its ultimate end, I leave it knowing I tried. Highland Products has had opportunities to correct past practices, and to show real intent to correct this adverse impact, but you elected not to act.

In closing I am asking the same question as I started with — Why?

Sincerely,

Susan E. Lesley

MEDICAL AND ENVIRONMENTAL
ELECTRONIC DEVICES CORPORATION (B)

In October 1979, Barbara Hamlin had been assigned the job as manager of human resource development and planning (HRDP) in the IC Group (ICG) of Medical and Environmental Electronic Devices Corporation (MEED). The IC Group was organized to supply MEED with up to 20 percent of its semiconductor requirements, particularly custom-made semiconductors required by MEED for its sophisticated medical and environmental systems. MEED's increasing needs for semiconductors had led to ICG's rapid growth. Growth had created a significant gap between needed managerial and engineering talent and the available supply. A forecast of new hires through fiscal year (FY) 1985 [see Exhibits 16–1 and 16–2 in (A) case in casebook] showed that this gap would continue.

Tom Douglas, ICG manager, had been convinced by several of his managers and personnel people that some of ICG's problems were caused by the human resource gap. This had led him to create the HRDP job. Indeed, he himself was a victim of the talent shortage. With the resignation of Kenny Lash, manager of operations in the plant, Douglas was temporarily wearing three hats, group manager, plant manager, and operations manager. Now, one year later some steps had been taken in developing a human resource planning process.

A False Start

The task of forecasting human resource needs for all of ICG seemed like a monumental task to Barbara Hamlin. How accurate would these forecasts be? What effect would numbers generated by Hamlin have on top management's commitment to develop and hire talent? She decided to recommend that the human resource planning process focus on only the top three levels of the organization. Drawing on the work of Edgar H. Schein, she developed a model of human resource planning which guided her recommendations to Tom Douglas (Exhibit 1). The process was to involve Douglas and his staff in defining the FY 1983 organization, describing requirements for the top 26 managerial and technical positions in FY 1983,

This case was prepared by Michael Beer, Lecturer, as a basis for class discussion rather than to illustrate either effective or ineffective handling of an administrative situation.

identifying internal candidates to fill these positions based on assessments of their potential and career goals, committing to a development plan for this group, and committing to a hiring plan for the gap which remained. A data base on employees—their past experience, skills, and estimated potential—would be needed. Barbara Hamlin recommended an improved performance appraisal system which would supply this data and also proposed a computerized system for recording data on employees in ICG.

The process proposed by Hamlin would require Douglas and his staff to attend a series of meetings in which *they* would do the work. When Barbara Hamlin made her presentation to Douglas, he rejected the idea because he could not commit to such a heavy investment of time and energy given the immediate and urgent problem in ICG. Hamlin was back to where she had started. Douglas wanted human resource planning but the pressures created by the human resource gap were preventing the very planning needed.

The Board of Directors

In order to develop broader commitment to HRDP, Hamlin talked with individual line managers within ICG, including Raffaelli, Hogan, and two managers in corporate research and development (R&D) who had product development responsibility for ICG and needed the same type of technical people as ICG. Indeed, both these managers and Raffaelli had been talking about a merger of their groups with ICG. All these managers agreed that human resource planning was necessary for ICG's survival. She called a meeting of all these managers and Douglas to discuss the role of human resource planning in ICG. The group agreed to act as a "board of directors" (BOD) for human resource planning and meet once a month to review the human resource planning process.

While they identified school relations, management development, technical development and training, and total employee population profiles and forecasts as important HRDP activities, the BOD gave priority to identifying and developing candidates for the top 25 managerial and technical positions as projected for ICG in FY 1983. This came to be known as the "fill-the-gap" pilot project. Board members working with Hamlin in between sessions and making decisions as a group during monthly meetings committed themselves to the following main steps:

1. Based on business plans, define the organization for FY 1983.
2. Define the personal and knowledge requirements for the top 25 positions using a form to be developed by Hamlin (see Exhibit 2).
3. Based on available performance appraisal data, identify a pool of candidates (probably 100 people) potentially developable for the top 25 positions.

4. Using an individual assessment form comparable to the position requirement form in step 2 above (see Exhibit 3), board members meet to discuss strengths and weaknesses of each candidate.
5. Identify at least three candidates for each of the 25 positions and insure that personal development plans are created and carried out by their bosses.
6. Develop a hiring plan for positions which have insufficient candidates inside of ICG.

Progress by November 1980

By November 1980, Tom Douglas and his staff had completed the first five steps in the planning process and reported a number of beneficial side effects.

The BOD had met for the past six months with everyone attending. Though organizational scenarios for FY 1983 had not been fully completed, the BOD had identified 35 key (difficult to fill and critical to success) positions they expected to exist by FY 1983. They also described the requirements for each position using the form in Exhibit 2. This process had led them to discover a number of key technical positions they had not anticipated and to clarify the knowledge requirements for these positions. This was the reason for 35 rather than 25 positions. Writing position profiles had helped nonsemiconductor people in ICG realize what semiconductor jobs in FY 1983 would look like. For example, Hamlin's interviews with semiconductor people in manufacturing led to a realization that semiconductor equipment specialists would be critical by FY 1983 in defining the manufacturing process. Similarly the importance of computer-aided design specialists also surfaced. In the management area discussions by the BOD hastened the reorganization of ICG. It now included the two groups from corporate R&D which Raffaelli had felt needed to work closely with his Advanced Design Group.

Tom Douglas felt that the process of human resource planning had forced him and his staff to identify a number of organizational and people issues that would not otherwise have been dealt with. He was pleased with the process.

A pool of 150 candidates for the top 35 jobs were identified by Barbara Hamlin from performance appraisal data. To enhance opportunities for blacks and women and to meet affirmative action goals she included in this pool *all* blacks and women with a rating of 1 (top performance rating). She presented this list to the BOD who cut it down to 75 and then to 30. These were individuals BOD members wanted to take *personal responsibility* for developing. Individuals on the list did not have to be approved by other members of the BOD. The list constituted a pooling of employees nominated by BOD members from their own departments.

A pilot project for 30 employees, BOD members felt, would allow them to learn about the process of human resource planning and development through direct involvement. In some cases individuals on the list were two levels below a BOD member. Nonetheless, the BOD member was to meet with these individuals directly.

By November BOD members had met once with each person on the list and communicated to them about the fill-the-gap project (see Exhibit 4 for a memo written by Barbara Hamlin to guide this communication). Though the selection of the 30 candidates was not intended to communicate a promise that they would be promoted this proved to be difficult to do in practice. One person was reported to have said:

> My boss has singled me out for a special job. I have a big responsibility to develop myself so I can take one of these key jobs.

In addition to the fill-the-gap project a number of programs to recruit and develop human resources were launched on a decentralized basis. For example, cooperative education programs were being discussed with universities, some funding for university research had been started and technical training was being beefed up in several areas. In Materiel and Advanced Design, fill-the-gap planning for all positions below the top 30 was beginning. Indeed, the personnel people for these departments wanted to take over this activity from Barbara Hamlin who had involved them in the planning process.

The November BOD Meeting

The November BOD meeting was the first meeting at which not all members attended. Absent were Tom Douglas and two others. Nevertheless, the meeting was productive. BOD members reported about their first interviews with the 30 candidates. Some of the employees had never thought ahead to what they were going to do to develop (that is, education, job rotation, and so forth). Raffaelli reported that he learned a lot about his people that he did not previously know, their motivation, aspirations, and expectations. He reported that his people had high expectations as a result of being selected and that much of his time was spent playing these expectations down. For example, one person, who was known to be ambitious, said that "this process was long overdue." Other BOD members described similar problems and raised concerns about what ICG would do next to meet expectations. All agreed that minimizing expectations was a critical problem for the future.

At the meeting Barbara Hamlin reported about fact-finding visits to several semiconductor companies in Silicon Valley to identify what they did in humans resource planning and development. She reported that several had large technical training efforts coordinated with universities. These included classes by television or classes on the premises. Several companies reported multimillion dollar failures in new plant startup because these plants had been staffed by experienced people hired from other companies rather than by experienced people from their own banks. One company reported extensive organization and management development programs which they claimed had improved supervision and reduced turnover. None, however, reported a human resource planning and development process as sophisticated as the one undertaken by MEED's IC Group.

Despite this positive note, the November meeting broke up on a sobering note. Would ICG be able to meet expectations raised by the HRDP process? How would the process be broadened and how would managers be trained to conduct developmental interviews (a proposed training film was viewed and discussed)? Most important, did the poor attendance at the November meeting signal a loss of commitment to HRDP among BOD members?

MEDICAL AND ENVIRONMENTAL
ELECTRONIC DEVICES CORPORATION (B)

EXHIBIT 1
HRDP Model

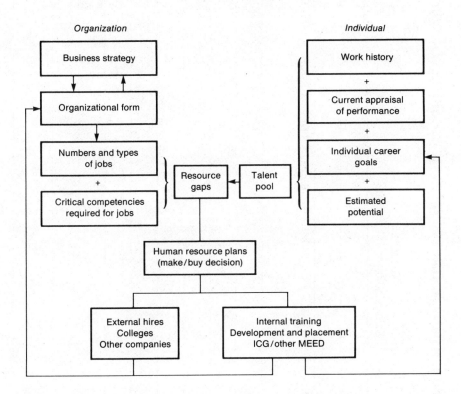

MEDICAL AND ENVIRONMENTAL ELECTRONIC DEVICES CORPORATION (B)

EXHIBIT 2

Semiconductor Job Profile

TITLE: _____   DATE: _____

DATE TO BE FILLED: _____   JOB CODE: _____

SUMMARY DESCRIPTION (INCLUDING CRITICAL INTERFACES, BUDGETS, NUMBER OF PEOPLE/GROUPS MANAGED, AND SO FORTH)

_____

_____

_____

_____

_____

_____

_____

_____

_____

REPORTING TO: _____   SALARY RANGE: _____

PREFERRED EXPERIENCES

EDUCATION: _____

EXPERIENCES (INTERNAL/EXTERNAL DEC): _____

COMMENTS: _____

EXHIBIT 2 (*continued*)

POTENTIAL SOURCES OF APPLICANTS

1. _____

2. _____

3. _____

4. _____

5. _____

6. _____

PREFERRED KNOWLEDGE AND SKILLS

TECHNICAL DIMENSIONS

	L H 1 2 3 4 5
1. SYSTEM ARCHITECTURE	....
2. LOGIC DESIGN	....
3. COMPUTER-AIDED CIRCUIT DESIGN	....
4. BIPOLAR CIRCUIT DESIGN	....
5. MOS CIRCUIT DESIGN	....
6. DEVICE ENGINEERING	....

BUSINESS DIMENSIONS

	L H 1 2 3 4 5
1. WRITING/ DOCUMENTATION	....
2. MEED ACCOUNTING SYSTEMS	....
3. BASIC INVESTMENT THEORY ROI/ROA	....
4. MEED BUSINESS REPORT SYSTEM	....
5. PRODUCT COST ELEMENTS	....

LEADERSHIP/ MANAGERIAL DIMENSIONS

	L H 1 2 3 4 5
1. GOAL AND TASK ORIENTATION (motivated toward practical results)	....
2. FORMAL COMMUNICATION SKILLS (oral/written)	....
3. TOLERANCE FOR UNCERTAINTY	....

7. TEST ....

8. DEVICE PHYSICS ....

9. SEMICONDUCTOR EQUIPMENT ....

10. COMPUTER-CONTROLLED SYSTEMS ....

11. PROCESS DESIGN ....

12. PHOTO/ETCH ....

13. DIFFUSION/IMPLANT ....

14. EPI ....

15. ELECTRON BEAM ....

16. METALLIZATION ....

17. CVD ....

18. MATERIALS ....

19. RELIABILITY/QUALITY ....

20. PACKAGING ....

21. PROGRAMMING ....

6. PRODUCTION CONTROL/OPERATIONS ....

7. MEED PERSONNEL POLICIES AND PROCEDURES ....

8. MEED CULTURE, VALUES, NORMS, ORGANIZATIONS ....

9. STRATEGY FORMULATION/PLANNING ....

10. KNOWLEDGE OF COMPETITORS ....

11. VENDOR KNOWLEDGE ....

12. MARKETING PRINCIPLES ....

13. PRODUCT STRATEGIES ....

14. CONTRACT WRITING/NEGOTIATION ....

4. SUBORDINATE DEVELOPMENT ....

5. PROJECT MGMT. SKILLS (balancing, controlling, prioritizing, planning, checking up) ....

6. COLLABORATIVE (listens to others) ....

7. TOUGH-MINDEDNESS/CONFRONTIVE ....

8. INFLUENTIAL/IMPACT DECISIONS ....

9. COURTEOUS/NONABRASIVE ....

10. DECISIVENESS (exercises judgment) ....

11. OPENNESS ....

12. COACH, ADVISE, COUNSEL, TEACH, AND ASSIST ....

EXHIBIT 2 (*continued*)

PROBLEM-SOLVING ORIENTATION

ANALYSIS/TAKING APART AND
UNDERSTANDING WHAT EXISTS

1————————5————————10

SYNTHESIS/CREATING WHAT
DID NOT EXIST

DO NOT COMPLETE THIS SPACE

POTENTIAL CANDIDATE: _____
    CURRENT POSITION: _____

POTENTIAL CANDIDATE: _____
    CURRENT POSITION: _____

POTENTIAL CANDIDATE: _____
    CURRENT POSITION: _____

MEDICAL AND ENVIRONMENTAL ELECTRONIC DEVICES CORPORATION (B)

EXHIBIT 3

Semiconductor Human Resource Planning Profile

NAME: _____   DATE: _____

CURRENT POSITION: _____   LOCATION: _____

CURRENT MANAGER: _____   MONTHS IN CURRENT POSITION: _____

EDUCATION: _____

_____

PROFESSIONAL EXPERIENCES
(BEGINNING WITH CURRENT POSITION)

POSITION AND DATES	RESPONSIBILITIES AND SIGNIFICANT CONTRIBUTIONS
(19 –19)	
(19 –19)	
(19 –19)	
(19 –19)	

EXHIBIT 3 (*continued*)

CHARACTERISTICS OF DESIRED NEXT JOBS

DESIRED FUTURE POSITIONS

1. _____
2. _____
3. _____

TECHNICAL DIMENSIONS

     L H
    1 2 3 4 5

1. SYSTEM ARCHITECTURE   ....
2. LOGIC DESIGN   ....
3. COMPUTER-AIDED CIRCUIT DESIGN   ....
4. BIPOLAR CIRCUIT DESIGN   ....
5. MOS CIRCUIT DESIGN   ....

BUSINESS DIMENSIONS

     L H
    1 2 3 4 5

1. WRITING/ DOCUMENTATION   ....
2. MEED ACCOUNTING SYSTEMS   ....
3. BASIC INVESTMENT THEORY ROI/ROA   ....
4. MEED BUSINESS REPORT SYSTEM   ....

LEADERSHIP/ MANAGERIAL DIMENSIONS

     L H
    1 2 3 4 5

1. GOAL AND TASK ORIENTATION (motivated toward practical results)   ....
2. FORMAL COMMUNICATION SKILLS (oral/written)   ....

6. DEVICE ENGINEERING ....
7. TEST ....
8. DEVICE PHYSICS ....
9. SEMICONDUCTOR EQUIPMENT ....
10. COMPUTER-CONTROLLED SYSTEMS ....
11. PROCESS DESIGN ....
12. PHOTO/ETCH ....
13. DIFFUSION/IMPLANT ....
14. EPI ....
15. ELECTRON BEAM ....
16. METALLIZATION ....
17. CVD ....
18. MATERIALS/PHYSICS ....
19. RELIABILITY/QUALITY ....
20. PACKAGING ....
21. PROGRAMMING ....

5. PRODUCT COST ELEMENTS ....
6. PRODUCTION CONTROL/OPERATIONS ....
7. MEED PERSONNEL POLICIES AND PROCEDURES ....
8. MEED CULTURE, VALUES, NORMS, ORGANIZATIONS ....
9. STRATEGY FORMULATION/PLANNING ....
10. KNOWLEDGE OF COMPETITORS ....
11. VENDOR KNOWLEDGE ....
12. MARKETING PRINCIPLES ....
13. PRODUCT STRATEGIES ....
14. CONTRACT WRITING/NEGOTIATION ....

3. TOLERANCE FOR UNCERTAINTY ....
4. SUBORDINATE DEVELOPMENT ....
5. PROJECT MGMT. SKILLS (balancing, controlling, prioritizing, planning, checking up) ....
6. COLLABORATIVE (listens to others) ....
7. TOUGH-MINDEDNESS/CONFRONTIVE ....
8. INFLUENTIAL/IMPACT DECISIONS ....
9. COURTEOUS/NONABRASIVE ....
10. DECISIVENESS (exercises judgment) ....
11. OPENNESS ....
12. COACH, ADVISE, COUNSEL, TEACH, AND ASSIST ....

PROBLEM-SOLVING ORIENTATION

ANALYSIS/TAKING APART AND UNDERSTANDING WHAT EXISTS

1 ———— 5 ————10

SYNTHESIS/CREATING WHAT DID NOT EXIST

EXHIBIT 4
Interoffice Memorandum

TO: ICG HRDP Board of Directors

FROM: Barbara Hamlin

DATE: August 26, 1980

SUBJECT: Communication to our Employees
           RE: Fill-the-Gap Pilot Project

We have reached the point in our Fill-
The-Gap Plan that we want to increase the communication with our organizations about the plan. I believe that we should let people know that for the past
five months we've been working to define a pilot project which will support our rapidly growing, high-
technology semiconductor organization with regard
to the human resources which will be needed two-to-
five years from now.

I believe that our employees realize that
the acquisition and development of ICG's human resources will determine, in part, our rate of growth
and chances for success. Industrywide there is a
growing need for, and the increasing shortage of
technical and managerial resources. The IC Group
plans to grow at about 35 percent per year for the
next three years. In order to be ready to deal with
the environment, we need to take definitive actions.

In addition, I think that there are at
least three major things employees are going to

want to know about the project. <u>What are we going</u>
<u>to do?</u> <u>How will it affect them?</u> <u>How is this attempt</u>
<u>at human resource planning and development planning</u>
<u>going to be any different from the others?</u>

<u>What are we going to do?</u>

The pilot project (see attached pert for detail)
committed to a set of deliverables which are:

0. Organizational scenarios for FY '82

1. A list of 25 of the key[1] openings, both managerial and technical for ICG

2. A list of the critical competencies needed to
   do these key[1] jobs

3. Names of some current MEED employees
   who may be capable of these jobs two years
   from now

4. A matching process to correlate current human resources with future openings

5. Development activities to provide career
   planning skills to individuals

6. Development activities to provide development planning skills to managers in the
   organization

7. A process to convene personnel specialists
   (employment and training) to write project
   plans to deliver the necessary human resources to the business

---

[1] Key is defined as: (1) difficult to obtain,
(2) in critical path of a program.

EXHIBIT 4 (*continued*)

How will it affect them?

Maybe we can best communicate what the project will and will not be. For example, the project will:

1. Be a small, limited pilot project

2. Provide employees with increased aware-ness of options and additional information about jobs and careers

3. Provide employees with support to do devel-opment planning

4. Continue to change and evolve over time

5. Require that each employee take responsibil-ity for his or her own career

The project will not:

1. Be a guarantee for a job, promotion, or career path

2. Imply any particular organizational form

3. Conflict with matrix activities

4. Be a decision-making process

5. Become a "high-potential pool"

6. Be a process that will exclude any employee from being considered for any job

This pilot project will require us to gather data on the critical competencies of those selected key jobs as well as data on a group of identified employees. We will also pilot a development planning process with those same employees. Our goal is that we will ultimately use a similar process for each job and and every employee.

How will this be different from other times when we've promised development?

Maybe it won't be. But, from all I've seen, it will be. There are five major reasons I believe that this project will be successful. They are:

1. Top management has done the planning, designing, and implementation with Personnel's support versus the other way around.

2. This project provides the horizontal breadth spanning manufacturing and R & D that has, in the past, been lacking.

3. We have the mechanics in place, including and emerging Management Information System (MIS), to back up our good intentions.

4. We've kept the project small enough to work out the bugs before trying it out on our entire population.

5. There's a commitment from top management for the long haul. You are all willing to go through the necessary redesigns and do everything to ensure that your replacements get committed to HRDP if and when you move on.

MEGALITH, INC.–HAY ASSOCIATES (B)

Exhibits 1 to 4 are excerpts of the Hay Associates report prepared for Megalith, Inc.

Exhibit 1 shows the Hay point value for each of the top 24 jobs in the Megalith Finance Group along with the base salaries for the jobs current incumbent.

Exhibit 2 compares the base salary practice in Megalith's Finance Group to the base salaries paid in 1975 by 350 other companies.

Exhibit 3 compares the total compensation practices in Megalith's Finance Group to the total compensation paid in 1975 by 225 other bonus-offering companies.

Exhibit 4 plots onto the data of Exhibit 3 salary ranges that Hay Associates felt would be appropriate for different levels of employee performance.

This case was written by John A. Seeger, with the cooperation of Hay Associates, under the supervision of Assistant Professors John P. Kotter and Anne Harlan. It is intended to serve as a basis for class discussion rather than as an example of either effective or ineffective handling of an administrative situation.

MEGALITH, INC.–HAY ASSOCIATES (B)

EXHIBIT 1

Position	Total Points	Current Base Salary
Senior Vice-president Finance	3,192	$90,000
Controller	1,976	59,000
General counsel	1,856	65,000
Treasurer	1,788	54,000
Vice-president Management Information	1,688	55,000
Vice-president Corporate Development	1,500	48,000
Director Systems and Data Processing	1,358·	46,000
Manager Taxation	1,358	30,000
Manager Accounting Operations	1,312	37,000
Assistant general counsel	1,303	52,000
Director Financial Analysis	1,136	40,000
Director Financial Planning and Analysis	1,096	25,000
Director International Financial Operations	1,028	36,000
Manager Computer Research and Planning	994	38,000
Manager Information Service	988	40,000
Director Computer Programming	954	26,000
Director Systems and Methods	954	23,000
Manager Corporate Control	954	33,000
Director Systems and Procedures	928	38,000
Director Domestic Financial Operations	894	21,000
Director Communications	860	25,000
Manager Cost Analysis	830	36,000
Director Data Processing	800	24,500
Assistant secretary	800	31,000

MEGALITH, INC.–HAY ASSOCIATES (B)

EXHIBIT 2

Hay Compensation Comparison, 1975, U.S.A.
Chart A: Actual Base Salary, Bonus and Nonbonus Companies.
(Data as of May 1st)

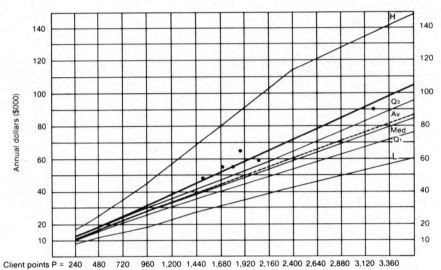

Client points P = 240   480   720   960   1,200 1,440 1,680 1,920 2,160 2,400 2,640 2,880 3,120 3,360

The bold line in this chart represents a "least squares" fit of the data in Exhibit 1 as well as point and salary
data on the rest of the jobs in the finance group not shown in Exhibit 1. It represents, in a sense, the current
base salary practice of the Megalith finance group. The six dots locate the base salary of the top six positions
in the group. The other lines on the chart indicate the range of "base salary practices" in 350 other companies in 1975. The base salary practices of 25% of all the companies fall between L and Q_1, another 25% between Q_1 and Med, another 25% between Med and Q_3, and the final 25% between Q_3 and H.

Source: Adapted from Hay Associates chart. © Hay Associates 1975.

EXHIBIT 3

Hay Compensation Comparison, 1975, U.S.A.
Chart B: Total Cash Compensation, Bonus Companies Only.
(Data as of May 1st)

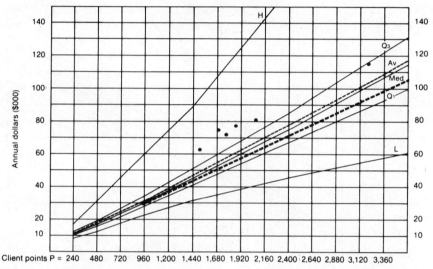

Chart B plots the total cash compensation paid to employees of 252 bonus-offering companies, against the point content of the jobs for which the salaries and incentives were paid. The dashed bold line represents the current base salary practice of the Megalith finance group. It is the same as the bold line shown in Exhibit 2. The six dots locate the total cash compensation of the top six positions in the group (base salary and M10 awards).

Source: Adapted from Hay Associates chart. © Hay Associates 1975.

EXHIBIT 4

Hay Compensation Comparison, 1975, U.S.A.
Chart C: Total Cash Compensation, Bonus Companies Only.
(Data as of May 1st)

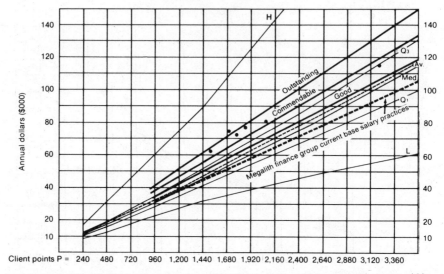

Onto the data of Chart B (Exhibit 3), we have here added three bold lines which represent the ranges within which we would expect compensation would fall, depending on an individual's performance and given an incentive policy consistent with Megalith's current policy statements and with Hay Associates' evaluations of the jobs involved.

Source: Adapted from Hay Associates chart. © Hay Associates 1975.

MEGALITH, INC.–HAY ASSOCIATES (C)

Exhibits 1 and 2 contain further excerpts from the Hay Associates report to Megalith, Inc. [see Megalith Inc.—Hay Associates (A) for the background surrounding the study and case (B) for other data from Hay's report]. These additional data are based on a 57-item "climate survey" questionnaire that was completed by 48 employees in the Finance Group, the seven top managers, and 41 other employees.

Exhibit 1 represents responses to seven of the questions contained in the Hay Climate Survey questionnaire. All responses have been scaled as percentiles in comparison with a data base consisting of several thousand other participants from many other companies.

For example, the Megalith Finance Group's top managers felt more positive about Megalith's reporting structure (question "A") than 72 percent of all the survey participants in the data base felt about their own reporting structures.

Exhibit 2 plots a "climate profile" based upon answers to all 57 questions. (The eight dimensions of climate shown in Exhibit 2 were created by using a mathematical technique called "factor analysis," and from climate survey data from hundreds of companies.) Scores for the Megalith Finance Group are displayed separately in percentile form (again relative to the large data base) for the top management respondents and for the general sample of respondents.

The eight dimensions of organizational climate are defined as follows:

1. *Organizational clarity.* Th degree to which the structures, functional patterns, and managerial intentions of the organization are clearly perceived by its members.
2. *Decision-making style.* The extent to which decisions are made in a timely and rational manner, with attention to the long-term effects of the actions being taken.
3. *Organizational integration.* The extent to which various subunits cooperate and communicate effectively toward the achievement of overall organization objectives.

This case was written by John A. Seeger, with the cooperation of Hay Associates, under the supervision of Assistant Professors John P. Kotter and Anne Harlan. It is intended to serve as a basis for class discussion rather than as an example of either effective or ineffective handling of an administrative situation.

4. *Management style.* The extent to which people perceive encouragement to use their own initiative in performing their jobs, feel free to question constraints, and sense support from higher levels of management when needed.
5. *Performance orientation.* The extent of emphasis placed upon individual accountability for clearly defined end results and high levels of performance.
6. *Organizational vitality.* The extent to which people see the organization as a dynamic one, as reflected by the venturesomeness of its goals, the innovativeness of its decisions, and its responsiveness to changing conditions.
7. *Compensation.* The extent to which the compensation system is seen as equitable, competitive, and related to performance.
8. *Human resource development.* The extent to which individuals perceive opportunities within the organization that will allow people to develop to their full potential.

MEGALITH, INC.–HAY ASSOCIATES (C)

EXHIBIT 1
Hay Management Climate Survey (1975):
Critical Specimen Questions

A. To what extent does the current reporting structure facilitate or hinder implementation of the organization's strategies?

Greatly hinders   1   2   3   4   5   6   7   **Greatly facilitates**

B. To what extent are people in this organization free to take independent actions that are necessary to carry out their job responsibilities?

To a very great extent   7   6   5   4   3   2   1   **To a very little extent**

C. To what extent are managers encouraged to take reasonable risks in their efforts to increase the effectiveness of this organization?

To a very little extent   1   2   3   4   5   6   7   **To a very great extent**

D. To what extent is open discussion of conflicts encouraged?

To a very little extent   1   2   3   4   5   6   7   **To a very great extent**

E. To what extent are the goals in this organization truly challenging?

To a very great extent   7   6   5   4   3   2   1   **To a very little extent**

F. Relative to its competition, this organization is:

A follower   1   2   3   4   5   6   7   **A pacesetter**

G. Considering the work you do, how would you describe your present compensation?

Very unsatisfactory   1   2   3   4   5   6   7   **Very satisfactory**

| 0 | 10 | 20 | 30 | 40 | 50 | 60 | 70 | 80 | 90 |

Megalith, Inc. finance group

T — Top management   7
G — General sample   41

385

MEGALITH, INC.–HAY ASSOCIATES (C)

EXHIBIT 2

Hay Management Climate Survey (1975): Subunit Results

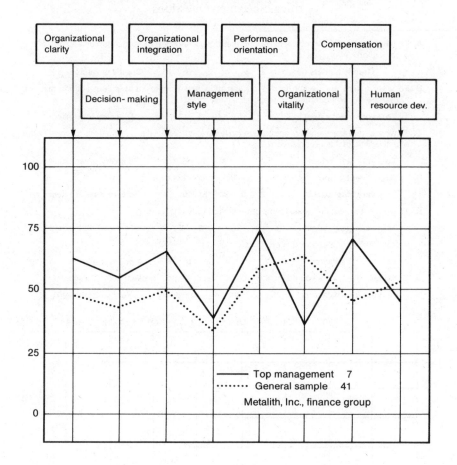

LEP CORPORATION (B)

ALTERNATIVES/RECOMMENDED ACTIONS

John Taylor proposed the following alternative measures for Dr. Campbell's consideration:

Engineering Compression in Pay Relationships

1. *Increase the rates for all engineers in the same proportion as the starting salary rates.*

Although this would maintain the previous pay relationship, it would result in paying salaries for all engineers far in excess of that which is necessary to retain above average employees.

2. *Constrain the stating salaries for engineers so they will grow no faster than the increases for the on-board population.*

This would negatively impact the ability to attract above-average candidates.

3. *Continue usual salary practices since attrition of engineers has not been a major problem in the past.*

The Division could wait until this issue becomes a serious concern. Action would then have to be taken quickly to minimize the number of employee losses when attrition does begin. In the meantime, there could be an impact on the ability to motivate engineers and a number of salary relationships would develop that would not be equitable.

4. *Construct a model to ensure that all on-board engineers receive an annual increase that would maintain their salary 5 percent ahead of engineers hired in previous years.*

Compression equity would be maintained with this approach. However, high performers may not receive higher increases than lower performers.

5. *Construct a combination model that would accelerate the movement of engineers based on performance and maintain a 5 percent ahead relationship with engineers hired in previous years. The model would be lim-*

This case was prepared by E. Mary Lou Balbaky under the direction of D. Quinn Mills as a basis for class discussion rather than to illustrate either effective or ineffective handling of an administrative situation.

ited by not allowing individuals to exceed their maximum pay based on their performance.

This model will allow for appropriate relationships in pay based on performance and maintain most salaries 5 percent ahead of previous engineer hires. Those employees limited by the maximum pay for their performance would tend to be the lower performers. Although the model would be complex, Dr. Campbell selected this alternative for implementation in the 1982 program.

Employees Questioning Pay Practices

The pay practices of LEP Corporation are based on the cost of labor. Although pay is not based directly on increases in the Consumer Price Index, it is taken into consideration to the extent that it affects the salaries of companies with which it competes for employees.

Since employees' use of company communication programs has increased regarding this issue, Dr. Campbell directed Personnel to develop an education/training package to enable managers to respond to employee concerns.

A salary system utilizing sound pay practices will not be effective if it is not properly administered by line management. Management must understand the principles and objectives of the company's pay program and effectively communicate this understanding to employees to ensure its success.

Transfer in of Nonexempt Technicians

Pay for nonexempts is based on the local labor market in which the location competes for employees. Therefore, pay differentials exist between locations. While paying all nonexempt employees the same rate of pay would solve the problem of transferring employees between locations, it would also result in paying unnecessarily high salaries at some locations.

One alternative is to adjust the pay of transferring employees either up or down depending on the labor market at the location to which they will transfer. This approach, however, would greatly reduce the ability of management to transfer employees from a high-paying labor market to a lower-paying labor market.

Therefore, LEP's approach is to transfer the employee at the salary they have merited based on past performance. Once at the new location, future salary increases will be determined by the new location's salary ranges and increase guidelines. This results in only a temporary situation of pay differences within a location and Dr. Campbell believed that it could be managed by explaining pay practices to employees.

Design Specialists

When differences in pay practices are necessary due to external pay comparisons, temporary program guidelines for affected groups should be implemented.

There were two major options available to Dr. Campbell:

—Additional percentages could be added to the increased guidelines used for the design specialists, thus raising their average salary increase above the 9 percent established guide.
—Salary increases could be generated based on performance ratings that are higher than those actually earned.

Both options generate higher salaries in a shorter time frame than typically achieved under normal guidelines. Additional percentages, however, affect the timing and percentage of future increases since individual salaries have become higher than normal guideline yield.

Dr. Campbell decided to administer design specialist salary increases using one higher performance rating than earned. He was thereby able to upwardly adjust the guideline yield for each individual and achieve a competitive salary position for this particular skill group without compromising the parameters of the established guidelines.

Since actions taken will affect future increases to the design specialists, and the long-term objectives are to administer salaries of all groups of similar skill levels comparably, Dr. Campbell asked Personnel to continue to review the reasons for current differences and recommend elimination of the temporary adjustments when the conditions no longer exist.

LEP CORPORATION (C)

Salary Program Implementation

In December 1981, the 1982 salary program was forwarded to LEP corporate headquarters for review and approval. The projected cost of the 1982 salary program, which was increased to $9.3 million to resolve major concerns that had arisen in 1981, was included in the financial planning for the coming year.

In early January 1982, the salary ranges and increase guidelines for the 1982 salary program were printed and distributed to line management, along with a training program explaining the concepts of the company's merit pay system.

Each year all managers are required to develop a salary plan, which is approved by the next level of management. Factors to be considered include compression, pay differentials based on performance, projected changes in performance, and so on. Planned increases can be plus or minus the guidelines so long as the plan is balanced at the major organization level. Any significant deviations from the plan at this level must be approved by Dr. Campbell.

Personnel consolidates the individual department plans into one total plan for the division, ensuring that all of the above factors have been considered and resolved and that the proper level of contingency remains in the final plan that is presented to Dr. Campbell for approval. When the plan has been approved, managers are expected to manage their plan.

MAJOR CONCERNS
Cost Overrun

In mid-March 1982 a letter was received from senior corporate management indicating that the cost of the salary program through February was overrunning the plan by 9 percent. Dr. Campbell had already been ad-

This case was prepared by E. Mary Lou Balbaky under the direction of D. Quinn Mills as a basis for class discussion rather than to illustrate either effective or ineffective handling of an administrative situation.

vised of this situation by his staff and had received the following analysis of the problem from the personnel manager:

1. A number of increases had been granted at a higher percentage or earlier than that indicated on the management salary plan.
2. The performance distribution for employees had begun to shift upward. Since the beginning of the year, the percent of level 1 and level 2 performers for the total population had gone from 50 percent to 55 percent. This compared to a projection by management to end the year at 51.5 percent. As a result, more employees were beginning to receive higher increase percentages than originally planned.
3. Due to business demands, implementation of the new technology was occurring faster than anticipated. To staff this activity, a number of employees had moved into new jobs. Many of these individuals had assumed positions of greater responsibility than their previous positions and this had resulted in promotions. In addition, more moves are projected to occur during the year which will add $100,000 to the total cost of the salary program.

To ensure that no other potential problems existed, other tracking programs such as Equal Opportunity salary equity, below-range minimums, manager/employee salary compression, and so on, were reviewed and found to be in satisfactory condition.

Although the overrun was only $17,000 through February, the salary plan for the year could be exceeded by as much as three quarters of a million dollars if action is not taken by Dr. Campbell. Again, the question was: What actions should he take, if any?

LEP CORPORATION (D)

The Cost Overrun

Dr. Campbell thought through each aspect of the cost overrun and acted on them as follows:

1. *Increases granted early or higher than the increase guideline.*

Management can and should vary from their salary plan during the year due to factors such as unexpected or unplanned changes in employee performance and changing pay relationships in the department. Occasionally, as in this example, managers will "round-up" increases for lower performers who should receive smaller increases.

Dr. Campbell covered the cost of the overrun with money available in the contingency fund ($50,000). If the problem had not been discovered until later in the year, he would have had to accept the overrun and not take action that would have negatively impacted employees who were yet to receive increases in the year.

2. *Performance distribution too high.*

An important objective of the merit system is to differentiate levels of performance and contribution to the business so merit pay differentials can be established and maintained. Performance distribution skewed too far to the high or low side impacts the attainment of this objective. The increase of level 1 and level 2 performers to 55 percent prompted Dr. Campbell to remind managers that a valid evaluation system requires close management involvement to accurately identify and reward the true high achievers.

3. *Additional promotions.*

As a direct result of changes in the direction of the business, additional promotions are needed in 1982 for the early implementation of the new technology. Therefore, Dr. Campbell will request an additional $100,000 from LEP corporate headquarters and revise the 1982 salary program.

After going through a complete salary plan cycle, Dr. Campbell became aware of the advantages of the merit system. He was convinced that proper evaluation of an employee's contribution is the most fundamental recognition of the employee's individual dignity—the cornerstone of the company's human relations efforts. He saw that the positive elements of the

This case was prepared by E. Mary Lou Balbaky under the direction of D. Quinn Mills as a basis for class discussion rather than to illustrate either effective or ineffective handling of an administrative situation.

merit system could be extended to touch on nearly all aspects of human relations. He has been impressed with the system's flexibility in adjusting to the vicissitudes of business while at the same time continuing to offer incentives to employees to excel.

Dr. Campbell believed that steps needed to be taken to underscore the company's belief that even with its well-endowed technological resources, people were still its most important assets. He asked John Taylor to ensure that ongoing management training reaffirm top management's commitment to the merit system. He also asked that employee–manager communication channels be reviewed to ensure the company's beliefs and efforts are effectively communicated to all employees.

FIRST FEDERAL SAVINGS (B)

Current State of Operations—1980

First Federal Savings now has 39 branch offices spread throughout the State of Arizona. Most of the branches are in the Metro-Phoenix area:

—Apache Junction	—Sun City (5)
—Glendale	—Scottsdale (2)
—Mesa (4)	—Tempe
—Phoenix (13)	—Youngtown

Other branches are scattered through the state:

—Northern Arizona:	Flagstaff, Payson, Prescott
—Central Arizona:	Casa Grande, Coolidge, Wickenburg
—Southern Arizona:	Tucson (2), Yuma (2), Green Valley (opened in 1980)

No branches were opened from 1976 to 1979, and one was sold. In addition to branches, a subsidiary, First Service Mortgage Corporation (FSMC), operates one office outside of Arizona in San Diego. Subsidiary operations have been gradually deemphasized so that only FSMC had significant operations in 1979.

Information on the size of the Association is contained in the updated exhibits as well as in the attached reports.

Review of Financial Results from 1974 to 1979

The rapid growth that had been prevalent at First Federal in the late 1960s and early 1970s slowed in 1974 and came to a virtual halt in 1975 due to the severe recession and overbuilding in Arizona.

In 1974 savings, lending and revenue all increased from 1973 levels, but income declined substantially due to:

—Increased cost of savings

—Increases in operations costs

—Disintermediation which required borrowing at higher rates

This case was prepared by Leonard Schlesinger as a basis for class discussion rather than to illustrate either effective or ineffective handling of an administrative situation.

—Declining housing market from the effects of housing cost inflation, high interest rates, and public apprehension resulting from the recession

In early 1975 growth nearly came to a complete halt as the national recession, already in effect for over a year, finally hit Arizona with full force. A drastic slowdown in construction and in the housing market, complicated by tight money markets and high interest rates, led to a sharp reduction in First Federal's profits. First Federal, however, remained the state's leading real estate lender, while all financial institutions experienced similar economic conditions.

The decline in the Arizona housing market reached its lowest point in 1976; First Federal still led the state in originating mortgages, but incurred a net loss of $2 million, much of the loss due to loan losses and creation of loss reserves. First Federal was less profitable than most financial institutions in 1975–1976. Its period of rapid growth had left the Association somewhat overextended and in weak financial condition. It should be noted that First Federal's relationships with several construction builders were prime causes of the 1975–1976 profitability problems.

The Arizona housing market began a strong upswing in 1977 as consumer spending increased. First Federal continued to maintain its stature as the leading residential lender while intentionally not increasing its assets or savings balances. This was accomplished through a program of heavy loan sales, which provided the financing for this volume of loan originations. (The loan sales program had been very active since 1973). The lack of growth in assets and savings in 1976 and 1977 was planned, giving First Federal a chance to improve its financial condition and net worth position. Profits improved, reaching $4.4 million.

The year of 1978 was a most profitable one for First Federal as earnings reached $10.6 million, although the return on assets was not as great as it had been in the early 1970s. The high profits were a result of high loan demand, increased internal efficiency and internal cost reductions. Efficiency and cost programs had been initiated in 1976 and 1977, years of no growth, with the fruits of these programs being realized in 1978. By 1978 First Federal's financial position had improved sufficiently to allow it to begin cautious growth once again.

Conditions in 1979 were similar to those in 1978. First Federal grew more in this year than any year since 1974 as the lending market in Arizona remained strong. Profits were about the same as in 1978. The changing economic conditions, especially the switch in savings to money market and jumbo accounts, had not yet had much of a impact on First Federal's growth, profitability, or strategies.

As 1980 began the savings and loan industry was facing a major challenge. Economic conditions were difficult to interpret. An extremely high level of interest rates and a rapidly increasing cost of money had cut the profitability spread between cost of funds and the lending rate. The demand and ability of people to qualify for lending was decreasing as interest rates soared. The possibility of a major recession was looming. First Federal is now in a much healthier position to ride out the hard times than in the previous recession. The financial position is strong after years of controlled growth and controlled costs. Loan sales afford First Federal money to lend when most institutions have a shortage due to the disintermediation of savings. But even First Federal is being faced with the need to change its thinking in order to cope with changing conditions as the threat of some unprofitable times becomes more likely.

MBO Program

The management-by-objective (MBO) program at First Federal first underwent changes in 1975. There was never a chance to test the effectiveness of the changes, however, as no bonus was paid from 1975 through 1977. Payment of bonuses was precluded by the economic conditions and First Federal's internal financial concerns that resulted in barely profitable conditions in these years. By the time First Federal again became profitable in 1978, the MBO program had been greatly deemphasized because of the lack of need for it during 1976 and 1977, when growth was not desired.

The theory behind MBO does still exist. Planning (budgeting) for the following year begins at the middle-management level. Managers are responsible for meeting their goals during the following year. The emphasis is not the same as it had been in the early 1970s, however.

Bonus Compensation Plan

The policy toward the payment of bonuses also changed in 1975. Payment of bonuses is now at the discretion of the board of directors. There is no longer a strict MBO bonus. Bonuses now paid are not as objectively determined as in the past and do allow for greater variation.

No bonuses were paid during the less-profitable years of 1975–1977. Bonuses were paid to all employees at the end of both 1978 and 1979, based primarily on salary, though a portion of *one's* bonus was also related to length of service to the Association. The vice presidential group may receive an additional bonus based upon their value to the association, performance, relative standing, and a host of other, largely discretionary criteria.

It is important to note that the philosophy embodied in MBO is still relevant and meaningful to the Association. Senior management encourages all management to practice MBO. Profit planning, goal setting, and strategy development are still conditioned on the belief that participation in setting objectives, and the successful negotiation and completion of those objectives, will be rewarded through pay, benefits, profit-sharing, and bonuses. Simultaneously, however, the pitfalls of blind loyalty to MBO without strict control mechanisms can lead to less than desirable results.

Below is the bonus policy in its entirety as presently stated:

> The Board of Directors of the Association, from time to time in the past, has voted a discretionary bonus to individuals who are in the active employ of the Association on a particular date. The decision as to whether any such payments will be made in the future, the amount of the payments, if any, and the individuals to whom the payments, if any, will be made, is entirely within the discretion of the Board of Directors of the Association.
>
> It is also recommended that Association management and personnel department representatives *do not* promise or imply, in conversation with present or prospective employees, the probability of a bonus.

The Use of MBO and Incentive Compensation Systems

First Federal Savings learned much from their MBO and bonus compensation experiences of the early 1970s. The way the programs were structured certainly did contribute to the growth and profitability of the early 1970s. However, the programs caused too much of a short-run outlook, disregarding long-range implications for immediate benefits. The result was the financial difficulties of 1975–1977, difficulties that were much more severe for First Federal than for its competitors.

Gene Rice would still like to see First Federal employ the MBO concept more directly; however, a number of problems in structuring the program need to be solved before MBO can again be used as a permanent and reliable management tool.

FIRST FEDERAL SAVINGS (B)

EXHIBIT 1
Consolidated Growth

	1979	1978	1977	1976	1975	1974
Deposits						
Passbooks	$ 223,571	$256,285	$280,408	$295,094	$261,313	$207,788
Certificates	842,677	670,265	595,702	596,679	611,597	542,660
Total	1,066,248	926,550	876,110	891,773	872,910	750,448
Loans						
First mortgage	996,679	868,474	767,901	751,635	807,255	802,889
Property improvement	100,977	81,530	66,522	71,012	64,928	74,022
Mobile home	23,122	27,477	31,939	44,717	44,943	64,214
Other	12,055	8,117	7,257	6,940	7,401	19,637
Total	1,132,833	985,598	873,619	874,304	924,527	960,762
Growth Statistics						
Number savings accounts	180,813	170,984	170,391	172,500	175,016	157,473
Number first mortgage loans	36,795	34,932	33,586	33,639	33,000	30,017
Number property improvement loans	17,634	17,752	18,055	21,019	21,000	19,462
Number mobile home loans	2,780	3,181	3,590	4,058	4,000	3,779
Number offices	38	38	39	39	39	34
Operating Results						
Total revenue	119,379	97,158	89,908	89,309	87,639	79,517
Total expenses	106,178	84,000	84,603	90,644	86,427	72,282
Income before taxes and extraordinary items	13,201	13,158	5,305	(1,335)	1,212	7,235
Income taxes	4,144	4,111	2,048	805	805	2,037
Income before extraordinary items	9,057	9,947	3,257	(2,140)	407	5,198
Extraordinary items	1,554	1,545	1,154	159	679	292
Net income	$ 10,611	$ 10,592	$ 4,411	$ (1,981)	$ 1,086	$ 5,490

FIRST FEDERAL SAVINGS (B)

EXHIBIT 2

Consolidated Statement of Income

Year Ended December 31	1979	1978	1977	1976	1975	1974	1973	1972	1971
Revenues									
Interest on loans	94,347	77,315	71,829	72,623	73,243	64,211	45,425	33,164	21,976
Loan fees and service charges	9,173	8,240	7,798	6,629	7,136	8,518	6,713	5,069	3,573
Interest and dividends on investments	10,717	7,968	7,651	6,797	6,205	5,357	3,396	1,635	1,214
Real estate operations: net	624	1,205	617	139	505	514	614	493	671
Gain on sales of loans and other income	6,073	3,975	2,549	3,280	2,525	1,209	944	963	978
Total	120,934	98,703	90,444	89,468	89,614	79,809	57,092	41,324	28,412
Expenses									
Interest on savings deposits	73,411	58,121	56,546	57,915	54,258	44,507	31,666	28,756	16,320
Other interest expense	9,270	6,505	8,709	9,972	13,694	10,615	3,594	1,558	892
Provision for losses		11	1,174	6,252	2,011	280	181	81	
General and administrative expenses	23,498	19,363	17,556	16,545	17,760	16,880	10,973	7,415	4,889
Total	106,179	84,000	83,985	90,644	87,723	72,282	46,414	32,810	22,101
Income before taxes	14,755	14,703	6,459	(1,176)	1,891	7,527	10,678	8,514	6,311
Provision for income taxes	4,144	4,111	2,048	805	805	2,037	2,850	2,100	494
Net income	10,611	10,592	4,411	(1,981)	1,086	5,490	7,828	6,414	5,817

FIRST FEDERAL SAVINGS (B)

EXHIBIT 3
Recent Financial Trends

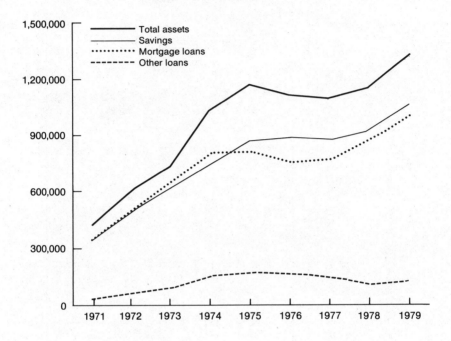

NEW TECHNOLOGY AND JOB DESIGN
IN A PHONE COMPANY (B)

Interviews with repair service answerers (RSAs) and their supervisors led to the following conclusions about why they reported feeling "frustrated" and "like robots."

1. *Small fragment of the whole task and little or no knowledge of the larger task.* The RSAs complain that they are totally isolated from the subsequent steps in the process of satisfying the customers whose complaints they take. They are isolated physically, organizationally, and informationally. The answer and service organizations are not closely tied by measurements or reporting structure. They do not know specifically what happens to a particular complaint they handled, nor do they know the people in the bureau to whom they pass along the complaint. And except for those who have worked in a repair bureau, they do not have a general understanding of what is involved in the repair cycle (although there have been attempts to provide slide presentations to fill the last information gap). In contrast, the former position of repair clerk had much more information about the repair cycle and felt more a part of the total cycle.

2. *Negative contacts.* Calls are initiated because subscribers have encountered a problem. Antagonism escalates when a "call back" by the service bureau has not been made after a RSA has promised it; and when repair commitments are promised but not kept. Customers making those repeat requests for service are often angry, impatient, and demanding of quick action. There is no balancing positive reaction from customers. This seemed to be an important aspect of the RSA's job.

3. *Short cycle time and repetition.* The job consists almost entirely of one short phone conversation after another for the entire day. The job becomes highly repetitive despite the variety of personalities and moods of subscribers who call, and the occasional challenges in dealing with difficult customers.

This case was prepared by Professor Richard E. Walton as the basis for class discussion rather than to illustrate either effective or ineffective handling of an administrative situation.

4. *Constant load and pacing.* The basic idea of the centralized bureau included better utilization of clerical time. Although there still are times during the day when the loads are lighter than others, and days that are lighter than others, the load is relatively more constant than for a repair clerk in a service bureau. This adds to the monotony and job pressure.

5. *Constraints on movement and social interaction.* RSAs are tied to their desks except for monitored official breaks and trips to the rest room. They are able to converse briefly with adjacent neighbors if and when both are free. The layout does not create many options for conversational partners.

6. *Lack of individualization—symbolic messages from the situations.* In many ways the situation itself, implicitly deemphasizes individuality. They are all in one large room, arranged in regimental fashion (rows and columns). Moreover, since any phone call can be routed to any station, the RSAs are literally interchangeable parts.

7. *Lack of discretion or latitude and decision making.* Although RSAs must exercise individual judgment in how to elicit the necessary information from irate customers, they are provided instructions about the schedule commitment they may make to customers, and are proscribed from giving customers certain information which could be helpful to the customer. Only supervisors may disclose this information. Many RSAs believe they are given too little latitude in both the information they supply and the commitments they make.

8. *Lack of effective authority to commit.* If the RSA and the customer cannot arrange for a mutually convenient repair time, then a RSA may promise that a representative of the local repair bureau will call the customer within a certain period to arrange for an appointment. But RSAs complain that repair bureaus often do not follow through—generating a sense of futility and powerlessness, and bad attitudes toward the bureaus. Such failures also can produce repeated angry calls from customers who want to know why they were not contacted.

9. *Lack of forthrightness.* When customers call back for some reason (no call yet from local bureau, repair personnel failed to come, or phone problem not solved), RSAs must be reassuring or make new promises, even though they lack confidence that the promise will be fulfilled. They do not like that feeling.

10. *Lack of relevant knowledge.* Customers are accustomed to dealing with a local repair bureau and expect the person answering their call to know local place names and landmarks. They don't. They can't, since they are serving a several-state area. As a result, they

may give incorrect information regarding the location of the nearest or most convenient phone store. In any event, they feel handicapped by not being able to refer to common landmarks, and so forth.

11. *Cumulative effects of negative job factors?* One supervisor repeated in many ways a question to which she would like an answer. Referring especially to the negative tone of the customer contact and to the repetitive nature of the task, she asked: "How long can you take it before you stop trying so hard, stop concentrating? When do you start getting negative yourself?" She had many time frames in mind. After how many hours a day, are you likely to slip? After how many weeks of overtime hours? After how many years? Clearly she had a hypothesis that there were cumulative effects of the job. She pointed out that repair clerks could get away from the customer, updating records, posting, and so on, and that others in the manual service bureaus were available who could share customer contact. Moreover, there was *un*level loading on this job in the service bureaus—an apparent efficiency disadvantage, but perhaps an effectiveness advantage.

Although they do not effectively offset the negatives, there were a number of positives. First, the pay is viewed as relatively good for this type of work. Second, for many phone employees displaced from other parts of the company, this job represents the best available means for staying in the company. They value their employment relationship with the company. Third, RSAs understand that their work is important. Fourth, management—aware of the lack of intrinsic satisfaction—has endeavored to generate opportunities for RSAs to participate in other office activities. Still, on balance, the quality of work life was judged to be very deficient.

SEDALIA ENGINE PLANT (B)

Sure, I had problems when I became plant manager. Like any other place, we've always had our problems. Maybe even more so, because of all that we're trying to do here. But if you ask me, the greatest asset of Sedalia Engine Plant has always been our ability to make midcourse corrections and to solve our problems. There are still some things up in the air. I don't kid myself about that. Still, I'm quite pleased with the way things have gone in the last year.

It was now the winter of 1980. Just over a year ago Danney Goble had taken over as plant manager of Sedalia Engine Plant (SEP), one of the plants of the American Diesel system. He had faced many serious problems in that intervening time: the breakdown of the corrective action process among teams; the twin crises of possible layoffs and dissatisfaction with the compensation system among nonexempt employees caused by the severe economic downturn of 1979; and the upheaval in plant leadership that developed out of a major turnover in the plant's top management team, as well as the sharp contrast between Goble's style and that of his predecessor, Don St. Clair.

As Goble candidly admitted, there were still some loose ends that would take more attention in the upcoming months. Yet, Goble believed, he and everyone else at SEP had good reason to be proud of what they had accomplished in the past year.

Corrective Action in Teams

From the beginning of SEP, team advisers were expected to deal with any and all behavioral problems among their team members. Absenteeism, not making up time off, and disruptive behavior were all to be handled by the advisors through an informal counseling procedure known as the corrective action process. When Goble became plant manager, he had perceived a complete breakdown in the procedure. There were more and more behavioral problems within the plant, and nothing was being done.

Bert A. Spector, Research Associate, prepared this case under the direction of Lecturer Michael Beer as the basis for class discussion rather than to illustrate either effective or ineffective handling of an administrative situation.

To meet this problem, Goble created a special task group to investigate. That group conducted an exhaustive poll of SEP to find out what employees thought of the problem and what suggestions they might have for solutions. The task group also studied other plants to determine how they handled disciplinary problems, then the group went off-site for two days of intensive meetings and discussions. The group's suggestion, accepted by Goble and his plant operating team (POT), called for the corrective action process to be replaced by the more positive sounding performance improvement process (PIP).

While PIP added some specificity to performance expectations, its main innovation was a new orientation program designed to emphasize problem-solving skills, constructive feedback, and expectation setting. The early response to PIP seemed positive. "Participation in PIP is purely voluntary, of course," commented Connie Kelleher, a plant director. "We find that most manufacturing teams participate; most staff support teams do not. But those that do, find it tremendously helpful." The question of rising absenteeism was placed in the hands of a separate task force. Connie Kelleher, a member of that group, explained that they were considering three possible recommendations:

1. POT providing teams with a specific definition of what constitutes excessive absenteeism for SEP employees.
2. A more rigorous record system that would tell each team weekly what percentage of the previous 40-hour week each employee had been at work.
3. The above record system would be combined with a policy that would not allow overtime pay to any employee who had not made up lost time from the previous 40-hour week. Thus, if an employee missed three hours during the week and worked six extra hours on the weekend, he or she would receive overtime pay for only three of those hours.

The committee recommended, and POT accepted, the second idea—reporting on each member's attendance. Teams were urged to take special steps—they could decide themselves on what those steps might be—whenever an individual's attendance fell below 98 percent.

Plant Leadership

Although Goble felt that he could do little about the large turnover in plant leadership except wait until things settled down, he had moved immediately to define more sharply and precisely the roles of directors and business managers. Under St. Clair, the managers had often bypassed the director's level to work directly with the plant manager. Goble wanted his business managers to remain strong, but within their own businesses so as not to bypass the directors. That shift, he hoped, would meet the needs of a rapidly growing plant. Goble said:

> As soon as I got the job, I found that the business managers were constantly coming to me rather than their directors with their problems. Well, I just didn't have the time for that. Besides, I was afraid that we were seriously undermining the role of my directors. So I decided what I needed to do was go more by the book, push down the level of responsibility so that business managers would run their own businesses while I and the directors would, through POT [composed of the plant manager and directors] take overall responsibility for running the plant.

In attempting to strengthen the role of POT, Goble felt that he had made one mistake. He had discussed his intentions extensively with manufacturing teams and with POT, but he had not brought the business managers themselves into the discussions. He said:

> I didn't even know they were upset until it spilled over into a meeting of the Organizational Review Group. I happened to be out of town the day of a meeting, and I guess the business managers really laid it all out on the table. They didn't know for sure what was going on, but they sure didn't like it.
>
> Then I promoted one of the business managers to be a director. He was now part of my operating team. And one day he sat me down in my office and said, "Danney, just what the hell is going on here?" It was then that I knew we had a problem.

While regretting that mistake, Goble said that he had taken major steps to overcome the suspicions of the business managers and develop a more smoothly operating management team:

> Things worked out pretty well after that. I started meeting informally with the business managers, often over a few beers, and assured them that I had no hidden agenda. Far from weakening their positions, I was actually trying to strengthen them. Now, I know they're still a little edgy, still testing me. But I'm confident this is going to work out. I know it's working, because they are no longer coming to me with all their problems.

Possible Layoffs

With the economic downturn and the distinct possibility of layoffs throughout the American Diesel system, Goble decided to commit himself to the protection of all present SEP jobs. Immediately after taking over as plant manager, he announced a five-step plan that would cut costs and, he hoped, meet the crisis without layoffs:

1. Cost reductions whenever possible, and a freeze on new hiring
2. The creation of "swing teams"

3. Voluntary, temporary layoffs
4. Cutbacks on contract help
5. 37½-hour work weeks for all plant employees

The plant would move from one step to the next as economic conditions warranted, he explained, and to layoffs only after everything else had been tried.

Once cost reductions were implemented, SEP moved to create a swing team. "That was my brainchild," said Goble. "The idea was to allow for fair and effective management of temporary people movement." The swing team was made up of excess personnel from manufacturing teams—personnel who were excess because of cutbacks in SEP's build rate (from 22 engines per day down to 18). For instance, team number 1—an assembly team—was told that it needed to reduce its work force by one person. Instead of being laid off, however, that person would be assigned to the swing team. Team number 1 was free to decide for itself which of its members would go to the swing team. In that case, as in most others, the team decided against going by strict seniority. Instead, it would rotate the assignment by sending a new person each month.

Once created, the swing team would send its members out wherever there was a need in the plant. Demand for some parts like the cambox remained high throughout the crisis, so the swing team often sent one of its members to work on the cambox line during third shift. Because of the elimination of outside contract work, there were also certain chores within the plant that needed to be done. The plant was about to be painted, for instance. Instead of hiring painters from the outside, Goble assigned the task to the swing team.

People assigned to the swing team found their work schedules to be somewhat uncertain, not knowing exactly what they might be doing on any given day, or what shift they would be working on during the week. Still, swing-team assignments entailed no cut in pay, and they promised to forestall any future layoffs.

When it became clear that, because of worsening economic conditions, further action might well be needed, Goble approached the board of representatives (BOR). At his request, it issued a call for voluntary, temporary layoffs. By allowing people to take a month off without pay, BOR might be able to save a few jobs. Fifteen people volunteered to take August off without pay. When volunteers became more difficult to find in the next three months, Goble allowed two people, even four, to "share" a month off.

In the fall of 1980, Goble told SEP employees, "I am now willing to stick my neck out and make a commitment to you." At existing business levels, there would be no work reduction—either through 37½-hour work weeks or layoffs. That could change again, however, so he warned against undue optimism: "The future is still in doubt, so please understand this may change later." But by late in the year, Goble was able to say with confidence: "We can get back to normal."

SEP had weathered the storm with some disruptions, but not a single layoff. That accomplishment was even more dramatic when compared with the large number of layoffs that had occurred within American Diesel. And all during those months, Goble had sent out weekly *Business Updates*, providing team advisers with "all information available on a continuous basis." He asked that all the material be shared with everybody in the plant.

During his first year as plant manager, nearly 1,500 American Diesel workers had been laid off—not one of those had come from SEP. Now, how did employees view Don St. Clair's successor?

—*Connie Kelleher*, director: I don't think Danney or the company got nearly enough credit for what they did.

—*Bob Greene*, team member: Sure, the way Danney handled the layoff thing helped a lot. He said he was going to try to avoid layoffs here, and, by God, there weren't any. That really builds trust when you see he's a man of his word.

—*Tom O'Donnell*, business manager: Danney was trying to be entirely open and honest. He passed along all sorts of new data to the plant, stuff that wasn't censored or filtered by the management team. And that created a great deal of uncertainty, perhaps more than was necessary. I kind of think maybe we did too much sharing.

—*Ed Fremder*, team adviser: It was great what the company did, and everybody knows that, believe me. And the whole thing was St. Clair's idea, wasn't it?

—*Dave Palmer*, director: People really pulled together around here. There was a sense of solidarity. Within a few months, we were back to fighting over the compensation thing. But I'm convinced that the spirit of unity of purpose is still with us.

Nonexempt Compensation Problems

Goble stood by his feeling that, despite the short-term problems it might cause, the plant ought to stick literally with the old formula for calculating salaries of nonexempt employees. Instead of making adjustments as St. Clair had done in the past, Goble insisted that SEP salaries be tied precisely to the average union-negotiated hourly wage for four-year employees at the Beacon plant. The economic downturn in early 1979 had led to the large layoffs at the Beacon, Illinois plant, so the average wage for four-year employees there began to drop (four-year employees at Beacon found themselves bumped down to lower-paying job classifications within the plant). Thus, the two economic reviews in 1979 and 1980 brought only small raises for SEP employees. Furthermore, the traditional gap between team members and the skilled trades was widened by the fact that the skilled trades received raises almost double those of the team members. They had been tied separately to the skilled trades at Beacon, whose wages were not affected by layoffs.

Goble knew, of course, that there would be some concern on the part of nonexempts about his decision to stick with the old formula, so he held several large meetings to explain to employees what he had done and why. He was taken by surprise by the level of vehemence of the dissatisfaction.

> —*Frank McCarthy*, team member: First, in 1979, we got hit with no overtime because of the lousy economy. Then this came along. A lot of people I know had come to count on that overtime and those raises. They had bills to pay. They probably shouldn't have done that, but that's what happened. So, when Danney told them they weren't going to get the raises they expected, they exploded.

By awarding skilled tradespeople significantly greater raises than team members, Goble laid open the emotional matter of internal equity.

> —*Mike Cassity*, team member: I don't think there would have been any problem at all if it hadn't been for those skilled trades. They're not a very popular group in the plant anyway. A lot of us feel that they shouldn't be getting more money than us in the first place. After a few years, most team members can do the same work as skilled tradespeople. And then to have them receive a raise twice the size of ours—that's what made us mad.

In reviewing the decision to stick with the old formula and weather the consequences, Dave Palmer, the plant's director of organizational development and training, decided that Goble and POT seriously miscalculated on two points:

> First, we overestimated the degree to which nonexempts would subordinate their own interests to the interests of the plant, or at least to what we in management thought was the interest of the plant. Second, we really underestimated the emotional impact surrounding the issue of equity. We knew the difference in raises between the team members and the skilled tradespeople was going to be large, and we knew just how large it was going to be. What we didn't realize was how emotional our people were going to get.

In July 1980 Goble moved to respond to this growing dissatisfaction. Wanting to leave BOR free to handle day-to-day plant matters, Goble established a special task force—the economic review group (ERG)—to review the compensation formula. Goble recalled that the very act of setting up that group raised certain difficulties:

> The first problem we had was selecting representatives to ERG. I told the business managers to pick somebody from their own business. That caused a real stink because a lot of the team members felt that the representatives were being handpicked to speak for management rather than them. So I had to send the

business managers back and told them to use a more participative process in making their selection. There were no elections, but they did solicit volunteers.

That raised another question. I'm afraid that some of the team members came to look upon ERG as a kind of bargaining unit for them. Emphatically, that wasn't the case. I told them that ERG could make recommendations, but all compensation decisions would be made by POT and POT alone. What we were doing was seeking input and participation before we made our decisions.

ERG was made up of one representative for each of the five businesses, plus one team advisor, one representative from BOR, the personnel director, and Dave Palmer as facilitator. Twice a week, often for eight hours at a time, ERG undertook a sweeping, detailed reevaluation of Sedalia's nonexempt compensation system. ERG surveyed the plant for employee reaction and looked at other plants with redesigned work throughout the country. Goble attended ERG meetings twice, and then only when specifically invited. In response to a query from ERG for some corporate parameters to any new compensation package, he brought in a representative from American Diesel to speak to the group. The only other limit he imposed was that SEP salaries could not outstrip salaries offered by the surrounding community.

In October ERG made its proposal for the next economic package. Much of the original formula—the tie-in with Beacon, the separate and higher salary schedule for skilled trades—remained intact. ERG did call for a change, however, in the way that four-year Sedalia employees were tied to Beacon. Sedalia wages would be pegged to certain job classifications, rather than to an average of all four-year employees. SEP's four-year employees would be paid on the basis of the average wage of Beacon's classifications 2 through 11.

The new proposal would offer SEP workers greater protection against the impact of future layoffs. It would also raise the pay of Sedalia workers in comparison to their Beacon counterparts. Dave Palmer observed: "In fact, if we follow this scheme, it will mean that some of our four-year employees will be earning the same as some Beacon employees with 15 or 20 years of experience. I remember turning to the team members on ERG and asking directly, 'Are you really worth that?' They responded just as directly, 'Yes, we are.' "

Goble felt that the ERG proposal was modest: "What they were asking for would raise salaries an average of 20 cents an hour more than the old formula would have done. So, it was worth allowing all this participation? Did I allow too much? I'm really not sure."

As of December 1980, Goble and his organizing team had not decided on what parts, if any, of ERG's proposal to accept. Dave Palmer hoped that the controversy had been a healthy one for SEP, and that the process through which the debate had been channeled a healing one: "The whole process was open and participatory. We encouraged dialogue and communication. If POT doesn't accept part of the proposal, people will be angry. Sure. But will they still trust us? I'm not sure."

Machine Workers of America Union

About halfway through ERG's deliberations on the compensation system, the Machine Workers of America—the union representing most other American Diesel plants—came to Sedalia to mount its first serious campaign at SEP, but the union drew little support. Most of the management team within the plant dismissed the union efforts. But at least one director cautioned against overconfidence, even complacency, on the part of management:

It's true that the union didn't get much support this time. But I'm afraid most of the management people will misinterpret that to mean that everything is fine. But we still have problems. The expectations and demands of our nonexempts are rising faster than most of us are willing to recognize. Look at the package proposed by ERG. What's going to happen, I wonder, if POT rejects those proposals?

OFFICE TECHNOLOGY, INC. (B)

In September 1979, Robert Dorr, administrative manager for the Scientific Markets Group of Office Technology, Inc. (OTI), decided to redesign the order administration (OA) work system into teams. Changes had occurred at both Menlo Park and Los Altos, although this case will focus primarily on the OEM group at Los Altos. That group had been reorganized from a production-line work organization to one in which all order administration functions were assigned to small regional teams. But by the summer of 1981, the reaction of the manager and group members to this reorganization was decidedly mixed.

Implementing the Change

One of the first things that was done prior even to any attempts at implementation of the team concept was to deal with the strong resistance from the original equipment manufacturing (OEM) manager, Tim Everhart. First, Robert Dorr suggested that Tim Everhart take a couple of days off—a long weekend—to get away from work and give himself some time to think about the whole issue. According to Robet Dorr, Tim did return from his mini-vacation more relaxed and less emotional about the restructuring but still opposed. it was then suggested that he might benefit from a one-to-one consultation with Michael Russell to explore his resistance and discuss further what the team structure would involve. According to Tim Everhart:

> Until this meeting, I really hadn't been able to articulate what really bothered me about teams. As I talked with Michael, these objections took better form: The team concept smacked to me of management by committee. I didn't think we could accomplish anything like that. In addition, we would be putting our fate in the hands of people who didn't have experience in decision-making or the ability to see the larger overall picture. Our operation would become bogged down and chaotic. It was difficult for me to conceive of groups of people running the organization.

This case was prepared by Bette Witcraft, Research Assistant, and Richard O. von Werssowetz, Associate Fellow, and revised by Bert Spector, Research Associate, under the supervision of Michael Beer, Lecturer, as the basis for class discussion rather than to illustrate either effective or ineffective handling of an administrative situation.

Once I could express these feelings, we could talk them out. All of a sudden this light went off in my head and I could see how teams might work. When Michael talked about giving people total responsibility for their work and for solving their own problems, it made sense. I would be able to set down some general guidelines. And I realized what an opportunity it could be. I could take the time to do special projects or take classes and help develop my people—be a manager.

It was decided that Jeff Chaney and the Scientific Markets Group personnel people would be responsible for training at the Menlo Park facility [engineering products (EGP), education products (EDP), government products (GVP)] and that the Los Altos facility personnel people, who worked for manufacturing, would be responsible for training the OEM and laboratory and medical products (LMP) groups which were located at the Los Altos facility. On November 15, 1979, a meeting was held that introduced the Los Altos personnel staff to the project. Their initial reaction was one of concern. They were not terribly pleased about the fact that they hadn't been involved in the process from the beginning, they didn't feel they had enough information to understand the total standardization project, and they were concerned that while the standardization project had been in the works for 18 months and the decision made to restructure almost two months prior, implementation was set for only two months away and therefore time was critical. The Los Altos personnel people raised the additional issues of concern—that there was no top-level management "ownership" at Los Altos for the project. Furthermore, they were concerned that there was no strategy in place for ensuring that people would be ready to work in teams.

The following month was spent in developing a transition plan for the OA groups at Los Altos that included involving plant management in the project and a training plan to get people ready. The initial phase of the training plan focused on Tim Everhart and the two supervisors, Jim Hancock and John Fortier (although Fortier, as a leader of this concept was clearly more a resource than a trainee), and revolved around the issue of how to manage effectively a team organization (that is, issues of delegation of responsibility, participative work systems, the role of supervisors and managers, and so forth).

In the meantime, the implementation proceeded at the Menlo Park facility. Consistent with his earlier assertion that it would be easy to impose a new structure on the Menlo Park unit (easier because he was onsite and could exercise greater control), Robert Dorr, while John Hanley was on vacation, did just that. He began to hire the dozen or so people needed and assigned them into teams organized along product lines as they came into the unit. By the first of January, the Menlo Park OA group was fully staffed, moved to new quarters, formed into teams, and had met all the OA demands (including the end of the quarter crunch). Robert Dorr handled strong resistance from one of the two supervisors (neither of whom had been involved in the September 24 meeting), by issuing an ultimatum—if she didn't like the reorganization, she could leave. This particular supervisor was accustomed to a more autocratic supervisory style and was reluctant to delegate responsibility to the teams.

In February 1980, the time frame for restructuring the OEM group was moved forward with the new deadline for implementation set for April 1, 1980. This delay was caused by a change in the way that OEM product line did business and this in turn was going to affect the OA task. According to Tim Everhart: "until we get this figured out and up to speed on our new line, we don't want to cause trouble for the business."

Training efforts in Los Altos had begun, however, and were to continue in spite of the delay. In addition to training efforts directed toward the manager and supervisors, the Los Altos personnel staff assisted OA management in providing training for the OA staff. The training involved activities such as development and discussion of minicases describing potential scenarios. For example, one minicase discussed was the following:

> Team number 3 is composed of three experienced order processing personnel. Six weeks after joining the group, the order editor approached the supervisor and said she was bored with her job in the team. It was suggested that the order editor assist the OA specialist in problem-solving, but a few weeks later the problem still persisted.
> Question: How do we keep employees motivated in an OA atmosphere?

One exercise initiated and conducted by Tim Everhart and Jim Hancock for the OEM group involved an attempt to involve OA employees in the process of team design by having them assign themselves to teams and having each team, then, structure its own organization. The "name the organization" exercise resulted in the following:

1. The teams proceeded immediately to place the available personnel into slots based on expertise or potential.
2. There was little concern about the personalities of the individuals that would be on any particular team.
3. The teams placed exempt and nonexempt personnel in jobs with exempt and nonexempt responsibilities.
4. Only three individuals of the thirteen to be placed were assigned to the same block by all three teams.

About a week after this practice session, the OA employees were told they would be divided up into teams and that the teams would be organized on a regional basis rather than by products or product lines. This meant that the teams would be composed of a mix of people from each of the OEM groups who had not actually worked together before. One OA-1 recalled how she learned of the decision to implement regional teams:

> There was an awful lot of discussion on the team concept. There was a lot of discussion about how we were going to break up into regions and how the

teams were to be selected. For a while, they were talking about writing down your top three preferences about who you'd like to work with. All of a sudden out of nowhere we came to a meeting that was on employee benefits or something and management told us we have an hour to pick teams. It caught everybody totally by surprise. We picked the teams, and after that the OA specialists were asked to choose what regions they wanted to have. So we did it in an hour. We had no idea we were going to do it on that particular day. We really took nothing into consideration.

As members of the OA groups struggled with the new ideas associated with the team concept, other groups in the plant began to wonder if OA wasn't out of control. One of Robert Dorr's important contributions was to buffer OA from the other areas while they learned to cope with the frustration and anxieties of finding new ways to make decisions and resolve conflicts.

In April 1980, the deadline for restructuring OEM was once more pushed back for at least another quarter due to the still unresolved problems in how orders were going to be processed in the OEM product line.

Jeff Chaney made the following observation:

The way things have developed, the process at Los Altos is the total opposite of the process at Menlo Park. At Menlo Park, they have the new team structure but they have had to get right down to doing the work and haven't had the training needed to support the new structure. As a result, people had to deal with a number of unanticipated problems inherent in working with teams. At Los Altos, however, the opposite situation exists in that the people have been involved in training for the team structure but haven't had a chance to operate in teams. Every delay in implementation creates distrust of the project and has a negative impact on morale. The training gets them psyched-up and then there's another delay.

At the end of April, Robert Dorr resigned from OTI and joined a financial institution as vice president of administration. A consideration in his decision to accept an attractive offer was that he felt that he had moved the standardization project to the point where implementation was a matter of course.

In August 1980, the changes in the way OEM business was to be done at Los Altos had been resolved and by September 1980 the OEM and LMP groups were physically adjacent to one another, Tim Everhart had been made manager of the two consolidated groups, the supervisory positions held by John Fortier, and Jim Hancock had been upgraded to manager. "Contribution to the team" had been added to the performance evaluation of OA personnel.

The OEM group had formed teams of four to five members organized according to geographical regions. Instead of establishing standardized procedures for OA within OEM, each regional team was told to develop its own procedures.

At the end of September 1980, John Fortier left his position at the LMP Group to take over as manager of an OA department in another part of the company. Progress continued but, in May 1981, Tim Everhart felt that:

> The people within the team are just skimming the cream—they're taking the money that came with the elevated positions and the freedom they have in operating as teams, but they're leaving the less-desirable aspects untouched. As teams, they don't want to get involved in solving personal confrontations. They're not working out how to make decisions. They're not self-starting. They feel less ownership than we would have liked and can't seem to break the mold of automatically electing the salaried professional as "team leader," either officially or unofficially. It's also obvious from meetings where we talk about professionalism that they have very different ideas on what the team concept is.
>
> Management has allowed this to happen. We have been so busy trying to meet our demands that we haven't been able to be as involved as we should in facilitating the new process. We have not been able to follow through on additional training until the last three or four months. Now we've recently hired an additional OEM supervisor, Joy Caldwell, with great skills as a facilitator and in giving feedback. We need the extra skills and the time.
>
> I have been disappointed with some resistance I've seen to taking on the new responsibilities. We promoted several people on the expectation that their jobs would include working the float (orders in process and unentered because of material shortages). This was delayed until the work was transferred to us. They had gotten used to the more limited jobs and looked at the float as additional work. The biggest bone was that now with complete responsibility, their effectiveness could be measured.
>
> We're still working out the problems of team leaders. Under the team concept, we said that anybody can become the team spokesperson. These were really meant to be the focal point for communication, not a supervisor or work coordinator. However, in some teams people have assumed the role of leader. The team begins to revert to management by directive. Some take this because they are used to it. Others resist, saying, "You're not my boss!"

For some team members, the adjustment to a new style of operating was a difficult one. According to Marion Hardy, an OA-1 within OEM:

> It's a different world. You are used to being on your own and used to a supervisor over you telling you what to do. It's a big adjustment and a hard adjustment, learning to function as a team, being open with each other. That's very hard, too, I find. Being open and learning not to fear it. It was a big fear for me to be able to sit down with these people and say, "There's a problem here." It *is* different.

But the OA specialist on that same regional team felt that Marion Hardy and others on that team had made great progress:

> I think we've come a long way in the last year in that our team meetings didn't used to be all that productive. We used to discuss operational issues and things

like that. But as far as getting out any of the things that bothered us, I don't think we did it a year ago. Now, I think we've come a long way. If something is bothering Marion, she will come out at a team meeting and say it. If something is bothering me, we'll iron it out. So our team has progressed a long way in a year as far as that's concerned. I guess we've opened up more to each other, probably developed a real team feeling in the course of a year.

Likewise, Tim Everhart's assessment of OEM's performance was not entirely negative:

> We've had some signs of success. Except for two or three promotions and new hires, there has only been one change in the team structures, and that was negotiated between two teams when the order volume switched. The team with the increased load sought a particular skill from the team with the lessened load. That team discussed it, agreed, and found a member who didn't mind moving. Another good sign is that the OEM revenue accounting group has been watching our operation and has expressed serious interest in trying the team concept themselves.
>
> It is apparent that working in teams is good for the individuals in OA. They are growing much faster and becoming more professionally mature. They're learning how to make decisions earlier and how to deal with pros and cons and compromise. They normally wouldn't have dealt with these until they were made supervisors. They may not recognize it, but they are forming a much better candidate pool for promotion.

Special Projects

One particular problem faced in 1981 by the order administration function in OEM had to do with what was called "special projects." Because of the rapidity with which the OEM product line was growing, material shortages regularly produced major backlogs of orders. Periodically, as materials became available, the product marketing group would insist that backlogged orders be filled. Members of the various regional teams would then be pulled out of their team and be placed on a special project team that would fill back orders on a *national* rather than *regional* basis. Once that special project was completed, members would then return to their regional teams. Because the backlog of unprocessed orders was great, one special project usually followed on the heels of another, continually causing individuals to be pulled out of teams. OEM personnel expressed concern over the stress this continual displacement placed on them personally as they moved from a team operation to special projects and back again.

A NOTE ON THE 1982 AUTO NEGOTIATIONS

"This contract opens a new chapter in American labor relations," said Al Warren, vice president for labor relations and chief negotiator at General Motors, "and clearly signals a move for us in a new direction: away from confrontation and toward cooperation." But Douglas Fraser, president of the United Auto Workers (UAW), did not believe any fundamental change had taken place in the attitudes of the rank-and-file. "There's no doubt about the attitude of our members toward GM," he noted after the new contract had been approved. "They view them as rich even when they aren't rich, and arrogant."

GENERAL MOTORS' "BATTLE FOR SURVIVAL"

In 1980, as the domestic automobile industry reported a combined loss of $4 billion, it became clear that the traditional pattern built up over the previous three decades was likely to undergo significant change. In 1948, following a devastating and bitter 113-day strike against General Motors, GM and the auto industry adopted a formula of establishing wage agreements which provided a 3 percent "annual improvement factor" designed to reflect continually increasing worker productivity, and allowances for increases in the cost of living. Under that formula, GM reached a national settlement with the UAW seven of ten times (although local disputes often proved more troublesome). The most serious work disruptions involved one-week shutdowns in 1958 and 1964 and a 67-day strike in 1970. Today, auto workers earn an average $12 per hour with fringe benefits that increase their total package to nearly $20 an hour.

But the drastic slump in the automobile industry during the late 1970s brought pressures on the UAW to help companies control labor costs, particularly to help reduce the gap between the earnings of American auto workers and those of their Japanese counterparts (who make approximately $9 per hour in wages). In 1980 Chrysler won wage concessions from the UAW that would save the corporation more than $1 billion, and allowed a board seat for UAW President Fraser. Immediately thereafter, Ford aggres-

This note was written by Bert A. Spector, Research Associate, under the supervision of Professor Michael Beer, as the basis for class discussion.

sively warned workers of the need for wage concessions, telling employees at their Shefield, Alabama aluminum casting plant, for instance, that their jobs were in danger if they failed to reduce wages and benefits by 50 percent. American Motors asked its workers to give up future pay and benefit increases equal to 10 percent of their income. And GM Chairman Roger Smith has called for significant union concessions that "could send positive signals throughout the economy . . . [and] represent an enormously important contribution to the welfare of the entire country."

Hyatt Bearing

In October 1981, after GM announced its intention to close a 43-year-old bearing plant in Clark, New Jersey and purchase less-costly parts elsewhere, including Japan, local UAW leaders responded with a plan to buy the plant. After the purchase they would cut wages 30 percent and reduce employment 50 percent, cuts that would otherwise have been difficult to achieve. Under the purchase plan, all employees would receive equal amounts of stock in the new company. Employees would have voting rights which would give them a voice in how the company is managed.

GM set the purchase price for the plant at $60 million, and agreed to $20 million in funding and $100 million in orders in each of the next three years. While UAW national leadership declined comment on the situation, local labor leaders said that Fraser had been generally cool toward the idea. "I'm not saying what we're doing is the only answer," said the chair of the UAW local, "but the UAW has done nothing to save any jobs or help its membership facing plant shutdowns." The purchase was completed in November 1981.

UAW Leadership

At a meeting of the UAW executive board in July 1981 Donald Ephlin, union vice president and chairman of their Ford division, urged consideration for reopening the Ford and General Motors contracts. The current contracts were due to expire in September 1982 but the automobile companies were asking for talks to be held early so that the contract could be renegotiated and concessions made. Ephlin was one of the few members of the board who supported reopening talks. He explained:

> At that point, the question was whether it would be to our advantage to open negotiations, whether our bargaining posture would be better than it would be in September 1982. We had something they [the auto companies] wanted: concessions.

At that time it seemed clear to the three top members of the UAW board—Fraser, Ephlin, and Owen Bieber who headed the GM division—that there would be more opposition to new talks by GM workers than by Ford workers, reasoning that Ford's more serious economic problems would make the need for concessions there more obvious. Fraser and Bieber decided to explore the idea of having GM agree to some initial concessions in order to build support for reopened talks. Specifically, Fraser wanted GM to agree, as a precondition to any discussion of concessions, that any resulting savings be passed along to car buyers through lower prices, and that an independent auditor working for the union be allowed to verify compliance. Explained Fraser:

> These were two principles we've been after for years: a voice in prices and an opening of GM's books to outsiders.

A November 1981 meeting with Roger Smith and Al Warren produced exactly the agreement Fraser had been hoping for. This willingness by GM to offer initial concessions, however, was only one factor in Fraser's support for reopening talks. That November, both American Motors and International Harvester had also asked their 35,000 UAW employees to consider wage and benefit concessions. Fraser was convinced that the UAW had more to gain by talking now than by waiting:

> If you do nothing now, then what can you do on September 14, when the current contract expires? The companies could unilaterally try to take away much more than we might be willing to give now. Our only alternative, a strike, isn't viable. Then were would we be?

In early December Fraser got the UAW executive board to reverse the union's no contract revision policy. He then dispatched staffers to locals across the country to build support for new talks. In January 1982 GM and Ford councils (representatives of the rank-and-file) met in Chicago and cautiously authorized "collective bargaining discussions" with GM and Ford.

News that GM would pass labor savings costs on to car buyers generated much interest in the press, but was greeted with skepticism by some automobile industry experts. Labor costs constitute about 23 percent of the average GM car, and less on small cars. Of the $19.65 average hourly labor cost, $11.53 is direct payment of wages, an amount that the UAW placed off limits for possible concessions. Another $.92 is Social Security and unemployment taxes paid by GM, leaving $7.20 for such things as holidays, vacations, overtime, shift premiums, pensions, and insurance.

Some industry analysts insisted that GM, by concentrating on reducing labor costs and car prices, was addressing the wrong problem. Japanese cars made dramatic inroads into the American market, they insisted, as much because of quality as cost. Observed one analyst:

> We're never going to get down to Japanese cost levels, so we've got to build cars that people will perceive as better and be willing to pay more to own.

GM's Campaign

As Fraser worked to build support for concessions among the rank-and-file, GM Chairman Roger Smith worried about how successful Fraser might be. "They've stampeded this herd of buffalo," said Smith of the leadership and their members, "by telling them that they're underpaid. Now they've got to tell them that they're overpaid in relation to the competition." In order to convince employees of the "hard realities that may be required for survival," GM launched a campaign of its own. Part of that campaign included a 22-minute filmed presentation by Smith entitled "The Battle for Survival," which was designed to be shown to GM's 440,000 UAW workers on company time. In that film, Smith tells workers that they make considerably more than many of their foreign counterparts, and that "our corporation is in serious trouble."

Many UAW members found Smith's comparison to Japanese auto workers less than persuasive. Noted one:

> General Motors is constantly comparing my wages to those of the Japanese auto worker, but I'm sure that GM doesn't want to enter into a relationship such as the Japanese firms enjoy with their workers. GM has never offered to guarantee me a job for life as the Japanese do, or subsidize my housing, or provide me with opportunities for low-cost vacations. Instead, General Motors wants to cut my pay to that of my Japanese counterparts and close the plants whenever by doing so it will maximize their profit.

Smith also announced that he hoped the campaign to get workers to "know everything" would become part of various quality of work life (QWL) programs. But that idea ran into strenuous opposition from the UAW. An official union statement said QWL "was never intended to be a vehicle to propangandize or parrot the current views of the chairman of the board of GM as to how to serve General Motors through worker sacrifice." Owen Bieber called the attempt to tie the "Road to Survival" campaign to QWL programs a "perversion" of the intent of QWL.

Negotiations

As the new year opened, the UAW was meeting with both Ford and GM representatives to discuss new contract terms. Agreement proved somewhat easier at Ford where, on February 13 the two sides announced agreement on concessions designed to save the company $1 billion during the term of the contract (which would run through September 1984). Among the major provisions of the contract were:

— *Wages.* Three percent annual wage increase was cancelled; quarterly cost of living assessment (COLA) increases for 1982 were deferred until 1983; a letter of understanding agreeing to the principle of

421

equal sacrifices for white-collar workers; profit-sharing was introduced for hourly workers (when profits reach 2.3 percent of sales, 10 percent of that profit would be divided among hourly workers according to wage levels).

—*Benefits.* Reduction in personal days off; benefits to be phased in more gradually for new hires; increase in special early retirement benefits to encourage attrition.

—*Job security.* Ford would use "every effort" to avoid permanent work force reduction and to replace jobs lost through outsourcing (buying products from outside, less expensive suppliers); 24-month moratorium on plant closings due to outsourcing.

Ford announced two further steps to help ensure job security. One was an experimental project to be launched at two locations in which 80 percent of the work force would be given lifetime job security. The second was the guaranteed income stream (GIS), which guaranteed between 50 and 75 percent wages for workers with at least 15 years seniority to be paid by the company until retirement. Other features included continued insurance coverage for idled workers, a system to find new work for laid-off employees, and a rule that the amount of payment would be reduced if a worker finds other income. Ford's director of hourly benefits commented that GIS was designed to send a new message to employees:

> It says we, the company, will guarantee to find you a job or pay you at a certain level. Supplemental unemployment benefits (SUB) were designed to address the cyclical ups and downs of the industry. In essence, the company has now decided to accept a greater social responsibility for its employees.

Ford's UAW workers approved the new contract by a 3 to 1 margin. Especially noticeable was the impact of the joint Ford–UAW Employee Involvement (EI) program. Designed in 1979 as a counterpoint to the GM/UAW QWL undertaking, EI was meant to "enhance employee creativity, contribute to improvements in the work place, support goals of achieving the highest quality products, heighten efficiency, and reduce unwarranted absenteeism." Twenty-two of Ford's 92 bargaining units approved the contract by 85 percent or more; 21 of those 22 had active EI programs. In total, of the 58 units with active EI programs, 50 approved the new contract, 8 rejected it.

The first round of negotiations between GM and the UAW were not so successful. In early February, less than two weeks before Ford and the UAW announced their agreement, the talks broke down. Inside sources said that GM was seeking concessions amounting to $5 per hour, but according to Fraser the talks stalled over two nonmonetary issues: job security and outsourcing. The day the talks ended, Chairman Smith announced that GM executives would now have to make their own sacrifices for the good of the company. The press reported that Smith would deduct $135 per month from his four hundred thousand dollar plus salary.

Pressures built in the following weeks for GM and the UAW to meet again. First, of course, there was the Ford agreement. At the same time, GM announced its intention to close several major plants resulting in the indefinite layoff of nearly 10,000 workers. In March the talks resumed and an agreement was reached. Among the major provisions were:

—*Wages.* Three percent annual pay increases cancelled; 1982 COLAs deferred until 1983; a letter of understanding agreeing to the principle of equal sacrifices for white-collar workers; profit-sharing for hourly workers.

—*Benefits.* Decrease in personal days off; new prepaid legal services for workers; increased employee discount on new GM cars; increased tuition benefits for laid-off workers.

—*Job security.* Twenty-four-month moratorium on plant closings due to outsourcing; reopen four plants scheduled to close; guarantee of 50 percent or more pay for laid-off workers with either 15 years seniority or 10 years seniority if plant is permanently closed.

The plan which, according to estimates, would save GM $2.5 billion, also included UAW agreement to economic penalties for chronic absenteeism and local negotiations to eliminate restrictive work rules.

It immediately became clear that ratification by the rank-and-file would be more difficult for GM than it had been at Ford. Two local members explained their reluctance to go along with concessions. Said Carole Travis:

If people thought that jobs would be created by some minimal take-aways, they'd do it. But we think what the auto industry really needs is a general economic recovery. I'm not interested in any concessions. I'm paying for GM's shoddy management.

Martin Douglas, a laid-off UAW member, wrote:

Once there was a time when GM had customers standing in line and couldn't produce enough cars to satisfy demand. The profits rolled in, but did the company offer to share them with the workers? Not on your life. But when it is announcing losses of hundreds of millions of dollars, the company is willing to share profits if I, along with Gomez, Frank, Smittie, and LeRoy sacrifice our pay and benefits. Now that the gravy is reduced to a trickle, GM is more than willing to share—for a price. . . . I say, "You should have come a little earlier when times were good and we could have gotten to know each other. If you had, I would now be more willing to help."

In April the rank-and-file approved the new contract by a vote of 114,000 to 105,000. "The closeness of the vote," noted Fraser, "makes it clear this was a very difficult and painful step for our members." Opposition to the pact, he said, centered at final assembly plants (plants least likely to be closed because of outside suppliers) or plants with historically poor labor relations. Plants in Lordstown and Framingham, for instance, rejected the contract by nearly a 3-to-1 margin. Early indications were that there was a significant correlation between active QWL programs and contract approval.

Executive Bonuses

Immediately after the new contract was ratified, Chairman Smith sent a letter to all GM salaried employees saying, in part,

> I know that salaried employees may be wondering whether further sacrifices may be required as a result of concessions by hourly employees. Please be assured this is *not* the case. In fact, we will continue a merit increase program for salaried employees.

At the same time, he announced that GM would pay top executives a bonus based on the company's $333 million profit in 1981. That new bonus plan had been agreed to some time earlier by the GM board's compensation system as a way of stopping the loss of GM executives to higher-paid jobs. Such a bonus, Smith went on to explain, was management's equivalent of the hourly workers' new profit-sharing plan.

Douglas Fraser did not accept Smith's explanation, saying the bonus scheme "shows a lack of sensitivity to how people react to perceptions." He asked Smith to reconsider the scheme, warning him that "I've never seen a situation where workers were so upset. They felt they were doublecrossed." Smith agreed to cancel the new bonus plan.

UPDATE ON PEOPLE EXPRESS—APRIL 1983

The People Express news releases reproduced on pages 426–440 tell the story of the company's progress from February through April 1983.

February 18, 1983	"People Express Experiences Net Profit for 1982" (Exhibit 1)
March 2, 1983	"People Express Experiences Highest Load Factor to Date" (Exhibit 2)
March 21, 1983	"People Express Airlines and Braniff Airways Enter into Purchase and Lease Agreement" (Exhibit 3)
March 24, 1983	"Civil Aeronautics Board Approves People Express's Application for Newark-to-London Route" (Exhibit 4)
March 30, 1983	"Braniff and People Express Reach Agreement" (Exhibit 5)
April 4, 1983	"People Express Achieves Highest Load Factor Ever in March" (Exhibit 6)

Harvard Business School case 8-483-114.

EXHIBIT 1

Contact: Bob McAdoo
People Express
(201) 961-2935

Russell Marchetta or Ed Stukane
Keyes Martin
(201) 376-7300

For Immediate Release — February 18, 1983

People Express Announces Net Profit for 1982

Newark, N.J., February 18, 1983 — People Express Airlines, Inc. (OTC-PEXP) today announced that for the year ended December 31, 1982, it earned $1,002,000, or $.17 per share, compared with a loss of $9,205,000, or $1.92 per share, during the nine months ended December 31, 1981. Comparisons to the full year 1981 are not meaningful because the company began airline service in April 1981.

For the quarter ended December 31, 1982, the company had an operating income of $584,000 versus an operating loss of $136,000 in the fourth quarter of

1981. The company's net loss in the quarter was $1,676,000 versus $1,740,000 in the prior year.

	Year Ended 12/31/82	9 Months Ended 12/31/81
	(in thousands of dollars except per share figures)	
Operating revenues	$ 138,688	$ 38,383
Operating expenses	$ 128,230	$ 45,584
Operating income/(loss)	$ 10,458	$ (7,201)
Net income/(loss)	$ 1,002*	$ (9,205)
Net income/(loss) per common share	$ .17	$ (1.92)
Weighted average share outstanding	6,059	4,805

	3 Months Ended 12/31/82	3 Months Ended 12/31/81
	(in thousands of dollars except per share figures)	
Operating revenues	$ 39,925	$ 20,426
Operating expenses	$ 39,341	$ 20,562
Operating income/(loss)	$ 584	$ (136)
Net income/(loss)	$ (1,676)	$ (1,740)
Net income/(loss) per common share	$ (.21)	$ (.35)
Weighted average share outstanding	7,855	4,930

* After tax benefit relating to net operating loss carry forward.

EXHIBIT 1 (*continued*)

The company previously announced that it expected to incur a net loss for the fourth quarer primarily attributable to generally poor industry conditions, the result of the recessionary economy.

The company attributed its achievements during the year to a number of factors, including successfully integrating six additional Boeing 737s and six new cities to its system, while maintaining its position as one of the most efficient airlines in the industry. By year-end, with more than 65 departures per day to 15 destinations, the company had the largest airline operation at Newark International Airport in terms of both departures and passengers.

For the year, the company carried nearly three million passengers and, as previously announced, will soon add 2 aircraft to its fleet, bringing to 22 the total number of Boeing 737s it operates.

EXHIBIT 2

Contact: Ed Stukane or Russell Marchetta
Keyes Martin
(201) 376-7300

For Immediate Release—March 2, 1983

PEOPLExpress Experiences
Highest Load Factor to Date

Newark, N.J., March 2, 1983—PEOPLExpress
Airlines, Inc. (OTC-PEXP) announced today that
during the month of February it flew 257.5 million
available seat miles, carrying 317,783 passengers
197.1 million revenue passenger miles. The load
factor for the month was 76.5 percent, the highest
since the airline started service in April 1981.

Last year for the month of February, the airline
flew 143,297 passengers a total of 92.3 million revenue passenger miles for a load factor of 56.0 percent.

PEOPLExpress attributed its unprecendented
high load factor of 76.5 percent to its Florida ser-

EXHIBIT 2 (*continued*)

vice and a continued strengthening of its Newark hub.

The airline provides 19 daily nonstop flights from

New York/Newark to Florida with additional nonstop

flights to Florida from Baltimore, Buffalo, Columbus,

Pittsburgh, Syracuse, and Washington, D.C.

PEOPLExpress announced yesterday that it has

signed a letter of intent to purchase eight Boeing

727-200 aircraft from McDonnell Douglas with an op-

tion to purchase nine additional Boeing 727-200s.

McDonnell Douglas will obtain these aircraft from

Alitalia Airlines.

	Feb. 1983	Feb. 1982
Passengers	317,783	143,297
Revenue Passenger Miles	197,124,000	92,380,000
Available Seat Miles	257,547,000	164,879,000
Load Factor	76.5 percent	56.0 percent

	TOTALS FOR FIRST TWO MONTHS OF 1983	TOTALS FOR FIRST TWO MONTHS OF 1982
Passengers	674,777	288,239
Revenue Passenger Miles	403,781,000	179,844,000
Available Seat Miles	547,296,000	319,627,000
Load Factor	73.8 percent	56.3 percent

EXHIBIT 3

Contact: Russell Marchetta or Ed Stukane
Keyes Martin
(201) 376-7300

For Immediate Release—March 21, 1983

PEOPLExpress Airlines and Braniff Airways
Enter into Purchase and Lease Agreement

PEOPLExpress Airlines and Braniff Airways today announced that they have reached an agreement
in principle for the sale by Braniff to PEOPLExpress
of Boeing 727-200 aircraft at a purchase price of
$4.0 million per aircraft and the lease by Braniff to
PEOPLExpress of a Boeing 747-200 aircraft. The
agreement is subject to the approval of the Bankruptcy Court having jurisdiction over Braniff's bankruptcy, government approval of the application by
PEOPLExpress to provide nonstop Newark-London
authority, and certain other conditions.

The agreement contemplates that the 727-200
aircraft will be delivered to PEOPLExpress between

November 1983 and March 1985 with PEOPLExpress having the right to accelerate delivery of six of the aircraft to the summer of 1983. The 747-200 aircraft lease is for a term of five years expiring September 1988, with the right on the part of PEOPLExpress to terminate the lease at the end of one year. PEOPLExpress will pay a lease rate of $50,000 per month from delivery through September 30, 1983, and $250,000 monthly for the balance of the lease term. PEOPLExpress will also have an option to convert such a lease arrangement into a conditional sales agreement after one year and the option to purchase the aircraft at the end of the lease term.

PEOPLExpress has also agreed to purchase from Braniff a Boeing 727-200 simulator, certain ground equipment, technical assistance, and flight training in connection with the start-up of Boeing 727 and 747 operations.

Recently, PEOPLExpress announced that it had entered into a letter of intent with McDonnell Douglas

EXHIBIT 3 (*continued*)

(MDC) for the purchase of eight Boeing 727-200 air-

craft that MDC is acquiring from Alitalia Airlines

with an option on nine additional such aircraft, if

MDC acquires such aircraft from Alitalia.   Under

the terms of the letter of intent PEOPLExpress has

until March 29, 1983, to terminate the agreement

without penalty.

EXHIBIT 4

Contact: Ed Stukane or Russell Marchetta
Keyes Martin
(201) 376-7300

For Immediate Release—March 24, 1983

Civil Aeronautics Board Approves PEOPLExpress'
Application for Newark-to-London Route

Newark, N.J.—PEOPLExpress Airlines today

announced that the Civil Aeronautics Board (CAB)

has approved its application to provide nonstop ser-

vice between Newark, New Jersey, and London,

England.

The CAB's decision to select PEOPLExpress

was made at a public meeting and was based on

PEOPLExpress' ongoing successful domestic opera-

tion, its significant traffic feed at Newark Internation-

al Airport, and its uncompromising commitment to

low-priced service.

PEOPLExpress further announced that it would

file with the British government for the operation of

EXHIBIT 4 (*continued*)

its service at an unrestricted price of $149 coach

class and $439 premium class. These prices would

be the lowest transatlantic prices offered by any

scheduled airline. PEOPLExpress announced on

Monday that it has filed an agreement in principle

with Braniff Airways for the lease of a Boeing 747

for use on this route.

PEOPLExpress President Don Burr stated,

"All of us at PEOPLExpress are extremely pleased

with the CAB's decision. The support of our applica-

tion that we received from Governor Kean, the New

Jersey Congressional Delegation, the Port Authority

of New York and New Jersey, and the Greater

Newark Chamber of Commerce was very helpful and

greatly appreciated. We look forward to providing

low-priced Boeing 747 nonstop service between

Newark and London in time for the peak summer

season."

When PEOPLExpress receives approval of its

proposed prices, it will begin accepting reservations

for London. The company presently expects to begin service in late May or early June. The airline will announce its prices and schedule as soon as the necessary government approvals are received.

UPDATE ON PEOPLE EXPRESS—APRIL 1983

EXHIBIT 5

<u>Contact</u>: Ed Stukane or Russell Marchetta
Keyes Martin
(201) 376-7300

<u>For Immediate Release</u>—March 30, 1983

<u>Braniff and PEOPLExpress Reach Agreement</u>

<u>Newark, N.J.</u>—PEOPLExpress Airlines today announced that it has received court approval to purchase from Braniff Airways 20 Boeing 727-200 aircraft and to lease a Boeing 747-200 aircraft.

The approval was given by Judge John C. Flowers of the U.S. Bankruptcy Court for the Northern District of Texas, Ft. Worth Division, which has jurisdiction over the Braniff's bankruptcy case.

"We are very pleased with the ruling and Judge
Flowers' expeditious handling of the case," said Don
Burr, president of PEOPLExpress, adding, "We feel
it is an excellent agreement for both Braniff and
PEOPLExpress."

The 20 Boeing 727s will be purchased at a price
of $4.2 million each and will be delivered between
November 1983 and March 1985 with PEOPLExpress
having the right to accelerate delivery of 6 of the aircraft to the summer of 1983. The 747-200 aircraft
will be used on the Newark-London route PEOPLExpress was given authority to serve last week by the
Civil Aeronautics Board. The airline hopes to begin
London service by late May or early June.

EXHIBIT 6

<u>Contact</u>: Russell Marchetta or Ed Stukane
Keyes Martin
(201) 376-7300

<u>For Immediate Release</u>—April 4, 1983

<u>PEOPLExpress Achieves Highest
Load Factor Ever in March</u>

<u>Newark, N.J.</u>—PEOPLExpress Airlines

(OTC-PEXP) today announced that during the month

of March it flew 313.6 million available seat miles,

carrying 396,364 passengers 252.7 million revenue

passenger miles. The load factor for the month was

80.6 percent, the highest in the 23-month history of

the airline.

Last year for the month of March, PEOPLEx-

press flew 194,974 passengers a total of 127.9

million revenue passenger miles for a load factor

of 64.0 percent.

March is the third consecutive month that

PEOPLExpress has surpassed its previous month's

load factor. The airline attributed the 80.6 percent load factor for March to its nonstop service to Florida and its continued low-cost, high-frequency service to cities throughout its system.

	March 1983	March 1982
Passengers	396,364	194,974
Available Seat Miles	313,640,000	199,724,000
Revenue Passenger Miles	252,738,000	127,900,000
Load Factor	80.6%	64.0%

	TOTALS FOR FIRST THREE MONTHS OF 1983	TOTALS FOR FIRST THREE MONTHS OF 1982
Passengers	1,071,141	483,213
Available Seat Miles	860,936,000	519,351,000
Revenue Passenger Miles	656,519,000	307,744,000
Load Factor	76.3%	59.3%

How to Order Course Material

HBS Case Services is committed to processing your orders quickly and managing your account efficiently. We would appreciate your cooperation in filling out the order form completely. Particularly, we need your customer code, your phone number, and the order number for each item. Orders with complete information from the customer are now being processed in four working days. Allow three weeks for processing collated case packets.

Phone Orders. Placing orders by phone expedites order processing and provides you with immediate information on the availability of what you order. Have your customer code and order numbers ready when you call. To place an order, call (617) 495-6117.

Prices. Effective April 1, 1984, and subject to change without notice:

Type of Item	Price to Educational Institutions	Price to Others
Cases	$1.00 per copy	$2.00 per copy
Teaching Notes	$1.00 per copy *To verify your teaching status, telephone number of Dean's office must be included.*	$2.00 per copy *To verify your teaching status, telephone number of Personnel office must be included.*
Working Papers	$5.00 per copy	$5.00 per copy
Course Modules	Individually priced *Please inquire*	Individually priced *Please inquire*
Teacher's Manuals	Individually priced *Please inquire*	Individually priced *Please inquire*
Videotapes	$75.00 per cassette	$150.00 per cassette
Directory of Course Material	Individually priced; prepayment required *Please inquire*	Individually priced; prepayment required *Please inquire*

Quantity Discount. A quantity discount on cases, notes and working papers is now available:

Quantity Ordered	Cases/Notes Price per Copy Educational	Cases/Notes Price per Copy Other	Working Papers Price per Copy Educational/Other
1–249	$1.00	$2.00	$5.00
250–499	.95	1.90	4.75
500–1,999	.90	1.80	4.50
2,000–4,999	.85	1.70	4.25
5,000–9,999	.80	1.60	4.00
10,000+	.75	1.50	3.75

Shipping Costs. For orders *prepaid in full*, shipping via UPS or surface mail will be paid by HBS Case Services. You will be billed for any other method you specify. For orders that are not prepaid, please specify the preferred shipment method; you will be billed for the shipping costs.

Copyright Notice. Harvard Business School cases are protected by U.S. copyright laws. Unauthorized duplication of copyrighted material is a violation of federal law.

5/84

Order Form
HBS Case Services
Harvard Business School
Boston, MA 02163

Ref. No. _____

Batch No. _____

Please fill in completely, to speed processing.

Customer Code _____

Ordered by _____

Phone No. (_____)

Purchase Order No./Buyer _____

Charge to my ☐ VISA ☐ MasterCard

Account Number | | | | | | | | | | | | | | | |

Expiration Date _____

Cardholder's Signature _____
☐ Check enclosed. Include Customer Code on check, made payable to HBS Case Services.

Returns not accepted. Products are sold FOB shipping point. Title and risk pass to customer when product is delivered to carrier.

Billing Address

_____

_____

_____

_____

Shipping Address

_____

_____

_____

_____

Prepaid orders are shipped at no charge via UPS in the U.S. and by surface mail outside the U.S. For another shipping choice, and for all non-prepaid orders, you will be charged the costs of the shipping method you specify here.

☐ UPS   ☐ Express Mail   ☐ Surface Mail
☐ UPS Blue Label ☐ Federal Express   ☐ Air Printed Matter
☐ Air Mail   ☐ Emery Air Freight   ☐ Air Parcel Post

Orders for teaching notes require verification of teaching status.
Please provide the phone number of Dean's Office/Personnel Office (_____) _____

Order Number	Title (one line per title)	No. of Copies	× Price (see reverse)	= Total
-	-			
-	-			
-	-			
-	-			
-	-			
-	-			
-	-			
-	-			
-	-			
-	-			
-	-			
-	-			
-	-			
-	-			

Total Due $